Key Duties of International Investment Arbitrators

Katia Fach Gómez

Key Duties of International Investment Arbitrators

A Transnational Study of Legal and Ethical Dilemmas

Springer

Katia Fach Gómez
Tenured Professor (Profesora Titular) at the Law School
University of Zaragoza
Zaragoza, Spain

This book is part of a research project financed by the Humboldt Stiftung, and has also been published by Springer with a financial subsidy from the former scientific institution. Additionally, the editing of the book has been kindly funded by LegMIBIO S12_17R DGA.
The author is also member of the Institute of European Law and Regional Integration (IDEIR) at the Complutense Univesity of Madrid (Spain) as well as member of the following Spanish Research Projects: LegMIBIO S12_17R DGA, DER2016-80568-R and DER2017-85585-P.

ISBN 978-3-030-07455-5 ISBN 978-3-319-98128-4 (eBook)
https://doi.org/10.1007/978-3-319-98128-4

This Springer imprint is published by the registered company Springer Nature Switzerland AG
The registered company address is: Gewerbestrasse 11, 6330 Cham, Switzerland

Foreword

In the aftermath of World War II, the United States and other Western countries made considerable intellectual efforts to establish minimum standards for the protection of private property against expropriation as customary principles under international law. These efforts were doomed to failure at a time when socialist ideas and decolonization prevailed in large parts of the world. However, it soon became clear that the national development in many countries of the Third World depends on capital inflows from abroad and that foreign investors need some kind of assurance that the terms of the agreements underlying their investment would be honoured in the future. As a result, more and more bilateral investment treaties (BITs) were concluded between capital-exporting and capital-importing countries. Alongside substantive principles on the protection of the foreign investment they provide for dispute settlement mechanisms, nowadays more and more in the form of investor state arbitration.

Over many years, the proceedings between foreign investors and host states have attracted little attention outside the group of those involved. The cases have not been numerous and from the closed club of the lawyers and arbitrators participating in the system little insider information transpired. The public interest grew when the capital flows changed direction. When the industrialized countries of the Western world became destinations of foreign investment, it turned out that regulatory interventions in the host states could be challenged under the investment protection treaties. Investor state arbitration now became a tool allowing private business to contest legislation that had been approved in democratic procedures of the host states. The number of such cases is still small, but they have aroused the interest of a wider public for investor state arbitration, in particular for the recruitment of arbitrators, for their powers and obligations and for possible conflicts of interest.

This is the political environment of this book. It is meant to shed light on some key duties of investment arbitrators and, by their analysis, contribute to a rationalization of the debate. Caught between the duty of impartiality, the loyalty to the appointing party and their own interests, arbitrators will invariably have to take difficult ethical decisions, relating both to the procedure and to the substance of the litigation. Various intergovernmental and private bodies have tried to stake out a clear path for arbitrators' conduct, but the dilemma underlying this book is inherent and inevitable. In the light of the existing literature, the author does not tackle the fundamental issues of independence and impartiality but rather focuses on more specific duties which are of central significance nevertheless: the duties of disclosure, of confidentiality and of personal diligence and integrity.

The reader who is less familiar with investment arbitration will be surprised about the multiple sources which give evidence of a broad discussion in arbitral circles about these issues. Not only has the author drawn from various instruments adopted in recent years and from a broad literature; she has also analysed a large number of arbitrations which give evidence of the frequent occurrence of, and the broad discussions on, the issues treated in this investigation.

The enquiry leads to the proposal of a code of conduct for arbitrators that would establish a number of rules and duties concerning their action in particular phases of the proceedings. This code may also help to improve the competitive position of investment state arbitration as compared with the multilateral investment tribunal that is currently negotiated. The author's proposal to require for example truthful information on the arbitrators' availability at the appointment stage relates to a problem that will be common to both investor state arbitration and the multilateral investment tribunal. Just like an investment arbitration panel, such a tribunal will have to deal with few cases only. As a consequence, it will likely be composed of part-time judges who will face the same difficulty as arbitrators, i.e. to reconcile their various other activities with their judicial office. The example shows that the choice between investment arbitration and an international arbitration tribunal depends, beyond the ethical dilemma outlined above, on a number of issues which will be discussed in the future. The author's enquiry provides an excellent basis for such comparison and thereby for the future development of investment dispute settlements, both in arbitration and by a future multilateral tribunal.

Professor Dr. Dr. h. c. mult. Jürgen Basedow, LL.M. (Harvard Univ.); Director em. of the Max Planck Institute for Comparative and International Private Law; Member of the Institut de droit international

1 July 2018

Preface and Acknowledgements

Given the title of this book, I feel I have an ethical duty to begin by recounting some of the events that have been taking place around me as my work on this book progressed over the last 2 years.

At the risk of crossing the line of what the academic establishment would consider appropriate, I feel compelled to underline the fact that this book has been developed during the recent problems that have shaken the academic community in Spain. The project has unfolded and come to fruition in the midst of a devastating economic and financial crisis, which has weakened the state university system in Spain to a shocking extent.

In addition to what has become a classic debate about the lack of funding for research in Spain and the absence of any genuine commitment to education and research from the political class,[1] a new battlefront has recently been opened regarding higher education. Following a series of events in national politics, part of Spanish society has accused state universities of turning their back on the principle of equality, of ignoring transparency and of quashing meritocracy. This may be a new front for public opinion, but to those of us who form part of the university system, it certainly is not.

Contrary to the approach taken by some of the media and part of social debate, there is nothing new either about the reasons that sparked another recent event: the women's strike on International Women's Day in 2018, which was supported on a massive scale and with particular intensity in Spain. In spite of the indisputable progress that has been made in recent years, where gender issues are concerned, my country still lags behind at both general and academic level.

As a result of these factors, this book could not have been written had I not been granted a Humboldt Research Fellowship for Experienced Researchers. This has undoubtedly been one of the most outstanding milestones in my academic career. Becoming a Humboldt Senior Research Fellow enabled me to visit Germany several

[1]Fach Gómez K (2014) Europe and the Legal Lost Generation: Spain's Dysfunctional University System is Also to Blame. German Law Journal 15(6): 1209–1222.

times for research purposes in the best possible conditions and also to take advantage of the countless academic resources to which Humboldt Stiftung scholars have access. I am particularly indebted to the individual mentoring scheme run by two engaged and generous German academics of world renown, Prof. Dr. Dr. h.c. mult. Jürgen Basedow, LL.M. (Harvard Univ.), at the Max-Planck-Institut für ausländisches und internationales Privatrecht in Hamburg, and Prof. Dr. Dr. h.c. Matthias Herdegen at the Universität Bonn. They have left their tacit footprint on every page of the book, and my enormous debt of gratitude to them far exceeds the space available in this short preface. I am also grateful to the academic authorities at the University of Zaragoza, the Law Faculty and the Private Law Department, to whom it was not necessary to explain that a research stay abroad, far from bearing any resemblance to a holiday, is in fact a period of intense work and sacrifice. Such visits are, moreover, an absolute necessity for those of us who wish to carry out high-quality research but unfortunately lack the resources we need at our *alma maters*.

The series of research periods in Germany gave me access to bibliographic sources that were essential for writing this book. They also enabled me to enjoy the great pleasure of rigorous academic conversation with numerous university colleagues. I am especially grateful to Prof. Dr. Karsten Nowrot for his intense personal involvement in the many research-related projects (international conferences, special issues of journals and edited volumes) that arose from the Humboldt scholarship. All this serves to highlight the great honour of being a fellow of a foundation that fully understands that research projects that aspire to quality need to be allowed to develop slowly and also require suitable physical and intellectual surroundings if they are to be carried out properly.

However, my gratitude to the Humboldt Stiftung increases even more if personal and family circumstances are taken into account—circumstances which, nonetheless, are nothing out of the ordinary. The family and parental support section in the Humboldt Guidelines and Information for Research Fellows was a key factor in the successful completion of the research project presented in this book. I wish to express my most sincere thanks for the Humboldt Stiftung's unwavering support in the difficult task of combining my academic and research work with bringing up my beloved daughter Inés. Thanks to this support, Inés was able to come with me on my research visits to Germany and go to school there. Because of this experience, the seed of love for German language and culture that was planted in me many years ago has now taken root in her, and as it is still alive in me, I am deeply grateful to the Humboldt Stiftung for helping me to cultivate it in my daughter.

Unfortunately, a set of family and parental means such as that provided by the Humboldt Stiftung is still entirely alien to many national research schemes. I therefore wish to take advantage of this excellent opportunity to commend all the research contexts that take the human dimension into account, with all the consequences, and regardless of gender.[2] A great deal has been written about the life-work

[2]Regarding the EU research framework, Fach Gómez K (2014) La nueva política de Investigación e innovación de la Unión Europea: Horizonte 2020 y el tratamiento de las Ciencias Sociales y Humanidades. Revista General de Derecho Europeo 33:1-36.

balance from many different angles, but I feel that the reality requires still more reflection and especially more resolute decision-making.

I would also like to express my gratitude to Jesús, my partner and Inés' father, for his support throughout the lengthy and intense process of writing this book. I would be lying if I did not say that being the absent mother at many school, social and family events was a frankly painful experience. I want to believe that these absences have their positive side and that through them our beloved daughter has understood the real implications of notions such as responsibility, effort and discipline. I also want to believe, in many different ways, that the best is yet to come.

I could not bring this final section of acknowledgements to a close without mentioning my dear parents. All my previous academic works have been dedicated to them, and deservedly so; however, during the long process of writing this book, I have realized that what I really need to dedicate to them from now on is more time. It is sometimes impossible to achieve the right balance between the many lives that we are obliged to manage on a day-to-day basis. Unfortunately, it is often those whose love we know we have won that bear the brunt of this. In spite of everything, my parents continue to prove their generosity and unswerving loyalty to me.

Finishing the research component of this book in late spring 2018 meant that my family and personal life began to make more demands on me than previously. This prevented me from continuing to procrastinate over writing this preface, which is a very emotional act for me. I trust that some of the issues mentioned here manage to capture not only my personal circumstances, but also the reality and sentiments of other academics, whether female or otherwise. We are living in an era in which public visibility seems to be awakening sleeping consciences and inspiring a range of positive actions and I wish this preface to be my contribution. It is a contribution from an extremely shy person in this sense, but one who understands that it is her academic duty to publish her reflections on the professional and human circumstances surrounding her research work.

Hamburg, Germany Katia Fach Gómez
25 June 2018

Contents

List of Abbreviations

ABA	American Bar Association
ADR	Alternative Dispute Resolution
AI	Arbitrator Intelligence
AIAC	Asian International Arbitration Centre (formerly known as KLRCA)
ASA	Swiss Arbitration Association
ASIL	American Society of International Law
CAM	Camera Arbitrale di Milano (Milan Chamber of Arbitration)
CAM (Sp)	Corte de Arbitraje de la Cámara de Comercio de Madrid (Madrid Court of Arbitration)
CAS	Court of Arbitration for Sport
CEA	Corte Española de Arbitraje (Civil and Commercial Arbitration Court)
CEA	Club Español de Arbitraje (Spanish Arbitration Club)
CEDCA	Centro empresarial de conciliación y arbitraje
CETA	European Union-Canada Comprehensive Economic and Trade Agreement
CIArb	Chartered Institute of Arbitrators
CIETAC	China International Economic and Trade Arbitration Commission
CIMA	Corte Civil y Mercantil de Arbitraje (Civil and Commercial Court of Arbitration)
CJEU	Court of Justice of the European Union (see also ECJ)
CRCICA	Cairo Regional Centre for International Commercial Arbitration
CV	Curriculum Vitae
DCCP	Code of Civil Procedure of the Netherlands
DIA	Danish Institute Arbitration
DIS	Deutsche Institution für Schiedsgerichtsbarkeit (German Arbitration Institute)
DRD	Dispute Resolution Data
DSU	Understanding on Rules and Procedures Governing the Settlement of Disputes

EC	European Commission
ECHR	European Court of Human Rights
ECJ	European Court of Justice
EFILA	European Federation for Investment Law and Arbitration
EP	European Parliament
EU	European Union
EUR	Euro
EUSFTA	European Union–Singapore Free Trade Agreement
FAI	Finland Arbitration Institute
FDI	Foreign Direct Investment
FINRA	Financial Industry Regulatory Authority
FTA	Free Trade Agreement
KLRCA	Kuala Lumpur Regional Centre for Arbitration
GAR	Global Arbitration Review
GAR ART	Arbitrator Research Tool
HKIAC	Hong Kong International Arbitration Centre
HS	Host State
IBA	International Bar Association
ICC	International Chamber of Commerce
ICCA	International Council for Commercial Arbitration
ICDR	International Centre for Dispute Resolution
ICJ	International Court of Justice
ICS	Investment Court System
ICSID	International Centre for Settlement of Investment Disputes
IPA	Investment Protection Agreement
ISDS	Investor State Dispute Settlement
JAMS	Judicial Arbitration and Mediation Services
JEFTA	European Union-Japan Free Trade Agreement
KLRCA	Kuala Lumpur Regional Centre for Arbitration
LCIA	London Court of International Arbitration
MIC	Multilateral Investment Court
NAFTA	North American Free Trade Agreement
NAI	Netherlands Arbitration Institute
OGEMID	Oil, Gas, Energy, Mining, Infrastructure and Investment Disputes Forum (Mailing list of TDM)
OUP	Oxford University Press
PCA	Permanent Court of Arbitration
SADC	Southern African Development Community
SCC	Stockholm Chamber of Commerce
SIAC	Singapore International Arbitration Centre
TAB	Tribunal Arbitral de Barcelona (Barcelona Arbitration Court)
TDM	Transnational Dispute Management
TNI	Transnational Institute
TTIP	Transatlantic Trade and Investment Partnership

UK	United Kingdom
UNCITRAL	United Nations Commission on International Trade Law
UNCTAD	United Nations Conference on Trade and Development
USA	United States of America
USD	United States Dollar
VIAC	Vienna International Arbitral Centre
WB	World Bank
WIPO	World Intellectual Property Organization
WTO	World Trade Organization

Chapter 1
Introduction. A Transnational Study of Legal and Ethical Dilemmas

This book focuses on the duties of international investment arbitrators.[1] Its aim is to examine their current profile, while also reflecting on how and why their duties may evolve at a time in which even these individuals' job title appears likely to change. This introductory chapter moves from the general to the specific, and its first task is to pin down the main characteristics of the Investor State Dispute Settlement (ISDS) regime in the current global context. To this end, specific attention is paid to recent developments in this area that have arisen from European Union (EU) initiatives. Readers are assumed to be familiar with the classic investment arbitration system epitomised by ICSID.

The focus of this chapter then shifts to the fundamental importance of investment adjudicators in the ISDS framework, and to the way in which their duties have been defined up to now. This chapter closes by outlining a series of fundamental uncertainties and challenges that cut across the range of investment adjudicators' duties, and which will very probably require deep analysis and decision-making in the future.

1.1 The ISDS in Flux

The ISDS regime is at a particularly tumultuous stage in its existence. Criticisms of the current system, some little short of merciless, have been raised in different forums: "ISDS is a caricature of a legal system".[2]

[1]Unless otherwise noted, the reference to the "investment arbitrator" throughout this book should be understood as replaced by the notion of "member of de tribunal" or "judge" when referring to the EU-MIC framework. Sometimes, the book resorts to the term "investment adjudicator" to cover all these possible realities.

[2]Kahale (2018), p. 5. Taking a more neutral approach, the EU identifies a list of significant concerns with the existing ISDS system. EU (2018).

K. Fach Gómez, *Key Duties of International Investment Arbitrators*,
https://doi.org/10.1007/978-3-319-98128-4_1

The EU has been one of the stakeholders to shake the foundations of ISDS since it acquired competence in the foreign direct investment (FDI) sphere. Following the entry into force of the Treaty of Lisbon, the EU has implemented a wide range of initiatives whose guiding principle is the desire to take the lead in constructing global governance in the international investment field. More specifically, the EU wishes to support a new legal structure for the resolution of disputes arising from international investments. What is known about this new structure indicates that it is clearly incompatible with the current scenario, which is characterized by ICSID's hegemony as the institution in charge of handling investment arbitration.[3]

In simple terms, the EU began to lay out its current roadmap in January 2015 as a consequence of the "Online public consultation on investment protection and investor-to-state dispute settlement (ISDS)".[4] The results of the consultation prompted Commissioner Malmström to stop defending what was known as ISDS 2.0,[5] and instead to promote a new dispute resolution model managed by a permanent two-instance investment court.[6] The reason given at the time that was the "[. . .] fundamental and widespread lack of trust by the public in the old ISDS model."[7]

The EC position was also supported by the European Parliament's (EP) stern July 2015 recommendation "[to] replace the ISDS system with a new system for resolving disputes between investors and states which is subject to democratic principles and scrutiny, where potential cases are treated in a transparent manner by publicly appointed, independent professional judges in public hearings and which includes an appellate mechanism, where consistency of judicial decisions is ensured, the jurisdiction of courts of the EU and of the Member States is respected, and where private interests cannot undermine public policy objectives."[8]

---

[3]ICSID has been defined as an "absolute monarchy" where its policy of appointing arbitrators is concerned. Thomson (2016).

[4]The text indicates that one of the main outcomes of the consultation is that: "the collective submissions reflect a widespread opposition to Investor-State Dispute Settlement (ISDS) in TTIP or in general. There is also quite a majority of replies opposing TTIP in general." European Commission (2015a).

[5]This term, which refers to an improved ISDS system, is used by authors such as Bungenberg (2015).

[6]The Commissioner launched a balloon probe on this subject in her blog on May 5, 2015, following the presentation of the EU concept paper, which dealt with ICS *in extenso* for the first time. Malmström (2015a).

[7]Malmström (2015b). She proclaimed that: "We want the rule of law, not the rule of lawyers. If we are to continue with investment protection and international arbitration, it will need to be a very different animal. (. . .)". Malmström (2015c).

[8]The text goes on to say: "[a new system] where potential cases are treated in a transparent manner by publicly appointed, independent professional judges in public hearings and which includes an appellate mechanism, where consistency of judicial decisions is ensured, the jurisdiction of courts of the EU and of the Member States is respected, and where private interests cannot undermine public policy objectives". EP (2015), point (d) xv.

In the same year the EC issued a concept paper entitled "Investment in TTIP and beyond - The path for reform"[9] and has subsequently remained very active in this area. It has proposed a new CETA text which includes an investment court system (ICS) with a bilateral approach[10]; energetically defended this model vis-à-vis its US counterpart in TTIP[11]; continued to include the ICS in other recent texts that will be analysed throughout this book (such as the EU-Singapore IPA text, published in April 2018),[12] and will also probably include its new approach to investment policy in other free trade agreement negotiations.[13] Furthermore, the EC is not the only EU institution to be involved in international investment issues, and recent ECJ judgments such as Slovak Republic v Achmea BV and Micula v Commission have the potential to turn the current global ISDS picture on its head. Meanwhile, member states have also shown an interest in and expressed doubts about this issue. For example, Belgium recently requested the CJEU's opinion regarding the compatibility of Chapter 8, Section F of CETA ("Resolution of investment disputes between investors and states") with European Treaties, including basic rights.[14]

Since this introductory chapter begins by presenting the bigger picture of the subject of this book (Key Duties of International Investment Arbitrators), it should be noted that an essential feature of the EU's ICS proposal is that the system should be viewed as a public justice system.[15] As academics have pointed out, the pre-ICS system—the ISDS system whose flagship is ICSID—is a true reflection of its creators' world view and the times in which it originated; that is, the 1960s. This

---

[9]EC (2015b).

[10]EC (2016a).

[11]EC (2015c).

[12]EC (2018a). Likewise, "the EU-Mexico agreement fully implements the new EU approach to investment protection and investment dispute resolution by fundamentally reforming the old-style ISDS system". EC (2018b).

[13]For instance, regarding Australia and New Zealand: EC (2018c).

[14]More specifically, Belgium is requesting the ECJ to provide an opinion on the compatibility of the ICS with: "1) The exclusive competence of the CJEU to provide the definitive interpretation of European Union law; 2) The general principle of equality and the 'practical effect' requirement of European Union law; 3) The right of access to the courts; 4) The right to an independent and impartial judiciary. Regarding the right to an independent and impartial judiciary, the Kingdom of Belgium wishes to obtain an opinion regarding the following aspects: -the conditions regarding the remuneration of the members of the Tribunal and the Appeals Body; -the appointment of members of the Tribunal and the Appeals Body; -the release of members of the Tribunal and the Appeals Body; -the guidelines of the International Bar Association regarding conflicts of interest in international arbitration and the introduction of a Code of Conduct for the members of the Tribunal and the Appeals Body; -the external professional activities related to investment disputes of members of the Tribunal and the Appeals Body". Kingdom of Belgium (2017).

[15]Malmström stated: "Some have argued that the traditional ISDS model is private justice. What I'm setting out here is a public justice system – just like those we're familiar with in our own countries, and the international courts which Europe has so actively promoted in the past". Malmström (2015b).

explains why the system, which was created to depoliticize investment disputes, sometimes juggles several areas of international law and commercial arbitration.[16]

As indicated above, the EU is fully aware that many twenty-first century analysts reject the classic ISDS system, accusing it of lacking democratic legitimacy. This is expressed for instance in stark terms in the titles of various policy papers drafted by NGOs, such as "Profiting from Injustice" or "ISDS-The devil is in the details".[17] In an attempt to overcome those criticisms, the EU presents its proposal for ICS as a public justice system[18] which prides itself on resembling national judicial systems at various points.

Apart from terminological novelties, such as judge, member of the court or tribunal, in the new EU texts, the notion of public justice is reflected in a number of this court-like system's defining elements, which differ markedly from the defining features of the ICSID regime. Very simply, the judges or members of the court are selected by a committee and acquire quasi-civil servant status: the system has an appeal mechanism, and cases are randomly assigned to the adjudicators—formerly known as arbitrators, who may receive a fixed salary to ensure their continuing commitment.

The new adjudicators have a smaller margin of interpretation than previously, in part because some substantive provisions on investment protection have been defined more clearly and in greater detail—e.g., fair and equitable treatment, indirect expropriation—but also because the FTAs allow states to adopt binding interpretative decisions on controversial provisions through their committees. There is thus a clear desire in the EU—and the non-EU countries that have accepted or will accept the ICS mechanism—to retain its political-legislative contribution, not only while the texts are being negotiated, but also while they remain in force.[19] The texts also reveal the EU's firm will to restrict party prerogatives. The eliminating of party autonomy when choosing adjudicators, for instance, effectively dynamites one of the foundations of the classic ISDS.[20]

---

[16]Howse (last accessed June 2018), pp. 6–7.

[17]Transnational Institute (2012), Jacques Delors Institute (2015) and Seattle to Brussels Network (2013).

[18]Malmström (2015b).

[19]Referring to the political-legislative input of the States, Venzke (2016), p. 391. In this sense, the Government of Thailand recently demanded "ways of implementing the joint interpretation mechanism". Government of Thailand (2018), 3.

[20]This legislative option may be justified by a policy of "double standards" implemented by the parties: "The fact that "issue conflict" is perceived as a problem may derive, in part, from a sense that the proper balance between party autonomy and impartiality has not yet been adequately identified in investment arbitration. As stated, disputing parties enter the arbitral process with the expectation (not found in litigation) that they can shape the profile of the decision maker through their choice of arbitrator and any participation in the appointment of the chair. Their expectations are thus raised by the hope that they can appoint arbitrators who have displayed past practice sympathetic to their particular case, and perhaps their desired outcome. There is, however, a frequent disparity between a party's expectations when appointing an arbitrator, and its expectations when considering the other party's arbitrator appointment. When considering the independence and

A bilaterally-based ICS, which the EU aims to implement swiftly, has to be interpreted as a half-way point on the EU's ambitious roadmap. As early as 2005 the EC stated that: "In parallel to the EU-US negotiations, the European Commission will start work, together with other countries, on setting up a permanent International Investment Court. The Commission is also currently exchanging views with several international organisations in this field. The objective is to, over time, replace all investment dispute resolution mechanisms in EU agreements, in EU Member States' agreements with third countries, and trade in investment treaties concluded between non-EU countries, with the International Investment Court. This would lead to the full replacement of the "old ISDS" mechanism with a modern, efficient, transparent and impartial system for international investment dispute resolution."[21] In line with this, various recent EU texts expressly refer to a transition towards a Multilateral Investment Court (MIC),[22] as well as the 2018 Netherlands draft model BIT.[23]

The United Nations Commission for International Trade Law (UNCITRAL), and more specifically its Working Group III, can be expected to play a major role in this global reconfiguration. This Group was the driving force behind the "Reform of the Dispute Resolution System between Investors and States" initiative, and its regular meetings since 2017 have produced a series of documents that provide essential information on the issue's present and future. Its 35th session was held in New York between April 23 and 27, 2018 and the Group is expected to continue to make progress on key issues in the reform of the ISDS.[24] In this context, on March 1, 2018, the Council of the EU issued some negotiating directives authorizing the EC to participate in the negotiation of a Convention establishing a multilateral court for the settlement of investment disputes.[25] This is consistent with the Trade Commissioner's clear positioning in favour of "the EU [taking] a global role on the path of reform, to create an international court based on public trust."[26]

Many other current developments outside the EU sphere and the MIC project also deserve mentions throughout this book, among them the ICSID Rules Amendment

impartiality of the other party's arbitrator, a party and its counsel typically apply pronounced scrutiny, leaving the expectation of how the standards of independence and impartiality should protect the process from prejudgment to be arguably asymmetric. This pattern has been accentuated as the pool of investment arbitrators is better known through their decisions". ASIL-ICCA (2016), pp. 12–13.

[21]EC (2015c).

[22]Article 3.12: "Multilateral Dispute Settlement Mechanism. The Parties shall pursue with each other and other interested trading partners, the establishment of a multilateral investment tribunal and appellate mechanism for the resolution of international investment disputes. Upon establishment of such a multilateral mechanism, the Committee shall consider adopting a decision to provide that investment disputes under this Section will be resolved pursuant to that multilateral mechanism, and to make appropriate transitional arrangements". EU-Singapore IPA (2018).

[23]Article 15. Kingdom of Netherlands (2018).

[24]UNCITRAL Working Group III (2018).

[25]Council of the EU (2018).

[26]EC (2015c).

Process[27] and the renegotiation of NAFTA.[28] In short, it is clear that ISDS is in a state of ferment and the figure of the investment adjudicator cannot escape from this process of change.

1.2 Investment Adjudicators and Their Duties: Present and Future

It is well known that claims brought by foreign investors against the investment's host state (HS) have been traditionally resolved by talented and successful multilingual legal professionals in their capacity as international investment arbitrators. However, these have come under attack from many different fronts and for highly

[27] The 2017 Public Comments to Amendment of ICSID's Rules and Regulations offer multiple proposals for improving the current ICSID arbitrator disqualification system. The following proposals, while by no means comprehensive, are noteworthy since they connect to a greater or lesser extent with the subject of arbitrator duties. Among them: (1) Preventing last minute challenges by setting a time limit for filing challenges [N.A. (2017), 6.]; (2) Granting the ICSID Chairman a more active role in the decision to challenge [the option of limiting the power of ICSID co-arbitrators regarding challenges is supported by academia. The innovations implemented by the EU are also an incentive in this respect vis-à-vis the continuity reflected in TTIP and EU-Vietnam FTA texts (Articles 11.3 and 14-3 "the President of the Tribunal or the President of the Appeal Tribunal, respectively, shall (...) issue a decision"). On the other hand, JEFTA, EU-Singapore FTA and 2016 CETA resort to external authorities (the Secretary General of ICSID- Art 8.10 and 9.18-, and the President of the International Court of Justice –Article 8.30. On this issue, see also the ABA Investment Treaty Working Group (2016), 60]; (3) Creating an ICSID Challenge Committee [various proposals have been outlined, depending on whether a reform of the ICSID Convention would be needed or not. Baker McKenzie (2017), pp. 5–6. A further option would be to create a collegial bod, responsible for ruling on challenges to appointments made by the Secretary General. Derains and Gharavi (2017), 6]; (4) Shortening various deadlines in the challenge procedure (the importance of this issue has also been underlined in different texts in the commercial context, such as Rule 20 of CEA Code of Good Arbitration Practices); (5) Not suspending the proceedings when a disqualification proposal is initiated [Law Council of Australia (2017), pp. 7–8. Indirectly, Coleman and Innes (2015)]; (6) Prohibiting second or subsequent challenges except in limited circumstances [Debevoise and Plimpton (2017), p. 3]; (7) Providing detailed reasoning for decisions and always publishing them (N.A. (2017), 6); and (8) charging fees to parties that bring challenges without merit [EFILA (2017). There is a growing tendency in ICSID arbitrations to consider that the party filing the disqualification is responsible for the associated costs if the filing is considered to be improper. For instance, the two other arbitrators in the Fábrica v. Venezuela case stated: "It was legitimate and proper for the respondent to seek [the arbitrator's] clarification in respect of the employment status of Ms. MN in these circumstances. The same cannot be said for the Respondent's decision to proceed to file its Third Proposal for Disqualification. For these reasons, the Two Members have decided that the Respondent shall be responsible for the costs associated with this Third Proposal for Disqualification and that an order to that effect will be made in the final award to be issued by the Tribunal in these proceedings". Fábrica v. Venezuela (2016b), par 62].

[28] A detailed analysis of developments and trends can be found in UNCTAD (2018a, b).

diverse reasons,[29] all of which highlight the process of legitimacy erosion of the ISDS system.

It is for this reason, as stated above, that a not inconsiderable part of the key modifications to the ISDS regime proposed by the EU currently focuses on changing the investment arbitrator profile. It is no secret that adjudicators are the stepping stones in any dispute resolution system; hence stakeholder interest in shaping the characteristics, rights and duties of these individuals is not new either.[30] The EU proposal to eliminate party-appointed arbitrators in international investment provides a good example of this; the issue has long been discussed in the commercial arbitration context,[31] and is also extremely controversial in the investment arbitration setting.

Moving closer towards the central theme now, this book focuses on the duties attributable to international investment arbitrators. Within the very complex legal profile that comes together in the figure of the investment arbitrator, it is argued that the issue of arbitrators' duties is of decisive significance in this legal sector's present and future. It has been stated that: "Confidence in the ethical standards of arbitrators and arbitral institutions is the Alpha and Omega of the legitimacy of the process".[32]

This work therefore aims to undertake a detailed study of the current situation regarding some key duties of international investment arbitrators, together with a desire to encourage in-depth debate on the matter. If any proposals linked to either moderate or substantial changes[33] arise from this analysis, they would not necessarily be unwelcome. As has already been pointed out, we are at a crucial point, and the machinery of change is unlikely to come to a complete standstill.

---

[29]Investment arbitrators are obviously not the only recipients of such reprovals, and other types of international adjudicators have also been and still are in the spotlight. An example of this broader reality is the problem that underpins Lazareff's enlightening text: "Sur la plupart des arbitres dits "professionnels", il y a peu à écrire. Fidèles à leur éthique, connaissant et appliquant les procédures choisies par les parties, respectueux de leurs collègues, ils constituent l'immense majorité silencieuse. Mais les autres! On aurait pu peindre l'arbitre absent (qu'il soit ou non présent), l'arbitre muet, l'arbitre partial, le salomonique (dit aussi 50/50), le bon arbitre, le juriste tatillon, celui qui privilégie l'équité sans verser dans l'amiable composition, le président indécis, le président tranchant, le président (ou l'arbitre) maniaque, l'arbitre lièvre et l'arbitre tortue, l'arbitre au compteur, l'arbitre surmené, entre deux (importantes) audiences, l'ensommeillé, le professoral (qu'il soit ou non professeur), le grincheux, le sautillant, l'atrabilaire. La galerie eût été sans limite. Le titre était tout trouvé: des *arbitris illustribus* ou de la pathologie des arbitres. Pathologie, car, fort heureusement, ils sont encore –pour longtemps, espérons-le- minoritaires". Lazareff (2005), p. 477.

[30]Reflecting extensively on the profile of investment adjudicators, Fach Gómez (2019).

[31]Summarising the bitter positions adopted on the issue, Brower and Rosenberg (2013).

[32]Paulsson (2013), p. 147.

[33]Supporting a more conservative approach: "while there are clearly tensions between independence and impartiality on the one hand, and other characteristics or objectives of investment arbitration on the other hand, [the book] concludes that there is no irreconcilable contradiction, and that the suggested comprehensive reforms would therefore be unwarranted and unsuitable to resolve existing deficiencies of the system", Cleis (2017), p. 189. This more static approach should not be underestimated, taking into account the fate of previous proposals for system change. St. John and Chernykh (2018).

In general, neither conventions, IIAs nor institutional arbitration rules in the investment sphere have traditionally addressed the international investment arbitrators' duties in any systematic sense. These texts do allude to some issues—mostly, independence, impartiality, confidentiality—but tend not to deal with them very thoroughly, in addition to which there is no exhaustive list of the possible duties of international investment arbitrators.

At academic level, a good number of authors have dealt with the duties of international commercial and investment arbitrators. These studies could be divided into those that present a generalist approach using umbrella terms that are difficult to ring-fence, such as ethics, deontology and morals, and those that focus on a specific duty, which is usually independence and impartiality—another concept that almost defies clear definition.

An interesting novelty that has begun to emerge in the investment arbitration milieu over recent years is the code of conduct. Codes of conduct were already known in the commercial arbitration context,[34] in other ADR spheres—mediation, WTO, etc.—and also in the international judicial sector, but they had not been established so far in the ISDS sphere.

The most recent EU-inspired IIAs contain Codes of conduct for members of the tribunal, the appeal tribunal and mediators.[35] Likewise, references to the future creation of Codes of conduct have been included in the 2016 ICSID Rules Amendment Process,[36] alternative ISDS mechanisms to ICSID,[37] recent Model BITs,[38] and proposals coming from academics.[39]

---

[34]The growing need for a Code of ethics for international commercial arbitrators was affirmed as far back as 1985. Hunter and Paulsson (1985).

[35]The Council has recently stated that a Code of Conduct is also required in the MIC setting: "strong rules on ethics and conflict of interests, including a Code of Conduct for the Members of the Court and challenge mechanisms shall be included in the Convention." Council of the European Union (2018).

[36]Potential Areas for Amendment: "Code of Conduct for Arbitrators: the ICSID rules currently require a declaration that an arbitrator meets the required qualifications in the Convention, however some recent treaties have included more elaborated Codes of conduct outlining expectations. This could be incorporated in the ICSID process". ICSID (2016).

[37]An example of an initiative that has not yet prospered is Article 32 bis of the UNASUR Draft Constitutive Agreement: "The requirements that must be met by members of the Permanent Court (…) The Code of Conduct contains provisions for ensuring the independence of the members of the Permanent Court from all Parties involved in a dispute, whether they will be States or investors". Sarmiento (2015).

[38]"Article [15] – Conflict of Interest and Code of Conduct: Members of the Tribunal shall comply with the International Bar Association Guidelines on Conflicts of Interest in International Arbitration and any Code of Conduct adopted by the Joint Committee pursuant to Article [The Joint Committee]". Draft Model Agreement (2015). This provision does not appear in the 2017 version of this Draft Model Agreement.

[39]Article 22.2: "Code of Conduct. The Committee of the Contracting Parties shall establish a Code of Conduct specifying the conduct of the panel members and the grounds for excusing a Panel member. The Code shall be binding on the members of the Tribunal. In adopting the Code, the

A priori, these Codes of conduct should be welcomed as a clear contrast to the previous scenario of scattered references to one or more arbitrator duties. The availability of a separate document that contains the whole set of adjudicators' duties reflects an effort to be systematic, while also representing progress in terms of transparency.[40] Likewise, making the duties more visible seems to reflect an attempt to establish a distinction between the usual procedural rules and these new Codes of conduct, which possibly aspire to become an essential part of a new legal sector dealing with adjudicators' ethics. It can also be argued that Codes of conduct provide adjudicators with better protection from unjustified party attacks. The EU has clearly positioned itself in favour of including Codes of conduct in the ICS/MIC context.[41] A recent study devised by the EP provides a twofold justification for drawing up such Codes: they represent a gesture of rapprochement to highly critical public opinion, as well as an increased desire to achieve government control over the issue.[42] Creating Codes of conduct, in short, appears to be a response to pre-existing concerns over accountability.[43]

However, and as will be discussed in detail throughout this book, there are major shortcomings in the way international investment arbitrators' duties are currently systemised. Both single provisions and recent Codes of conduct are drafted in general and ambiguous terms.[44] Moreover, and given that the literal wording of these duties has sometimes been taken from other legal contexts, the question arises as to whether the content of these provisions is adequate for the complex and highly specific reality of conflicts developing from international investments. A further point of criticism is that not even the new Codes comprehensively cover the duties of investment adjudicators.[45]

On the basis of this set of circumstances, this book aims to provide a detailed analysis of a significant set of duties that are attributed to investment adjudicators—both traditional international investment arbitrators and also prospective members of the tribunal/judges. The book does not devote a chapter specifically to the duty of

Committee shall take the IBA Guidelines on Conflicts of Interest in International Arbitration into consideration." Krajewski (2014), pp. 17–18.

[40]These values have been very positively viewed in the judicial context. Action 2.3 of the Council of Europe plan of action on strengthening judicial independence and impartiality states: "to shield judges from inducement to corruption, member state must ensure that the remuneration and working conditions of judges are adequate and that standards of professional conduct and judicial ethics are clearly defined and made public". Council of Europe (2016).

[41]It is stated that: "We have included, for the first time, a Code of Conduct for arbitrators, ensuring the respect of high ethical and professional standards". EC (2015b).

[42]EP (2017), p. 106.

[43]Kaufmann-Kohler (2016), p. 146.

[44]In Cleis' opinion: "The Code of Conduct is otherwise rather rudimentary and vague". Cleis (2017), p. 220.

[45]The NGO milieu affirms that: "loopholes in the proposed ethics code for the arbitrators also give rise to concerns". Corporate Europe Observatory (2016), p. 5. "The Code of Conduct and ethics provisions of the ICS proposal are not solid enough". TACD (2016), p. 5.

independence and impartiality, as this is by far the most widely discussed duty at both practical and academic levels,[46] and there are also extensive recent studies in the field.[47] Instead, a perhaps more novel and challenging approach has been adopted: focusing on other pre- and post-appointment duties, which have thus far been viewed as less clearly-defined, or even secondary.[48] This does not mean that the principle of independence and impartiality is absent of the pages of this book; on the contrary, it is frequently referred to in the context of other arbitrator duties.[49] This is also because these duties should not be regarded as watertight compartments,[50] as will be detailed later.

It should also be noted that the book does not deal comprehensively with the duties of commercial arbitrators or international or national judges.[51] However, there are reflections on comparative law at several points; as analysing the origins and application of these duties in other legal contexts is important for a better understanding of the—more recent—international investment sector. This comparative analysis is based on a set of representative texts with conventional, national and arbitral origins, drafted at different times and in different legal cultures.

This book's main aim is therefore to make a significant contribution to the in-depth study of the duties of investment adjudicators, regardless of the soft or hard law mechanisms through which they may be systematised.[52] As has already been pointed out, the current system is in flux. The reflections contained here may be useful for tackling the content of existing provisions, promoting reforms in this area within existing institutions such as ICSID, or providing theoretical and practical foundation for new institutions such as the MIC. An additional aim is to suggest further research lines which may be relevant with respect to future practice.

On the basis that defining the specific perimeters of investment adjudicators' duties is a highly controversial issue in itself, this work aims to stimulate debate among all investment stakeholders. While being far from accommodating, the book

---

[46]Although the author does not completely share this approach, it could also be argued that "the existing framework provide[s] adequate mechanisms to ensure independence and impartiality of the arbitrators". UNCITRAL (2018), par 50.

[47]Cleis (2017).

[48]In this sense, if the UNCITRAL Commission concludes that there is a need for a harmonized and authoritative source of ethics in international arbitration, it is the author's view that this should cover the entire content of ethical standards (i.e. not be limited to impartiality and independence, but also encompassing other obligations such as those analysed in this book). UNCITRAL (2017), par. 43.

[49]The author has examined some facets of this duty of independence and impartiality in a recent publication: Fach Gómez (2018).

[50]Indicating that there may be tensions between the range of duties falling to arbitrators, Park (2011a). Developing this approach in other scholarly pieces: Park (2011b, c).

[51]There are various works devoted to this area: Shetreet and Forsyth (2011), Langbroek and Fabri (2007). Apart from other English pieces cited throughout this book, there are also noteworthy works in other languages: Ruiz Fabri and Sorel (2010) and van Compernolle and Tarzia (2006).

[52]Pointing out the need to draft revised arbitrator Codes of conduct, see Joint Working Group on Trade & Investment Law Reform (2017).

aims to treat international investment arbitrators with the greatest respect. There is no doubt that the individuals that make up this honourable group have not only duties but also rights.[53] The fact that the book is based on the premise that investment adjudicators act in good faith goes without saying.

1.3 Key Duties of International Investment Adjudicators: Some Transversal Uncertainties and Challenges

As pointed out above, the book dissects some of the key duties of international investment adjudicators,[54] aiming to pin down their current content and reflecting on which specific aspects of the duties could be more clearly defined or enhanced in the future. The choice of this methodology does not however imply a lack of awareness of the fact that these individual duties are cross-cut by several major issues.

This chapter therefore concludes with a brief reference to challenging questions such as these: the fact that there are so many sources that refer to international investment arbitrators' duties and the ways in which these sources relate to each other; the need to give these duties teeth and, linked with this, the role that arbitral tribunals, arbitration institutions and other entities may play in terms of the enforcement of adjudicators' duties.

1.3.1 Plurality of Sources

The claim that "international arbitration dwells in an ethical no man's land" has become a classic.[55] In the commercial arbitration framework this statement can be extended to both arbitrators and counsels, as the fact that international arbitration has now become a powerful global industry[56] is by the same token the source of many ethical problems and practical doubts for its participants.[57]

---

[53]This was adequately reflected in an extensive Special Issue dealing with the Duties, Rights and Powers of International Arbitrators, jointly coordinated by the author. Álvarez Zárate and Fach Gómez (2018). Other recent works in the field are: Bjorklund and Brosseau (2017) and Jacquet (2015).

[54]The question of the ethical standards applicable to counsels, arbitral secretaries, and expert witnesses involved in international arbitrations (called "micro issues" or "behavioral concerns" by Menkel-Meadow) lies outside the scope of this book. "Macro" or "policy concerns" (institutional or social justice issues) are not covered either. Menkel-Meadow (2002), p. 952. These issues have generated an ever-increasing number of publications in recent years: Rauber (2014), Harris (2013) and Moses (2012), etc.

[55]Rogers (2001), p. 342.

[56]Menon (2013), p. 4.

[57]Sussman and Ebere (2011).

Where the figure of the commercial arbitrator is concerned, the numerous scholars and practitioners that have addressed this issue agree that "the ethical standards of arbitrators (...) is perhaps the most fractured area of international arbitration (...) remain[ing] a work in progress".[58] In simple terms, the lack of consistency in this area has given rise to a number of disturbing and inefficient scenarios: situations in which commercial arbitrators have to deal with conflicting or unclear obligations; and arbitration parties claiming that they did not receive fair treatment due to these ethical inconsistencies[59] or using a range of procedural strategies to take advantage of such uncertainties (arbitrator challenges, annulment or non-recognition of arbitral awards, etc.).

This context has naturally prompted some commentators to suggest creating rules to define the way in which the potentially applicable texts should interconnect, while others have called for a uniform code of ethics for arbitrators to be created.[60] However, reality shows that these desiderata have not completely taken shape yet; moreover, creating a global code of ethics has recently been described as a quixotic endeavour[61] that will have to face many crucial difficulties: ineffectiveness deriving from being over-general and from the lack of sanctions for arbitrator misconduct; the true impossibility of coordinating or overcoming diverse national and regional specificities, and the risk that a standardised Code, which may be seen as over-regulation, could further complicate arbitral proceedings, among others.

The picture in investment arbitration is very similar: investment scholars point out that what exists at present is a true "patchwork of laws, rules and guidelines" referring to arbitrators' duties. Identifying all the components referred to is no small task, since multiple and varied texts with different levels of binding force may come together vis-à-vis a single pattern of facts in a case, for instance: national procedural laws (domestic laws/acts or texts drafted by national bar associations)[62]; institutional arbitration rules and ethical Codes (drawn up by arbitral institutions, practitioners' associations, or as joint initiatives), and international conventions.[63] In the face of such fragmented reality, it is natural that stakeholders like the EU have found it necessary to point out that "an issue to consider will be the potential overlap of multiple applicable Codes of conduct" when developing projects such as the ICS or the future MIC.[64]

---

[58]Ng (2016), pp. 24 and 41.

[59]Niedermeyer (2014), p. 496.

[60]This feeling of insecurity has produced conflict of law proposals in favour of applying the strictest ethical requirements to arbitrators from among those potentially applicable to the case, for example. Michaelson (2007–2008).

[61]Menon (2013), p. 18.

[62]For instance, Article 61 of the Code of Conduct for Lawyers. Italian National Bar Council (2014).

[63]Bernasconi-Osterwalder et al. (2010), p. 2.

[64]EC (2016b). Likewise, the UNCITRAL Secretariat has stated with reference to both commercial and investment arbitration that: "Different approaches could be envisaged, for instance, providing guidance to determine whether and when the ethical standards are applicable, while noting the limits of application of such standards, since arbitrators are likely to come from different jurisdictions and

With regard to the current scenario, there is already a need for a provision that would enable legal actors to predict the applicable instrument when various texts covering investment adjudicators' duties clash. The FTAs recently created in the EU context fail to address this issue in a general sense, and neither is it completely clear how references to the specific relationship between the FTA Codes of conduct and the IBA guidelines ("take into consideration", "supplement", "replace")[65] will be implemented in practice.

Looking to the future, and focusing on a global context such as that envisaged by the prospective MIC, *a priori* UNCITRAL appears to be a suitable forum for tackling the question of the interrelationship of multiple texts dealing with arbitrators' duties.[66] If this approach is to be prioritized,[67] a provision such as that in the UNCITRAL Rules on Transparency in Treaty-based Investor-State Arbitration might serve as an inspiration at ethical level. The transparency provision contains individual solutions for conflict between the Rules and arbitration rules, IIAs, and mandatory and non-mandatory provisions pertaining to the law applicable to the arbitration.[68]

---

would thus be subject to different ethical standards. Work could be undertaken to provide clarity regarding the interrelationship among ethical rules (i) of the arbitrator's home jurisdiction, (ii) of the jurisdiction in which the arbitration is being held (both the legal seat and physical venue), (iii) provided for in the applicable law, (iv) of the arbitral institutions, and (v) contained in soft law standards agreed to by the parties or set by the arbitral tribunal (...) arbitral tribunals could be bound by more than one ethical standard depending on the nationality of the arbitrators, affiliation with bar associations, as well as the place of arbitration. Therefore, multiple norms may apply at the same time, without any clear indication on which shall prevail in case of conflict." UNCITRAL (2017), pars 38–39.

[65]*Infra*, Chap. 3.

[66]As stated in the April 2018 Working Group III Report: "the consideration of the topic by UNCITRAL constituted a unique opportunity to make meaningful reforms in the field, and that active and wide participation by both developing and developed States was essential to ensure the effectiveness and legitimacy of the UNCITRAL process in implementing the mandate". UNCITRAL (2018), par 15.

[67]The options for future work are currently open, with the choice being between: "Whether there is a need for a harmonized and authoritative source on ethics in international arbitration, or whether guidance on articulation among the possible applicable ethical standards would be more appropriate". UNCITRAL (2017), par 43.

[68]Article 1.7 and 1.8 of the UNCITRAL Rules: "Applicable instrument in case of conflict. Where the Rules on Transparency apply, they shall supplement any applicable arbitration rules. Where there is a conflict between the Rules on Transparency and the applicable arbitration rules, the Rules on Transparency shall prevail. Notwithstanding any provision in these Rules, where there is a conflict between the Rules on Transparency and the treaty, the provisions of the treaty shall prevail. Where any of these Rules is in conflict with a provision of the law applicable to the arbitration from which the disputing parties cannot derogate, that provision shall prevail." UNCITRAL (2014).

1.3.2 Sanctions and Enforcement

It is clear that if arbitrators comply with their duties, regardless of how and where they are set out in writing, this benefits not only the arbitrators' careers, but also the entire arbitration collective, the institution managing the arbitration, and ultimately all participant stakeholders. However, praxis shows that international adjudicators sometimes disregard their duties, and this book contains several examples. The question therefore arises as to what kind of action such breaches of duty merit, and who is responsible for dealing with such situations.

In some legal sectors, such as the judicial, consolidated responses to these questions exist at both national and international levels. The Code of Conduct for Members and former Members of the CJEU, for instance, contains a provision for establishing a collective body that is responsible for ensuring the proper application of the Code of Conduct.[69] Likewise, the 2010 Kyiv Recommendations on Judicial Independence stipulate that disciplinary proceedings are to be initiated against judges in cases of alleged professional misconduct and also require an Independent Body Deciding on Discipline to be set up, which complies with a range of procedural and transparency safeguards.[70] Comparative studies reveal that similar mechanisms usually exist at national level.[71]

There has been much discussion in the international commercial arbitration world about the most appropriate body for enforcing ethical duties and imposing sanctions. The possibility of creating a new international structure to respond to issues of counsel ethics in arbitration proceedings was considered.[72] However, the Global Arbitration Ethics Council, as it was called, in fact came to nothing.[73]

When dealing with international commercial arbitrators, the critical focus is not on creating a new global institution, but rather on the competences of existing arbitration institutions. Indeed, both academic commentators and participants in

[69] Article 10 of the Code of Conduct: "Application of the Code. The President of the Court of Justice, assisted by a Consultative Committee, shall be responsible for ensuring the proper application of this Code of Conduct. The Consultative Committee shall be composed of the three Members of the Court of Justice who have been longest in office and the Vice-President of the Court of Justice if he or she is not one of those Members. Should a Member or a former Member of the General Court be the person concerned, the President, the Vice-President and another Member of the General Court shall take part in the deliberations of the Committee. The Committee shall be assisted by the Registrar of the Court of Justice. Without prejudice to the provisions of the Statute of the Court of Justice of the European Union, the Committee may, in an individual case, give its opinion to the Member or the former Member concerned after hearing him or her". CJEU (2016).

[70] Part III – Accountability of Judges and Judicial Independence in Adjudication. Provisions 25 and 26. OSCE-ODIHR (2010).

[71] Seibert-Fohr (2013) and Clark (n.a).

[72] ASA (2016).

[73] Geisinger (2015).

international arbitration[74] are presently calling for arbitration institutions to adopt a much more energetic role in preventing, policing and sanctioning cases of arbitral misconduct,[75] which are crucial issues that many arbitration institutions are felt to have failed to address. Expressed in other words: "Self-regulators, however, tend to be self-satisfied".[76] For this reason, initiatives such as that implemented by CIArb, which focuses on investigating complaints of misconduct against its members,[77] are positively valued by a school of thought[78] that also calls for this type of "institutional activism" to become more widespread.[79] This approach would result in these managing institutions implementing a broad range of possible initiatives, such as devoting more material resources to the investigation of misconduct complaints; specifying the subjects that are authorized to submit such complaints; ensuring increased transparency in disciplinary processes, and strengthening the sanctions arising from misconduct, among others.[80]

Academics have also noted that a series of similar problems to those already detected in the commercial context exist in the investment arbitration setting as well. The practical hurdles resulting from international investment arbitrators' failure to comply with their duties are addressed throughout this book. It is also pointed out that some crucial stakeholders currently consider both the normative scenario for

---

[74]Focusing on the adequacy of an *ex post* evaluation of the arbitrators' performance, and also suggesting that arbitral institutions should be more proactive in other contexts, the 2018 White & Case International Arbitration Survey reveals that: "The overwhelming majority of respondents (80%) indicated that they would [like to be given the option of evaluating arbitrators at the end of proceedings] (...) The overall results show that reporting to an arbitral institution, provided that the arbitration was administered by that institution, would be by far the preferred method of providing an assessment of arbitrators (88%). This longstanding trend adds to the perception that arbitral institutions occupy a central position in the arbitration framework, which also suggests that users' expectations from them are accordingly high. It seems that the users increasingly expect the role and duties of arbitral institutions to evolve in accordance with changing trends and user needs, such as the desire for more transparency on arbitrator performance, based on both measurable and intangible metrics." White & Case (2018), pp. 22–23.

[75]Fernández Rozas (2010), p. 449. As Menon states: "As we contemplate these problems of moral hazard, ethics, inadequate supply and conflicts of interest associated with international arbitrators, it seems surprising that there are no controls or regulations to maintain the quality standards and legitimacy of the industry (...) is it time then for us to give up our cherished notions of autonomy and subscribe to an international regulatory regime?". Menon (2012), pars 43 and 71. Warwas (2017).

[76]Paulsson (2013), p. 147.

[77]CIArb (last accessed June 2018).

[78]Oyre states: "If the Institute is truly to promote arbitration and ADR as a viable alternative to litigation it has a concomitant duty to investigate allegations of members' inappropriate conduct in a fair and independent manner and to ensure that its practicing members are as up-to-date and competent as they can be. If it fails in this one fundamental aspect, it cannot honestly claim to be one of the foremost and respected international education and training bodies in the field of arbitration and ADR". Oyre (2002), p. 103.

[79]Reflecting on institutional activism, Nappert (2015).

[80]Hacking (2016), par 13.27.

investment arbitrators' duties[81] and the international investment arbitrators' corresponding accountability level[82] to be insufficient.

For reasons of this kind, some actors argue that intervention at multilateral level would constitute a decisive step forward. The novel approach of having a code of ethics drawn up by UNCITRAL[83] or jointly by UNCITRAL and ICSID has recently gained momentum.[84] This initiative raises a fundamental issue that is sketched out in various points in this book, to which it is difficult to find a wholly satisfactory solution: the dichotomy between self-regulation (endogenous) and top-down external intervention (exogenous)[85] in the legal framework of investment arbitrators'

[81]The latest surveys on the subject indicate that arbitration stakeholders support the imposition of sanctions on international arbitrators in specific cases of breach of their duties. For instance, the 2018 White & Case survey brings out into the open the fact that: "most users would welcome provisions regulating the conduct of arbitrators: a large majority of about 80% of respondents think that arbitration rules should address "standards of independence and impartiality for arbitrators," "consequences for delay by arbitrators" and "deadlines for issuing awards." White & Case (2018) pars 34 and 35. Focusing on the dilatory conduct of an arbitrator, the survey indicates that: "Some interviewees argued that inefficient conduct of this kind by arbitrators should not go unsanctioned and that arbitral institutions should entertain with more interest the idea of applying strict sanctions in cases of unreasonable delays. As for the appropriate sanction, various views were expressed. A number of interviewees were of the opinion that pecuniary sanctions should be put in place. Others were reluctant as to their effectiveness, arguing that the busiest, most sought-after arbitrators are likely to be the ones least deterred by such measures. Yet another group of interviewees proposed that arbitrator profiles made available to users by arbitral institutions should include performance indicators such as the average time a certain arbitrator has spent on an arbitration. The counterargument advanced by others was that the relevance of such data is rather limited since every arbitration has its own particularities. That being said, there was a consensus among interviewed respondents that arbitration rules should indeed contemplate a more efficient mechanism for sanctioning delays by arbitrators." White & Case (2018), 34 y 35.

[82]Tung (2016), p. 57.

[83]It has been recently proclaimed that: "Two possible approaches could be considered for future work on ethics. The first being the preparation of a substantive Code of ethics seeking to provide harmonization and clarity, for instance with regard to the disclosure and challenge procedures; and the second being the preparation of guidelines on relevant and applicable ethical standards". UNCITRAL (2017), par. 18.

[84]ICSID has recently announced that the organization is working with the UNCITRAL Secretariat on a Code of Conduct for Arbitrators. ICSID Secretariat, Proposals for Amendment of the ICSID Rules—Synopsis, Volume 1, August 2, 2018, par. 33. This document is not going to be analysed in detail in this book, as it was presented after completing the elaboration of the present book.

[85]Paulsson stresses the existing difficulties in the following reflections: "The stakes are too high to leave these matters to be dealt with by self-appraisal, peer pressure, or other forms of self-regulation. It is not clear that all arbitral institutions have adequate structures to meet the challenge. But unless these bodies fully embrace their role in protecting the interests of arbitrants rather than those of arbitrators, it is likely that occasional judicial intervention will not be perceived as enough and pressure will build on political actors to step in and provide stricter regulations notwithstanding their lack of familiarity with the arbitral process. The result might be unwelcome bureaucratization, and a gradual erosion of arbitrations´ advantages". Paulsson (2013), p. 149. On the other hand, Rogers makes a clear case for ethical self-regulation in international arbitration: "the international arbitration community should explicitly assume primary responsibility for ethical regulation of its participants (. . .) Taking up the call for ethical self-regulation provides an opportunity to develop

duties. In the case of the initiative newly promoted by UNCITRAL on Investor-State Dispute Settlement Reform, the autopoietic approach seems to be considered insufficient.[86]

The proposal to draw up a standard Code of conduct for international arbitrators is undoubtedly an ambitious initiative that will require time for serious debate and implementation where appropriate. This is an extremely complex legal and political issue, which requires the confluence of a specific set of circumstances to succeed. In the interim, however, there is still a need to reflect on investment arbitrators' duties and the level of enforcement in the immediate future.

It was recently stated in the investment arbitration milieu that: "we do not need more rules. What is needed is someone to enforce the rules".[87] Regardless of whether or not the first sentence is true, there is little doubt that international investment arbitration has been less than pioneering in terms of enforcing sanctions when investment arbitrators have breached their ethical duties. As will be pointed out in the course of this book, commercial arbitration seems to be more developed in this matter. Of course, there are mechanisms such as investment arbitrator´s disqualification in the ICSID sphere.[88] Nevertheless, Article 21 of the ICSID Convention,[89] combined with the lack of any detailed development of disciplinary powers attributable to investment arbitration tribunals, arbitration institutions and other entities has led to a contemporary scenario that can be defined in many ways, ranging from excessively protectionist to simply considerate of investment arbitrators' idiosyncrasies.

As already indicated, the EU's intervention in the ISDS system via its latest generation of FTAs has resulted in the establishment of a more cohesive ethics regime through the incorporating of Codes of conduct into FTAs. These texts contain classic legal institutions in the investment arbitration sphere, such as adjudicator disqualification as a consequence of a notice of challenge submitted by a disputing party. The texts also introduce a new figure into the framework of their

collective understanding about what constitutes proper and improper conduct, an understanding that transcends national legal cultures (...)" Rogers (2014), introduction. Although both authors might have commercial arbitration as their first reference in mind, it is understood that their reflections also cover investment arbitration.

[86]Wai (2002).

[87]Kaufmann-Kohler (2016), p. 146.

[88]Article 57 ICSID Convention (1966) and Rule 9 of the ICSID Arbitration Rules. ICSID (2006).

[89]Article 21 of the ICSID Convention states that: "arbitrators (...) shall enjoy immunity from legal process with respect to acts performed by them in the exercise of their functions, except when the Centre waives this immunity". ICSID (1966). Being in the antipodes of the referred article, it is relevant to point from the perspective of comparative law the existence of the still firmer Article 399 I of the Chinese Criminal Law: "Where anyone who undertakes the duties of arbitration according to law intentionally goes against the facts and law and makes any wrongful ruling in the process of arbitration he shall be sentenced to fix-term imprisonment of not more than three years of detention. If the circumstances are extremely serious, he shall be sentenced to fixed-term imprisonment of not less than three years but no more than seven years". Ruiping and Xiaosong (2014). *Infra* Chapter 2.8.

procedural rules, which reflects a regulatory interest in matters of disciplinary power: the removal of the adjudicator, which may occur in the following circumstances: "Upon a reasoned recommendation from the President of the Appeal Tribunal, or on their joint initiative, the Parties, by decision of the [. . .] Committee, may remove a Member from the Tribunal where his or her behaviour is inconsistent with the obligations set out in paragraph 1 [. . .] and incompatible with his or her continued membership of the Tribunal. If the behaviour in question is alleged to be that of the President of the Appeal Tribunal then the President of the Tribunal of First Instance shall submit the reasoned recommendation".[90]

In addition, the Code of Conduct for Members of the Tribunal, the Appeal Tribunal and Mediators contained in the 2018 EU-Singapore IPA incorporates a body that did not appear in previous FTAs negotiated by the EU: the Consultative Committee. Article 10 of the Code states that: "The President of the Tribunal and the President of the Appeal Tribunal shall each be assisted by a Consultative Committee, composed of the respective Vice-President and the most senior member by age of the Tribunal and the Appeal Tribunal respectively, for ensuring the proper application of this code of conduct, Article 3.11 (Ethics) and for the execution of any other task, where so provided".[91] Neither the new body's name nor the wording of Article 10 suggest that this innovation will wield much power. Besides that, getting the Consultative Committee running properly will require further and detailed regulation. It is however, a first intimation of the future that may await this sector.[92]

The UNCITRAL Working Group III has recently raised a number of issues in this ethical area: "In that light, the Commission may wish to consider the following questions (. . .) whether a new instrument should cover (v) effect of breach of ethical standards, and (vi) enforcement mechanisms (how should ethical rules be enforced and by whom (arbitrators, parties, institutions, others)?); (d) Whether the consequences of non-compliance with ethical standards are addressed in sufficient detail in existing instruments". Taking into account what is stated in the preceding paragraphs of this chapter, the questions posed by UNCITRAL should be answered in the future with a call to develop a range of disciplinary instruments, available should investment adjudicators fail to comply with their duties.

---

[90]Article 8. 30.4 of CETA; Article 3.11.5 EU-Singapore IPA; Article 14.5 EU-Vietnam FTA, Article 8.5 Ethics-JEFTA and Article 11.5 TTIP.

[91]Article 10 (paragraph 24) of the EU-Singapore IPA Code of Conduct (2018).

[92]It is also remarkable that the recent Code of Conduct contained in the EU Singapore IPA incorporates a procedure in case a former Member had breached his/her ethical obligations referred to in the Code: "If the President of the Tribunal or of the Appeal Tribunal is informed or otherwise becomes aware that a former Member of the Tribunal or of the Appeal Tribunal, respectively, is alleged to have breached the obligations set out in paragraphs 15 through 17, he shall examine the matter, and provide the opportunity to the former Member to be heard. If, after verification, he finds the alleged breach to be confirmed, he shall inform: (a) the professional body or other such institution with which that former Member is affiliated; (b) the Parties; and (c) the president of any other relevant investment tribunal or appeal tribunal. The President of the Tribunal or of the Appeal Tribunal shall make public its findings pursuant to this paragraph." EU-Singapore IPA (2018).

It must be taken into account that there are standing bodies of adjudicators in both the bilateral ICS structure and also at the level of a future MIC. *A priori*, this may be one of the factors facilitating the development of a disciplinary power exercised by the investment tribunal or other institution, if, as would be desirable, this legislative option were to be developed in the future.

References

Álvarez Zárate JM, Fach Gómez K (2018) The duties, rights and powers of international arbitrators. Special Issue. Law Pract Int Tribunals 17(1)

ASA (2016) ASA Working Group on Counsel Ethics Releases Latest Findings. https://www.arbitration-ch.org/en/asa/asa-news/details/993.asa-working-group-on-counsel-ethics-releases-latest-findings.html

ASIL-ICCA (2016) Report of the Joint Task Force on Issue Conflicts in Investor-State Arbitration. https://www.asil.org/sites/default/files/ASIL_ICCA.pdf

Baker McKenzie (2017) Submissions to the ICSID Secretariat on amendments to the ICSID rules and regulations. In: Public Comments to Amendment of ICSID's Rules and Regulations. https://icsid.worldbank.org/en/Documents/about/Public%20Comments%20to%20Amendment%20to%20ICSID%20Rules%20and%20Regulations.pdf

Bernasconi-Osterwalder N, Johnson L, Marshall F (2010), Arbitrator independence and impartiality: examining the dual role of arbitrator and counsel. International Institute for Sustainable Development. http://www.iisd.org/pdf/2011/dci_2010_arbitrator_independence.pdf

Bjorklund A, Brosseau J (2017) Sources of inherent powers in international adjudication. Eur Int Arbitr Rev 6(2):1–49

Brower CN, Rosenberg CB (2013) The death of the two-headed nightingale: why the Paulsson-van den Berg presumption that party-appointed arbitrators are untrustworthy is wrongheaded. Arbitr Int 29(1):7–44

Bungenberg M (2015) Towards a more balanced international investment law 2.0? In: Hermann C, Simma B, Streinz R (eds) Trade policy between law, diplomacy and scholarship. Liber amicorum in memoriam Horst G. Krenzler. Springer, Berlin, pp 15–37

Clark DS (n.a.) Chapter 3. The Organization of Lawyers and Judges. Section XI. Judicial Accountability and Independence. In: Cappelletti M (chief ed) International Encyclopedia of comparative law. Civil procedure, vol XVI. Mohr Siebeck, Tübingen and Martinus Nijhoff Publishers, Leiden Boston, pp. 97–101

Cleis MN (2017) The independence and impartiality of ICSID arbitrators. Brill Nijhoff, Leiden

Coleman M, Innes T (2015) Provisional measures during suspension of ICSID proceedings. ICSID Rev 30(1):713-728.

Corporate Europe Observatory (2016) The zombie ISDS. Rebranded as ICS, rights for corporations to sue states refuse to die. https://corporateeurope.org/sites/default/files/attachments/the_zombie_isds_0.pdf

Debevoise & Plimpton (2017) Proposed Amendments to 2006 ICSID Rules. In: Public Comments to Amendment of ICSID's Rules and Regulations. https://icsid.worldbank.org/en/Documents/about/Public%20Comments%20to%20Amendment%20to%20ICSID%20Rules%20and%20Regulations.pdf

Derains & Gharavi (2017) ICSID Rules Amendment Project. In: Public Comments to Amendment of ICSID's Rules and Regulations. https://icsid.worldbank.org/en/Documents/about/Public%20Comments%20to%20Amendment%20to%20ICSID%20Rules%20and%20Regulations.pdf

EFILA (2017) Response of the European Federation for Investment Law and Arbitration to the Invitation to File Suggestions for ICSID Rules Amendments. In: Public Comments to Amendment of ICSID's Rules and Regulations. https://icsid.worldbank.org/en/Documents/about/

Public%20Comments%20to%20Amendment%20to%20ICSID%20Rules%20and%20Regulations.pdf
Fach Gómez K (2018) Diversity and the principle of independence and impartiality in the future multilateral investment court. Law Pract Int Courts Tribunals 17(1):78–97
Fach Gómez K (2019) Los árbitros en el arbitraje internacional de inversiones. In: Zenkiewicz M, Álvarez Zárate JM (eds) Inversiones Internacionales, Universidad Externado de Colombia, Bogotá., in press
Fernández Rozas JC (2010) Clearer ethics guidelines and comparative standards for arbitrators. In: Fernández-Ballesteros MA, Arias D (eds) Liber Amicorum Bernardo Cremades. La Ley, Madrid, pp 413–449
Geisinger E (2015) "Soft Law" and hard questions: ASA's initiative in the debate on counsel ethics in international arbitration. In: Favalli D (ed) Sense and non-sense of guidelines, rules and other para-regulatory texts in international arbitration - ASA Special Series No. 37. Juris, Huntington, pp 17–32
Hacking BS (2016) Ethics in arbitration: party and arbitral misconduct. In: Betancourt JC (ed) Defining issues in international arbitration: celebrating 100 years of the chartered institute of arbitrators. Oxford University Press, Oxford
Harris TL (2013) Ethics in international arbitration: they're not just for lawyers. Constr Law Int 8 (3):37–40
Howse R (last accessed June 2018) Courting the critics of investor-state dispute settlement: the EU proposal for a judicial system for investment disputes. https://cdn-media.web-view.net/i/fjj3t288ah/Courting_the_Criticsdraft1.pdf
Hunter MH, Paulsson J (1985) A code of ethics for arbitrators in international commercial arbitration. Int Bus Lawyer 13:153–160
ICSID Secretariat, Proposals for Amendment of the ICSID Rules—Synopsis, Volume 1, August 2, 2018., https://icsid.worldbank.org/en/Documents/Amendments_Vol_One.pdf
Investment Treaty Working Group of the American Bar Association (2016) Task Force Report on the Investment Court System Proposal. http://apps.americanbar.org/dch/thedl.cfm?filename=/IC730000/newsletterpubs/ExecutiveSummaryDiscussionPaper101416.pdf
Jacques Delors Institute (2015) ISDS-The devil is in the details. http://www.institutdelors.eu/media/ttipisds-fabrygarbasso-nejdi-jan15.pdf?pdf=ok
Jacquet JM (2015) Les libertés de l'arbitre international. In: Mélanges en l'honneur du Professeur Pierre Mayer. LGDJ, Paris, pp 311–329
Joint Working Group on Trade & Investment Law Reform (2017) Principles for a 21st Century Investment Law Regime. https://www.bc.edu/content/dam/bc1/schools/law/academics/law-global-context/principles-towards-investment-regime.pdf
Kahale G III (2018) ISDS: the wild, wild west of international law and arbitration. Brooklyn J Int Law 44(1). https://www.curtis.com/siteFiles/AttorneyFiles/ISDS%20-%20The%20Wild,%20Wild%20West%20of%20International%20Law%20and%20Arbitration.pdf
Kaufmann-Kohler G (2016) Remarks. American Society of International Law, Proceedings of the 110th Annual Meeting 142–149
Krajewski M (2014) Modalities for investment protection and ISDS in TTIP from a trade union perspective. http://library.fes.de/pdf-files/bueros/bruessel/11044.pdf
Langbroek PM, Fabri M (2007) The right judge for each case. A study of case assignment and impartiality in six European judiciaries. Intersentia. Antwerp-Oxford
Law Council of Australia (2017) Potential rule amendments or improvements to the arbitration and conciliation procedures of ICSID. In: Public Comments to Amendment of ICSID's Rules and Regulations. https://icsid.worldbank.org/en/Documents/about/Public%20Comments%20to%20Amendment%20to%20ICSID%20Rules%20and%20Regulations.pdf
Lazareff S (2005) L'arbitre singe. Ou comment assassiner l'arbitrage. In: Aksen G et al (ed) Liber Amicorum in honour of Robert Briner. Global reflections on international law, commerce and dispute resolution. ICC Publishing, Paris, pp 477–489

Malmström C (2015a) Blog. Investments in TTIP and beyond-towards an international investment court. https://ec.europa.eu/commission/2014-2019/malmstrom/blog/investments-ttip-and-beyond-towards-international-investment-court_en

Malmström C (2015b) Blog. Proposing an Investment Court System. https://ec.europa.eu/commission/2014-2019/malmstrom/blog/proposing-investment-court-system_en

Malmström C (2015c) Opening remarks: discussion on investment in TTIP. http://trade.ec.europa.eu/doclib/docs/2015/march/tradoc_153258.pdf

Menkel-Meadow C (2002) Ethics issues in arbitration and related dispute resolution processes: what's happening and what's not. Univ Miami Law Rev 56:949–1008

Menon S (2012) International arbitration: the coming of a new age for Asia (and elsewhere). In: ICCA Congress. Opening Plenary Session. http://www.arbitration-icca.org/media/0/13398435632250/ags_opening_speech_icca_congress_2012.pdf

Menon S (2013) Some cautionary notes for an age of opportunity. Key Note. Chartered Institute of Arbitrators International Arbitration Conference. http://www.singaporelaw.sg/sglaw/images/media/130822%20Some%20cautionary%20notes%20for%20an%20age%20of%20opportunity.pdf

Michaelson PL (2007–2008) In international arbitration, disclosure rules at the place of enforcement matter too. Dispute Resolut J 62(3):82–88

Moses C (2012) Ethics in international arbitration: traps for the unwary. Loyola Univ Chicago Int Law Rev 10:73

N.A. (2017) Suggested Changes to the ICSID Rules and Regulations. In: Public Comments to Amendment of ICSID's Rules and Regulations. https://icsid.worldbank.org/en/Documents/about/Public%20Comments%20to%20Amendment%20to%20ICSID%20Rules%20and%20Regulations.pdf

Nappert S (2015) International arbitration and its users: ships passing in the night? A dialogue with Michael McIlwrath. Bahrain Chamber Dispute Resolut Int Arbitr Rev 2(1):15–29

Ng J (2016) When the arbitrator creates the conflict: understanding arbitrator ethics through the IBA guidelines on conflict of internet and published changes. McGill J Dispute Resolut 23(2):23–42

Niedermeyer MK (2014) Ethics for arbitrators at the international level: who writes the rules of the game? Am Rev Int Arbitr 25:481–496

Oyre T (2002) Ethical Codes of conduct for arbitrators and disciplinary proceedings of the Chartered Institute of Arbitrators. Arbitration 68(2):90–105

Park WW (2011a) The four musketeers of arbitral duty: neither one-for-all nor all-for-one. In: Derains Y, Lévy L (eds) Is arbitrator only as good as the arbitrator? Status, powers and role of the arbitrators. Dossiers ICC Institute of World Business Law 8:25–45

Park WW (2011b) Rectitude in international arbitration. Arbitr Int 27(3):473–526

Park WW (2011c) Maturity in arbitration. ICSID Rev Foreign Invest J 26(1):1–33

Paulsson J (2013) The idea of arbitration. Oxford University Press, Oxford

Rauber M (2014) The impact of ethical rules for counsel in international commercial arbitration- is there a need for developing international ethical rules? Int Arbitr Law Rev 17(1):17–36

Rogers AC (2001) Fit and function in legal ethics: developing a code of conduct for international arbitration. Mich J Int Law 23:341–423

Rogers AC (2014) Ethics in international arbitration. Oxford University Press, Oxford

Ruiping D, Xiaosong D (2014) Promoting impartiality of international commercial arbitrators through Chinese criminal law: arbitration by "perversion of law". Int Law Manage Rev 10:109–138

Ruiz Fabri H, Sorel JM (2010) Indépendance et impartialité des juges internationaux. Pedone, Paris

Sarmiento MG (2015) The 2014 Draft Constitutive Agreement of the Centre for the Settlement of Investment Disputes of the UNASUR. https://papers.ssrn.com/sol3/papers.cfm?abstract_id=2703651

Seattle to Brussels Network (2013) BITs that bite into budgets: will the EP let private lawyers decide? http://www.s2bnetwork.org/bits-that-bite-into-budgets-will-the-ep-let-private-lawyers-decide/

Seibert-Fohr A (2013) International judicial ethics. In: Romano CPR, Alter KJ, Avgerou C (eds) The Oxford handbook of international adjudication. Oxford University Press, Oxford, pp 757–776

Shetreet S, Forsyth C (2011) The culture of judicial independence: conceptual foundations and practical challenges. Brill Nijhoff, Leiden

St. John T, Chernykh Y (2018) Déjà Vu? Investment court proposals from 1960 and today. Kluwer Arbitration Blog. https://www.ejiltalk.org/deja-vu-investment-court-proposals-from-1960-and-today/

Sussman E, Ebere S (2011) All's fair in love and war – or is it? Reflections on ethical standards for counsel in international arbitration. Am Rev Int Arbitr 22(4):611–623

TACD (2016) Transatlantic Consumer Dialogue, Response to the European Commission's Investor-State Dispute Settlement "Reform" Proposal. http://tacd.org/wp-content/uploads/2015/02/TACD-resolution-ICS-proposal.pdf

Thomson D (2016) Is ICSID a "monarchy"? Glob Arbitr Rev. https://globalarbitrationreview.com/article/1034993/is-icsid-a-monarchy. Accessed 4 Jan 2016

Transnational Institute (2012) Profiting from Injustice. https://www.tni.org/files/download/profitingfrominjustice.pdf

Tung KY (2016) CETA and TTIP. A New Platinum Standard for ICSID? American Society of International Law. Proceedings of the 110th Annual Meeting, 54–59

Van Compernolle J, Tarzia G (2006) L'impartialité du juge et de l'arbitre. Etude de droit comparé. Bruylant, Bruxelles

Venzke VI (2016) ISDS in TTIP from the perspective of a public law theory of international adjudication. J World Invest Trade 17:374–400

Wai R (2002) Transnational liftoff and juridical touchdown: the regulatory function of private international law in an era of globalization. Columbia J Transnl Law 40:209–274

Warwas BA (2017) The liability of arbitral institutions: legitimacy challenges and functional responses. Asser Press, Springer, Berlin Heidelberg

White & Case (2018) International Arbitration Survey: The Evolution of International Arbitration. https://www.whitecase.com/sites/whitecase/files/files/download/publications/2018-international-arbitration-survey-the-evolution-of-ia.pdf

Legal and Arbitration References

IIAs

CETA (2016) http://ec.europa.eu/trade/policy/in-focus/ceta/ceta-chapter-by-chapter/

EU-Singapore IPA (2018) http://trade.ec.europa.eu/doclib/press/index.cfm?id=961

EU-Vietnam FTA (2016) http://trade.ec.europa.eu/doclib/docs/2016/february/tradoc_154226.pdf

JEFTA (2016) https://trade-leaks.org/jefta-leaks/investment-dispute-resolution/

Kingdom of Netherlands (2018) Netherlands draft model BIT. https://www.internetconsultatie.nl/investeringsakkoorden/document/3586

Kingdom of Norway (2015) Draft Model Agreement – Agreement between the Kingdom of Norway and ---- for the promotion and protection of investments. https://www.regjeringen.no/contentassets/e47326b61f424d4c9c3d470896492623/draft-model-agreement-english.pdf

TTIP (2016) http://trade.ec.europa.eu/doclib/press/index.cfm?id=1230

Arbitration Acts, Institutional Arbitration Rules, and Codes of Conduct

CEA (2005) Código de buenas prácticas arbitrales. Code of Good Arbitration Practices (author's translation). https://www.clubarbitraje.com/sites/default/files/090216_buenas_practicas_arbitrales_castellano_1.pdf

ICSID (2006) Arbitration Rules. https://icsid.worldbank.org/en/Pages/icsiddocs/ICSID-Convention-Arbitration-Rules.aspx

Italian National Bar Council (2014) Code of Conduct for Lawyers. http://www.consiglionazionaleforense.it/documents/20182/40227/Code+of+Conduct+for+Lawyers+traduzione+ufficiale+inglese+del++Nuovo+Codice+Deontologico+Forense/ea8f06e6-ba33-4eb0-a568-ba56b4198a3a

International Conventions

ICSID (1966) Convention on the Settlement of Investment Disputes between States and Nationals of Other States. https://icsid.worldbank.org/en/Documents/icsiddocs/ICSID%20Convention%20English.pdf

UNCITRAL (2014) UNCITRAL Rules on Transparency in Treaty-based Investor-State Arbitration. http://www.uncitral.org/uncitral/en/uncitral_texts/arbitration/2014Transparency.html

Legal Documents

CIArb (last accessed June 2018) How CIArb Investigates Complaints of Misconduct Against its Members. http://www.ciarb.org/docs/default-source/default-document-library/complaints-booklet1.pdf?sfvrsn=4

CJEU (2016) Code of Conduct for Members and former Members of the Court of Justice of the European Union. http://eur-lex.europa.eu/legal-content/EN/TXT/PDF/?uri=OJ:C:2016:483:FULL&from=FR

OSCE-ODIHR (2010) Kyiv Recommendations on Judicial Independence in Eastern Europe, South Caucasus and Central Asia. https://www.osce.org/odihr/KyivRec?download=true

Council of Europe (2016) Plan of Action on Strengthening Judicial Independence and Impartiality. https://rm.coe.int/1680700285

Council of the EU (2018) Negotiating directives for a Convention establishing a multilateral court for the settlement of investment disputes. http://data.consilium.europa.eu/doc/document/ST-12981-2017-ADD-1-DCL-1/en/pdf

EC (2015a) Report. Online public consultation on investment protection and investor-to-state dispute settlement (ISDS) in the Transatlantic Trade and Investment Partnership Agreement (TTIP). http://trade.ec.europa.eu/doclib/docs/2015/january/tradoc_153044.pdf

EC (2015b) Concept Paper-Investment in TTIP and beyond – the path for reform. Enhancing the right to regulate and moving from current ad hoc arbitration towards an Investment Court. http://trade.ec.europa.eu/doclib/docs/2015/may/tradoc_153408.PDF

EC (2015c) In: Press Release Database. EU finalises proposal for investment protection and Court System for TTIP. http://europa.eu/rapid/press-release_IP-15-6059_en.htm

EC (2016a) In: Press Release Database. CETA: EU and Canada agree on new approach on investment in trade agreement. http://europa.eu/rapid/press-release_IP-16-399_en.htm

EC (2016b) Discussion paper. Establishment of a multilateral investment dispute settlement system. http://trade.ec.europa.eu/doclib/docs/2017/january/tradoc_155267.12.12%20With%20date_%20Discussion%20paper_Establishment%20of%20a%20multilateral%20investment%20Geneva.pdf
EC (2018a) In: Memorandum. EU-Singapore trade and investment agreements (authentic texts as of April 2018). http://trade.ec.europa.eu/doclib/press/index.cfm?id=961
EC (2018b) New EU-Mexico agreement- The agreement in principle. http://trade.ec.europa.eu/doclib/docs/2018/april/tradoc_156791.pdf
EC (2018c) Commission welcomes green light to start trade negotiations with Australia and New Zealand. In: Press Release Database. http://europa.eu/rapid/press-release_IP-18-3881_en.htm
EP (2015) Resolution of 8 July 2015 containing the European Parliament's recommendations to the European Commission on the negotiations for the Transatlantic Trade and Investment Partnership (TTIP) (2014/2228(INI)), P8_TA(2015)0252, http://www.europarl.europa.eu/sides/getDoc.do?pubRef=-//EP//TEXT+TA+P8-TA-2015-0252+0+DOC+XML+V0//EN
EP. Directorate-General for External Policies. Policy Department (2017) In Pursuit of an International Investment Court: Recently Negotiated Investment Chapters in EU Comprehensive FTA in comparative perspective. http://www.europarl.europa.eu/RegData/etudes/STUD/2017/603844/EXPO_STU(2017)603844_EN.pdf
EU (2018) Possible Reform of Investor-State dispute settlement (ISDS). http://www.uncitral.org/uncitral/en/commission/working_groups/3Investor_State.html
Government of Thailand (2018) Possible reform of Investor-State dispute settlement (ISDS). Comments by the Government of Thailand. http://www.uncitral.org/uncitral/en/commission/working_groups/3Investor_State.html
ICSID (2016) ICSID Rules Amendment Process. https://icsid.worldbank.org/en/documents/about/icsid%20rules%20amendment%20process-eng.pdf
Kingdom of Belgium (2017) Minister Reynders submits request for opinion on CETA. https://diplomatie.belgium.be/en/newsroom/news/2017/minister_reynders_submits_request_opinion_ceta
UNCITRAL Working Group III (2017) A/CN.9/916 - Possible future work in the field of dispute settlement: Ethics in international arbitration. http://www.uncitral.org/uncitral/en/commission/working_groups/3Investor_State.html
UNCITRAL (2018) Report of the Working Group III (Investor-State Dispute Settlement Reform) on the work of its thirty-fifth session. http://www.uncitral.org/uncitral/en/commission/working_groups/3Investor_State.html
UNCTAD (2018a) Recent Developments in the International Investment Regime. IIA Issues Note. http://investmentpolicyhub.unctad.org/Publications/Details/1186
UNCTAD (2018b) World Investment Report. http://worldinvestmentreport.unctad.org/world-investment-report-2018/

Chapter 2
The Duty of Disclosure: An Overview

The duty of disclosure is connected with the duty of independence and impartiality that is imposed on arbitrators. At a very early stage in the proceedings, all investment arbitrators are obliged to disclose a series of circumstances that may connect them with the case or its participants. This disclosure exercise is viewed as crucial in an arbitration framework in which parties have the right to select their arbitrators.[1] The duty of disclosure is also relevant for the arbitration procedure itself because of its impact on the arbitration's organisation—e.g., the arbitrators' status in the panel,[2] the length and costs of the procedure, and even future requests for annulment.

The duty of disclosure and arbitrator challenges both give rise to opposing views among international arbitration stakeholders. While some consider excessive disclosure to be an impossible burden[3] that threatens freedom of choice over arbitrator

[1]This requirement derives from the need to eliminate explicit bias, a fundamental issue that underpins this section. Other relevant issues such as unconscious or implicit bias and systemic bias have been studied by various authors: Brekoulakis (2013), pp. 553–585. Davis (2014), pp. 1–39.

[2]The general impression is that a party that fails to challenge an arbitrator will lose the panel's goodwill, and that unsuccessfully challenged arbitrators are weakened in the eyes of their co-arbitrators. O'Brien and Nandivanda (2014), pp. 1–5.

[3]Brower refers to the California disclosure standards as an—non-international—example of "going too far", which "impairs the utility of the system" and "would likely be counter-productive and ultimately inefficient". The referred Californian standards imposed expansive disclosure obligations on commercial arbitrators, and failure to disclose was connected to arbitrator's disqualification and setting aside of the award. Brower (2010), pp. 15–16.

K. Fach Gómez, *Key Duties of International Investment Arbitrators*,
https://doi.org/10.1007/978-3-319-98128-4_2

selection,[4] allude to the "black art of bias challenge",[5] and prophesy that "excessive rigor can at times hide a deeply vicious soul"[6]; others refer to the right to challenge as a crucial element in guaranteeing a fair hearing, which is clearly connected with the due process benchmark.[7] Additional reasons put forward for implementing the duty of disclosure in the investment arbitration context include the lack of any ICSID appellate mechanism, the limitations of the current annulment mechanism,[8] and the impossibility of appealing in the investment context to national courts performing the role of *juge d'appui*.[9]

As a matter of fact, these two legal institutions (duty of disclosure and arbitrator challenge) can be viewed as communicating vessels, in the sense that broad disclosure may reduce the possibilities of challenges, and vice versa.[10] Some academics have commented that the duty of disclosure has a purifying effect in this sense,

---

[4]In the commercial arbitration context, it has also been pointed out that imposing full and exhaustive disclosure on arbitrators prevents parties from working with the most knowledgeable and experienced arbitrators. This issue has been the subject of debate for decades in some jurisdictions, such as the United States. For example, as early as 1968, the US Supreme Court nullified an arbitration award because the arbitrator's failure to disclose a repeated and significant relationship with one party presented sufficient evidence of the "evident partiality" referred to in the US Federal Arbitration Act. Dotseth (2012), pp. 347–354.

[5]Investment cases such as ConocoPhillips v. Venezuela and Victor Pey Casado v. Chile have indisputably become endless challenge sagas, for which expressions such as the "black art of bias challenge" have been coined. Luttrell (2009). As a mechanism to fight against the black art of harassing arbitrators, a later work of the same author proposes an amendment to ICSID Rule 9, which would allow either the other tribunal members or the chairman to decide that the challenging party may have to pay some of or all the fees and expenses incurred when deciding on the proposal to challenge, and would also take into account whether or not the challenging party had made more than one proposal in respect of the same tribunal member during the proceedings. Luttrell (2009), p. 615. Reflecting on the same topic, Greenberg (2010). Attempts to combat this "black art" in the field of international commercial arbitration include initiatives such as the Annex to the LCIA Rules (2014): "A legal representative should not engage in activities intended unfairly to obstruct the arbitration or to jeopardise the finality of any award, including repeated challenges to an arbitrator's appointment or to the jurisdiction or authority of the arbitral tribunal known to be unfounded by that legal representative". LCIA (2014). Academics have pointed out that one of the arbitration parties may in bad faith generate certain links with the arbitrator to subsequently take advantage of them through annulment action if the award does not meet their expectations. Fernández Rozas (2013), p. 808.

[6]Resorting to a Molière's citation, Mourre (2009).

[7]This statement from an ICSID decision is very clear in this sense: "the challenge of arbitrators is a procedural right of the Parties, granted under the ICSID regime (...) As there are no concrete circumstances indicating the contrary, the exercise of this procedural right cannot be characterised as abusive". RSM v. Saint Lucia, par 75.

[8]The situation is quite different in the context of commercial arbitration, as evidenced by cases such as the Tecnimont saga. Fouchard (2016) and Crivellaro (2014).

[9]Focusing on commercial arbitration, Sousa Uva (2009), pp. 480–511.

[10]In Rubins and Lauterburg's words: "the duty to disclose not only serves as a basis for an educated analysis of the prospective arbitrator's qualifications, but also insulates the arbitrator from a subsequent challenge based on the disclosed circumstances". Rubins and Lauterburg (2010), p. 156.

acting as life insurance for the arbitration system.[11] It brings with it that: "the best means to protect the international arbitration process is to have greater clarity regarding issues that may lead to disclosure or disqualification. Leaving parties, arbitrators and institutions to make decisions on an ad hoc basis will only continue to cause uncertainty, inefficiency and ultimately less faith in the process".[12] As indicated in Chap. 1, diverse actors have lost faith in the autopoietic approach that currently prevails in the contemporary investment arbitration milieu.

On the other hand, it is unquestionable that the implementation of duty of disclosure may be troublesome and that, in any case, this duty not a global panacea: "overemphasis on mechanical disclosure requirements may exclude the honest and do little to stifle true mischief. There comes a point of diminishing returns where excessive formalism serves only to assist an obstreperous party in fomenting delay and difficulty. As a result, scrupulous arbitrators may be removed from trivial reasons, while hypocritical rascals do not even have to break their stride (...) Disclosure is insufficient to cure all ills, and the answer cannot be yet more disclosure. It is an intrinsically limited tool". [13]

Starting from this highly controversial antinomy, a number of issues related to the duty of disclosure are discussed in detail in Chap. 2.

2.1 The Duty of Disclosure in ICSID: Preliminary Comments

In principle, ICSID praxis recognizes the possibility that "nondisclosure [may be] an aberration on the part of the conscientious arbitrator".[14] For this reason, the Decision to disqualify an arbitrator in Fábrica v. Venezuela includes the following assertion: "if an arbitrator, when facing an application for disqualification, were found to have deliberately concealed or misrepresented a fact in a declaration to the parties, then such conduct would provide a conclusive justification for the disqualification of the arbitrator".[15]

Despite the severe tone of this text, an analysis of ICSID practice shows that challenge adjudicators—mainly co-arbitrators, and at times the Chairman of the World Bank (WB) Administrative Council[16]—have never considered that they

[11]Sousa Uva (2009), pp. 480–511; Fernández Rozas (2013), p. 811; Matheus López (2015), p. 270.

[12]Cárdenas and Rivkin (2005), p. 200.

[13]Paulsson (2013), pp. 152–153.

[14]Suez v. Argentine Republic, par 44 (paragraph cited in Tidewater v. Venezuela, par 47).

[15]Fabrica v. Venezuela (2016a), par 57.

[16]Article 58 ICSID Convention. ICSID (1966). An analysis of ICSID decisions on proposals to disqualify arbitrators shows some differences depending on who the challenge adjudicator is. In a formal sense, the chairman's decisions, which are sometimes requested from third parties such as the Secretary-General of the PCA, are often more succinct than those issued by the co-arbitrators.

were facing a "deliberate aberration" in the disclosure context; that is, one which should be sanctioned by disqualifying the arbitrator.[17]

The overriding impression when dealing with arbitrator disclosure is that challenged arbitrators have been treated with kid gloves on the vast majority of occasions, especially by their unchallenged colleagues.[18] A priori, this is not a bad thing. It is always positive when arbitration proceedings of the magnitude of investment claims take place in a context of good manners and gallantry, and arbitrators have sometimes taken pains to emphasize this in their rejections of challenges to fellow arbitrators.[19] Moreover, as arbitrators are clearly entitled to the presumption of innocence in this and every other possible context, the starting point should be the assumption that all their actions are governed by the principle of good faith.

Quantitatively speaking, the chairman is more likely to uphold a disqualification than the unchallenged arbitrators are. Luttrell also points out that the chairman's centralized decision-making role is more likely to generate a predictable body of authority; so much so that the author suggests that there is a growing tendency to challenge more than one arbitrator—double-barrelled challenges—perhaps because this guarantees the chairman's intervention under the current ICSID system. Luttrell (2016), pp. 597–621. More updated statistics can be found in: Secretariat UNCITRAL (2018), p. 13. More generally, criticisms of the ICSD system are raised in Vasani and Palmer (2015).

[17]None of the few ICSID cases in which challenges have been upheld has primarily dealt with the issue of the arbitrator's duty of disclosure. It is symptomatic that most of these cases have so far been resolved by the ICSID Administrative Council.

[18]It is difficult to find any challenge decision statements that reproach an arbitrator. Perhaps the two that follow are the most symptomatic in this sense: first, "it might have been possible at first to consider (the arbitrator's) attitude in these matters as a one–off serious lapse of judgment, but her removal by the Permanent Court of Arbitration in the Yukos cases after her refusal voluntarily to withdraw appears to confirm that she has more broadly a view of her independence and of the relevant criteria in this connection which do not longer accord with the minimum standards that now prevail in these matters" (Compañía v. Argentine Republic. par 231); second, "there is nothing in the IBA Guidelines that supports a special deference to the subjective positions of arbitrators based on their level of experience or standing international community. [The arbitrator] no doubt has extensive experience in international arbitration and is highly regarded in this field, but this fact is irrelevant in applying the IBA" (Perenco v. Ecuador, par 62). The Secretary-General of the PCA upheld the challenge in this later case under IBA Guidelines. This decision would presumably have been considered invalid within the ICSID convention framework, but the arbitrator in fact resigned. Campolieti and Lawn (2010).

[19]The co-arbitrators stated: "It should be noted that these written exchanges were all made courteously and professionally, as might have been expected from their authors; and that the Claimant raised its concerns at the earliest opportunity, first privately with the Respondent and then formally with the ICSID Secretary-General. This was no tactical device by a party acting in bad faith to thwart or delay the arbitral process. To the contrary, as the Claimant party with the first session imminent on 7th January 2008 [sic], it was not in the Claimant's interest to impede these arbitration proceedings unnecessarily. Further, the Claimant's proposal has carefully eschewed any personal attack on [the arbitrator]. As recorded in the Claimant's concluding submissions: Electrabel does not seek to embarrass [the arbitrator], or force her to resign (. . .)". Electrabel v. Hungary, par 27. However, the tone of some challenges has become stronger lately; for instance, one claimant recently stated that the arbitrator "lied when he stated that he learnt at the jurisdictional hearing, for the first time, that (. . .)". Victor Pey Casado v. Chile (2017b), par 25.

It may be true that no ICSID arbitrator has ever deliberately concealed or misrepresented information in the statement of impartiality and independence. It therefore makes sense to be "confident that if there were ever a problem, we would learn of it promptly from [the challenged arbitrator] herself".[20] It may also be true that no ICSID arbitrator has ever weakened in respect of his/her duty to investigate.

However, when the various issues set out below are analysed in detail, a somewhat different picture emerges. In the first place, ICSID practice has used an excessively soft interpretation of certain aspects of the duty of disclosure, and co-arbitrators' use of sophisticated arguments cannot remove the shadow of endogamy and cronyism that falls over this scenario. Furthermore, current ICSID provisions on the issue do not help to redress the balance.[21] If the self-policing strategy on challenges is far from ideal, as Paulsson recognizes,[22] the same can be said of the specific duty of disclosure.

Any short and medium-term solutions will probably come hand in hand with regulatory reforms. A potential restructuring of the duty of disclosure could be channelled through the ICSID's work to update and modernise current Rules and Regulations, initiated on November 2016.[23] The EU's willingness to set up a MIC[24] also leaves room for introducing major changes in the duty of disclosure in the investment arbitration context—via instruments such as for instance Codes of conduct.[25]

As a result of the study detailed in this chapter, the comment that "practices that seem reasonable and normal one day can quickly become out-dated, counterproductive or subject to radically different ethical expectations"[26] may well become a prophecy in this context. A more effective system of institutional measures against conflict of interests is expected to be established in the future,[27] and this will undoubtedly have an impact in the context of the disclosure duty.

---

[20]Electrabel v. Hungary, par 45.

[21]Perhaps for these reasons, the survey carried out by the IBA Subcommittee on Investment Treaty Arbitration concluded that: "a large percentage of the respondents specifically identified the procedures for challenging arbitrators in ICSID and ICSID Additional Facility arbitrations as in need of reform. The challenge procedures under other arbitration rules (such as the UNCITRAL Arbitration Rules and the ICC Arbitration Rules) were generally not identified as areas where reform is needed): IBA Subcommittee on Investment Treaty Arbitration (2016), p. 5.

[22]Paulsson (2012), p. xix.

[23]ICSID (2016).

[24]EC (2016).

[25]It should be borne in mind that the MIC would be a permanent body consisting of tenured members/judges. Statements of impartiality and independence would thus be issued and updated by a member/judge who works for the MIC on a permanent basis. Practical differences could be created with respect to the investment arbitration implemented to date, in which every arbitrator selected for a specific arbitration has to issue the relevant statement for each arbitration.

[26]Rogers (2014), par 10.10.

[27]The statements from Howard Mann in the Ghana v. Telekom case are prime examples: "That the arbitral Tribunal in the Ghana arbitration ruled there was no conflict is symptomatic of the gulf between the "inside the tent" view and the outside view of the Court. That the Permanent Court of

2.2 Formal Aspects of the Statement of Impartiality and Independence

An analysis of ICSID's disclosure rules is essential in the investment arbitration context, as most challenges[28] have been raised within the framework of these rules.[29] The relevant section of current Rule 6 (2) of the ICSID Rules of Procedure for Arbitration Proceedings (Arbitration Rules)[30] dated 2006[31] reads as follows:

> (2) Before or at the first session of the Tribunal, each arbitrator shall sign a declaration in the following form:
>
> "To the best of my knowledge there is no reason why I should not serve on the Arbitral Tribunal constituted by the International Centre for Settlement of Investment Disputes with respect to a dispute between ____________________and____________________.
>
> "I shall keep confidential all information coming to my knowledge as a result of my participation in this proceeding, as well as the contents of any award made by the Tribunal.
>
> "I shall judge fairly as between the parties, according to the applicable law, and shall not accept any instruction or compensation with regard to the proceeding from any source except as provided in the Convention on the Settlement of Investment Disputes between States and Nationals of Other States and in the Regulations and Rules made pursuant thereto.
>
> "Attached is a statement of (a) my past and present professional, business and other relationships (if any) with the parties and (b) any other circumstance that might cause my reliability for independent judgment to be questioned by a party. I acknowledge that by signing this declaration, I assume a continuing obligation promptly to notify the Secretary-General of the Centre of any such relationship or circumstance that subsequently arises during this proceeding."

Following this rule, ICSID has created a Declaration (Template 4.2.3—Declaration Arbitration) which can be accessed from its website.[32] This single-page

Arbitration sides with the Tribunal is a sign of the deep systemic failure by key institutions to put the perception of conflict by outside stakeholders and objective observes above the interests of the current practitioners and practices of the international arbitration bar. Institutional or systemic safeguards are, in effect, almost nonexistent or are at a most rudimentary level (minimalistic disclosure requirements)". Mann (2005).

[28] Kinnear and Nitschke (2015).

[29] ICSID provides reasoned decisions on challenges, a pioneering approach in this sector. Other arbitral institutions have recently embraced this policy, in spite of the fact that most arbitration institutions still do not give reasons for their decisions. In this vein, the 2017 ICC Arbitration Rules have eliminated the statement in Article 11.4 which in the past read: "and the reasons for such decisions shall not be communicated"; LCIA Court Articles 10.5 and 10.6 state that reasons for the challenge must be given unless the parties agree otherwise, and the VIAC board also provides rationales for its decisions. ICSID reasoned decisions on challenges are also published. Hacking (2006).

[30] For the sake of simplicity, the comments to the rule in this chapter also apply to Article 13(2) of ICSID Arbitration (Additional Facility) Rules, unless indicated to the contrary.

[31] An analysis of the different versions of this precept since its 1978 incorporation into ICSID Arbitration (Additional Facility) Rules shows that the scope of the duty of disclosure has increased over time.

[32] ICSID (last accessed in June 2018a).

document reproduces the content of the four paragraphs in Rule 6 (2) and the last paragraph in the ICSID Declaration refers to the "attached statement". The Declaration itself does not offer a template for the statement of relationships and/or circumstances referred to; it simply contains a box in which one of two options has to be marked with a cross: "statement attached" or "no statement attached". Prospective ICSID arbitrators therefore enjoy considerable formal freedom when drafting the statement—if one is required. Where form is concerned, ICSID praxis shows that the statement typically contains the case name, the stage of the proceedings, the date and the arbitrator's signature, as well as any relevant relationships or circumstances.[33]

It must be taken into account that not all arbitral institutions have baptized this general document with the term "Declaration". Interestingly enough, ICC models not only vary in length, but also have different titles: ("Statement of Acceptance and Independence",[34] "Statement of Acceptance, Independence and Impartiality",[35] and "Statement of Acceptance, Availability, Impartiality and Independence"[36]). Nevertheless, they all use the same defining term—"Statement"—and enable prospective arbitrators to make the specific disclosure regarding independence and impartiality either in the statement itself or "on a separate sheet". These ICC Statements can be fairly complex from a technical perspective, (boxes to be ticked; boxes for identifying facts or circumstances regarding independence, impartiality or availability; tables for currently pending cases, detailed calendars to indicate pre-existing commitments and availability,[37] etc.).

Still in the commercial context,[38] the CAM calls its document a "Declaration of Acceptance and Statement of Independence of the Arbitrator",[39] and SIAC uses the term "Disclosure Sheet".[40] Neither requires a separate document to deal with the arbitrator's independence and impartiality, although this issue is addressed in the main document. These documents are also less sophisticated from a technical

[33]The author would like to thank Ms. Frauke Nitschke for the practical information provided on this issue.

[34]ICC (last accessed in June 2018a).

[35]ICC (last accessed in June 2018b).

[36]ICC (last accessed in June 2018c).

[37]*Infra,* Chap. 4.2.

[38]Various arbitral institutions have been consulted by the author with regard to their policy on the accessibility of their statement of independence and impartiality. Three of the commercial arbitration institutions that kindly responded to the queries (LCIA, ICDR and FAI) confirmed that this statement is not available online. In the case of ICDR, for example, the Notice of Appointment is only available to arbitrators through its online portal once they have been selected for a case. Perhaps there could be a case for making these documents accessible without restrictions so that they could be compared, which may lead to the creation of new and more complete versions.

[39]CAM (last accessed in June 2018).

[40]SIAC (last accessed in June 2018).

perspective: for instance, SIAC provides a file containing two very simple headings ("Disclosure pursuant to paragraph 1.2 of the Code of ethics", referring to time constraints, and "Disclosure pursuant to paragraph 2 of the Code of ethics", referring to impartiality or independence) and allows relatively unlimited space.

In other legal contexts, the PCA calls the document "Model Statements of Impartiality and Independence"[41] and the WTO simply uses the term "Disclosure Form".[42] In these cases—as with the UNCITRAL rules—[43] the annexes to their respective rules do specify the content of these documents. However, the fact that it has not been possible to confirm whether or not the forms exist and are available online[44] may be reason to believe that prospective arbitrators have some formal freedom in these contexts. The PCA and the UNCITRAL rules seem to provide the same freedom when dealing with the specific statement of relationship and circumstances, merely indicating "attached is a statement"[45] and "[Include statement]".[46]

Focusing specifically on what is referred to here as the "statement of independence and impartiality"[47]—not to be confused with the ICSID Declaration, a document with broader content—, a brief comparative analysis of the main characteristics of this kind of statement in the investment and commercial arbitration contexts reveals the following: first, all the texts examined agree on the requirement for a written statement, which is a reasonable minimum condition. Second, the texts do not provide a model statement: while each institution refers to the statement's specific content to a greater or lesser extent, arbitrators have some freedom where the formal aspects of the document are concerned. Third, while the UNCITRAL rules and the PCA also offer the content to be included in model statements for arbitrators with no circumstances to disclose,[48] the 2006 wording of ICSID Arbitration Rule

[41]PCA (last accessed in June 2018). In the UNCITRAL context, it is called "Model statements of independence pursuant to Article 11 of the Rules". UNCITRAL (last accessed in June 2018).

[42]WTO (1996b).

[43]UNCITRAL (2010).

[44]However, following an inquiry by the author, the Permanent Court of Arbitration kindly provided this clarification on the matter: "A Model of a Declaration of Acceptance and Statement of Impartiality and Independence for Cases under the PCA 2012 Rules is available as Appendix XV of the book "A Guide to the PCA Arbitration Rules" co-written by our Deputy Secretary-General, Brooks Daly, our Senior Legal Counsel, Evgeniya Goriatcheva and one of our previous Assistant Legal Counsels, Hugh A. Meighen (2014). This Model is also used in cases under the UNCITRAL Rules, with minor modifications."

[45]The model referred to in the previous note states: "I attach a statement (. . .) Use separate sheet for disclosure".

[46]Note that, unlike the ICSID binomial "Declaration/Statement", the double use of the term "statement" in these contexts may be misleading.

[47]This document is referred to as the "Statement of Independence and Impartiality" in this chapter, in spite of the fact that this is not a universal designation, and that in some cases there is only one document covering a wider range of issues.

[48]UNCITRAL Model Statement: "No circumstances to disclose*:* I am impartial and independent of each of the parties and intend to remain so. To the best of my knowledge, there are no circumstances, past or present, likely to give rise to justifiable doubts as to my impartiality or

6 (2) and the subsequent Declaration form do not require arbitrators who have no circumstances to disclose to expressly proclaim their independence and impartiality.[49]

The existence of divergence among arbitral institutions with regard to the content and formal characteristics of these documents—Declaration and attached statement, to follow ICSID nomenclature—may ultimately lead to uncertainty between arbitration parties and the arbitrators themselves.

Where ICSID investment arbitration is concerned, an Alpha v. Ukraine arbitrator who was challenged in 2010 explained that he had not attached a statement to his 2007 Declaration "because he deemed that the relationships to which Arbitration Rule 6 (2) refers, did not "exist" in this case and that, consequently, no statement was warranted".[50] In Tidewater v. Venezuela an arbitrator deleted two sentences from her declaration ("Attached is a statement of (a) my past and present professional, business and other relationships (if any) with the parties and (b) any other circumstance that might cause my reliability for independent judgment to be questioned by a party"). Following the claimant's request "to provide a complete declaration in accordance with ICSID Arbitration Rule 6 (2), since in Tidewater's submission, the Rule does not contemplate deletions or alternative texts",[51] the arbitrator argued that: "First I consider that there is no circumstance that could cause my reliability for independent judgment to be questioned, which explains that I deleted that (b) in order to indicate that I will not attach a document containing such information, as there was none. Moreover, I deleted also (a), as I always thought that there was a necessity to disclose only unknown facts, not facts in the public domain that can be seen by anyone on the ICSID webpage".[52]

Although the arbitrator's deleting these two paragraphs from her declaration did not help to uphold the proposal for her disqualification filed by the claimant in this particular case,[53] it is true that the current wording of ICSID Arbitration Rule 6 (2) has sometimes led to misunderstandings, procedural delays and additional

independence. I shall promptly notify the parties and the other arbitrators of any such circumstances that may subsequently come to my attention during this arbitration". UNCITRAL (last accessed in June 2018). PCA: "I am impartial and independent of each of the parties and intend to remain so. To the best of my knowledge, there are no circumstances, past or present, that need be disclosed because they are likely to give rise to justifiable doubts as to my impartiality or independence".

[49]To the contrary, it has been stated that the 2006 wording of ICSID Arbitration Rule 6 (2): "does not provide a fixed form of wording to cover the contingency where a declarant considers that there is no basis on which to attach such a statement; that is, there are no separate words supplied in the text of Arbitration Rule 6 (2) to the effect that, as far as the declarant is concerned, there are no relationships or other circumstances that fall within the form of declaration found in Arbitration Rule 6 (2) (e.g., there is no provision allowing a declarant to place a checkmark in favour of an assertion akin to: "There is no such relationships or circumstances"". Alpha v. Ukraine, par 50.

[50]Alpha v. Ukraine, par 15.

[51]*Ibid,* par 7.

[52]*Ibid,* par 8.

[53]*Ibid,* par 56. In Universal v. Venezuela, the same arbitrator had also crossed out the sentence and afterwards submitted a letter to ICSID on the issue, par 10.

costs for the parties. Modifying certain aspects of this rule—and the Declaration—would therefore be justified, and the work to update and modernise the current ICSID Rules and Regulations issued in November 2016 would provide the ideal opportunity,[54] as will be outlined in subsequent paragraphs.

It therefore seems that not only should a standard text referring to independence and impartiality be added to both the ICSID Rule and the Declaration to cover cases in which arbitrators consider that there is no basis for attaching a statement, but that the content of the Declaration should also be expanded. The investment arbitration system's credibility would be enhanced if, for example, the ICSID Declaration also referred in detail to other crucial issues such as arbitrator availability.[55]

In addition, it would certainly be convenient if ICSID provided a freely available statement for cases where disclosure is needed. Given ICSID's pre-eminent role in investment arbitration, the "attached statement" referred to in Rule 6 (2) should not only be created in a formal sense, but it should also be a true milestone in the international arbitration context. The statement should be both user-friendly from a technical perspective and extensive and detailed in terms of content—a question that is covered more thoroughly in a later section of this chapter.[56]

For reference purposes, it is now worth looking back at some texts from the commercial arbitration context, the contents of which reveal an awareness of the importance of limiting arbitrator freedom in this delicate matter. Accordingly, ICC statements affirm that: "Any disclosure should be complete and specific, identifying inter alia relevant dates (both start and end dates), financial arrangements, details of companies and individuals, and all other relevant information". Article 18 of the CAM arbitration rules states that "In the statement of independence the arbitrator shall disclose, specifying the time and duration: a. any relationship with the parties, their counsel or any other person or entity involved in the arbitration which may affect his/her impartiality or independence; b. any personal or economic interest, either direct or indirect, in the subject matter of the dispute; c. any bias or reservation as to the subject matter of the dispute". The CAM Filling In Notes to the Statement of Independence of the Arbitrator are more specific, stating that: "the statement of independence may concern any facts / circumstances/relationships, either direct, or indirect. Duration of any aspect shall be disclosed, specifying its beginning and ending. When filling in the statement of independence, the arbitrator shall take into

---

[54] ICSID (2016).

[55] It has been suggested that the following information be incorporated : "ICSID should require each arbitrator to confirm as part of the same declaration (i) his/her commitment to conduct the proceedings fairly and efficiently, by adopting procedures suitable to the circumstances of the arbitration, (ii) the days or weeks in the next two years that he/she has already committed to other cases or other obligations that make him/her unavailable, and (iii) his/her commitment that he/she will not take on new appointments that will conflict with his/her responsibilities to the case subject to the appointment". Debevoise & Plimpton (2017). This proposal has also recently been incorporated, in the context of mediation, in the "Model Statement of Independence and Availability" proposed by the Investor-State Mediation Task Force (2017).

[56] *Infra,* Chap. 2.3.

consideration the firm/organization where he/she performs an ongoing professional relationship. As for point a) of Art. 18, Para. 2, of the Rules, the statement of independence may concern any facts /circumstances/relationships in regards of: the parties and, where a company is involved, any other entity /individual that is owned by, or related to the same group of any of the parties; the legal representative of the parties; the parties' counsels, as well as their law firms".[57]

Outside the arbitration context there are also relevant examples of adjudicators' obligation to comply with certain parameters regarding disclosure content. For instance, Article 5 of the Code of Conduct for Members and Former Members of the Court of Justice of the European Union (CJEU), which in turn refers to the "Declaration of financial interest" states that: "On taking up their duties, Members shall submit a declaration of their financial interests, within the meaning of paragraph 3, to the President of the Court or Tribunal of which they are a Member. The declaration shall identify every entity in which the Member has a direct financial interest which, because of its scale, might reasonably be perceived as being capable of giving rise to a conflict of interest if the Member were to hear a case involving that entity. In this declaration, the Member shall identify each entity in which he or she has such a financial interest, which may be in the form of a specific financial holding in its capital, in particular, shares, or any other form of financial interest, for example, bonds or investment certificates. This paragraph does not apply to entities in which the Member owns holdings managed on a discretionary basis by a third party".[58] The arbitrators' statement could also be focused by including the type of proposal contained in the WTO Rules of conduct for the understanding on rules and procedures governing the settlement of disputes, which provides an illustrative list of information to be disclosed.[59]

In short, irrespective of whether we are dealing with ICSID's party-appointed arbitrators or prospective members of initiatives such as the MIC, the major

[57]CAM (2010a).

[58]CJEU (2016).

[59]Annex 2: "This list contains examples of information of the type that a person called upon to serve in a dispute should disclose pursuant to the Rules of Conduct for the Understanding on Rules and Procedures Governing the Settlement of Disputes. Each covered person, as defined in Section IV:1 of these Rules of Conduct has a continuing duty to disclose the information described in Section VI:2 of these Rules which may include the following: (a) financial interests (e.g. investments, loans, shares, interests, other debts); business interests (e.g. directorship or other contractual interests); and property interests relevant to the dispute in question; (b) professional interests (e.g. a past or present relationship with private clients, or any interests the person may have in domestic or international proceedings, and their implications, where these involve issues similar to those addressed in the dispute in question); (c) other active interests (e.g. active participation in public interest groups or other organisations which may have a declared agenda relevant to the dispute in question); (d) considered statements of personal opinion on issues relevant to the dispute in question (e.g. publications, public statements); (e) employment or family interests (e.g. the possibility of any indirect advantage or any likelihood of pressure which could arise from their employer, business associates or immediate family members)." WTO (1996).

challenge of setting multiple formal aspects of the statement of impartiality and independence should be faced sooner rather than later.

2.3 The Content of the Statement of Impartiality and Independence, and Disclosure Standards

As indicated above, ICSID Arbitration Rule 6 (2) specifies that arbitrators must produce a statement of "(a) his/her past and present professional, business and other relationships (if any) with the parties, and (b) any other circumstance that might cause his/her reliability for independent judgment to be questioned by a party".

The wording relating to arbitrators' "a) past and present professional, business and other relationships (if any) with the parties" creates a very broad duty of disclosure. All types of relationship with the parties are covered, no time limits are established, and no minimum threshold is incorporated with regard to the relevance of the relationship[60] or the risk of undermining arbitrator reliability.

It is interesting to point out that the recent Public Comments to Amendments of ICSID's Rules and Regulations propose adding the following reference to Rule (2) a): "and a non-party having a substantial interest in the proceedings (if any)".[61] This addendum is aimed at third-party funders, who—as recognized by the 2014 IBA Guidelines on conflicts of interest—[62] may have a direct financial interest in a dispute. It therefore seems logical for the proposal to link third-party funders with parties. In short, this is a good example of how such new realities may justify modifying the ICSID Rules.

At this point, the first impression of Rule 6 (2) a) is that ICSID demands a great deal from its arbitrators. However, if one looks at the wording of b) of Rule 6 (2) and

[60]The 1984 ICSID wording required only "other *relevant* relationships" (author's emphasis). Daele (2012), p. 7. "Relevant" is still included in the wording of the UNCITRAL Model Statement, which establishes a minimum requirement. In Alpha v. Ukraine, the co-arbitrators stressed the differences between: "6(2)(a) [which] by its plain verbiage only addresses relationships with parties whereas 6 (2)(b) is not similarly or unambiguously constricted in its reach. Further, 6(2)(b) is broader than 6(2) (a) in another significant feature through its use of the word "circumstance" rather than of the word "relationship." According to Webster's Dictionary, "relationship" connotes the "state of being related or interrelated", thereby requiring in this instance a personal connection of some sort, whereas "circumstance," connotes a "condition, fact or event accompanying referencing certain facts or situations that are attendant to, or are surrounding, certain other facts or situations. In effect, a circumstance is more inclusive than is a relationship". Alpha v. Ukraine, par 53.

[61]N.A. (2017), p. 7.

[62]Standard 6: "Third-party funders and insurers in relation to the dispute may have a direct economic interest in the award, and as such may be considered to be the equivalent of the party. For these purposes, the terms 'third-party funder' and 'insurer' refer to any person or entity that is contributing funds, or other material support, to the prosecution or defence of the case and that has a direct economic interest in, or a duty to indemnify a party for, the award to be rendered in the arbitration." IBA (2014).

compares this with the way other arbitral institutions and mega-regionals approach the content of the statement of impartiality and independence, the conclusion is that the current ICSID text still leaves room for improvement. As will be explained below, it would be a positive step for ICSID to refine and strengthen its demands in matters of arbitrator disclosure.

It is worth taking a closer look at the wording of clause "b) any other circumstance that might cause [the arbitrator's] reliability for independent judgment to be questioned by a party". Like a), this text sets no explicit limits regarding either time or the nature of the relationship. In dealing with personal scope, b) covers all individuals not considered parties in the sense of a).[63] It is important to note that many other texts analysed do not make this distinction between "relationships with the parties" and "other circumstances",[64] but opt for more generic terminology such as "facts or circumstances"[65] or "any interest, relationship or matter".[66] As will be discussed in more detail below, the latter option is preferable, especially if accompanied by a detailed list of situations that would need to be disclosed by the investment arbitrator.

There are notable differences between the way ICSID Rule 6 (2) b) deals with the relevance of the relationship and the risk of undermining arbitrator reliability in comparison with a), in which every possible relationship has to be disclosed. In accordance with b), only circumstances that might be questioned by a party in terms of independent judgment need to be disclosed. Even hypothetical doubts therefore have to be disclosed and the wording used by ICSID asks arbitrators to put themselves in the parties' shoes, which is no easy task.[67]

The UNCITRAL Arbitration Rules,[68] which do not make ICSID's distinction between a) and b), have adopted an antithetical position on the two issues that analysed with regard to b) of the ICSID Rule: "When a person is approached in connection with his or her possible appointment as an arbitrator, he or she shall disclose any circumstances likely to give rise to justifiable doubts as to his or her impartiality or independence". Article 11 of the UNCITRAL Rules thus bases the

[63]Doubts may arise as to the scope of the concept of party. The issue may therefore be raised with regard to persons with a controlling influence on the claiming company or senior official representatives of the respondent state. Daele (2012), p. 8. It may also be raised by new phenomena such as third-party funding, in spite of the fact that texts such as CETA seem to rule out this possibility. ("Third party funding means any funding provided by a natural or legal person who is not a party to the dispute but who enters into an agreement with a disputing party in order to finance part or all of the cost of the proceedings either through a donation or grant, or in return for remuneration dependent on the outcome of the dispute"). This is not a trivial question, especially in the ICSID context, where the wording of Rule 6 (2) b) is controversial.

[64]UNCITRAL model statements of independence pursuant to Article 11 of the Rules (Circumstances to disclose) do reflect this distinction.

[65]General Standard 2. IBA (2014).

[66]Code of Conduct NAFTA, TTIP, EU-Vietnam FTA, Singapore IPA.

[67]Daele uses ICSID's *travaux préparatoires* to point out that an understanding seemed to exist regarding the standard's objective nature at that time. Daele (2012), pp. 11–12.

[68]UNCITRAL (2010).

duty of disclosure on fewer circumstances ("likely")[69] than b) of ICSID Rule, but it does adopt the objective reasonable third-party standard ("justifiable doubts"). Some commercial arbitration texts also duplicate the UNCITRAL terms "likely to arise" and "justifiable doubts".[70] However, other texts in the commercial arbitration milieu choose a different option, reflecting a blend of ICSID and UNCITRAL Rules: "may or might or could give rise", combined with "justifiable or reasonable doubts".[71]

The latest generation of EU investment texts[72] (the EU-Singapur IPA,[73] the former EUSFTA,[74] TTIP,[75] the EU-Vietnam FTA,[76] and the leaked EU-Japan

---

[69]The same idea is embodied in the UNCITRAL model statement "any other *relevant* circumstance" (emphasis added). UNCITRAL (last accessed in June 2018).

[70]In commercial arbitration, CIArb for instance. Outside that context, the PCA and the WTO.

[71]SIAC ("may give rise to justifiable doubts"), KLRCA ("may give rise to justifiable doubts"), Barcelona Arbitration Court ("might give rise"), ICDR (might reasonably), DIA ("might give rise to reasonable doubts"), ICC ("might be of such a nature as to call into question . . . could give rise to reasonable doubts"). The Netherlands Arbitration Institute (NAI) uses novel terminology when indicating that "an arbitrator who suspects that there could be justifiable doubts as to his impartiality or independence. . ." The reference to "directly or indirectly" in Article 13.2 of the Procedural Rules of the Spanish Court of Arbitration (CEA) is of some interest: "[the proposed arbitrator] must also immediately inform the Court of any circumstance that (. . .), directly or indirectly, may raise justifiable doubts".

[72]In the context of the 2016 CETA, the Code of Conduct has not yet been created. Article 8.44 indicates:"The Committee on Services and Investment shall, on agreement of the Parties, and after completion of their respective internal requirements and procedures, adopt a Code of Conduct for the Members of the Tribunal to be applied in disputes arising out of this Chapter, which may replace or supplement the rules in application, and may address topics including: (a) disclosure obligations; (b) the independence and impartiality of the Members of the Tribunal; and (c) confidentiality. The Parties shall make best efforts to ensure that the Code of Conduct is adopted no later than the first day of the provisional application or entry into force of this Agreement, as the case may be, and in any event no later than two years after such date". CETA (2016).

[73]Article 3.1 of the Code of Conduct: "Prior to his or her appointment as a Member, a candidate shall disclose to the Parties any past or present interest, relationship or matter that is likely to affect his or her independence or impartiality or that might reasonably create an appearance of impropriety or bias." EU-Singapore IPA (2018).

[74]Article 3.1 of the Code of Conduct: "Prior to confirmation of his or her selection as an arbitrator under Section B (Investor-State Dispute Settlement) of Chapter Nine (Investment), a candidate shall disclose any past or present interest, relationship or matter that is likely to affect his or her independence or impartiality or that might reasonably create an appearance of impropriety or bias in the proceeding." EUSFTA (2015).

[75]Article 3.1 of the Code of Conduct: "Prior to their appointment candidates shall disclose any past and present interest, relationship or matter that is likely to affect their independence or impartiality or that might reasonably create an appearance of impropriety or bias in the proceeding". TTIP (2016).

[76]Article 3.1 of the Code of Conduct: "Prior to confirmation of her or his selection as an arbitrator under Chapter X (Dispute Settlement), a candidate shall disclose any interest, relationship or matter that is likely to affect his or her independence or impartiality or that might reasonably create an appearance of impropriety or bias in the proceeding". EU-Vietnam FTA (2016).

Trade Agreement [JEFTA])[77] reproduce in their respective Codes of conduct the wording[78] in the NAFTA Code of Conduct.[79] They make a distinction between "any interest, relationship or matter that is likely to affect the candidate's independence or impartiality" and those that "might reasonably create an appearance of impropriety or an apprehension of bias". These texts differentiate between independence and impartiality on the one hand, and impropriety and bias on the other. In relation to the latter, an objective reasonable third-party standard is prioritized.

The subjective test in ICSID Rule 6 (2) b) (queries from the parties' perspective as to the reliability of arbitrators' independent judgement) is also reflected in Article 11.2 of the 2017 ICC Rules of Arbitration[80] and in Standard 3 of the IBA Guidelines on conflicts of interest.[81] However, the brief comparative analysis above shows that the option formally chosen by ICSID is not the most common. Academic opinion has pointed out that there are various disadvantages to this subjective parameter, such as the difficulty of applying it to arbitration parties from different cultural and legal backgrounds.[82] The fact that this criterion may generate frivolous challenges has also been highlighted, together with the risk of overstating the duty of disclosure and subsequently causing an enormous increase in the number of challenges.[83]

Irrespective of the veracity of these arguments, which will be dealt with later, the reality in the field of arbitrator disclosure standards is as follows: regardless of the current wording of ICSID Rule 6 (2) b), an analysis of diverse ICSID decisions on disqualification leads to the conclusion that the subjective standard referring to the

---

[77]Article 3.1 of the Code of Conduct: "Prior to their appointment candidates shall disclose any past and present interest, relationship or matter that is likely to affect his or her independence or impartiality or that might reasonably create an appearance of impropriety or bias in the proceeding." JEFTA (2016).

[78]Part II: "A candidate shall disclose any interest, relationship or matter that is likely to affect the candidate's independence or impartiality or that might reasonably create an appearance of impropriety or an apprehension of bias in the proceeding". NAFTA (1994).

[79]Throughout this book, various references are made to the NAFTA Code of Conduct, which is considered a pioneering text in this matter. It should not be forgotten, however, that the said text only applies to a specific subtype of Chapter 11 disputes. Holbein and Greenidge (1995), p. 62.

[80]A literal reading of the text shows that the reference to the "eyes of the parties" is only linked to the duty of independence, whereas the duty of impartiality is assessed by applying the reasonable doubt test: "The prospective arbitrator shall disclose in writing to the Secretariat any facts or circumstances which might be of such a nature as to call into question the arbitrator's independence in the eyes of the parties, as well as any circumstances that could give rise to reasonable doubts as to the arbitrator's impartiality". ICC (2017b).

[81]The standard indicates: "If facts or circumstances exist that may, in the eyes of the parties, give rise to doubts as to the arbitrator's impartiality or independence, the arbitrator shall disclose such facts or circumstances to the parties, the arbitration institution or other appointing authority (if any, and if so required by the applicable institutional rules) and the co-arbitrators". IBA (2014).

[82]Academic commentators typically use the following example: if a party is not familiar with the functioning of the English bar, an arbitrator will be forced to disclose membership of the same barrister's chamber(s) as one of the co-arbitrators or one of the arbitration's counsels. Stanic (2009), p. 220.

[83]Daele (2012), pp. 10–11.

parties has in most cases been replaced, de facto, by either a subjective standard referring to the arbitrators or by an objective standard. This means that the ICSID Rule's reference to being "questioned by a party" has so far failed to have any substantial impact.

First of all, various ICSID cases show that arbitrators sometimes impose their subjective perspectives by ignoring the distinction between a) and b) in Rule 6 (2). In Nations Energy v. Panama the arbitrator was challenged on the basis of his professional relationship with a counsel at the law firm that had appointed him. The two members of the Annulment Committee endorsed the arbitrator's declaration regarding his independence, which was entirely based on the arbitrator's own opinion and not on the party's perspective.[84] After affirming that "the non-disclosure of the relationship between him and [the counsel], although prudent and advisable, was only the result of an honest exercise of discretion",[85] the Commission accordingly rejected the proposal for disqualification pursuant to Arbitration Rule 6 (2). It should also be noted that the Commission wrongly based its decision on Rule 6 (2) a) instead of b) and also that this is not the only ICSID case which seems to have avoided any explicit reference to b).

[84]The Decision, which is not available in English, states: "En adición, en fecha 16 de junio de 2011, presentó sus observaciones de conformidad con la Regla 9(3) de las Reglas de Arbitraje. En ese sentido el [árbitro] claramente expresó "(...) [c]uando hice mi declaración, *estaba al tanto* de que la firma Arnold & Porter era la representante legal de la República de Panamá y que el Sr. Patricio Grané había sido miembro del equipo de abogados en los procedimientos de arbitraje. *Mi opinión fue* entonces, y sigue siendo ahora, que el trabajo que desempeñó el Sr. X con la firma Sidley Austin LLP no es un factor que pueda afectar mi habilidad de juicio independiente, tal y como lo requiere el artículo 14 del Convenio". (In addition, on 16 June 2011, [the arbitrator] submitted his observations in accordance with Rule 9 (3) of the Arbitration Rules, stating,"(...) [When I made my statement, *I was aware* that Arnold and Porter was the legal representative of the Republic of Panama and that Mr. X had been a member of the team of lawyers during the arbitration proceedings. *My opinion* at that time was, and continues to be, that Mr. X's work with Sidley Austin LLP is not a factor that could affect my ability of independent judgement as required by Article 14 of the Convention) (English translation by the author). Nations v. Panama, par 75. In the same vein, in Suez v. Argentine Republic, the arbitrator—without making any reference to "mind-stretching", declared that she "saw no reason to advise all the parties in her pending arbitrations of an unrelated appointment as a UBS board member". Suez v. Argentine Republic, p. 18. Another example of this practice is Total v. Argentine Republic, in which it was stated that the arbitrator "explained that when she was filling out her Form of Acceptance for this case, *she did not consider it necessary* to disclose the matters Argentine Republic questioned owing to the nature of the parties and of the dispute, the legal issues, and the identity of the lawyers involved in the matters". Nations Energy v. Panama, par 140, (emphasis added).

[85]The Decision states: "la no divulgación de la relación existente entre él y el señor X, aunque hubiera sido prudente y aconsejable, no fue más que el resultado de un honesto ejercicio de la discrecionalidad. Asimismo, los Dos Miembros estiman que dicha información puede considerarse como de dominio público" (The non-disclosure of the relationship between [the arbitrator] and Mr. X, although prudent and advisable, was merely the result of an honest exercise of discretion. In addition, the two Members believe that such information can be considered to be in the public domain) (English translation by the author). Nations v. Panama, par 76.

In Tidewater v. Venezuela the company claimed that the undisclosed multiple appointments made by the same party and the same counsel gave rise to "objective and justifiable doubts regarding her independence and impartiality". The co-arbitrators reproduced[86] this wording, which does not contain a subjective standard, in their decision. The phrasing, which originally comes from the UNCITRAL Rule, was later reflected by the ICSID Secretariat in the 2004 Discussion Paper on Possible Improvements of the Framework for ICSID Arbitration.[87]

In another case, when laying the foundations for the decision, the arbitrators devoted a section to the "non-disclosure of other ICSID arbitral appointments by the same party", that is, Rule 6 (2) a), concluding that the arbitrator's failure to disclose "was an honest exercise of judgment on her part".[88] The non-disclosure of the multiple appointments performed same counsel,[89] which would have led to the application of Rule 6 (2) b), was also pushed into the background in this case. In conclusion, in some current ICSID praxis, an arbitrator's subjective criterion has superseded the parties' subjective criteria regarding the duty to disclose any other circumstances.

This is also true of Total v. Argentine Republic, although the decision does incorporate a formal reference to the parties' perception. In this case, the state submitted an application for the award to be annulled and subsequently filed a proposal for the disqualification of one of the ad hoc committee members, claiming that she had an undisclosed contractual relationship with the investor's law firm. The other two members rejected the proposal and stated: "when the arbitrators and

[86]Tidewater v. Venezuela, pars 36 and 39.

[87]It is worth noting that the ICSID Secretariat Discussion Paper dated October 22 2004 made no reference to the eyes of the parties. However, the Secretariat's suggestion for the 2006 version required arbitrators to disclose "more generally, any circumstances likely to give rise to justifiable doubts as to the arbitrator's reliability for independent judgment". ICSID (2004), p. 13.

[88]Total v. Argentine Republic, par 55. In general terms, various ICSID decisions use the expression "honest exercise of judgment" to approve the arbitrator's modus operandi. However, on some occasions the party bringing the challenge states that certain conduct constitutes a "dishonest exercise of judgment". In Highbury v. Venezuela, for instance, the investor's lawyers claimed that: "las Directrices de la IBA califican dentro del Listado Naranja más de tres designaciones por parte del mismo abogado o de la misma Firma de abogados. De manera que no puede ser un ejercicio honesto del árbitro revelar solo un número de casos que esté por debajo de esa cifra y ocultar los restantes. Omitir la revelación de casos que evidencian que el árbitro ha sido designado 4 o más veces por parte de los mismos abogados evidencia un ejercicio deshonesto por parte del árbitro y genera una apariencia manifiesta de parcialidad y dependencia" (Under IBA Guidelines, more than three appointments by the same attorney or law firm merits inclusion on the Orange List. Therefore, it cannot be an honest exercise of judgment to reveal only a number of cases below that figure and hide the remaining ones. Omitting to disclose cases that show that the arbitrator has been appointed 4 or more times by the same lawyers shows dishonesty on the part of the arbitrator and creates a manifest appearance of partiality and dependence) (English translation by the author). Highbury v. Venezuela (2015a), par 97.

[89]It is advisable to make this distinction, since a law firm may have appointed the arbitrator when the country in question—in this case Venezuela—was not the defendant. The same situation arose in Universal v. Venezuela.

annulment committee members make the declaration referred to in Rule 6 (2) they are making an honest exercise of discretion. The arbitrator or annulment committee member determines, in his sole discretion, that is, with a subjective criterion, if in his opinion a particular circumstance may be perceived by the parties as a circumstance that affects his ability to make an independent judgment."[90] As will be indicated below, this appears to be the wrong interpretation of Rule 6 (2) b).

The wording of the ICSID Rule "to be questioned by a party" should clearly not mean that "if the party considers that a circumstance should have been disclosed and the arbitrator or committee member did not disclose it, that is enough for the challenge to be successful".[91] However it is debatable whether the approach advocated in the ICSID cases referred to above complies with the wording of Rule 6 (2) b), which is more in line with the following interpretation, which is supported by academic opinion: "arbitrators are required to 'stretch their mind' so as to consider how particular facts and circumstances may be perceived by the parties".[92]

Secondly, other ICSID decisions seem to have been behind a shift towards objectivism with regard to the disclosure of "any other circumstances" referred to in Rule 6 (2). In Suez v. Argentine Republic, an arbitrator was challenged because she was a director of the USB group, a minority shareholder in two of the claimant companies. In this case the co-arbitrators once again referred generically to Rule 6 (2) and did not clarify whether the fact was to be subsumed in a) or b), in spite of the issue's consequences for the case.[93] The co-arbitrators' decision stated that "a reasonable interpretation of the ICSID Arbitration Rule 6 is that an arbitrator is required to disclose a fact only if he or she reasonably believes that such fact would reasonably cause his or her reliability for independent judgment to be questioned by a reasonable person". That is, objectivity applies to both letter a) and letter b) of ICSID Rule 6 (2).

In a further case, the members of the Alpha v. Ukraine tribunal mixed disclosure and disqualification standards, considering that "in order to accomplish the dual goal of a full disclosure of the relationships defined in 6 (2) a), but of a more flexible and limited level of disclosure of any other circumstance based on likelihood, the drafters chose, for the purposes of 6 (2) b), to adopt a justifiable doubts test such as that

---

[90]Total v. Argentine Republic, pars 133 and 134.

[91]*Ibid,* par 136.

[92]Referring to the former Article 7(2) of the ICC rules—which shares ICSID's drafting on this point—Derains and Schwartz (2005), p. 135.

[93]The following approach is revealing: "The term parties is not defined. In the strict sense, the parties are the disputants that are indicated in the first paragraph of the arbitrators' declaration of acceptance. In the broad sense, the parties may also include other entities or persons. One of the parties in an ICSID arbitration is usually a legal entity. It is reasonable to consider the managers, directors and members of the supervisory board of such a legal entity and any person having a similar controlling influence on the legal entity to be the equivalent of the legal entity. (...) Other categories, such as employees or companies belonging to the same corporate group as the legal entity involved in the dispute should probably not be considered as being the equivalent of the parties". Daele (2012), p. 8.

encapsulated in Article 9 of the UNCITRAL arbitration rules rather than to follow the much higher "manifest" threshold that must be met in order to sustain a challenge under the ICSID Convention".[94]

Thirdly, one decision appears to conform to the wording of the ICSID Rule 6 (2) b) on disclosure of "any other circumstances" by using the party's approach as a yardstick. In Compañía de Aguas v. Argentine Republic, the state requested the annulment of the ICSID award, claiming that the arbitral tribunal had not been constituted properly (Article 52.1.a ICSID Convention) and that the non-disclosure of an arbitrator's conflict of interest had led to a departure from a fundamental rule of procedure (Article 52.1.d ICSID Convention). Although the ad hoc committee members rejected Argentina's request, their opinion is the most critical with reference to non-compliance with arbitrators' duty of disclosure ever expressed by ICSID arbitrators.[95] Adopting the parties' perspective,[96] the ad hoc committee members were highly critical of the arbitrator's actions, concluding that "it is, in any event, difficult to understand why the bank was notified by [the arbitrator] of her existing arbitrations but not the arbitrating parties of her (impending) directorship of the bank at the same time".[97]

In the light of all these considerations with regard to ICSID's disclosure standard, it has to be concluded that prioritizing arbitrators' volitional element is not the best solution; or at least, not in the current version as practised. Arbitrators have frequently alleged their ignorance of a particular circumstance,[98] and this has been

---

[94]Alpha v. Ukraine, par 54.

[95]A possible interpretation could be that the ad hoc committee members were trying to suggest that ICSID arbitrators that have been freely chosen by the parties have different levels of independence and impartiality from those who come from the "official" Panel of Arbitrators—a very alarming hypothesis: "In annulment cases, members of ICSID ad hoc committees are chosen exclusively from the Panel of Arbitrators, and serve at the invitation of ICSID to address this concern. Their position is therefore different from that of arbitrators. In this connection, the ad hoc Committee noted the claim contained in Professor X's Report that there has been a demonstrable inclination of international arbitrators to raise the threshold for a challenge of their fellow arbitrators. This was not contested in cross-examination or commented upon by the parties after they were invited to do so. It may be that such an attitude more easily results amongst arbitrators who are called upon to determine a challenge in respect of an arbitrator with whom they sit (...) Ad hoc committees are not in a similar position". Compañía de Aguas v. Argentine Republic, pars 207–210.

[96]The decision states: "the bank could not decide these issues for others, particularly parties to an arbitration, who from the perspective of their arbitration may have a very different view of conflicts that result or could result for them from the involvement of their arbitrator with the bank. Rather, having properly and adequately investigated and established any relationship between the bank and any of the parties to the arbitrations, it is for the arbitrator personally first to consider such a connection in terms of a voluntary resignation as arbitrator. *Such connection must otherwise be properly disclosed* to the parties through an adequate amendment of earlier declarations under Rule 6." (emphasis added) Compañía de Aguas v. Argentine Republic, pars 225–226.

[97]*Ibid*, par. 229.

[98]It is declared that: "She had no knowledge of the business relationship between (...)", EDF v. Argentine Republic, par 59; "she states that she did not know that UBS held shares in the

accepted. As will be discussed in the framework of the duty to investigate,[99] arbitrator subjectivism should not be the criterion for assessing the duty of disclosure. Conversely, the deciding bodies in disqualification proceedings should be encouraged to take the reference to "by a party" in ICSID Rule 6 (2) b) into account in a meaningful sense.

Given that this has not happened so far, it might be useful if ICSID texts included some additional support that would enable a shift away from arbitrator-centred towards more party-centred standards. For instance, ICSID could officially duplicate the idea of in dubio pro disclosure contained in some commercial arbitration texts,[100] as arbitrators challenged by ICSID have sometimes pointed out to justify their conduct.[101] This aphorism is taken to the limit in the IBA Guidelines, which state that "if the arbitrator finds that he or she should make a disclosure, but that professional secrecy rules or other rules of practice or professional conduct prevent such disclosure, he or she should not accept the appointment, or should resign".[102]

Other expressions found in ICSID decisions[103] ("out of an abundance of caution" or "ex abundante cautela") may become more generalised and thus provide a boost to the duty of disclosure by forcing arbitrators make what they may feel are unnecessary disclosures, but the party may consider necessary. As will be explained below, a party leading a challenge to an arbitrator views the latter as a professional of high moral character and recognized competence in the fields of law, commerce, industry or finance[104] who has to handle her inquiry and disclosure duties meticulously.[105]

Alternatively, should ICSID texts be redrafted in the near future, omitting the reference to "by a party" in ICSID Rule 6 (2) b) could perhaps be the most convenient solution to bridging the gap between the Rule's wording and current

Claimants. Can she be required to disclose a fact that he does not know? The answer to that question is plainly "no" (. . .)". Suez v. Argentine Republic, par. 46.

[99] *Infra*, Chap. 2.7.

[100] They proclaim that: "Any doubt as to whether or not disclosure is to be made should be resolved in favour of disclosure" (AAA (2004) ICDR Code of Ethics); "Any doubt must be resolved in favour of disclosure" (ICC 2017a); "any doubt should be resolved in favour of disclosure" (Article 7, Code of Ethics, CAM (2010b); and "en la duda, el candidato deberá optar por la revelación", CEA (n.a.).

[101] For instance, "For the avoidance of doubt", "for the sake of transparency", Fábrica v. Venezuela (2015), par 6.

[102] Explanation to IBA General Standard 3. IBA (2014).

[103] Total v. Argentine Republic, pars 9 and 137.

[104] Article 14.1 ICSID Convention (1966).

[105] The claimant company issued following very forceful statement: "Resulta difícil imaginar que un árbitro con más de 40 años de experiencia, que ha participado en más de 50 arbitrajes de inversión y que es profesor emérito de una de las universidades más prestigiosas del mundo no sea meticuloso". (It is difficult to imagine that an arbitrator with more than 40 years of experience who has participated in more than 50 investment arbitrations and is Emeritus Professor of one of the most prestigious universities in the world is not meticulous) (English translation by the author). Highbury v. Venezuela (2015a), pars 108–109.

ICSID praxis. In that case, it would be preferable to interpret ICSID wording in such a way that objective standards can be approximated, in the same way as those operating in the various contexts mentioned above. For some, the "justifiable doubts" standard already exists, "inherent in Arbitration Rule 6 (2)".[106]

2.4 Timing, Celerity, Duration and Addressees of the Duty of Disclosure

In terms of the timing of the duty of disclosure, the ICSID Rules establish an unusual regime, which gives the arbitrators considerable scope time-wise.

When dealing with arbitrator appointment and acceptance, Rule 3 of the ICSID Arbitration Rules indicates the way in which arbitrators should be appointed to ICSID Tribunals constituted in accordance with Article 37 (2) (b) of the Convention—that is, a panel made up of one arbitrator appointed by each party, and a third, who is president of the tribunal, appointed by agreement of the parties. Rule 4 stipulates the way in which the chairman of the Administrative Council should appoint arbitrators, while Rule 5 focuses on accepting appointments and establishes a specific deadline: "If an arbitrator fails to accept his appointment within 15 days, the Secretary-General shall promptly notify the parties, and if appropriate the Chairman, and invite them to proceed to the appointment of another arbitrator in accordance with the method followed for the previous appointment". This means that: "the Tribunal shall be deemed to be constituted and the proceeding to have begun on the date the Secretary-General notifies the parties that all the arbitrators have accepted their appointment" (Rule 6 (1)).

When addressing the duty of disclosure, ICSID Arbitration Rule 6 (2) indicates that the arbitrator's declaration containing the statement of impartiality and independence[107] should be signed before or at the first session of the tribunal.[108] In short, the ICSID regime does not oblige arbitrators to make a pre-appointment disclosure: the disclosure can be postponed until the tribunal's first session. As some commentators have pointed out, this is not the optimal regime; once the arbitral tribunal has

[106]Alpha v. Ukraine, par 64.

[107]Declaration frequently accompanied by an attached statement, as explained above.

[108]Consequently, the last sentence of this Rule 6(2) states: "Any arbitrator failing to sign a declaration by the end of the first session of the Tribunal shall be deemed to have resigned." This Rule does not make an express reference to who the recipients of this declaration are. The time frame for the celebration of this first session is contained in Rule 13.1: The Tribunal shall hold its first session within 60 days after its constitution or such other period as the parties may agree." ICSID (2006).

been constituted, any objections to an arbitrator deriving from his/her disclosure can only be channelled through the challenge mechanism.[109]

In the broad context of commercial arbitration, a few institutions also seem to postpone the disclosure to the post-appointment stage[110] or this sometimes takes place when the appointment is accepted.[111] However, the general rule in commercial arbitration is to impose a pre-appointment disclosure on the arbitrators. This duty is articulated by many arbitral institution rules, which are sometimes inspired by Article 11 of the UNCITRAL rules: "When a person is approached in connection with his or her possible appointment as an arbitrator, he or she shall disclose any circumstances likely to give rise to justifiable doubts as to his or her impartiality or independence".[112] In most cases, this pre-appointment duty of disclosure is reinforced by post-appointment and on-going disclosure duties (Article 11 ICC,[113]

[109]Daele (2012), pp. 39–41.

[110]For instance, Article 18.2 of the CIMA Arbitration Rules states: "Within ten (10) days of being informed by the Court of their appointment, an Arbitrator shall disclose any circumstances likely to create justifiable doubts as to their impartiality, independence or availability, by means of a signed statement". CIMA (2015).

[111]Article 12.2 ICDR Arbitration Rules: "Upon accepting appointment, an arbitrator shall sign the Notice of Appointment provided by the Administrator affirming that the arbitrator is available to serve and is independent and impartial. The arbitrator shall disclose any circumstances that may give rise to justifiable doubts as to the arbitrator's impartiality or independence and any other relevant facts the arbitrator wishes to bring to the attention of the parties". ICDR (2014). Article 13.2 of the Procedural rules of the Spanish Court of Arbitration states: "Once the arbitrator is proposed or appointed, the said individual shall be notified so that in a term of three days he or she may accept the appointment and sign a written declaration of independence and impartiality and stating that their personal and professional circumstances shall allow them to diligently comply with the post of arbitrator, and in particular, with the terms established in these Rules". CEA (2005).

[112]UNCITRAL (2010).

[113]Article 11.2 and 11.3 of the ICC Arbitration Rules: "Before appointment or confirmation, a prospective arbitrator shall sign a statement of acceptance, availability, impartiality and independence. The prospective arbitrator shall disclose in writing to the Secretariat any facts or circumstances which might be of such a nature as to call into question the arbitrator's independence in the eyes of the parties, as well as any circumstances that could give rise to reasonable doubts as to the arbitrator's impartiality. The Secretariat shall provide such information to the parties in writing and fix a time limit for any comments from them. An arbitrator shall immediately disclose in writing to the Secretariat and to the parties any facts or circumstances of a similar nature to those referred to in Article 11(2) concerning the arbitrator's impartiality or independence which may arise during the arbitration". ICC (2017).

Article 5 LCIA,[114] Article 18 SCC,[115] Article 20 FAI,[116] Article 11 CRCICA,[117] Article 11 KLRCA,[118] etc.). The IBA Guidelines on conflicts of interest

---

[114]Articles 5.4 and 5.5 of thte LCIA Arbitration Rules: "Before appointment by the LCIA Court, each arbitral candidate shall furnish to the Registrar (...) the candidate shall sign a written declaration stating: (i) whether there are any circumstances currently known to the candidate which are likely to give rise in the mind of any party to any justifiable doubts as to his or her impartiality or independence and, if so, specifying in full such circumstances in the declaration; and (ii) whether the candidate is ready, willing and able to devote sufficient time, diligence and industry to ensure the expeditious and efficient conduct of the arbitration. The candidate shall furnish promptly such agreement and declaration to the Registrar. If appointed, each arbitral candidate shall thereby assume a continuing duty as an arbitrator, until the arbitration is finally concluded, forthwith to disclose in writing any circumstances becoming known to that arbitrator after the date of his or her written declaration (under Article 5.4) which are likely to give rise in the mind of any party to any justifiable doubts as to his or her impartiality or independence, to be delivered to the LCIA Court, any other members of the Arbitral Tribunal and all parties in the arbitration. LCIA (2014).

[115]Article 18 of the SCC Arbitration Rules: "Every arbitrator must be impartial and independent. Before being appointed, a prospective arbitrator shall disclose any circumstances that may give rise to justifiable doubts as to the prospective arbitrator's impartiality or independence. Once appointed, an arbitrator shall submit to the Secretariat a signed statement of acceptance, availability, impartiality and independence, disclosing any circumstances that may give rise to justifiable doubts as to the arbitrator's impartiality or independence. The Secretariat shall send a copy of the statement of acceptance, availability, impartiality and independence to the parties and the other arbitrators. An arbitrator shall immediately inform the parties and the other arbitrators in writing if any circumstances that may give rise to justifiable doubts as to the arbitrator's impartiality or independence arise during the course of the arbitration. SCC (2017).

[116]Article 20 of the FAI Arbitration Rules: "Each arbitrator shall be and remain impartial and independent of the parties. Before confirmation or appointment, a prospective arbitrator shall sign and submit to the Institute a statement of acceptance, availability, impartiality and independence (the "Statement"). The prospective arbitrator shall disclose in the Statement any circumstances likely to give rise to justifiable doubts as to his or her impartiality or independence. The Institute shall transmit a copy of the Statement to all parties and set a time limit within which they may submit comments on the Statement or object to the confirmation or appointment of the arbitrator. An arbitrator shall promptly disclose in writing to the Institute, the parties and the other arbitrators any circumstances referred to in Article 20.2 which may arise during the course of the arbitration". FAI (2013).

[117]Article 11 of the CRCICA Arbitration Rules: When a person is approached in connection with his or her possible appointment as an arbitrator, he or she shall disclose any circumstances likely to give rise to justifiable doubts as to his or her impartiality or independence. An arbitrator, from the time of his or her appointment and throughout the arbitral proceedings, shall without delay disclose any such circumstances. Any doubts as to the duty to disclose a fact, circumstance or a relationship shall be interpreted in favour of disclosure. The appointment of an arbitrator shall be completed only upon the acceptance of his or her mission. The arbitrator thus appointed shall submit, within one week after being notified with his or her nomination, a written declaration confirming his or her impartiality and independence. CRCICA (2011).

[118]Article 11 of the KLRCA Arbitration Rules: "When a person is approached in connection with his or her possible appointment as an arbitrator, he or she shall disclose any circumstances likely to give rise to justifiable doubts as to his or her impartiality or independence. An arbitrator, from the time of his or her appointment and throughout the arbitral proceedings, shall without delay disclose any such circumstances to the parties and the other arbitrators unless they have already been

reproduce the framework,[119] which is also advocated in various national arbitration acts.[120]

This structure is both more comprehensive and stricter with arbitrators' duties than the ICSID approach, and the recent drafting of texts in the investment arbitration context, such as Article 10 of the SIAC Investment Arbitration Rules, is therefore a positive step. The provision states: "A nominated arbitrator shall disclose to the Parties and to the Registrar any circumstances that may give rise to justifiable doubts as to his impartiality or independence as soon as reasonably practicable and in any event before his appointment. An arbitrator shall immediately disclose to the Parties, to the other arbitrators and to the Registrar any circumstances that may give rise to justifiable doubts as to his impartiality or independence that may be discovered or arise during the arbitration".[121]

Likewise, judges and members of the tribunal referred to in texts such as TTIP,[122] the EU-Vietnam FTA, and JEFTA, who are no longer party-appointed arbitrators, are also bound to a pre- and post- appointment as well as an on-going duty of disclosure by their respective Codes of conduct. The standard provision reads[123]: "Disclosure obligations. Prior to their appointment, candidates shall disclose to the Parties any past and present interest, relationship or matter that is likely to affect his or her independence or impartiality or that might reasonably create an appearance of impropriety or bias. To this end, a candidate shall make all reasonable efforts to become aware of any such interests, relationships or matters. Members shall communicate matters concerning actual or potential violations of this Code of Conduct in

---

informed by him or her of these circumstances". KLRCA (2017). The references contained in this book to the *KLRCA have to be understood as currently referring to the* Asian International Arbitration Center (AIAC).

[119]Standard 3 (a) of the IBA Guidelines: "If facts or circumstances exist that may, in the eyes of the parties, give rise to doubts as to the arbitrator's impartiality or independence, the arbitrator shall disclose such facts or circumstances to the parties, the arbitration institution or other appointing authority (if any, and if so required by the applicable institutional rules) and the co-arbitrators, if any, prior to accepting his or her appointment or, if thereafter, as soon as he or she learns of them." IBA (2014).

[120]For instance, Article 1456.2 of the French Code of Civil Procedure (Book IV, Title II- International Arbitration): "Before accepting a mandate, an arbitrator shall disclose any circumstance that may affect his or her independence or impartiality. He or she also shall disclose promptly any such circumstance that may arise after accepting the mandate"; Section 1036 of the German Arbitration Act (Zivilprocessordnung), "1) When a person is approached in connection with his possible appointment as an arbitrator, he shall disclose any circumstances likely to give rise to justifiable doubts as to his impartiality or independence. An arbitrator, from the time of his appointment and throughout the arbitral proceedings, shall without delay disclose any such circumstances to the parties unless they have already been informed of them by him." German Arbitration Act (1998).

[121]SIAC (2017).

[122]Article 3.1 of the Code of Conduct. TTIP (2016).

[123]There is nevertheless a relevant difference between the texts: while Article 3 of the EU-Vietnam FTA indicates that the Parties are the recipients of the pre-appointment disclosure exercised by the candidate, Article 3 of JEFTA and TTIP's Codes of conduct do not specify this. JEFTA (2016), EU-Vietnam FTA (2016), TTIP (2016).

writing to the disputing parties. Member shall at all times continue to make all efforts to become aware of any interests, relationships or matters referred to in paragraph 1 of this Article. The member shall disclose such interests, relationships or matters by informing the disputing parties."[124]

In relation to the last points to be developed in this section, if the references in various commercial arbitration rules to the celerity, duration and addressees of the duty of disclosure were to be taken into account both in the context of a reform of ICSID arbitration rules and the creation of a MIC, this would indeed be a positive development.

Specifying the temporary diligence (speed) with which the pre-appointment disclosure duty should be exercised would be beneficial, for example. This could be achieved by incorporating time references such as: "in a term of [X]",[125] "promptly",[126] or "as soon as".[127] The temporary diligence regarding the post-appointment duty could also be specified by using time expressions references along the lines of: "within [x] days, weeks or months",[128] "promptly",[129] "without delay",[130] "as soon as"[131] or even "immediately".[132]

Where the addressees of the duty of disclosure are concerned, while TTIP, the EU-Vietnam FTA, and JEFTA only refer briefly to the parties, the SIAC Investment Arbitration Rules for instance extend this obligation to "the other arbitrators and to the Registrar". In the context of commercial arbitration, one or two of the addressees referred to are normally included within the post-appointment duty of disclosure.[133]

---

[124]Article 3.1 Code of Conduct. EU-Vietnam FTA (2016).

[125]Article 13.2 of the Procedural rules of the Spanish Court of Arbitration. CEA (2005).

[126]Article 5. LCIA (2014).

[127]Article 10. SIAC Investment Arbitration Rules (2017).

[128]Article 4 of the Code of Conduct for Members and Former Members of the CJEU: "In the event of changes in the list of entities identified in the declaration within the meaning of paragraph 3, a new declaration shall be submitted at the earliest opportunity and, at the latest, within 2 months after the change in question". CJEU (2016).

[129]Article 1456.2 of the French Code of Civil Procedure (2011); Article 20 FAI (2013) and Article 18.2 CIMA: "From the time of appointment and throughout the entire procedure, all Arbitrators shall disclose promptly to the parties, to the Court and to the other Arbitrators—in the case of collegiate tribunals—any new circumstances". CIMA (2015).

[130]Article 11 of the UNCITRAL rules: "An arbitrator, from the time of his or her appointment and throughout the arbitral proceedings, shall without delay disclose any such circumstances to the parties and the other arbitrators unless they have already been informed by him or her of these circumstances", UNCITRAL (2010); Article 1. KLRCA (2017).

[131]IBA Guidelines (2014).

[132]Article 10. SIAC Investment Arbitration Rules (2017); Article 18 SCC (2017), and Article 11.2 and 3 CAM: "the arbitrator must give immediate written notice to both the Court and to the parties of any circumstances of a similar nature to the ones described in the section above that arise during the arbitration". CAM (2015).

[133]Article 11.3 UNCITRAL Arbitration Rules, Article 5.5 LCIA, Article 18 SCC, Article 20 FAI, Article 11 KLRCA, Standard 3 of the IBA Guidelines; and Article 11.5 NAI: "An arbitrator who, during the arbitral proceedings, suspects that there could be justifiable doubts as to his impartiality or independence shall communicate the same in writing to the administrator, the parties and, if the

Both the texts analysed and national case law also include explicit references to the on-going nature of the duty of disclosure,[134] basing their justification of this continuous duty on the relationship of trust that must exist between the adjudicator and the parties.[135] It would therefore also be positive to stress this notion in future investment arbitration texts. In the ICSID framework, the relevance of the continuing obligation to disclose has been already highlighted in the case Saint-Gobain v. Venezuela. In this controversy, the claimant's proposal to disqualify the arbitrator is dismissed, but is dependent "on condition that [the arbitrator] completes, signs and transmits to the ICSID Secretary General a new Declaration under Rule 6 of the ICSID Arbitration Rules within 10 days of the date of this Decision".[136]

2.5 The Scope of the Duty of Disclosure

A number of challenge proceedings have referred to a peculiarity of the ICSID system: its pioneering nature as regards certain transparency issues.[137] Once a tribunal has been constituted, the ICSID website provides information about the case, such as the arbitrators' names, relevant documents, dates and procedural details.

Some arbitrators have relied on this to justify failure to disclose certain information, such as prior ICSID appointments, in their ICSID declarations, "because it was her understanding at that time that only facts that are undisclosed or unknown, and not publicly available information, must be disclosed".[138] So far, in various ICSID challenge decisions where non-disclosure needed to be justified, ICSID appointments have been successfully categorised as information in the public domain. In cases such as Tidewater v. Venezuela the co-arbitrators began by stating that

arbitral tribunal consists of multiple arbitrators, to the co-arbitrators in writing, stating the suspected reason(s)". NAI (2015).

[134]Article 5.5 LCIA, Article 11 KLRCA.

[135]Fernández Rozas (2013), p. 818.

[136]In this case, the arbitrator accepted his appointment as arbitrator on 25 October 2012, being an employee of the Argentine government. As of 1 January 2013, he resigned from his position to pursue doctoral studies. The co-arbitrators considered that "the present challenge arose due to the unfortunate timing of his appointment and the disclosure requirement imposed by Rule 6 of the ICSID Arbitration Rules. Saint-Gobain v. Venezuela, par. 86.

[137]Other international -commercial- arbitration institutions have eventually followed this path. The ICC Note to Parties deals with the publication of information regarding arbitral tribunals (a publication system that requires the parties' agreement, however). ICC (2017a). Likewise, the various ICC Statements of Impartiality and Independence include the following sentence: "I accept that my name, nationality, role and the method of my appointment as well as the termination of my assignment will be published on the ICC Court's website". ICC (2017a). Dealing with transparency, *infra* Chap. 5.1.

[138]Universal v. Venezuela, par 92.

"Arbitration Rule 6 (2) does not limit disclosure to circumstances which would not be known in the public domain. The wording of this rule is all encompassing without distinguishing among categories of circumstances to be disclosed."[139] However, they subsequently developed a rationale that de facto plays down the importance of non-disclosure when determining whether a challenged arbitrator may be relied upon to exercise independent judgement. The practical consequence may be expressed as follows: publicly available arbitral appointments ought to be disclosed solely out of an abundance of caution.[140]

In the duty of disclosure context, the concept of the public domain has been stretched far beyond what is accessible on ICSID's website. In Nations Energy v. Panama the co-arbitrators argued that information referring to the professional relationship between the arbitrator and one of the lawyers at the law firm that appointed him was also in the public domain.[141] Apart from the lack of sufficient argument in this case, in general terms this position can be qualified as both inadequate and unreasonable. As Tidewater pointed out, "arbitrators will always be in the best position to gather, evaluate, and disclose accurate information relevant to their potential conflicts".[142] Imposing these duties on the challenging party would represent a huge burden and could also lead to false negative results as a consequence of the inability to access certain sources due to data protection or confidentiality issues.[143]

For these reasons, the deciding arbitrators' non-acceptance of a broad definition of the "notorious fact" concept in Suez v. Argentine Republic is to be positively valued. They stated that the bank directorship given to the challenged arbitrator "is not so public and wide-spread that one can reasonably assume that the Respondent actually knew or should have known of that fact."[144]

[139]Tidewater v. Venezuela, par 46.

[140]The decision states: "while the Two Members consider that an arbitrator's disclosure statement ought to include even publicly available arbitral appointments, in the case of ICSID appointments, this must be *out of an abundance of caution*, given the ready accessibility of this information in the records of the very Centre with which the parties are dealing. In any event, the Two Members consider that the fact that this information is publicly available can and should be taken into account by them in determining the separate question of whether that non-disclosure may itself amount to a manifest lack of independence or impartiality". Tidewater v. Venezuela, par 54, (emphasis added). The same conclusion is also reached in Universal v. Venezuela, par 92: "In order to ensure that parties have complete information available to them, an arbitrator's Arbitration Rule 6 (2) declaration should include details of prior appointments by an appointing party, including, out of an abundance of caution. However, in assessing whether an arbitrator's non-disclosure of such appointments results in a manifest lack of independence or impartiality, the *public nature* of that information must be taken into account", (emphasis added). Tidewater v. Venezuela, par 54.

[141]Nations Energy v. Panama, par 76.

[142]Tidewater v. Venezuela, par 17.

[143]The co-arbitrators in Tidewater rightly point out that: "this is necessarily so, since otherwise, submits Tidewater, the parties would need to conduct intrusive investigations and rely on indirect and not always reliable sources". *Ibid,* par. 17.

[144]Suez v. Argentine Republic, par 45.

It can be seen from the above that texts such as the footnote to the EU-Vietnam FTA Code of Conduct for Members of the Tribunal, the Appeal Tribunal and Mediators[145] do not represent substantive progress. The footnote states that: "for greater certainty, Article 3 paragraph 1 [disclosure obligations] does not extend to information which is already in the public domain or was known, or should have reasonably been known, by all disputing parties". In spite of aiming to cast light on the issue, provision's use of generic expressions and lack of definitions would seem to lead to ad casum decisions and thus perpetuate uncertainty and the risk of failing to produce homogeneous results. Other EU texts such as CETA[146] have not yet developed a code of conduct for tribunal members and it would be a step in the right direction if any future texts adopted a clearer position regarding the scope of the duty of disclosure.

In these matters, erring on the side of pedantry and over-disclosure would seem preferable to carelessness or opacity. An important basic idea that needs reinforcing is that the duty of disclosure should be dedramatized.[147] As the IBA Guidelines stress, disclosure should not be considered a synonym for a lack of independence or impartiality; on the contrary, an arbitrator who discloses information has previously concluded that there is no reason to either decline the appointment or resign.[148]

These reflections on the concept of public domain in the context of the duty of disclosure are linked to another question: the degree of relevance of the facts that should be disclosed.

---

[145] EU-Vietnam FTA (2016).

[146] Article 8.44.2 CETA: "The Committee on Services and Investment shall, on agreement of the parties, and after completion of their respective internal requirements and procedures, adopt a Code of Conduct for the members of the tribunal to be applied in disputes arising out of this chapter, which may replace or supplement the rules in application, and may address topics including: disclosure obligations, the independence and impartiality of the members of the tribunal and confidentiality". CETA (2016).

[147] For instance, the—sucessful—structure developed by the Financial Industry Regulatory Authority (FINRA) securities arbitration has been stressed as an example of legal framework that "heavily rely on comprehensive disclosure obligations to address and prevent conflicts of interest". Bernasconi-Osterwalder, Johnson and Marshall, at 41.

[148] Explanation to IBA General Standard 3: "A disclosure does not imply the existence of a conflict of interest. An arbitrator who has made a disclosure to the parties considers himself or herself to be impartial and independent of the parties, despite the disclosed facts, or else he or she would have declined the nomination, or resigned. An arbitrator making a disclosure thus feels capable of performing his or her duties. It is the purpose of disclosure to allow the parties to judge whether they agree with the evaluation of the arbitrator and, if they so wish, to explore the situation further. It is hoped that the promulgation of this General Standard will eliminate the misconception that disclosure itself implies doubts sufficient to disqualify the arbitrator, or even creates a presumption in favour of disqualification. Instead, any challenge should only be successful if an objective test, as set forth in General Standard 2 above, is met. Under Comment 5 of the Practical Application of the General Standards, a failure to disclose certain facts and circumstances that may, in the eyes of the parties, give rise to doubts as to the arbitrator's impartiality or independence, does not necessarily mean that a conflict of interest exists, or that a disqualification should ensue". IBA (2014).

Some of the phrases in ICSID's disqualification decisions have become true classics in the investment arbitration context. There is a striking degree of creativity behind sentences such as the following: "Arbitrators are not disembodied spirits dwelling on Mars, who descend to earth to arbitrate a case and then immediately return to their Martian retreat to await inertly the call to arbitrate another".[149] This argument was put forward in Suez v. Argentine Republic and specifically refers to the alleged connection between a party and an arbitrator and the possible impact in terms of a manifest lack of arbitrator impartiality and independence.

Such co-arbitrator allegations transcend specific cases and constitute a general assertion: the combination of modern life and globalization with the duty of disclosure can impose an unreasonable burden on arbitrators.[150] One ICSID decision stated very viscerally that "without some link of materiality, an arbitrator would be called upon to reveal all (or almost all) elements of his or her life, a situation that would paralyze any arbitral process."[151] Reference has also been made to the "need to respect the personal privacy of the arbitrators" in other contexts.[152]

The arbitration collective has expressed its support for the materiality link that is required by refusing to disclose trivial, superficial or insignificant facts.[153] From this perspective, broad disclosure obligations may limit party freedom by depriving them of their chosen arbitrators, and may also support frivolous challenges. Once again, doubts arise as to how these adjectives should be defined. For instance: are the situations which do not need to be disclosed according to the IBA Green List trivial,

---

[149]Suez v. Argentine Republic, par 32.

[150]The co-arbitrators stated that: "such connections are increasingly easy to make as globalization of modern life rapidly advances and countless institutions engage in activities that are global in scope. At the same time, it is perfectly possible for a person to be unaware of the links that connect him or her to others or at least to be unaware of their full implications. For example, arbitrators in this case might unknowingly have a connection to UBS by virtue of the fact that their law firms have bank accounts with a UBS foreign branch, that their university pension fund is managed by UBS, or that they or their family members own shares in mutual funds which in turn hold UBS securities", Suez v. Argentine Republic, par 33.

[151]EDF v. Argentine Republic, par 123.

[152]The section dealing with the self-disclosure requirements for covered persons in the WTO Rules of Conduct for the Understanding on Rules and Procedures Governing the Settlement of Disputes states that: "They shall take into account the need to respect the personal privacy of those to whom these Rules apply and shall not be so administratively burdensome as to make it impracticable for otherwise qualified persons to serve on panels". WTO (1996a).

[153]"Trivial" and "superficial" are used in Alpha v. Ukraine: "Further, the Two Other Members view the position taken in the IBA Guidelines as reflective of the legitimate concern that a requirement to disclose trivial or superficial facts will prove burdensome to parties and arbitrators, will unnecessarily circumscribe the freedom of choice in the selection of party-appointed arbitrators and will encourage frivolous challenges". Alpha v. Ukraine, par 66. Likewise, national case law tries to draw a dividing line between trivial and non- trivial: Daele (2012), pp. 56–65. In the WTO context, the US Communication also opposes disclosing trivial facts. US (1994). The WTO Rules of Conduct for the Understanding on Rules and Procedures Governing the Settlement of Disputes uses the term "insignificant".

superficial and insignificant?[154] Even if they were, it should be recalled that the Green List is non-exhaustive.

2.6 Arbitrators' Curricula Vitae

The parties' interest in being fully informed of all circumstances that may affect arbitrator independence and impartiality has been affirmed in various forums.[155] Within this general context, an issue that deserves detailed analysis is that of arbitrators' CVs.[156] Although it has become clear that these are not the only relevant documents in relation to the duty of disclosure, at first glance they would seem to be important for participants in an international arbitration. The claim made in the ICSID Compañía v. Argentine Republic case is therefore logical: "it is also proper that at least an updated CV be circulated to all the parties to the arbitrations so that each party can decide for itself whether there are reasons why the arbitrator/board member should no longer serve, even if any subsequent challenge is ill-founded."[157]

When dealing with arbitrators' CV, he current ICSID website contains a user-friendly tab labelled "Arbitrators", which lists arbitrators, conciliators and ad hoc committee members and includes a link to their CVs. ICSID also provides a search engine enabling the search for arbitrators to be narrowed, using the parameters of nationality, language, ICSID panel designation, experience in ICSID cases, and party representative.[158] CVs displayed by ICSID have a standard format and include sections covering personal details including photograph; language; panel designation; professional experience; education and professional qualifications; experience in ICSID proceedings, professional membership, and publications. The standard CV also includes the following disclaimer: "The information in this form has been provided by the relevant arbitrator/conciliator. Every effort is made to ensure it is

[154]Explanation to General Standard 3 of the IBA Guidelines: "However, situations that, such as those set out in the Green List, could never lead to disqualification under the objective test set out in General Standard 2, need not be disclosed". IBA (2014).

[155]The ICC Note states: "The parties have a legitimate interest in being fully informed of all facts or circumstances that may be relevant in their view in order to be satisfied that an arbitrator or prospective arbitrator is and remains independent and impartial or, if they so wish, to explore the matter further and/or take the initiatives contemplated by the Rules". ICC (2017a), par. 17: The Chairman of the ICSID Administrative Council in Universal v. Venezuela stated that: "parties have an interest in knowing any facts or circumstances that may exist that may give doubts about an arbitrator's independence and impartiality. Indeed, as reflected in Arbitration Rule 6 (2), disclosure by arbitrators of any such facts or circumstances is required". Universal v. Venezuela, par 90.

[156]These reflections on some of the issues surrounding CVs have been enriched by the debate generated in OGEMID following a comment posted by the author. I am grateful to OGEMID members for their helpful comments.

[157]Compañía v. Argentine Republic, par 227.

[158]ICSID (last accessed in June 2018b).

accurate and current. However, persons relying on this information must conduct their own due diligence research."

The fact that this information is freely available on the ICSID website is certainly welcome for various reasons. Not only are arbitration parties provided with these details about potential arbitrators, but the data are also very useful for other groups—third parties, researchers, and civil society in general. In addition, the fact that this transparency-related initiative has arisen from ICSID itself rather than being imposed by external stakeholders is highly positive. The drive for transparency in international investment arbitration alluded to previously does not seem to have been imposed on arbitrators' CVs, and these do not appear on the list of documents to be made available to the public in the UNCITRAL Rules on Transparency in Treaty-based Investor-State Arbitration.[159]

Nevertheless, an analysis of the kind of arbitrator CVs currently posted on the ICSID website raises some doubts as to how detailed and up-to-date they are. Some arbitrators have failed to fill in one or more sections, in which case the section contains the comment "no records to display". In other cases, CVs contain only brief summaries that do not reflect the authors' full qualifications and experience. It is also clear that specific sections such as publications are not regularly up-dated, circumstances that explain the inclusion of the disclaimer quoted below.

The gaps in CVs may lead to situations similar to those already reported before ICSID began including such information on its public website. For instance, the Vito v. Canada case—an arbitration case brought under Chapter 11 of NAFTA—contains a veiled criticism of inaccuracies in the arbitrator's CV. The ICSID Deputy Secretary-General declared that "it would have been preferable for [the arbitrator] not to have stated in a CV provided to the parties that he intended to retire as counsel if his intentions were not entirely certain".[160]

A full updated CV undoubtedly offers more information about the arbitrator than a document that is both brief and out-of-date. Likewise, it is clearly preferable for arbitration institutions to strive to offer free access to full updated CVs on their websites. However, outside the ICSID context, this is not generally the case in either commercial or investment arbitration, and some major organizations still apply a confidentiality policy in the sense of not providing public access to arbitrators' CVs.[161]

Additionally, an analysis of various rules on investment and commercial arbitration reveals that not only that most of them do not contain explicit references to

---

[159] UNCITRAL (2014).

[160] Vito v. Canada, par 29. Commercial arbitration seems to have more resources to deal with such situations. Faced with a very extreme case: "A San Francisco court has set aside an arbitral award after it emerged that the chair of the tribunal had lied about his qualifications and impersonated a retired lawyer in California—a ruling that may threaten awards in nearly 40 US securities arbitrations conducted from 1998 to 2011". Yong (2016).

[161] Some arbitration institutions that may manage investment arbitrations do not have a publicly available arbitrator database. For instance, LCIA- LCIA (last accessed in June 2018); the ICC; and Stockholm Chamber of Commerce Arbitration Institute.

arbitrator CVs, but the few references that are provided are vague in the extreme. For instance, Article 12.2 of the 2013 Arbitration Rules of the DAI states that: "before being confirmed (...) the arbitrator shall also produce information on his or her professional and educational background, etc. (CV/ résumé)."[162]

A complementary analysis of various investment and commercial arbitration institution websites also proves how difficult it is to find arbitral institutions that oblige their arbitrators to keep their CVs up-to-date. While there is a growing trend for investment and commercial arbitration institutions websites to allow easy—or sometimes not so easy—access to the institution's list of arbitrators, only a few also supply their arbitrators' full CVs.

Among these minority initiatives[163] is the not-for-profit Singapore International Arbitration Center (SIAC), which supplies a list of the arbitrators that make up the SIAC panel. Although each arbitrator's name is linked to a SIAC CV template with various sections (personal details; educational and professional memberships; current position; professional experience/areas of expertise; arbitration experience, publications and languages),[164] there does not seem to be any formal obligation to update CVs on a regular basis.[165] The list of practitioners published by the Vienna International Arbitral Centre (VIAC) also links to a standard questionnaire with thirteen sections[166] and culminates with the practitioner's signature and the useful reference to the date.[167] The biographies of JAMS neutrals are also available,[168] although it should be taken into account that JAMS (formerly known as Judicial Arbitration and Mediation Services) is a US for-profit organization and that some of its practises—fee-sharing agreements and annual administrative fees charged to the neutrals on the list—are alien to investment arbitration institutions such as ICSID.[169]

In short, ICSID's policy of making its arbitrator CV database available to the public is far from being the norm in the international arbitration context. Besides

---

[162]DIA (2013).

[163]While not exhaustive, reference is made to other arbitration institutions that provide their adjudicators' CVs to some extent: AAA, referring solely to mediators. AAA (last accessed in June 2018); CEDCA, providing very brief CVs. CEDCA (last accessed in June 2018).

[164]SIAC (last accessed in June 2018).

[165]Panel members who wish to update their details or CV can e-mail panel@siac.org.sg.

[166]Namely: name; date of birth; citizenship; contact information; current position; education; experience in arbitration practice; publications and other arbitral activities; membership of arbitral institutions; languages, legal system in which the practitioner trained; main jurisdiction of practice, and special expertise or specializations).

[167]VIAC (last accessed in June 2018).

[168]JAM (last accessed in June 2018).

[169]These fees are also charged by some not-for-profit organizations that deal with commercial arbitration, such as AAA or CPR (International Institute for Conflict Prevention and Resolution). CPR (last accessed in June 2018). These two US organizations keep the arbitrators/neutrals list themselves and it is not available to the public. (The AAA/ICDR has nevertheless introduced a new procedure such that the parties can access the entire panel database for a specific period once a case has been filed with the AAA. AAA/ICDR (last accessed in June 2018). Analysing some characteristics of these US "for-profit" entities, Matthews (2005).

that, even in the ICSID context, the publicly available information supplied by the arbitrators on their CVs does not appear sufficiently detailed to be used as the cornerstone for decisions, either when selecting or challenging arbitrators. Taking into account the disclaimers incorporated by various arbitration organizations,[170] they clearly do not wish to impose a higher degree of diligence on arbitrators with regard to the accuracy of their CVs as yet.

In fact, practice in the international investment arbitration context seems is moving in a different direction. In a recent decision issued in the Victor Pey Casado v. Chile case, the World Bank Administrative Council chairman recognized that: "it is a standard practice for a party to perform a conflict search of arbitrators at the time they are appointed".[171] In cases where thorough knowledge of an arbitrator's CV is necessary—especially, if the arbitrator has been appointed by the other party, which may have more direct access to him/her[172]—lawyers currently resort to various, mainly informal mechanisms to reconstruct the arbitrator's full CV, including carrying out internet searches themselves,[173] accessing databases containing legal news and academic papers, and obtaining information from colleagues. The 2018 White&Case International Arbitration Survey reveils that: "the most selected source of information about arbitrators was "word of mouth" (77%), followed by "from internal colleagues" (68%) and "publicly available information (e.g. industry reviews, legal directories and other databases or review tools" (63%)."[174] They also use more formal mechanisms such as hiring companies that specialise in this type of research.

Other interesting advanced online initiatives providing information about the arbitrators' CV have been launched recently, such as Arbitrator Intelligence (AI), a resource which aims to provide information about arbitrators and their decision-making. The information is gathered from responses from users and counsels and is

---

[170]JAMS disclaimer: "This page is for general information purposes. JAMS makes no representations or warranties regarding its accuracy or completeness. Interested persons should conduct their own research regarding information on this website before deciding to use JAMS, including investigation and research of JAMS neutrals"; VIAC disclaimer: "I have completed this questionnaire to the above to the best of my knowledge and believe they are accurate. I understand that the above information will be used for VIAC's internal use and may be given to interested persons and may be put on VIAC's website"; ICC disclaimer: "We encourage users to log in to their profile from time to time and make any updates that might be useful".

[171]This search is understood to be based on the information that would be found in a full CV. Victor Pey Casado v. Chile (2017a), par 92.

[172]For instance, in the Alpha v. Ukraine case there was a ""brief phone call" from Dr. S. to Dr. T. in 2007 inquiring as to whether Dr. T. was available to serve as an arbitrator in this proceeding". The award stated that the ""brief phone call" was in keeping with common practice". Alpha v. Ukraine, par 40.

[173]Some investment awards recognize that the parties analyse information in the media about arbitrators. For instance: "At the same time, media regularly reported on [the arbitrator] representing Chile in an unrelated case, and Claimants regularly relied on evidence from these same media outlets during the proceedings". Victor Pey Casado v. Chile (2017a), par 93.

[174]White&Case (2018), p. 20.

expected to promote transparency, fairness, accountability and diversity in the selection of international arbitrators.[175] In the same vein, the Global Arbitration Review (GAR) has introduced an Arbitrator Research Tool (GAR ART),[176] and in the commercial context ICC has entered a cooperation agreement with Dispute Resolution Data (DRD).[177]

This type of cyber-information network is likely to become increasingly important in the future.[178] In the medium or long term, artificial intelligence will have a relevant role not only in recreating the objective content of arbitrators' CVs, but also in trying to detect subjective aspects such as unconscious bias.

Until that time comes, the question arises as to whether the EU's vigorous activity in the context of ISDS may alter the scenario outlined above with regard to arbitrators' duty to disclose their CVs. More specifically, the creation of a MIC would also entail the need to make decisions regarding the duty of disclosure of court members, as well as their obligations regarding their own CVs.

In an attempt to find a reference in the European context, the European Court of Justice (ECJ) website includes an introduction to Court members, but this certainly does not amount to a comprehensive CV for each individual.[179] The European Court of Human Rights (ECHR), which is not an EU institution, also offers a list of all judges as well as brief CVs.[180] However, recent events in the ECHR seem to suggest that neither the proponent state nor the international institution has to provide sufficient proof as to the veracity of its content.[181] A kind of post-truth seems to have broken into the current scenario. Therefore, extrapolating these criteria to the international investment context would not therefore seem to raise the bar of CV requirements for arbitrators or members of a future international investment court.

---

[175]http://www.arbitratorintelligence.org.

[176]The introduction of this tool affirms that GAR ART has information on who has recently seen whom—so that a lawyer can contact a person he/she knows directly—, as well as interviews with the arbitrators about their case-management style. It has been recently reported that GAR ART already gathers more that 200 arbitrators' profiles. GAR (2018).

[177]It is indicated that: "The International Chamber of Commerce (ICC) has announced it has entered into a cooperation agreement with Dispute Resolution Data (DRD)—a research service for international commercial arbitration and mediation." ICC (last accessed in June 2018).

[178]Hanke (2017) and Rose (2017).

[179]ECJ (last accessed in June 2018).

[180]The ECHR has stated: "In addition to the criteria set out in Article 21, paragraph 1, of the Convention (...) the Assembly has introduced linguistic requirements based on Article 21, paragraph 1, of the Convention, the need for gender balance, as well as other requisites, such as the standard curriculum vitae for candidates. Before proceeding to the election of judges, the Assembly also invites candidates to take part in personal interviews before a sub-committee set up for that purpose". ECHR (2009).

[181]The Diplomatic "PSOE considers asking for revocation of Elósegui's election to ECHR", http://thediplomatinspain.com/en/psoeconsiders-asking-for-revocation-of-eloseguis-election-to-echr/ (last accessed in June 2018); RTVE http://www.rtve.es/noticias/20180129/psoe-asegura-juez-elosegui-falseo-su-curriculum-estudia-como-revocar-sunombramiento-estrasburgo/1669760.shtml (last accessed in June 2018). At the time of sending this book to the publisher, the aforementioned judge has reportedly initiated legal actions against the information contained in the referred websites.

However, it should be pointed out here that several sectors in the EU are much more demanding in terms of CV detail and length, and the EU database of independent experts assisting in evaluating research and innovation proposals and monitoring actions is an example.[182] The database—created for European Commission (EC) internal use—obliges experts to fill in a standard CV form, which is not only extremely detailed but also expires, meaning that registered experts are forced to update their CVs regularly if they want the EU to take their profiles into account. There are of course obvious differences between the two sectors (research and innovation, and, on the other hand, investment claims), as well as clear dissimilarities deriving from short or long term professional connections between individuals and institutions in these fields (short term research and innovation contracts versus the quasi-civil servant status of future members of the ICS-MIC). In spite of all this, the question arises as to why this example should not be taken into account with the aim of initiating a serious debate on the issue of investment adjudicators' CVs.

In a more general context, national legislation in many countries normally requires candidates for the civil service to first prove that the information on their CV is correct by providing the originals or certified copies of certificates and qualifications. In the context of a prospective international investment court, this kind of example raises questions such as the following: would it be desirable to make the arbitrators/MIC court members' comprehensive CVs freely accessible to everyone? What might the negative effect of this obligation be? Are there any legal restrictions to prevent this new obligation being imposed, or is it rather that customs or lobbies do not favour change?

Although it seems to be preferred by arbitrators, the current situation is not the most efficient one, in the sense that individual ad hoc inquiries about an arbitrator's CV do not lead to all the relevant information being disclosed, and the information obtained is not always reliable.[183] In addition, since the results are not made public, efforts made in one particular case are of no use for subsequent cases. Obtaining this less than full information is also costly in terms of both time and money, and arbitration parties bear the expense. All the referred shortcomings lead to the conclusion that the most reliable mechanism would seem to be the arbitrators' own disclosure of their full updated CVs. There are other reasons why this obligation should fall to them alone: apart from the investment arbitrators' ethical duties vis-à-vis the parties, their own obligations as a careful professional, and their high remuneration, this is undoubtedly the most reasonable option from the cost

[182] EC (last accessed in June 2018).

[183] An example of the importance of professional CVs and the legal consequences that may result from unreliable information occurred during in the ICSID Factory v. Venezuela case. The case dealt with the issue of the CV of one of the assistants working for the arbitrator in his chambers. The assistant's LinkedIn profile claimed that she had worked at a specific law firm from a specific date. As a result of Venezuela's request to disqualify the arbitrator, he declared that "[she - the assistant] has never worked for the law firm and is not an attorney. She is a secretary who assists me clerically in my arbitration files including the present one. The entry in her LinkedIn profile is inaccurate". The other two members of the tribunal considered that "a reasonable third person would conclude that [the assistant] has committed an error on her LinkedIn page". Fábrica v. Venezuela (2016b), pars 43 and 53.

efficiency perspective, given that nobody but the arbitrators themselves hold all the relevant information.

As will be discussed below, the adjudicators' duty to disclose their full and updated CVs should be reinforced through an obligation imposed by the arbitration institution or the investment arbitration court. This might also produce interesting side benefits in the fight against gender discrimination or discrimination against minorities in arbitration.[184] An example of this approach are the Criteria for the appointment of arbitrators by the Centre approved by the Board of the Arbitration Centre of the Portuguese Chamber of Commerce and Industry, which state that: "From 1 July, 2015, no arbitrator shall be appointed by the Chairman unless they have submitted their arbitration curriculum to the Centre, according to the model to be duly published."[185]

On the other hand, any doubts that may arise regarding the confidentiality of personal data, for example, does not seem to be insurmountable. Current arbitration statements used by arbitral institutions such as the ICC ("By accepting to serve as arbitrator under the Rules, unless otherwise agreed by the parties, I accept that my name, nationality, role and the method of my appointment as well as the termination of my assignment will be published on the court website") could therefore be extended to include references to a full and up-to-date CV.[186] Where the optimum structure for this institutional CV model is concerned, the key criterion should be whether the form is adequate for arbitrators to disclose all relevant circumstances. The issue of truthfulness is obviously crucial when dealing with investment adjudicators' CVs. It would be therefore useful to include a kind of warning such as: "a member shall not make or allow to be made on the member's behalf any representation about the member's experience or expertise which is misleading or deceptive or likely to mislead or deceive".[187]

2.7 Arbitrators' Duty to Investigate

Although the ICSID system does not expressly refer to arbitrators' duty to investigate in the context of the duty of disclosure,[188] the issue is expressly addressed in other commercial and investment texts.

---

[184]In the fight against gender or diversity bias, it has been proposed that in the first instance arbitration institutions should provide the parties with standardized CVs that omit in all personal references (name, gender, etc.) to the candidates. Greenwood (2015), pp. 1–9.

[185]Arbitration Centre of the Portuguese Chamber of Commerce and Industry (2005).

[186]The ICC Note highlights the importance of transparency and states that "by accepting to serve as an arbitrator under the Rules, a prospective arbitrator accepts that such information will be published on the ICC website". ICC (2017) par. 29.

[187]Rule 4.2 of the Code of Professional and Ethical Conduct for Members of the CIArb (2009).

[188]The co-arbitrators in Suez v. Argentine Republic, for instance, are aware of this fact: "On this question, the ICSID Arbitration Rules offer little guidance. They require only the making of a declaration. They contain no specific requirement that an arbitrator is to make an investigation of

Various texts in the commercial arbitration context refer to the duty to investigate (the IBA Guidelines; the ICC Arbitration Rules; the International Centre for Dispute Resolution Code of Ethics; the KLRCA Code of Conduct, and the Barcelona Arbitration Court Code of Ethics, etc.). In the investment milieu, the respective Articles 3.1 of the Codes of conduct included in the EU-Singapore IPA,[189] in the former EUSFTA,[190] TTIP,[191] the EU-Vietnam FTA,[192] and JEFTA[193] all state that: "To this end [disclosure obligations], candidates shall make all reasonable efforts to become aware of any such interests, relationships or matter", wording that is once again based on the NAFTA Code of Conduct.

In spite of the fact that ICSID rules lack any explicit reference to arbitrators' duty to investigate, the issue has been addressed in several cases. For instance, the question has been raised as to whether arbitrators can be considered to have fulfilled their duty of enquiry if the investigation is carried out by someone else. The Suez v. Argentine Republic case provides an example of a lenient approach to this issue: simplifying, the arbitrator, who was about to be appointed director of a bank, gave the financial institution a list of all her arbitrations and the bank later informed her that there were no conflicts of interest between the arbitrator and her future responsibilities in the financial milieu.[194] From her co-arbitrators' perspective, the challenged arbitrator had complied with her duty of disclosure, even though she did not disclose any of her relationships with the parties because of what she had been told by the bank.[195]

possible compromising circumstances and they prescribe no standards as to the extent and nature of such investigation", par 47.

[189]EU-Singapore IPA (2018).

[190]EUSFTA (2015).

[191]TTIP (2016).

[192]EU-Vietnam FTA (2016).

[193]JEFTA (2016).

[194]More precisely, "except with respect to her position as a member of the America's Cup jury (since UBS sponsored a yacht in the competition), from which she resigned." Suez v. Argentine Republic, par 14.

[195]The co-arbitrators stated: "We believe that she had reason to rely on the UBS examination of this question since UBS, under Swiss banking law and the corporate and stock exchange rules to which it is subject, had a strong incentive to ascertain her independence because the company would have encountered legal and regulatory difficulties should it represent her as an independent director and later find that a court, regulatory agency, or stock exchange had determined her to be non-independent director of the UBS board of directors. It was therefore reasonable to rely on the investigation by UBS that no conflict existed between [the arbitrator] and the parties in any of her arbitrations (with the exception of the America Cup) as a result of becoming a UBS director. Consequently, we do not believe that she had a duty to inquire further. Moreover, even if it were established that she did have such an obligation (which we do not believe is the case), her failure to do was in our opinion the result of an honest exercise of judgment and was not part of a pattern of circumstances raising doubts about impartiality. We therefore conclude that [the arbitrator] did not violate ICSID Arbitration Rule 6 with respect of her obligations of disclosure to the parties in these cases." Suez v. Argentine Republic, par 48.

The ad hoc committee members in the Compañía v. Argentine Republic case were much more severe with the same arbitrator with respect to her duty to investigate.[196] The committee appeared inclined to consider the position of bank director incompatible with that of an international arbitrator. Anyone deciding to continue in both roles was taking a risk, and should therefore be required to make special efforts in areas such as investigating and notifying the arbitration parties about potential conflicts of interest.[197] In this case the committee considered that the arbitrator had not investigated properly and had also neglected her duties of information.[198] The fact that the bank had carried out its own investigation was neither appropriate nor relevant in the investment arbitration context, and it was therefore an inadequate substitute for the investigation that the arbitrator should have undertaken personally.[199]

The latter approach is the most appropriate. In the absence of unanimity on this point, future ICSID amendments and MIC-type initiatives should expressly state that the duty to investigate is a personal obligation in the investment arbitration context—intuitu personae—that is, an obligation that can only be fulfilled by the arbitrator-obligor. For the sake of efficiency, transparency and good faith, it is inappropriate to delegate such a key obligation to someone else, let alone to someone completely alien to the complex world of international investment arbitration.[200] In the same vein, the fact that other participants in the arbitration, such as counsels, are also obliged to inform—and therefore to investigate—does not reduce the scope of the arbitrator's obligations in this matter.[201]

---

[196] In spite of which, the annulment was ultimately rejected.

[197] Compañía v. Argentine Republic, pars 217–224.

[198] Using strong wording: "The complications that have subsequently arisen in terms of agony, ICSID credibility, and cost, not only in this case, provide a vivid and abject example of the consequences when an arbitrator accepts a board position in a major international bank without properly investigating and disclosing any connections between the bank and parties to its arbitrations and also neglects its information duties". Ibid, par 230.

[199] The ad hoc committee members stated: "Whether there were any conflicts for the bank's own purposes was for the bank to decide. Naturally, the bank could subsequently also decide whether to continue with the board appointment or not, but the bank could not decide these issues for others, particularly parties to an arbitration, who from the perspective of their arbitration may have a very different view of conflicts that result or could result for them from the involvement of their arbitrator with the bank." *Ibid,* par 225.

[200] In favour of transforming arbitrators' ethical duty to investigate potential conflicts into a positive, legal mandate in the US commercial arbitration context, Windsor (2009).

[201] For instance, General Standard 7(a) of the IBA Guidelines on Conflicts of Interest in International Arbitration establishes that "(a) A party shall inform an arbitrator, the Arbitral Tribunal, the other parties and the arbitration institution or other appointing authority (if any) of any relationship, direct or indirect, between the arbitrator and the party (or another company of the same group of companies, or an individual having a controlling influence on the party in the arbitration), or between the arbitrator and any person or entity with a direct economic interest in, or a duty to indemnify a party for, the award to be rendered in the arbitration. The party shall do so on its own initiative at the earliest opportunity". IBA (2014). The importance of the parties' duty to inform may increase, for example in the context of third party funding. For these reasons, the following opinion

Arbitrators' duty to investigate (frequently carrying out what are known as conflicts checks) also encompasses a number of other challenging issues that have not been comprehensively dealt with in ICSID cases.

First, it is important to clarify exactly what standards of inquiry arbitrators have to apply. In the commercial arbitration context, various arbitration institutions use similar wording to address the question of arbitrators' duty to investigate: "an arbitrator is under a duty to make reasonable enquiries to identify any conflict of interest"[202]; "persons who are requested to accept appointment as arbitrators should make a reasonable effort to inform themselves of any interests or relationships described in paragraph A"[203]; "when completing his or her Statement and identifying whether he or she should make a disclosure (. . .) an arbitrator or prospective arbitrator should make reasonable enquiries"[204]; "an arbitrator shall conduct reasonable enquiries with regard to potential conflict of interest"[205]; and "each potential arbitrator must make a reasonable effort to learn of, and must disclose to the Director, any circumstances which might preclude the arbitrator from rendering an objective and impartial determination in the proceeding".[206] All these texts include the word "reasonable", a term that introduces the objective standard of a reasonable person into the duty to investigate. Likewise, in their claims to initiate ICSID challenge procedures the parties have sometimes linked the arbitrators' duty to investigate with the term "reasonable".[207]

Nevertheless, the author considers that the criterion of reasonableness is insufficient by itself. Given arbitrators' crucial role in international arbitration, it seems more appropriate to raise stringency standards and require them to investigate at a level that is in accordance with their high professional profiles. For instance, the Spanish Arbitration Club recommendations concerning the arbitrator independence and impartiality are thought-provoking in this sense, as they state that any arbitrator has to achieve the level of diligence required from a well-organized professional

---

is not shared: "we understand that the rigor of this obligation [the arbitrator's duty to investigate] must be tempered with the respective obligation of the parties to investigate (...) In this sense, it should not be expected that the arbitrator reveals those facts (...) that the parties may know by conducting a reasonable investigation." (English translation by the author). "entendemos que el rigor de esta obligación—de investigar del árbitro—debe ser atemperado con la respectiva obligación de las partes de investigar (...) En este sentido no debería esperarse que el árbitro revele aquellos hechos (...) que las partes puedan conocer llevando a cabo una investigación razonable". Mantilla-Serrano and Pinsolle (2013), p. 899.

[202]Standard 7 (d) IBA Guidelines. IBA (2014).

[203]Canon 2 B. ABA (2004).

[204]ICC (2017a).

[205]KLRCA (2017).

[206]12405. Disclosures Required of Arbitrators. FINRA (2007).

[207]"Investigate by all reasonable means available to him", Fábrica v. Venezuela, par 19.

(profesional ordenado).[208] A comparable solution would be to replace "reasonable" with a stronger term, such as "careful",[209] "meticulous",[210] or "exhaustive".[211]

Applying the proposed parameters to the investment arbitration milieu would bring about certain consequences, which have already been recognized in some national case law[212] and several commercial texts. Some are worded negatively ("Failure to disclose an indirect relation unknown to a prospective arbitrator shall not be grounds for disqualification unless it could have been discovered by making reasonable enquiries"),[213] and others in more positive terms ("Failure to disclose a conflict is not excused by lack of knowledge, if the arbitrator does not perform such reasonable enquiries").[214]

Accepting this kind of parameter—lack of knowledge does not always release arbitrators from the duty of disclosure—would have major practical consequences in the ICSID context. In a number of cases it has been concluded that the arbitrators did not breach their duty of disclosure, on the grounds that they did not know, or it was not proved that they did know, about a given matter. The deciding arbitrators seem to have admitted this type of probatio diabolica through statements such as the following: "There is nothing in the record to suggest that [the arbitrator] tried to hide information that she should have disclosed. It is true that the timing of the disclosure, given the proximity of the hearings, might not have been the most convenient, but it cannot be derived from this circumstance that this is a malicious act or a breach of [the arbitrator's] duties as a member of this Committee"[215]; and "there was, in other words, no conceivable incentive for [the arbitrator] to conceal or misrepresent the facts."[216]

---

[208]For instance: Recommendations of the Spanish Arbitration Club (CEA) concerning arbitrator independence and impartiality: "Antes de informar sobre la existencia de Circunstancias de Abstención o de Revelación, el candidato deberá realizar una labor de investigación razonable, con la diligencia exigible a un profesional ordenado." (Before informing of the existence of circumstances of abstention or disclosure, the candidate must carry out a reasonable investigation, with the diligence of a well-organized professional) (English translation by the author). CEA (n.a.).

[209]"Make careful inquiry of whether (the bank) had connections to either party" is Prof. W.'s proposal, which was not accepted in the case. EDF v. Argentine Republic, par 109.

[210]Highbury v. Venezuela (2015a), pars 108–109.

[211]Fill in notes of the CAM Statement of Independence of the Arbitrator: "When filling in the statement of independence, the arbitrator undertakes to enquire exhaustively into any potential conflict of interest, and any doubt should be resolved in favor of disclosure". CAM (last accessed in June 2018).

[212]Daele (2012), pp. 56–59. Obviously, there is no unanimous opinion on the matter in the context of comparative law. For example, the Japanese Supreme Court has recently rejected the following standard: this duty encompasses the duty to conduct research to uncover any potential sources of conflicts that the arbitrator can find "without substantial effort". Maeda and Bloomenthal (2018).

[213]TAB (2009).

[214]Standard 7 (d) IBA Guidelines (2014).

[215]Total v. Argentine Republic, pars 137, 139, 141–142.

[216]Fábrica v. Venezuela, par 57.

Were ICSID to establish this criterion (arbitrators who do not undertake reasonable enquiries are not excused from their duty to disclose conflicts), the statement repeatedly used in ICSID decisions ("the arbitrator neither knew nor had reason to know")[217] would no longer lead to arbitrator challenges being dismissed in all cases.

However, if tougher stance along the lines proposed here were to be adopted, this would certainly not be welcomed by stakeholders. Some of them would consider it inconsistent with the current multiple connections deriving from the "flat legal world", or even unworkable in international arbitration practice.

Second, the issue of establishing the scope of enquiry is also highly relevant. Although ICSID challenge procedures do not frequently addressed the topic, there are a few references to the degree of detail arbitrators currently find necessary when writing and updating their personal records. The resulting impressions are twofold.

In the first place, no binding parameters or simple guidelines on personal records' management are publicly available, which means that arbitrators manage their records—assuming that they have some—however they deem appropriate. This gives the impression of a high degree of heterogeneity in the matter of arbitrators' personal files. While some arbitrators working in law firms may have a paralegal to help to manage their paperwork and/or use specialized computer software that may be shared by several arbitrators in the law firm, in principle it seems less likely that others who are for example university lecturers will have such professional or technical assistance. File management can also be influenced by cultural and even generational issues, such as familiarity with new technologies.[218]

Furthermore, as a consequence of the above, arbitrators do not always seem to adopt the most suitable practice when handling their personal files. In Highbury v. Venezuela, for instance, the investor's lawyers challenged an arbitrator and then criticized her responses in the course of the procedure: "her database is organized in a way that only refers to the law firms and lawyers leading the case, but not to the numerous individual counsels and witnesses who may appear in front of her in an audience", and "[the arbitrator] acknowledges that she clearly recalls having been arguing against her "some" of [law firm]'s current partners [sic], but that she cannot relate each of those names to specific cases".[219] If the parameters of the well-

[217]EDF v. Argentine Republic, par 105.

[218]Dealing with the difficult relationship of some arbitrators with new technologies.

[219]It is stated that: "La respuesta de [la árbitro] fue la de que su base de datos está organizada de una forma que solo se refiere a las Firmas de abogados y abogados líderes del caso, pero no a los numerosos consejeros individuales y testigos que pueden aparecer enfrente de ella en una audiencia. (. . .) [la árbitro] reconoce que "algunos" de los socios actuales de Foley Hoag recuerda claramente haberlos tenido argumentando enfrente de ella, pero que ella no puede relacionar cada uno de esos nombres con casos específicos. Y de esa manera pretende insólitamente arrojarle la carga de revelación que le impone la Regla 6 de las Reglas de Arbitraje a las Demandantes" ([the arbitrator] responded that her database is organized in such a way that it only refers to the law firms and lawyers leading the case, and not to the numerous individual counsellors and witnesses who may appear before her in a hearing. (...) [the arbitrator] acknowledges that she clearly remembers "some" current Foley Hoag members appearing before her, but she can not connect every name to a specific case. She therefore intends to throw the burden of disclosure imposed by Rule 6 of the Arbitration

organized professional are to be applied, it seems clear that investment arbitrators' personal files should contain more detail than those in the case mentioned above.

Besides that, the scope of the duty to investigate should include more sources of information, over and above the arbitrator's personal file. The 2017 ICC Note to Parties and Arbitral Tribunals on the Conduct of the Arbitration offers some reasonable guidelines: "an arbitrator or prospective arbitrator should make reasonable enquiries in his or her records, those of his or her law firm and, as the case may be, in other readily available materials".[220] These pointers can be extrapolated to the investment arbitration field and act as a starting point for setting limits to the definition of "due enquiry".[221] However, more detail is needed; for example, further clarification of what the term 'readily' means in this context, and which sources arbitrators who do not work in law firms should investigate. Other complementary issues that should also be addressed include the obligation to keep all material from any arbitrations participated in for a specific period, and what kind of information arbitrators' law firms' records should hold.[222]

On a practical level, requiring investment arbitrators to organise their personal files in accordance with a potential set of rules to be imposed by institutions such as ICSID is not the most feasible way of establishing homogeneous criteria in the context of the duty to investigate's scope. There should exist a clear set of the circumstances that arbitrators are obliged to disclose. That is, freedom of form where arbitrators' personal files are concerned may continue to be the applicable criterion, provided that these files and any additional materials can offer suitable answers to all the matters that need to be to disclosed. As indicated, the key question is therefore to determine just what issues all arbitrators have to disclose.

Thirdly, it is universally accepted that the duty of disclosure is an on-going obligation. The 2006 version of ICSID Rule 6 requires arbitrators to state their acceptance of "a continuing obligation promptly to notify the Secretary-General of the Centre of any such relationship or circumstance that subsequently arises during

---

Rules on the plaintiffs, which is most unusual.) (English translation by the author). Highbury v. Venezuela (2005a), pars 92 and 94.

[220]Note (2017), par. 23.

[221]"Due enquiry" is the terminology used in the various ICC Statements of Impartiality and Independence.

[222]The challenge decision in Azurix v. Argentine Republic contains a negative comment regarding the law firm's files: "one may regret that, in relation to the most recent events, (the arbitrator's law firm's) internal systems have not proven to be up to the task". Daele (2012), p. 50. Daele puts forward a proposal on the scope of the research an arbitrator belonging to a law firm should carry out with respect to business relationships: "at a minimum, the arbitrator should check the names of the parties, legal counsel and known witnesses against the law firm's conflict database. One level up, the arbitrator could send an e-mail to partners and associates with the same list of parties, counsel and witnesses, to solicit responses as to whether anyone knows of a connection with the persons, entities or matter identified. If a positive response is received, it is incumbent upon the arbitrator to follow-up, assess the information obtained and determine whether disclosure is required". Daele (2012), p. 54.

this proceeding".[223] As detailed above,[224] the existence of an on-going duty of disclosure is also affirmed in the EU and commercial arbitration contexts.[225] This leads to the logical conclusion asserted in some ICSID decisions: the continuing duty of disclosure imposes a continuing duty of investigation,[226] and these duties must continue to be equally binding throughout the entire arbitration procedure[227]—that is, arbitrators should not lower their guard in these matters as the arbitration draws to a close.[228] This approach is also proposed in the IBA Guidelines: General Standard 3 e: "When considering whether facts or circumstances exist that should be disclosed, the arbitrator shall not take into account whether the arbitration is at the beginning or at a later stage". In this sense, the clarification included in texts such as the Arbitration Rules of the CAM is useful: "The statement of independence shall be re-submitted during the course of the arbitration until its conclusion in the event of supervening facts or at the request of the Secretariat".[229] Therefore, the approach advocated by for instance some UK courts in the context of commercial arbitration (the duty of inquiry depends on what stage the proceedings are at) is not considered appropriate. In the same sense, practices such as the issuance of advance declarations or waivers by prospective arbitrators[230] should not discharge an arbitrator's on-going duties of investigation and disclosure.

2.8 The Role of Arbitral Institutions Regarding the Disclosure Duty

The appropriate starting point for briefly assessing the role played by arbitral institutions in terms of the duty of disclosure is double-sided. It has already been discussed that the commercial and investment arbitration worlds are extremely wide, and that comparative analysis and cross-fertilization is sometimes, but not always useful. Besides that, it can not be ignored that the duty of disclosure raises issues that

---

[223] In the ICSID context, there have been some cases where the disclosure took place after the celebration of the tribunal's first session. Daele (2012), p. 40.

[224] *Supra,* Chap. 2.4.

[225] Among the national case law referring to arbitrators' on-going duty of disclosure: Tecnimont SPA v. J&P Avax. Fouchard (2016).

[226] Compañía v. Argentine Republic, par 222.

[227] In the ICSID context, there is no certainty as to when the arbitrator's duty of disclosure ends. Academic opinion has pointed out that it could be terminated either when the proceedings are closed or could even continue until the final award has been issued. Daele (2012), p. 41.

[228] Chan (2007), p. 260.

[229] Article 18.5 CAM (2010a).

[230] Topic addressed in Guideline 3 b) of the IBA Guidelines (2014) and also in the ICC Note (2017a). Both texts consider that the advance declaration or waiver does not discharge an arbitrator from his or her ongoing duty of disclosure.

are closely linked to the practices of every single arbitration institution. In many cases they do not transcend the private sphere and can therefore only be surmised.

Where the statements of impartiality and independence submitted by prospective arbitrators are concerned, no express reference has been found to arbitral institutions carrying out active investigations linked to the arbitrators' duty of disclosure. On the contrary, academics point out that no such a policy exists, or that it is quantitatively limited or random.[231] An academic paper written by a former ICC Secretary-General a few years ago indicated that this court is sometimes aware of information that, in the arbitral institution's view, a future arbitrator should have disclosed but did not. Although the court contacts the individual to raise the issue in such circumstances, the decision on disclosure is always left in the prospective arbitrator's hands. Only one case has been reported in which a nominee's decision not to disclosure resulted in the ICC court's deciding not to confirm her appointment, even though neither party had questioned it.[232]

The question therefore arises as to why arbitration institutions do not assume a more active role in these matters. For example, why does institution staff not review the content of arbitrators' statements and CVs, either independently or with the arbitrators? It could probably be argued that arbitral institutions are not equipped to take on these new functions because of staff availability issues and increased costs. However, a range of mechanisms could be put in place to reduce the burden of this new task, such as online meetings with arbitrators and mandatory training courses for newcomers to arbitration lists and adjudication in arbitral institutions.[233] Issues such as ethics and integrity, how to fill out the statement of independence and impartiality, and how to draft a CV to suit institutional and parties' needs could be covered. The courses could also be useful for raising arbitrator awareness of exactly how to comply with the duty of disclosure.[234] Such training would of course need to be constructive, which is to say, the starting point should not be the arbitrators' bad faith, but rather the presumption that new arbitrators simply do not know the arbitration institution's disclosure policy in detail, or that, though they may have previously analysed these rules, doubts are likely to arise when they are put into practice—and so personalized institutional guidance on the matter would therefore

[231]Nathan states: "Although arbitral institutions make a fuss about the relationships with the parties, in practice none of them actually seriously review their relationships and take appropriate action except on a selective basis. Even if they do, the matter becomes deeply controversial and leads often to allegations against an activist arbitral institution on bias. Much of the scrutiny is left to the parties themselves (...)". Nathan (2006), p. 18.

[232]Whitesell (2007).

[233]In this sense: "Arbitrators must acquirer a thorough understanding of the various statutory directives and ethical codes that are applicable. Arbitrators must familiarize themselves with not only the rules of the arbitral association with which they are affiliated, but any professional or statutory standards that have been incorporated into those rules either expressly or by implication". Larson (2008), p. 919.

[234]*Infra*, Chap. 6.2.

be very useful. In short, arbitration institutions have an essential role to play in removing the tension from the duty of disclosure.

Another major issue connected with the role played by these institutions is the following: a comparative analysis—taking into account the limitations pointed out above—shows that few commercial arbitration institutions have envisaged any penalties for arbitrators who do not fulfil their duty of disclosure.[235] In the rare cases when they have, sanctions to the arbitrator[236] sometimes materialize either as a refusal to confirm the arbitrator in the case in question, provided the arbitration institution has this right of veto,[237] or as the ad casum replacement of the arbitrator.

In other cases, the institution goes a step further by reducing the arbitrator's fees[238] or by temporarily or even permanently expelling the arbitrator from its arbitrator list (e.g., CAM[239]). This sanction—referred to as "going on inactive

[235]Addressing potential improvements to the IBA Guidelines, Cinelli suggests that the 2014 Guidelines should refer to a presumption of sanction if arbitrators do not disclose facts listed in the waivable red list and the orange list; and the Guidelines should refer to explicit sanctions if the non-disclosed fact is to be included in the non-waivable red list. Cinelli Moreira (2014). In the—different—context of professional membership organizations, the CIArb has published a document explaining how it investigates complaints of misconduct against its members. A CIArb member who acts as arbitrator and commits a significant breach of professional or ethical conduct may be sanctioned by the CIArb Disciplinary Conduct Committee. The list of sanctions is varied (reprimand, suspension, expulsion, payment of the procedure costs, etc.). CIArb (last accessed in June 2018).

[236]It has been stated that other stakeholders are currently paying the price of arbitrators' misconduct. For instance, Park considers that "the price of misconduct thus falls more directly on the prevailing party, which must suffer annulment of an award for breach of fundamental procedural integrity". Park (2011), p. 27.

[237]For instance, Article 19 CIMA Arbitration Rules affirms: "Appointment and confirmation of Arbitrators. The Court shall confirm the appointment of party-appointed Arbitrators, sole Arbitrators and the Presidents of collegiate Arbitral Tribunals—carried out by the parties, jointly or individually, pursuant to the Rules—provided that the candidates have no reservations as to their availability, impartiality or independence or, should they have made a declaration of any reservation, this has not been the subject of any objections by the parties. The Court shall notify such decisions to the parties and to the Arbitrators. The Court shall ensure compliance with conditions as to the capacity of Arbitrators, and transparency in their appointment, as well as their independence and availability. The Court will assess the relevant circumstances in cases of repeated appointments of one or more Arbitrators by one of the parties or its affiliates or by their representatives or by other members of the Arbitral Tribunal, and in doing so will respect the rights of a fair hearing, presentation of their case and equality of the parties". CIMA (2015).

[238]Assuming that the duty of disclosure is covered for example by the following provision: Article 1.3 of the SIAC Code of conduct for an arbitrator: "The prospective arbitrator confirms that he understands that the Registrar of SIAC will take into account any failure by the prospective arbitrator to discharge his duties to ensure the fair, expeditious, economical and final determination of the dispute when fixing the quantum of fees payable to the arbitrator". SIAC (2015).

[239]Article 7.3 of the CAM Code of Ethics: "Where facts, circumstances and relationships that should have been disclosed are subsequently discovered, the Chamber of Arbitration may deem that this fact is a ground for replacing the arbitrator during the proceedings or not confirming him in other arbitral proceedings". In more general terms, Art. 13: "Violation of the Code of Ethics. The arbitrator who does not comply with this Code of Ethics shall be replaced by the Chamber of

status" within the AAA context-[240] may be applied "even if the non-disclosed facts or circumstances are not one that justifies removal or disqualification" (KLRCA).[241]

As analysed in Chap. 1, very few voices dare to utter more serious words such as "liability" in this context. Those who do so are usually confined to the commercial arbitration milieu,[242] where national courts have indeed annulled arbitral awards as a consequence of an arbitrator's breach of the duty to disclose.[243] The dominant overall impression remains that if the time has not yet come for initiatives such as a Global Arbitration Ethics Council for penalising counsel misconduct,[244] a scenario in which investment arbitrators are punished for violation of their duties seems even further away. The basic idea that underlies the matter is undoubtedly that of investment arbitrator immunity,[245] which has so far proved to be an almost unshakable principle in the investment arbitration context.[246]

Arbitration, which may also refuse to confirm him in subsequent proceedings because of this violation". CAM (2010b).

[240]Rogers indicates that he AAA "touts a "one-strike-you're out policy (. . .) Unter this policy, any arbitrator whose award is challenged for improper non-disclosure goes on inactive status and will not be nominated to future arbitrations while the judicial challenge is pending. Even after a final judicial decision, the AAA apparently makes a separate determination of whether the arbitrator should ever be restored to active status on the roster. For those institutions that do not have formal or published enforcement policies, they inevitably take into account perceived ethical transgressions when making future appointment decisions". Rogers (2014) par 2.82.

[241]Article 3.6 of the KLRCA Code: "Additionally, Article 5.1 of the 2013 KLRCA's revised Code of Conduct for Arbitrator states that: "without prejudice to any other rights of the KLRCA, if the Arbitrator is convicted by any court of law for corruption or any unlawful or illegal activities in relation to this Code of Conduct or any other agreement that the Arbitrator may have with the KLRCA, KLRCA shall be entitled to the removal or disqualification of the KLRCA Arbitrator at any time". KLRCA (2017).

[242]Cinelli Moreira (2014), p. 146. On the subject of investment arbitration, Bottini proposes "developing tough rules for failures on the arbitrators to disclose relevant circumstances". Bottini (2009), pp. 341–365.

[243]When dealing with the arbitrator's duty of disclosure in commercial arbitration, Judge Dominique Hascher states: "In the case of the non-disclosure of a fact that is known by the arbitrator and a party, shared liability between them could be considered. As between the parties, the other party may claim for a breach of the obligation of loyalty, which flows from the arbitration agreement". Hascher (2012), p. 794. His words find support in French judicial decisions such as Raoul Duval v. V, where the arbitrator was found liable and ordered to pay damages.

[244]Geisinger (2015) pp. 17–32; Newsham (2016).

[245]For instance, Article 21 (a) of the ICSID Convention states that: "The Chairman, the members of the Administrative Council, persons acting as conciliators or arbitrators or members of a Committee appointed pursuant to paragraph (3) of Article 52, and the officers and employees of the Secretariat: (a) shall enjoy immunity from legal process with respect to acts performed by them in the exercise of their functions, except when the Centre waives this immunity" ICSID (1966); and the 2017 SIAC Investment Arbitration Rules proclaim an exclusion of liability of any arbitrator "for any negligence, act or omission in connection with any arbitration administered by SIAC". SIAC (2017).

[246]A breach of this principle might be generated by article 11 of the 2014 version of the Draft Constitutive Agreement of the Centre for the Settlement of Investment Disputes of the UNASUR, which addresses the matter of privileges and immunities of the Centre and -in contrast to Article

By way of a summary, this chapter has made a case for arbitral institutions reinforcing their role and powers in key areas such as arbitrator conflicts of interest and the duty of disclosure.[247] The recent EU initiatives towards the creation of Codes of conduct in the context of investment treaty arbitration represent an improvement that should be assumed by a future MIC, and which in turn may also produce a knock-on effect among arbitration institutions that manage arbitrations with party-appointed arbitrators. In the latter context, it is worth noting that in Universal v. Venezuela the Chairman of the ICSID Administrative Council stated that "parties have an interest in knowing any facts or circumstances that may exist that may give doubts about an arbitrator's independence and impartiality. Indeed, as it reflected in Arbitration Rule 6 (2), disclosure by arbitrators of any such facts or circumstances is required".[248] It would clearly be an overstatement to say that a comment from an isolated disqualification decision set out an official "pro-stretching" ICSID policy, but such comments could provide clues as to the existence of a greater institutional awareness where this matter is concerned at ICSID level.

References

Bottini G (2009) Should arbitrators live on Mars? Challenge of arbitrators in investment arbitration. Suffolk Transnational Law Rev 32:341–365

Brekoulakis S (2013) Systemic bias and the Institution of International Arbitration: a new approach to arbitral decision-making. J Int Dispute Settlement 4(3):553–585

Brower CN (2010) Keynote address: the ethics of arbitration: perspectives from a practicing international arbitrator. Berkeley J Int Law Publicist 5:1–31

Campolieti F, Lawn N (2010) Perenco v. Ecuador: was there a valid arbitrator challenge under the ICSID Convention? In: Kluwer Arbitration Blog. http://kluwerarbitrationblog.com/2010/01/28/perenco-v-ecuador-was-there-a-valid-arbitrator-challenge/

Cárdenas E, Rivkin DW (2005) A growing challenge for ethics in international arbitration. In: Aksen G et al (eds) Global reflections on international law commerce and Dispute Resolution. Liber Amicorum in honour of Robert Briner. ICC, Paris, pp 191–200

Chan LS (2007) Arbitrators' conflicts of interest: bias by any name. Singapore Acad Law J 19:245–266

Cinelli Moreira NF (2014) The arbitrator's duty of disclosure analyzed through case-law: are the IBA guidelines on conflict of interest in international arbitration enough to create consistency? Revista de Arbitragem e Mediaçao 40:115–150

Crivellaro A (2014) Does the arbitrators failure to disclose conflict of interest fatally lead to annulment of the award? The approach of the European state courts. Arbitr Brief 4(1):121–141

Daele K (2012) Challenge and disqualification of arbitrators in international arbitration. Kluwer, Alphen aan den Rijn

21 of the ICSID Convention- makes no express reference to conciliator and arbitrator immunity. Fach Gómez and Titi (2016).

[247]The idea of shifting the focus from the institutions to the arbitration community by creating an opt-in certification system managed by ICSID does not fit in with the latest developments in the sector. Dimotropoulos (2016), pp. 371–434.

[248]Universal v. Venezuela, par 90.

Daly B, Goriatcheva E, Meighen HA (2014) A guide to the PCA Arbitration Rules. Oxford University Press, Oxford

Davis BG (2014) American diversity in international arbitration. In: University of Toledo Legal Studies Research Paper. https://papers.ssrn.com/sol3/papers.cfm?abstract_id=2364967

Debevoise & Plimpton (2017) Proposed amendments to 2006 ICSID rules. In: Public comments to amendment of ICSID's rules and regulations. https://icsid.worldbank.org/en/Documents/about/Public%20Comments%20to%20Amendment%20to%20ICSID%20Rules%20and%20Regulations.pdf

Derains Y, Schwartz EA (2005) A guide to the ICC rules of arbitration, 2nd edn. Kluwer Law International, Alphen aan den Rijn

Dimotropoulos G (2016) Constructing the independence of international investment arbitrators: past, present and future. Northwest J Int Law Bus 36(2):371–434

Dotseth KA (2012) Disqualifying arbitrators for failure to make complete disclosures after Scandinavian Re v. St. Paul Re: What is "Evident Partially". In: International Association of Defense Counsel Committee Newsletter. http://www.larsonking.com/files/Dotseth_IADC_Defense_Counsel_Journal_July_2012.pdf

EC (2016) The multilateral investment court project. http://trade.ec.europa.eu/doclib/press/index.cfm?id=1608

Fach Gómez K, Titi C (2016) UNASUR Centre for the settlement of investment disputes: comments on the draft constitutive agreement. In: Investment Treaty News 7(3). https://www.iisd.org/itn/2016/08/10/unasur-centre-for-the-settlement-of-investment-disputes-comments-on-the-draft-constitutive-agreement-katia-fach-gomez-catharine-titi/

Fernández Rozas JC (2013) Contenido ético del deber de revelación del árbitro y consecuencias de su trasgresión. Revista de arbitraje comercial y de inversiones 6(3):799–839

Fouchard C (2016) Tecnimont Saga: Episode V-The Paris court strikes back. In: Kluwer Arbitration Blog. http://arbitrationblog.kluwerarbitration.com/2016/08/03/tecnimont-saga-episode-v-the-paris-court-strikes-back/

Geisinger E (2015) "Soft Law" and hard questions: ASA's initiative in the debate on counsel ethics in international arbitration. In: Favalli D (ed) Sense and non-sense of guidelines, rules and other para-regulatory texts in international arbitration. Juris, Huntington, pp 17–32

Greenberg S (2010) Tackling guerrilla challenges against arbitrators: institutional perspective. Transnational Dispute Manag 7(2):1–12

Greenwood L (2015) Could "Blind" appointments open our eyes to the lack of diversity in international arbitration? Transnational Dispute Manag 12(4):1–9

Hacking D (2006) Arbitration challenges: theirs is to reason why. Glob Arbitr Rev 6(1):26–30

Hanke P (2017) Computers with law degrees? The role of artificial intelligence in transnational dispute resolution and its implications for the legal profession. Transnational Dispute Manag 14 (2):1–11

Hascher D (2012) Independence and impartiality of arbitrators: 3 issues. Am Univ Int Law Rev 27 (4):789–806

Holbein JR, Greenidge AD (1995) NAFTA code of conduct provides international guidelines for ethical behavior. Law Bus Rev Americas 1:50–68

IBA Subcommittee on Investment Treaty Arbitration (2016) Report on the Subcommittee's investment treaty arbitration survey. http://www.ibanet.org/Document/Default.aspx?DocumentUid=65C2AE58-752F-4E8C-900C-1A1FC0C2FD8B

ICSID (2004) Discussion paper on possible improvements of the framework for ICSID arbitration. https://icsid.worldbank.org/en/Documents/resources/Possible%20Improvements%20of%20the%20Framework%20of%20ICSID%20Arbitration.pdf

ICSID (2016) Work launched on updating ICSID rules and regulations. https://icsid.worldbank.org/en/Pages/News.aspx?CID=202

Investor-State Mediation Task Force (2017) Response to ICSID on its invitation to file suggestions for rule amendments, Annex 2, Appendix A of Annex C. https://icsid.worldbank.org/en/

Documents/about/Public%20Comments%20to%20Amendment%20to%20ICSID%20Rules%20and%20Regulations.pdf

Kinnear M, Nitschke F (2015) Disqualification of arbitrators under the ICSID convention and rules. In: Giorgetti C (ed) Challenges and recusals of judges and arbitrators in international courts and tribunals. Brill, Leiden, pp 34–79

Larson DA (2008) Conflicts of interest and disclosures: are we making a mountain out of a Molehill? South Texas Law Rev 49:880–919

Luttrell J (2009) Bias challenges in international commercial arbitration. The need for a real danger test. Wolters Kluwer, Alphen aan den Rijn

Luttrell S (2016) Testing the ICSID framework for arbitrator challenges. ICSID Rev 31(3):597–621

Maeda Y, Bloomenthal JM (2018) Japanese Supreme Court's first decision on arbitrator's non-disclosure. In: Kluwer Arbitration Blog. http://arbitrationblog.kluwerarbitration.com/2018/02/05/japanese-supreme-courts-first-decision-arbitrators-non-disclosure/

Mann H (2005) The Emperor's clothes come off: a comment on Republic of Ghana v. Telekom Malasya Berhard, and the problem of arbitrator conflict of interest. Transnational Dispute Manag 2(1):1–7

Mantilla-Serrano F, Pinsolle P (2013) La independencia del árbitro y su obligación de revelación, in Arbitraje internacional: pasado, presente y futuro. In: Libro homenaje a Bernardo Cremades e Yves Derains. Instituto Peruano de Arbitraje, Peru, pp 879–899

Matheus López CA (2015) Reflexiones sobre el deber de revelación del árbitro. Revista Vasca de Derecho Procesal y Arbitraje 27(2):267–273

Matthews J (2005) Consumer arbitration: is it working now and will it work in the future? Florida Bar J 79(4):22–27

Mourre A (2009) Conflicts of interest: towards greater transparency and uniform standards of disclosure. In: Kluwer Arbitration Blog. http://arbitrationblog.kluwerarbitration.com/2009/05/19/conflicts-of-interest-towards-greater-transparency-and-uniform-standards-of-disclosure/

N.A. (2017) Suggested changes to the ICSID rules and regulations. In: Public comments to amendment of ICSID's rules and regulations. https://icsid.worldbank.org/en/Documents/about/Public%20Comments%20to%20Amendment%20to%20ICSID%20Rules%20and%20Regulations.pdf

Nathan KVSK (2006) The independence of arbitrators. Amicus Curiae 68:18–22

Newsham J (2016) No need for Global Arbitration Ethics Council. In: Law360. https://www.law360.com/articles/847583/no-need-for-global-arbitration-ethics-council-group-says

O'Brien WT, Nandivanda SN (2014) Arbitrator challenges: warranted or abuse? Mealey's Int Arbitr Rep 29(10):1–5

Park W (2011) The four musketeers of arbitral duty. Status. Powers and role of the arbitrators. ICC Dossiers 8:27

Paulsson J (2012) Foreword. In: Daele K (ed) Challenge and disqualification of arbitrators in international arbitration. Kluwer, Alphen aan den Rijn, p xix

Paulsson J (2013) The idea of arbitration. Oxford University Press, Oxford

Rogers CA (2014) Ethics in international arbitration. Oxford University Press, Oxford

Rose A (2017) Is there a substitute for experience. Global Arbitration Review. http://globalarbitrationreview.com/article/1081058/is-there-a-substitute-for-experience

Rubins N, Lauterburg B (2010) Independence, impartiality and duty of disclosure in investment arbitration. In: Knahr C, Koller C, Rechberger W, Reinisch A (eds) Investment and commercial arbitration - similarities and divergences. Eleven International Publishing, Den Haag, pp 153–180

Secretariat UNCITRAL (2018) Possible reform of investor-State dispute settlement (ISDS). Submissions from International Intergovernmental Organizations and additional information: appointment of arbitrators. http://www.uncitral.org/uncitral/en/commission/working_groups/3Investor_State.html

Sousa Uva P (2009) A comparative reflection on challenge of arbitral awards though the lens of the arbitrator's duty of impartiality and independence. Am Rev Int Arbitr 20(4):480–511

Stanic A (2009) Challenging arbitrators and the importance of disclosure: recent cases and reflections. Croatian Arbitr Yearb 16:205–235

Vasani BS, Palmer SA (2015) Challenge and disqualification of arbitrators at ICSID: a new dawn. ICSID Rev 30(1):194–216

White&Case (2018) International arbitration survey: the evolution of international arbitration. https://www.whitecase.com/sites/whitecase/files/files/download/publications/2018-international-arbitration-survey-the-evolution-of-ia.pdf

Whitesell AM (2007) Independence in ICC Arbitration: ICC court practice concerning the appointment, confirmation, challenge and replacement of arbitrators. ICC Int Court Arbitr Bull, special supplement 18:7–49

Windsor KA (2009) Defining arbitrator evident partiality: the catch-22 of commercial litigation disputes. Seton Hall Circuit Rev 6:191–217

Yong L (2016) Imposter arbitrator's award set aside in California. Global Arbitration Review

Legal and Arbitration References

International Conventions

ICSID (1966) Convention on the Settlement of Investment Disputes between States and Nationals of Other States. https://icsid.worldbank.org/en/Documents/icsiddocs/ICSID%20Convention%20English.pdf

UNCITRAL (2014) UNCITRAL Rules on Transparency in Treaty-based Investor-State Arbitration. http://www.uncitral.org/uncitral/en/uncitral_texts/arbitration/2014Transparency.html

IIAs

CETA (2016) http://ec.europa.eu/trade/policy/in-focus/ceta/ceta-chapter-by-chapter/

EU-Singapore IPA (2018) http://trade.ec.europa.eu/doclib/press/index.cfm?id=961

EU-Vietnam FTA (2016) http://trade.ec.europa.eu/doclib/docs/2016/february/tradoc_154226.pdf

EUSFTA (2015) http://investmentpolicyhub.unctad.org/Download/TreatyFile/3247

JEFTA (2016) https://trade-leaks.org/jefta-leaks/investment-dispute-resolution/

NAFTA (1994) Code of Conduct. https://www.nafta-sec-alena.org/Home/Legal-Texts/Code-of-Conduct?mvid=1&secid=03428812-a551-4839-ab16-669c9d2a82e1

TTIP (2016) http://trade.ec.europa.eu/doclib/press/index.cfm?id=1230

Arbitration Acts, Institutional Arbitration Rules, and Codes of Conduct

ABA, AAA, CPR Institute (2004) Code of ethics for arbitrators in commercial disputes. https://www.americanbar.org/content/dam/aba/migrated/dispute/commercial_disputes.authcheckdam.pdf

Arbitration Centre of the Portuguese Chamber of Commerce and Industry (2005) Criterion 1.2.e) e). http://www.centrodearbitragem.pt/images/pdfs/Legislacao_e_Regulamentos/Criteria%20for%20the%20appointment%20of%20arbitrators.pdf

CAM (2010a) Arbitration Rules. http://www.camera-arbitrale.it/Documenti/cam_arbitration-rules_2010.pdf

CAM (2010b) Code of Ethics. https://www.camera-arbitrale.it/en/arbitration/arbitration-rules/code-of-ethics.php?id=104

CAM (last accessed in June 2018) Declaration of Acceptance and Statement of Independence of the Arbitrator. http://www.camera-arbitrale.it/Documenti/disclosure_en.pdf

CAM (2015) Reglamento de la Corte de Arbitraje de Madrid. http://arbitramadrid.com/web/corte/reglamento_corte

CEA (2005) Procedural rules of the Spanish arbitration court. http://corteespanolaarbitraje.es/wp-content/uploads/2014/06/Reglamento-Corte-Española-de-Arbitraje.pdf

CEA (n.a.) Recommendations of the Spanish Arbitration Club concerning arbitrator independence and impartiality. https://www.clubarbitraje.com/sites/default/files/recomendaciones_0.pdf

CIArb (2009) Code of professional and ethical Conduct for Members. http://www.ciarb.org/docs/default-source/ciarbdocuments/guidance-and-ethics/practice-guidelines-protocols-and-rules/code-of-professional-and-ethical-conduct-october-2009.pdf?sfvrsn=6

CIMA (2015) Arbitration Rules. http://arbitrajecima.com/wp-content/uploads/2015/12/Reglamento-CIMA-2015-ingles.pdf

CJEU (2016) Code of Conduct for Members and former Members of the Court of Justice of the European Union. http://eur-lex.europa.eu/legal-content/EN/TXT/PDF/?uri=OJ:C:2016:483:FULL&from=FR

CRCICA (2011) Arbitration Rules. http://crcica.org/Arbitration_rules.aspx#_idTOCAnchor-101

DIA (2013) Rules of arbitration procedure. https://voldgiftsinstituttet.dk/wp-content/uploads/2015/01/rules_1_may_2013_-_pdf-uden-logo.pdf

FAI (2013) Arbitration Rules. https://arbitration.fi/wp-content/uploads/sites/22/2017/10/arbitration-rules-of-the-finland-chamber-of-commerce-2013-1.6.2017.pdf

FINRA (2007) Code of Arbitration Procedure for Customer Disputes of the Financial Industry Regulatory Authority (FINRA). http://finra.complinet.com/en/display/display_viewall.html?rbid=2403&element_id=4096&record_id=5174&filtered_tag=

French Code of Civil Procedure (2011) http://www.jus.uio.no/lm/france.arbitration.code.of.civil.procedure.1981/doc.html#117

German Arbitration Act (1998) http://www.sccinstitute.com/media/29988/german-arbitration-act.pdf

IBA (2014) Guidelines on conflicts of interest in international arbitration. https://www.ibanet.org/Publications/publications_IBA_guides_and_free_materials.aspx#Practice%20Rules%20and%20Guidelines

ICC (2017a) Note to Parties and Arbitral Tribunals on the conduct of the arbitration under the ICC rules of arbitration. https://iccwbo.org/publication/note-parties-arbitral-tribunals-conduct-arbitration/

ICC (2017b) Arbitration Rules. https://iccwbo.org/dispute-resolution-services/arbitration/rules-of-arbitration/

ICC (last accessed in June 2018a) Ad hoc, non-Uncitral appointment. https://cdn.iccwbo.org/content/uploads/sites/3/2016/03/Ad-Hoc-Non-Uncitral-Appointment-Arbitrator-s-Statement-Acceptance-and-Independence-ENG.pdf

ICC (last accessed in June 2018b) Statement of Acceptance, Independence and Impartiality. Uncitral Appointment. https://cdn.iccwbo.org/content/uploads/sites/3/2016/03/Uncitral-Appointment-Arbitrator-s-Statement-Acceptance-Independence-Impartiality-ENGLISH-1.pdf

ICC (last accessed in June 2018c) Statement of Acceptance, Availability, Impartiality and Independence". ICC Arbitrator, https://www.iccgermany.de/fileadmin/user_upload/Content/Schiedsgerichtsbarkeit/8.2.ICC-Arbitrator-Statement-Acceptance-Availability-Impartiality-and-Independence-Arbitration-Rules-ENGLISH.pdf

ICDR (2014) International dispute resolution procedures. https://www.adr.org/sites/default/files/ICDR%20Rules_0.pdf

ICSID (2006) Arbitration Rules. https://icsid.worldbank.org/en/Pages/icsiddocs/ICSID-Convention-Arbitration-Rules.aspx

ICSID (last accessed in June 2018a) Template 4.2.3 – Declaration Arbitration. https://icsid.worldbank.org/en/Documents/arbitrators/Declaration%20-%20ICSID%20Convention%20Arbitration.pdf#search=declaration

ICSID (last accessed in June 2018b) Arbitrators, conciliators and Ad Hoc Committee Members. https://icsid.worldbank.org/en/Pages/arbitrators/CVSearch.aspx

KLRCA (2017) Arbitration Rules. https://aiac.world/wp-content/arbitration/Arbitration-Rules-2017.pdf

LCIA (2014) Arbitration Rules. http://www.lcia.org/Dispute_Resolution_Services/lcia-arbitration-rules-2014.aspx

NAI (2015) http://www.nai-nl.org/downloads/NAI%20Arbitration%20Rules%20and%20Explanation.pdf

PCA (last accessed in June 2018) Model Statements of Impartiality and Independence. https://pca-cpa.org/wp-content/uploads/sites/175/2015/11/PCA-Arbitration-Rules-2012.pdf

SCC (2017) Arbitration Rules. http://www.sccinstitute.com/dispute-resolution/rules/

SIAC (2015) Code of Ethics for an Arbitrator. http://www.siac.org.sg/our-rules/code-of-ethics-for-an-arbitrator

SIAC (2017) Investment Arbitration Rules. http://www.siac.org.sg/our-rules/rules/siac-ia-rules-2017

SIAC (last accessed in June 2018) Disclosure Sheet. http://www.siac.org.sg/images/stories/articles/rules/Disclosure%20Sheet.pdf

TAB/BAC (2009) Code of Ethics. http://www.tab.es/index.php?option=com_content&view=article&id=638:barcelona-arbitration-court-code-of-ethics&catid=29&lang=en&Itemid=426

UNCITRAL (2010) UNCITRAL Arbitration Rules. http://www.uncitral.org/uncitral/en/uncitral_texts/arbitration/2010Arbitration_rules.html

WTO (1996a) Rules of conduct for the understanding on rules and procedures governing the settlement of disputes. WT/DSB/RC/1 (96-5267). https://www.wto.org/english/tratop_e/dispu_e/rc_e.htm

Legal Documents

AAA (last accessed in June 2018) Find a mediator. https://www.aaamediation.org/index.php

AAA/ICDR (last accessed in June 2018) AAA arbitrator select. https://www.adr.org/sites/default/files/document_repository/AAA_Arbitrator_Select_2pg.pdf

CEDCA (last accessed in June 2018). List of arbitrators. http://www.cedca.org.ve/member_cat/todos-orden-alfabetico/

CIArb (last accessed in June 2018) How CIArb investigates complaints of misconduct against its members. http://www.ciarb.org/docs/default-source/default-document-library/complaints-booklet1.pdf?sfvrsn=4

CPR (last accessed in June 2018) Neutral administrative fees. https://www.cpradr.org/neutrals/neutral-administrative-fees

EC (last accessed in June 2018) Research & innovation. Participant portal. http://ec.europa.eu/research/participants/portal/desktop/en/experts/index.html

ECHR (2009) Nomination of candidates and election of judges to the European Court of Human Rights. http://assembly.coe.int/nw/xml/XRef/Xref-XML2HTML-en.asp?fileid=17704&lang=en

ECJ (last accessed in June 2018) Presentation of the members. http://curia.europa.eu/jcms/jcms/Jo2_7026/en/

GAR (2018) Welcome to Global Arbitration Review's Arbitrator Research Tool. https://globalarbitrationreview.com/arbitrator-research-tool?utm_source=mhtml&utm_medium=email&utm_campaign=art_over_200_profiles&dm_i=1KSF,5M9MO,9GPJKW,LU4CF,1

ICC (last accessed in June 2018) Dispute Resolution Data. https://iccwbo.org/media-wall/news-speeches/icc-dispute-resolution-data-enter-agreement-shed-light-arbitration/

JAM (last accessed in June 2018) All neutrals. https://www.jamsadr.com/neutrals/

LCIA (last accessed in June 2018) Frequently asked questions. http://www.lcia.org/Frequently_Asked_Questions.aspx#Eligible

RTVE (last accessed in June 2018) http://www.rtve.es/noticias/20180129/psoe-asegura-juez-elosegui-falseo-su-curriculum-estudia-como-revocar-sunombramiento-estrasburgo/1669760.shtml

SIAC (last accessed in June 2018) Application form for admission to SIAC Panel/SIAC IP Panel. http://siac.org.sg/images/stories/documents/application_form/SIACPanelApplicationForm_1Mar2016.pdf

The Diplomatic (last accessed in June 2018) "PSOE considers asking for revocation of Elósegui's election to ECHR", http://thediplomatinspain.com/en/psoeconsiders-asking-for-revocation-of-eloseguis-election-to-echr/

US (1994) Communication on rules of ethical conduct for the settlement of disputes. https://www.wto.org/gatt_docs/English/SULPDF/91820188.pdf

UNCITRAL (last accessed in June 2018) Model statements of independence pursuant to article 11 of the Rules. http://www.uncitral.org/pdf/english/texts/arbitration/arb-rules-2013/UNCITRAL-Arbitration-Rules-2013-e.pdf

VIAC (last accessed in June 2018) List of practitioners in international arbitration. http://www.viac.eu/en/arbitration/practitioners

WTO (1996b) Disclosure form. https://www.wto.org/english/tratop_e/dispu_e/rc_e.htm

Chapter 3
The Duty of Disclosure and Conflicts of Interest in Investment Arbitration Disputes

This chapter starts from the premise that if as complex an issue as arbitrators' conflicts of interest can be pinned down,[1] this will undoubtedly influence the way in which the duty of disclosure is outlined. For this reason, both the present and future of conflicts of interest in the investment arbitration field are examined. The development and general features of the IBA Guidelines on Conflicts of Interest in International Arbitration (IBA Guidelines), a decisive soft law document, provide a useful way into the discussion, after which focus shifts to the attention paid to the Guidelines in a fair number of ICSID disputes and investment-related conflicts handled by other international arbitral institutions and rules. Observations on the way the EU has approached the 2014 version of the IBA Guidelines when implementing its competence in Foreign Direct Investment (FDI) are also included, as is the possibility that the IBA may modify the Guidelines in the future with the aim of taking into account investment arbitration's specific characteristics. The likelihood that existing institutions such as ICSID and future initiatives such as the creation of a MIC will develop their own texts on investment arbitrators' conflicts of interest is also covered. This chapter concludes with reflections on the three highly controversial topics of repeat appointment, issue conflict and multiple hatting, with the aim of outlining the possible extent and content of conflicts of interest in the future of international investment disputes.

3.1 Key Aspects of the IBA Guidelines

The International Bar Association (IBA) Council approved its IBA Guidelines in May 2004. The Guidelines' inspiring introduction addressed many of the fundamental issues that are highlighted throughout Chap. 2, such as the parties' right to be

[1] This term has been chosen owing to its breadth and the fact that it is used by the IBA.

K. Fach Gómez, *Key Duties of International Investment Arbitrators*,
https://doi.org/10.1007/978-3-319-98128-4_3

judged by impartial and independent arbitrators; uncertainty among arbitrators as to what they should disclose; the risks linked to excessively detailed disclosures; arbitration parties that use challenges for opportunistic reasons, and the difficulties arising from the globalization of business. In the face of this uncertain scenario, the IBA Guidelines were presented as the culmination of the lengthy and painstaking work of a group of international arbitration experts, enriched by plentiful contributions from the arbitration community. Having examined national laws, judicial decisions, arbitration rules and the practical considerations relating to impartiality, independence and disclosure in international arbitration, the experts had concluded that the whole area lacked both clarity and uniformity.[2]

With the aim of shedding some light on the issue, the Guidelines are divided into two clearly differentiated parts. First, seven General Standards dealing with arbitrator impartiality, independence and disclosure and their respective explanations are set out (General Principle; Conflicts of Interest; Disclosure by the Arbitrator; Waiver by the Parties; Scope; Relationships, and Duty of Arbitrator and Parties). These are followed by the General Standards' application in practice, in which a wide range of situations are categorized into three non-exhaustive lists. The Red List contains both a non-waivable section that addresses severe situations that cannot be resolved, and a waivable section covering other serious situations that need to be disclosed, and also require the parties' agreement regarding arbitrators that are affected by this type of conflict. The Orange List refers to a further range of situations which require disclosure and that may produce timely objections if they result in justifiable doubts being raised by parties about an arbitrator's impartiality or independence. The Green List includes a series of situations in which no disclosure is needed, as there is neither any apparent nor actual conflict of interest according to the relevant objective point of view.[3]

The approval of these 2004 Guidelines attracted a great deal of attention from academic commentators as well as generating lively debate among international practitioners,[4] as a result of which arbitration and judicial decisions dealing with conflicts of interest in international arbitration began to obtain more interest. The IBA itself produced a lengthy document analysing the case law and the way arbitral institutions had approached the Guidelines during the first 5 years following their publication.[5] The Guidelines also received some criticism,[6] which was taken into account when they were subsequently revised by the IBA Arbitration Committee, a process that culminated with a new version in 2014.

---

[2]IBA Guidelines (2004).

[3]This is a simplified summary of the of the IBA Guidelines' essential content. A more detailed analysis can be found in the bibliography cited in throughout this chapter, and also in De Witt Wijner et al. (2004).

[4]Freyer and Bédard (2004), Ball (2005) and Lawson (2005).

[5]The IBA Conflicts of Interest Subcommittee (2010).

[6]Mullerat Obe (2012).

The new 2014 Guidelines open with a statement to the effect that that they were widely accepted in the international arbitration community during their first decade of life, and then focus on clarifying and improving various aspects relating to conflicts of interest in international arbitration. The General Standards of this new version of the IBA Guidelines address several major issues, of which the following are especially relevant: the effects of advance declarations or waivers; applying the Guidelines to administrative secretaries and assistants; whether arbitrators have to identify with their law firms, and the situation regarding barristers' chambers; third-party funding, and the disclosure of counsel identity. Changes in the Practical Application of the General Standards are also introduced, the broad approach being to set stricter standards for arbitrator disclosure.

3.2 The Current Significance of the IBA Guidelines in International Investment Disputes

From the beginning, the IBA Guidelines have expressly stated that they "should equally apply to other types of arbitration, such as investment arbitration".[7] In fact, a long section in the document covering the Guidelines' first 5 years (2005–2009) is devoted to analysing various ICSID cases in which they had been cited in party pleas, challenge decisions or annulment decisions.

The considerable increase in ICSID challenges in recent years has also led to an increase in references to the Guidelines, which have been referred to in multiple decisions in cases applying the ICSID Convention.[8] Not only do parties rely on them in varying degrees when this benefits their legal arguments,[9] but co-arbitrators and the Chairman of the Administrative Council have also expressly alluded to them in their decisions.

Most references, however, are characterized by a "carrot and stick" approach. That is, they begin by praising the Guidelines, which have been variously described as "useful references",[10] "instructive", "the preeminent set of guidelines for

[7]Nevertheless, this initial affirmation was in need of reinforcement from the 2014 Guidelines: "While the Guidelines were originally intended to apply to both commercial and investment arbitration, it was found in the course of the review process that uncertainty lingered as to their application to investment arbitration. Similarly, despite a comment in the original version of the Guidelines that their application extended to non-legal professionals serving as arbitrator, there appeared to remain uncertainty in this regard as well. A consensus emerged in favour of a general affirmation that the Guidelines apply to both commercial and investment arbitration".

[8]Other IBA texts have also been mentioned in these decisions, such as the Code of Ethics for International Arbitrators, in the case Compañía de Aguas v. Argentina, par 17.

[9]Stating that the Guidelines are soft law: Nations v. Panamá, par 26.

[10]Abaclat v. Argentina, par 78; Blue Bank v. Venezuela, par 62; Fábrica de Vidrios v. Venezuela (2016a), par 34.

assessing arbitrator conflicts",[11] "having persuasive authority",[12] "furnishing a useful indication",[13] and constituting "a most valuable source of inspiration".[14] Nevertheless, the final conclusion in most cases is clearly stated in the decisions and awards: ICSID adjudicators are solely bound by the standard set forth in the ICSID Convention.[15] Hence: "The IBA Guidelines are not binding in an ICSID challenge"[16]; they "are not law for ICSID tribunals",[17] but "merely indicative".[18]

In the Guidelines' favour, it should be stressed that the IBA has never explicitly stated that they were binding.[19] On the contrary, point 6 of the 2004 version expressly stated: "These Guidelines are not legal provisions and do not override any applicable national law or arbitral rules chosen by the parties. However, it is to be hoped that, as was the case for the 2004 Guidelines and other sets of rules and guidelines of the IBA Arbitration Committee, the revised Guidelines will find broad acceptance within the international arbitration community, as did the 2004 Guidelines and other IBA Arbitration Committee sets of rules and guidelines, and that they will assist parties, practitioners, arbitrators, institutions and courts in dealing with these important questions of impartiality and independence".[20]

Applying the IBA Guidelines has not been ruled out in all ICSID cases, however,[21] and adjudicators have even explicitly relied on them in some one-off decisions. The Alpha v. Ukraine decision, for instance, stated that: "the two other members are persuaded that the state of international law as to the duty of disclosure is best evidenced by the IBA Guidelines and not by the American and Canadian domestic law precedents cited by respondent (...) The two other members view the position taken in the IBA Guidelines as reflective of (...) In sum, based on their analysis of the IBA Guidelines, the two other members agree with the conclusion reached in the Suez Aguas Second Decision."[22]

Other investment arbitration tribunals outside the ICSID context have generally been more inclined to take into account and apply the IBA Guidelines. In the National Grid v. Republic of Argentina case, for instance, the LCIA determined the applicable

---

[11] Universal v. Venezuela, par 74.

[12] Alpha v. Ukraine, par 56.

[13] Tidewater v. Venezuela, par 41.

[14] Urbaser v. Argentina, par 37.

[15] Arbaclat v. Argentina, par 78; Blue Bank v. Venezuela, par 62; Tidewater v. Venezuela, par 41.

[16] Burlington v. Ecuador; par 69, Fábrica de Vidrios v. Venezuela (2016a); par 34, Getma v. Guinée, par 80; Opic v. Venezuela, par. 52.

[17] Urbaser v. Argentina, par 37; Repsol v. Argentina, par 74; ConocoPhillips v. Venezuela, par 59.

[18] Caratube v. Kazakhstan, par 59; PIP v. Gabon, par 24; Universal v. Venezuela, par 74. Reflecting on the reception of these Guidelines, IBA Arbitration Guidelines and Rules Subcommittee (2016).

[19] Highlighting the importance of soft law in the international arbitration sphere, Arias (2018).

[20] IBA (2004).

[21] Their possible applicability is alluded to in some cases: "The provisions of the IBA General Standard 7 c (were they applicable)", EDF v. Argentina, par 100; "en la hipótesis de que Directriz 3.3.9 de las Directrices de la IBA resultare aplicable", Total v. Argentina, par 144.

[22] Alpha v. Ukraine, pars 62 and 66.

standard on justifiable doubts as to the arbitrator's impartiality resorting to the IBA Guidelines, "to which both Parties refer".[23] In the same vein, the PCA decision sustaining a challenge against an arbitrator in the Perenco v. Ecuador case stated that: "it is a reasonable interpretation of the challenged arbitrator's comments and, applying the IBA Guidelines, would give rise to justifiable doubts about his impartiality".[24] Likewise, in the Vito v. Government of Canada case, which was heard under UNCITRAL Arbitration Rules and Chapter 11 of NAFTA, the Deputy Secretary-General of ICSID based his decision on the IBA Guidelines.[25]

To summarize the current scenario when dealing with investment "case law", various institutions that deal with challenges to investment arbitrators do apply the IBA Guidelines to decide whether the challenged arbitrator should be unseated. However, in the context of ICSID, the institution that issues most investment arbitration awards, the IBA Guidelines do not serve as a real basis for challenge decisions. The formal accolades for this international instrument have not culminated in their real application in controversial challenge cases. Firm backing in the investment milieu is still needed, and the following section aim to shed some light on how this might come about.

Turning the attention towards the role granted by diverse IIAs to the IBA Guidelines, it is relevant that these Guidelines are referred to in both versions of CETA (2014 CETA[26] and the consolidated 2016 CETA text[27]), which strongly emphasise the need for tribunal members to comply with them. Additionally, the Norwegian Draft Model Agreement and the Netherlands draft Model BIT contain the same obligation.[28] However, these texts from the investment context[29] establish the following caveats: they view the IBA Guidelines as a mere intermediate stage, compulsory or otherwise; as a convenient means in the quest for a final and satisfactory regulation of conflicts of interest in investment arbitration. Accordingly, both versions of CETA, the Norwegian Draft Model Agreement, and the Netherlands draft Model BIT first state that applying the IBA Guidelines is an imperative and then go on to indicate that the competent committee either may or will adopt supplementary rules[30] or a code of conduct in the

[23]National Grid v. Argentina, par 82.

[24]Perenco v. Ecuador, par 56. In this case, the parties agreed not to apply the ICSID disqualifications standards and the PCA resorted to the IBA Guidelines. *Supra*, Sect. 2.1. and *infra* Sect. 4.3.

[25]The Decision states: "in the instant case, from the point of view of a "reasonable and informed third party" (General Standard 2 c) of the IBA Guidelines (...) there would be justifiable doubts about the arbitrator's impartiality and independence as an arbitrator if (...)" Vito v. Canada, par 36.

[26]CETA (2014).

[27]CETA (2016).

[28]Article 15, Kingdom of Norway (2015), and Article 20.6. of the Netherlands draft Model BIT. Netherlands (2018).

[29]In commercial arbitration, the KLRCA Code of Conduct for arbitrators refers to the IBA Guidelines as a "point of reference" when determining the disclosure requirement and whether an Arbitrator is conflicted.

[30]So far, it is not known whether the reference to supplemental rules in Chapter 8 of CETA—Investment—could be covered by something similar to the contents of Annex B to Chapter 29—Dispute Settlement, in which a catch-all phrase ("a candidate shall disclose any interest, relationship

future.[31] The German Model BIT project opted for the non-compulsory approach, aiming to establish a binding code of conduct for panel members that will take the IBA Guidelines "into consideration".[32]

While most academics and practitioners who have either studied or applied the Guidelines agree that they represent an important advance in the clarification of the thorny issue of conflicts of interest, it should be noted that there is no such unanimity over the adequacy of their content and scope of application. Their drafting has been criticised in some quarters on the basis that certain relevant issues have been left unresolved or that the solutions provided are unsatisfactory,[33] and it has also been argued that the current text does not take into account the specificities of investment arbitration.[34] The fact that the IBA Guidelines apply to investment arbitration in a

or matter that is likely to affect her or his independence or impartiality or that might reasonably create an appearance of impropriety or bias in the proceeding"), is combined with the following breakdown: "Without limiting the generality of the foregoing, candidates shall disclose the following interests, relationships and matters: (1) any financial interest of the candidate: (a) in the proceeding or in its outcome, and (b) in an administrative proceeding, a domestic court proceeding or another panel or committee proceeding that involves issues that may be decided in the proceeding for which the candidate is under consideration; (2) any financial interest of the candidate's employer, partner, business associate or family member: (a) in the proceeding or in its outcome, and (b) in an administrative proceeding, a domestic court proceeding or another panel or committee proceeding that involves issues that may be decided in the proceeding for which the candidate is under consideration; (3) any past or existing financial, business, professional, family or social relationship with the interested parties in the proceeding, or their counsel, or such relationship involving a candidate's employer, partner, business associate or family member; and (4) public advocacy or legal or other representation concerning an issue in dispute in the proceeding or involving the same matters." Article 20.6. of the Netherlands draft Model BIT also refers to "any supplemental rules", but in this case they would be logically agreed upon by the Contracting Parties. Netherlands (2018).

[31] Article 15—Conflict of Interest and Code of Conduct. Kingdom of Norway (2015).

[32] The brief indication in Article 22—Code of Conduct ("A conflict of interests shall exist inter alia if a Panel member has served as legal counsel to one of the disputing parties in a previous matter"). Federal Ministry for Economic Affairs and Energy (2015).

[33] Joelson (2015), Cinelli Moreira (2014), pp. 142–147. These criticisms do not only come from the academic sector, but also from the judicial. For example, in March 2016, an English High Court of Justice decision stated that the controversy undoubtedly fell within the description in Paragraph 1.4 of the "Non-Waivable Red List" in the 2014 IBA Guidelines. Nevertheless, the judge decided that "the fair minded and informed observer, having considered the facts, would not conclude that there was a real possibility that the Canadian arbitrator was biased or lacked independence or impartiality". This outcome was decided under English law, but it was clearly stated that there were weaknesses in the 2014 IBA Guidelines from the judge's perspective. The judge did not take the shortcut of saying that the 2014 IBA Guidelines were not a statement of English law. On the contrary, he recognised that the arbitration was international and therefore did take into account the 2014 IBA Guidelines, explaining "why I do not, with respect, think they can yet be correct". [2016] EWHC 422 (Comm). Case No: CL-2015-000344. Analysing the case, Longley and Ngai (2016), pp. 1–5.

[34] For instance, Krajewski highlights that: "the IBA Guidelines only relate to an individual conflict of interests, and not to systemic interest in upholding investment arbitration for the benefit of investors". Krajewski (2014), pp. 17–18. In addition, investment arbitration involves aspects of public interest and the pool of potential arbitrators is limited, as is the likelihood of annulling ICSID awards. Fry and Stampalija (2014), p. 260; Rubins and Lauterburg (2010), p. 179.

formal sense but in practice their implementation does not fully convince stakeholders may be a plausible explanation of the trend outlined below.

In contrast to these above-mentioned texts, which do refer to the IBA Guidelines in one way or another, many others of the investment context have opted for approaches to arbitrators' conflicts of interest that ignore the IBA Guidelines—in a formal sense at least, because there is certainly a feeling that some were partially inspired by the Guidelines. For example, and as mentioned previously,[35] recent EU texts like the EU-Singapore IPA, the former EUSFTA, JEFTA, the EU-Vietnam FTA, and TTIP contain a brief general statement to the effect that members of the tribunal have to disclose any past or present interest, relationship or matter that is likely to affect their independence or impartiality or that might reasonably create an appearance of impropriety or bias in the proceedings, but there is no explicit reference to the IBA Guidelines in these IIAs.

The non-reference to the IBA Guidelines is also the general rule in other legal contexts. For instance, the NAFTA Code of Conduct combines a general statement with a non-exhaustive list of items to be disclosed: "Without limiting the generality of the foregoing, candidates shall disclose the following interests, relationships and matters: (1) any financial interest of the candidate (*a*) in the proceeding or in its outcome, and (*b*) in an administrative proceeding, a domestic court proceeding or another panel or committee proceeding that involves issues that may be decided in the proceeding for which the candidate is under consideration; (2) any financial interest of the candidate's employer, partner, business associate or family member (*a*) in the proceeding or in its outcome, and (*b*) in an administrative proceeding, a domestic court proceeding or another panel or committee proceeding that involves issues that may be decided in the proceeding for which the candidate is under consideration; (3) any past or existing financial, business, professional, family or social relationship with any interested parties in the proceeding, or their counsel, or any such relationship involving a candidate's employer, partner, business associate or family member; and (4) public advocacy or legal or other representation concerning an issue in dispute in the proceeding or involving the same goods".[36]

This combination of general statement and non-exhaustive list of varying length and detail is also quite common both in commercial arbitration texts where the IBA Guidelines are not referenced (the 2010 CAM Arbitration rules[37]; the 2015 Code of

[35]*Supra,* Chap. 2.

[36]NAFTA (1994) Code of Conduct.

[37]Article 18 CAM Arbitration Rules: "When giving notice of their acceptance the arbitrators shall submit their statement of Independence to the Secretariat. In the statement of independence, the arbitrator shall disclose specifying the time and duration: a) any relationship with the parties, their counsel or any other person or entity involved in the arbitration which may affect his/her impartiality or Independence; b) Any personal or economic interest, either direct or indirect in the subject matter of the dispute, c) Any bias or reservation as to the subject matter of the dispute". CAM (2010a).

Ethics for an Arbitrator-SIAC[38]; the 2017 Note to parties and arbitral tribunals on the conduct of the arbitration under the ICC rules of arbitration[39]; the ABA Code of Ethics[40]; and the TAB Code of Ethics,[41] among others), as well as in other

[38]Article 2.2 of the SIAC Code of Ethics for an Arbitrator.: "A prospective arbitrator shall disclose to the Registrar and any party who approaches him for a possible appointment: a) any past or present close personal relationship or business relationship, whether direct or indirect, with any party to the dispute, or any representative of a party, or any person known to be a potentially important witness in the arbitration; the extent of any prior knowledge he may have of the dispute". SIAC (2015).

[39]The ICC Note states: "Each arbitrator or prospective arbitrator must assess what circumstances, if any, are such as to call into question his or her independence in the eyes of the parties or give rise to reasonable doubts as to his or her impartiality. In making such assessment, an arbitrator or prospective arbitrator should in particular, but not limited to, pay attention to the following circumstances: The arbitrator or prospective arbitrator or his or her law firm represents or advises, or has represented or advised, one of the parties or one of its affiliates. The arbitrator or prospective arbitrator or his or her law firm acts or has acted against one of the parties or one of its affiliates. The arbitrator or prospective arbitrator or his or her law firm has a business relationship with one of the parties or one of its affiliates, or a personal interest of any nature in the outcome of the dispute. The arbitrator or prospective arbitrator or his or her law firm acts or has acted on behalf of one of the parties or one of its affiliates as director, board member, officer, or otherwise. The arbitrator or prospective arbitrator or his or her law firm is or has been involved in the dispute, or has expressed a view on the dispute in a manner that might affect his or her impartiality. The arbitrator or prospective arbitrator has a professional or close personal relationship with counsel to one of the parties or the counsel's law firm. The arbitrator or prospective arbitrator acts or has acted as arbitrator in a case involving one of the parties or one of its affiliates. The arbitrator or prospective arbitrator acts or has acted as arbitrator in a related case. The arbitrator or prospective arbitrator has in the past been appointed as arbitrator by one of the parties or one of its affiliates, or by counsel to one of the parties or the counsel's law firm. (...) For the scope of disclosures, an arbitrator will be considered as bearing the identity of his or her law firm, and a legal entity will include its affiliates. In addressing possible objections to confirmation or challenges, the Court will consider the activities of the arbitrator's law firm and the relationship of the law firm with the arbitrator in each individual case. Arbitrators should in each case consider disclosing relationships with another arbitrator or counsel who is a member of the same barristers' chambers. Relationships between arbitrators, as well as relationships with any entity having a direct economic interest in the dispute or an obligation to indemnify a party for the award, should also be considered in the circumstances of each case". ICC (2017), par. 20.

[40]CANON II of the ABA Code affirms: "An arbitrator should disclose any interest or relationship likely to affect impartiality or which might create an appearance of partiality. Persons who are requested to serve as arbitrators should, before accepting, disclose: (1) any known direct or indirect financial or personal interest in the outcome of the arbitration; (2) any known existing or past financial, business, professional or personal relationships which might reasonably affect impartiality or lack of independence in the eyes of any of the parties. For example, prospective arbitrators should disclose any such relationships which they personally have with any party or its lawyer, with any co-arbitrator, or with any individual whom they have been told will be a witness. They should also disclose any such relationships involving their families or household members or their current employers, partners, or professional or business associates that can be ascertained by reasonable efforts; (3) the nature and extent of any prior knowledge they may have of the dispute; and (4) any other matters, relationships, or interests which they are obligated to disclose by the agreement of the parties, the rules or practices of an institution, or applicable law regulating arbitrator disclosure". ABA (2004). Detailing the origins of this text, Feerick (2002).

[41]Article 4.2 of the TAB Code establishes that: "A prospective arbitrator must disclose: a) (Reformulated) Any relation past or present, whether direct or indirect as set out in Article 3.3.,

international ADR contexts such as the WTO Rules of Conduct for the Understanding on Rules and Procedures Governing the Settlement of Disputes.[42] Summarizing, the IBA Guidelines are not referenced so far in the vast majority of IIAs, a situation that is reproduced in other contexts such as commercial arbitration.

3.3 The Future of the IBA Guidelines in International Investment Disputes

It is not easy to predict future developments where the 2014 IBA Guidelines are concerned. In principle, they appear to be the most comprehensive text currently available: a document cooked on a slow heat that has already been amended to take into account the sector's needs, and whose drafting involved contributions from renowned jurists in various legal contexts. Mandatory referrals to the Guidelines as stipulated in CETA, for example, should be positively valued in principle as they provide investment dispute participants with certainty. If the EU were to support the implementing of an approach requiring compliance with the IBA Guidelines in the

including previous appointments as arbitrator, with any party to the dispute, or any representative of a party, or any person who is known to be potentially a relevant witness in the arbitration. As regards current relations, the duty of disclosure is applicable regardless of its magnitude, but as regards past relations it is only applicable if such relations were of a significant nature in relation to the professional or business relations of the arbitrator. Failure to disclose an indirect relation unknown to a prospective arbitrator shall not be grounds for disqualification unless it could have been discovered by making reasonable enquiries; b) the nature and duration of any social relation with any party or any person who is known to be potentially a relevant witness in an arbitration; c) the nature of any previous relation with any co-arbitrator (including previous joint services as arbitrators); d) the extent of any prior knowledge the prospective arbitrator may have of the dispute; e) the extent of any obligation which might affect his availability to discharge his duties as an arbitrator as far as is reasonably foreseeable". TAB (2009).

[42] Annex 2 of the Rules declares: "Illustrative List of Information to be Disclosed: This list contains examples of information of the type that a person called upon to serve in a dispute should disclose pursuant to the Rules of Conduct for the Understanding on Rules and Procedures Governing the Settlement of Disputes. Each covered person, as defined in Section IV:1 of these Rules of Conduct has a continuing duty to disclose the information described in Section VI:2 of these Rules which may include the following: (a) financial interests (e.g. investments, loans, shares, interests, other debts); business interests (e.g. directorship or other contractual interests); and property interests relevant to the dispute in question; (b) professional interests (e.g. a past or present relationship with private clients, or any interests the person may have in domestic or international proceedings, and their implications, where these involve issues similar to those addressed in the dispute in question); (c) other active interests (e.g. active participation in public interest groups or other organisations which may have a declared agenda relevant to the dispute in question); (d) considered statements of personal opinion on issues relevant to the dispute in question (e.g. publications, public statements); (e) employment or family interests (e.g. the possibility of any indirect advantage or any likelihood of pressure which could arise from their employer, business associates or immediate family members)." WTO (1996).

ICS -and/or in a prospective MIC setting, this would unquestionably be a definitive endorsement of the Guidelines in the international investment framework.

However, the claim that the Guidelines do not completely match the peculiarities of investment arbitration cannot be entirely ignored. It suggests that there is still room for improvement in the way investment arbitrators' conflicts of interest are currently regulated. For instance, the application of the IBA Guidelines and the supplementary text referred to in CETA might lead to more satisfactory results in terms of predictability and quality.

The EU's determination to include—or allude to the creation of—a code of conduct for members of investment courts in the most recent IIAs may have an impact on institutions that handle investment arbitration, leading to the emergence of a race to the top where the IBA Guidelines should not be necessarily absent. For instance, ICSID might follow in the EU's footsteps and issue a code of conduct for its arbitrators that addresses key issues such as arbitrators' conflict of interests in detail.[43] Within this framework, a recent proposal has suggested the incorporation of the IBA Guidelines as ICSID policy.[44] The IBA itself, for example, may decide to tackle this task by introducing specific references to investment arbitrators into the main body of its Guidelines.

Therefore, and regardless of some authors' views,[45] the developing of Codes of conduct or similar texts applicable to investment arbitrators should not necessarily be a cause for concern among stakeholders. If initiatives such as the referred to above continue to make headway in this area, their proposals may help to outline a more focused regime in the investment arbitration framework.[46]

---

[43]Cristani (2014), p. 177.

[44]Law Council of Australia (2017) and Fry and Stampalija (2014), p. 259.

[45]It has been affirmed that: "we can welcome this reference to a text developed by the best specialists in the field (IBA) .... However, we can only be concerned about the reference to any other supplementary rule .... In fact, it is not desirable that the states party to the treaty engage in a rewriting of texts such as the IBA Guidelines.... Similarly, the drafting of a code of ethics on communications between parties and arbitrators is unnecessary, as this issue is addressed in the texts such as the IBA Guidelines on party representation .... As for the confidentiality of arbitration, this is already dealt with in texts such as arbitration rules and in many arbitration laws. And it does not seem useful to add anything. Excessive regulation can therefore only lead to undesirable results" (author's translation) ("on peut se féliciter de cette référence à un texte élabore par les meilleurs spécialistes en la matière (IBA).... On ne peut cependant que s'inquiéter de la référence faite à toute autre règle supplémentaire.... In n'est en effet pas souhaitable que les états parties au traité s'engagent dans une réécriture de textes tels que les lignes directrices de la IBA.... De même, la rédaction d'un code de déontologie portant sur les communications entre les parties et les arbitres parait inutile, cette question étant traitée dans les textes telles que les lignes directrices de la IBA sur la représentation des parties.... Quant à la confidentialité de l'arbitrage celle-ci est déjà traitée dans les règlements d'arbitrage applicables et dans de nombreuses lois d'arbitrage. Et il ne parait pas utile d'ajouter quoi que ce soit. L'excès de réglementation ne pourra donc conduire qu'a des résultats indésirables"). Mourre and Fouret (2015), pp. 581–582.

[46]In the context of commercial arbitration, arbitral institutions such as CAM foresee that new regulations would supersede the IBA Guidelines, the document that this institution currently refers to: "When filling in the statement of independence, the arbitrator may consider the "IBA Guidelines

3.4 Three Case Studies on the Present and Future Regulation of Conflicts of Interest in the International Investment Context

It has been noted in previous sections of this chapter that there are various key supranational institutions such as the ICSID, IBA, UNCITRAL, and the EU which may update or draft texts tackling conflicts of interest among investment arbitrators -arbitrators who may be re-nominated as judges or tribunal members in the future. This final section presents some reflections on ways in which the peculiarities of investment arbitration could affect the regulation of conflicts of interest in the sector, as well as the existing links with the duty of disclosure. There can be no doubt that topics such as repeat appointments, issue conflict and multiple hatting all merit monographic studies. These three issues have been chosen from a much broader list of possible topics[47] and are dealt with as case studies here.

The survey performed by the IBA Subcommittee on Investment Treaty Arbitration might provide some preliminary clues as to specific concerns over conflicts of interest and investment arbitrator disclosure, as well as the challenges that will need to be faced in these legal areas. The follow-up 2016 Report stated that participants' responses overwhelmingly reflected the view that all appointments made either by the same party, or by different parties represented by the same law firm, should be disclosed. Respondents were evenly divided over the question of whether arbitrators should be permitted to participate in proceedings involving factual issues that they had previously decided on in other proceedings, but a majority felt that investment arbitrators should be allowed to sit in proceedings involving legal issues that they had already made decisions on in other cases.[48]

3.4.1 Multiple Arbitral Appointments

The issue of repeat or multiple arbitral appointments has frequently been raised in investment arbitration practice and has also attracted attention from academics. An

on Conflicts of Interest in International Arbitration", attached to the Secretariat's letter of appointment. Should the Arbitral Council decide on the statement of independence according to Article 18, Para. 4, of the Rules, then it will not be bound in its decision by the IBA Guidelines." CAM (2010c).

[47]For example, the classification regarding conflicts of interest proposed by Daele is very long and detailed: relationships of the arbitrator with a party, relationships of the arbitrator with a counsel of a party, relationships of the arbitrator with a barrister belonging to the same chambers, relationships of the law firm of the arbitrator with a party, relationships of the law firm of the arbitrator with counsel of a party, dual rule of the arbitrator, membership of other tribunals, writings and public statements, conduct of the arbitrator. Daele (2012).

[48]IBA Subcommittee on Investment Treaty Arbitration (2016).

immediate problem arises with regard to this phenomenon's definition and broad profile.[49] There can be no doubt that situations in which one arbitrator is repeatedly appointed by the same party, party affiliate, counsel or law firm are at its heart.[50] These situations are currently included in the IBA Guidelines Orange List, meaning that they are considered to be circumstances that "depending on the facts of a given case, may, in the eyes of the parties, give rise to doubts as to the arbitrator's impartiality or independence."[51] The Guidelines address the following types: "The arbitrator has, within the past three years, been appointed as arbitrator on two or more occasions by one of the parties, or an affiliate of one of the parties" (3.1.3)[52]; and "the arbitrator has, within the past three years, been appointed on more than three occasions by the same counsel, or the same law firm" (3.3.8)".[53]

Some authors have also suggested broadening the definition of repeat appointments by including situations in which the same arbitrator is repeatedly appointed by the same type of party (state or investor).[54] Finally, others feel that the notion of repeat appointments should equally include instances in which an arbitrator has previously been appointed to decide a case or cases involving similar facts or legal issues.[55] Although some ICSID praxis can be interpreted as supporting this broad

[49]As will be explained in Sect. 3.4.3, this broad definition is not a perfect match with the phenomenon of multiple hatting. This approach was also emphasized in the Tidewater v. Venezuela case: "the conflict which may potentially arise from multiple arbitral appointments by the same party is of a different character from other connections to one of the parties, including service as counsel or other professional capacity", par 60.

[50]Fernández Pérez (2018).

[51]IBA (2014).

[52]It is worth noting that the exception in footnote 5 of the IBA Guidelines does not refer to investment arbitration: "It may be the practice in certain types of arbitration, such as maritime, sports or commodities arbitration, to draw arbitrators from a smaller or specialised pool of individuals. If in such fields it is the custom and practice for parties to frequently appoint the same arbitrator in different cases, no disclosure of this fact is required, where all parties in the arbitration should be familiar with such custom and practice". IBA (2014).

[53]Sobota explains the numerical difference (two or more occasions/on more than three occasions) between 3.1.3 (party or an affiliate thereof) and 3.3.8 (council or law firm) in the following way: "The more liberal standard for repeat appointments by the same counsel stems from the fact that concerns of overlapping issues and extra-record knowledge are less acute where the cases involve different parties. In addition, it has been considered "nearly unavoidable" that incidental business contacts and "at least some degree of acquaintance" may exist between arbitrators and advocates". Sobota (2015), p. 298.

[54]Kuo (2011), p. 250; Hollander (2008). Sometimes the dividing lines between the three figures examined in this section are blurred. For instance, in the Saint-Gobain v. Venezuela case, the investor alleged that: "There is a danger that [the arbitrator] will decide a certain issue in favor of Venezuela because he has argued the same, or similar, issues in favor of Argentina in the past and potentially in the future, and, in doing so, that he will not have sufficient regard to the merits of the case". Saint-Gobain v. Venezuela, par 77. The investor—and the co-arbitrators, by discarding this argument- are not treating this circumstance as multiple appointments by the same type of party (State), but as an issue conflict.

[55]Kuo (2011), p. 250; Hollander (2008), p. 2.

definition,[56] in reality this scenario, which is included in Section 3.1.5 of the Orange List—similar facts or legal issues—is also connected with issue conflict, as discussed below.[57]

Repeat appointments may lead to questions over an arbitrator's independence and impartiality. There is a fear that they may not only cause arbitrators to become financially dependent on appointing individuals, but also that a sort of professional relationship may develop between them. Moreover, arbitrators who repeatedly deal with similar factual and legal issues may have an advantage over their co-arbitrators, or may be predisposed to re-apply analyses from previous cases.[58] These concerns over bias become more acute in a context such as that of investment arbitration, in which the pool of top-flight arbitrators is very small, many disputes arise from the same pattern of facts or the same decision by legislative or executive bodies, and the same or similar legal instruments raise recurring legal issues. The shadow of a breach of the principle of confidentiality also looms over these cases of multiple appointments,[59] and there is a fear that inequalities may arise, perhaps deriving from the overview acquired by a defendant state that is involved in multiple arbitrations.[60]

In fact, several ICSID decisions have included references to these delicate issues. As already noted at other points, these texts reflect an approach that cannot be described as tough on arbitrators. On the contrary, their guiding principle is that repeat appointments should not necessarily be seen as an indication of justifiable doubts about an arbitrator's independence and impartiality; they may also be the direct result of a praiseworthy degree of arbitrator independence and impartiality.[61]

[56]The analysis of ICSID awards shows that, when challenging an investment arbitrator, claimants sometimes pose a series of questions connected with the issue of repeated appointments to a greater or lesser extent. In Universal v. Venezuela, for instance, the investor put forward the following arguments to disqualify one of the arbitrators: multiple appointments by the same party, multiple arbitrations dealing with related issues, multiple appointments by the same counsel, and non-disclosure of other ICSID appointments by Venezuela. Universal v. Venezuela pars 75–96.

[57]*Infra*, Sect. 3.4.2.

[58]Giraldo-Carrillo (2011), pp. 75–106.

[59]*Infra*, Chap. 5.

[60]In EnCana v. Ecuador, the tribunal observed that: "The Respondent is also represented by the same legal firm, again something which is a matter for it to decide. Evidently, the Respondent and its legal advisers have a synoptic view of the various disputes related to the oil industry in Ecuador which may be denied to the Claimant and its legal advisers. But that is a natural inequality as between private companies and a host State, one which arises from their respective status and roles and which cannot be reversed *en tant que tel.*" In EnCana v. Ecuador, par 43.

[61]Tidewater v. Venezuela, par 61. This dichotomy is also reflected in Caratube v. Kazakhstan (2014): "Be it only said that the Unchallenged Arbitrators are impressed in particular by the fact that there exists a sufficient number of potential arbitrators for an appointment to be made without any appearance being given of an existing link, real or suspected, between the arbitrator and the appointing party and its counsel. And conversely, that it is quite natural that a party and its counsel will wish to appoint the "best" arbitrator available for a given case and that prior experiences with that potential arbitrator are of course adequate to give that assurance: it is a matter of public record that some high repute firms active in investment arbitrations and of the highest ethical standards will repeatedly call for the same arbitrators to serve in several arbitrations". Tidewater v. Venezuela, par 108.

In Universal v. Venezuela, the Chairman of the Administrative Council declared that "the international investment arbitration framework would cease to be viable if an arbitrator was disqualified simply for having faced similar factual or legal issues in other arbitrations".[62] ICSID decisions have generally adopted a case by case approach to analyse circumstances related to arbitrators' activity (number of appointments,[63] possible financial dependence,[64] the legal treatment of the appointing party by the arbitrator,[65] etc.). Although the initial statements in several ICSID decisions might lead one to conclude otherwise,[66] the reality is that repeat appointments are usually not sufficient to justify a successful arbitrator challenge.[67]

---

[62]Universal v. Venezuela, par 83.

[63]In some cases, ICSID decisions not only underscore the merely indicative nature of the IBA Guidelines in order to dismiss a proposal to disqualify the arbitrator, but also argue that their quantitative content—e.g. the 3-year timeframe and the number of appointments is random. For instance, in Tidewater v. Venezuela, the two Members "begin their analysis of this question by observing that the question whether multiple appointments to arbitral tribunals may impugn the independence or impartiality of an arbitrator is a matter of substance, not of mere mathematical calculation. Whilst it is useful to have the guidance provided by Section 3.1.3 of the IBA Guidelines, this can be no more than a rule of thumb. Depending on the particular circumstances of the case, either fewer or more appointments might, in combination with other factors, be needed to call into question an arbitrator's impartiality. There is perforce an arbitrary character about the limitation to two appointments within three years. Moreover, it is inherent in such a guideline that more than one appointment by the same party is not necessarily suggestive of a conflict". Tidewater v. Venezuela, par 59.

[64]Universal v. Venezuela: "[the arbitrator] has been appointed in more than twenty ICSID cases, evidencing that she is not dependent –economically or otherwise –upon respondent for her appointments in these [4] cases." Universal v. Venezuela, par 77.

[65]Tidewater v. Venezuela: "[the arbitrator] has joined unanimous preliminary decisions rejecting applications made by Venezuela. This fact tends to indicate that [the arbitrator] has been appointed on subsequent occasions because of her Independence, rather than the reverse." Tidewater v. Venezuela, par 64.

[66]The following statement, which nevertheless formed part of a decision dismissing the disqualification proposal submitted by the claimant, was promising in this sense: "We have reviewed with interest the decision of the remaining arbitrators on the proposal to disqualify an arbitrator in *Tidewater*. It is suggested by the arbitrators in that decision that multiple appointments as arbitrator by the same party in unrelated cases are a neutral factor in considerations relevant to a challenge. We do not agree. In our opinion, multiple appointments of an arbitrator by a party or its counsel constitute a consideration that must be carefully considered in the context of a challenge. In an environment where parties have the capacity to choose arbitrators, damage to the confidence that investors and States have in the institution of investor-State dispute resolution may be adversely affected by a perception that multiple appointments of the same arbitrator by a party or its counsel arise from a relationship of familiarity and confidence inimical to the requirement of independence established by the Convention. The arbitrators' suggestion in *Tidewater* that multiple appointments are likely to be explicable on the basis of a party's perception of the independence and competence of the oft appointed arbitrator is in our view unpersuasive. In a dispute resolution environment, a party's choice of arbitrator involves a forensic decision that is clearly related to a judgment by the appointing party and its counsel of its prospects of success in the dispute. In our view, multiple appointments of an arbitrator are an objective indication of the view of parties and their counsel that the outcome of the dispute is more likely to be successful with the multiple appointee as a member of the tribunal than would otherwise be the case". Opic v. Venezuela, par 47.

[67]Further examples of this trend: Saba v. Turkey and Electrabel v. Hungary.

The decision in Caratube v. Kazakhstan could nevertheless be considered a significant exception to this tendency, as the disqualification proposal was upheld by the co-arbitrators. However, it should be stressed that the question of repeat appointment in a strict sense was a secondary issue in the broad reasoning provided in the decision. The claimants in the case invoked two grounds for disqualifying the arbitrator: firstly, that he had been appointed arbitrator by a specific law firm on Kazakhstan's behalf in a previous case, and secondly that the same law firm and state had already appointed him on numerous occasions.[68] The decision focused mainly on the first ground, arguing that: "a reasonable and informed third party would find it highly likely that, due to his serving as arbitrator in the Ruby Roz case and his exposure to the facts and legal arguments in that case, [the arbitrator's] objectivity and open-mindedness with regard to the facts and issues to be decided in the present arbitration are tainted (...) [the arbitrator] has benefited from knowledge of facts on the record in that case which may not be available to the other two arbitrators on the present arbitration (or even be incompatible or contradictory with some facts on the record of the present arbitration) thereby giving rise to a manifest imbalance within the Tribunal to the disadvantage of the claimants".[69]

In this case, the co-arbitrators confirmed the notion that arbitrators cannot always maintain a Chinese wall in their minds, and that information acquired in a prior arbitration may affect their understanding of new cases.[70] Where the second ground is concerned, the co-arbitrators commented briefly that the existence of prior appointments "does not, without more, indicate a manifest lack of independence of impartiality on the part of [the arbitrator]".[71] Therefore, although the decision often referred to the notion of multiple appointments, it was the fact that there was an issue conflict that really justified the arbitrator challenge.

An analysis of other arbitration institutions' practice vis-à-vis repeat appointments shows that they seem more likely to uphold challenges raised in cases of repeat appointments.[72] ICSID may also opt to follow this path in the future, perhaps motivated by new decisions on the matter, or as the result of a stronger arbitrator disclosure policy incorporated via its current amendment process.

As indicated, in certain circumstances it is difficult to prevent the Chinese wall falling from arbitrators' minds. Given that using information obtained in one arbitration in subsequent cases creates procedural inequality between the parties, the

---

[68]This decision makes an internal clarification of the term "numerous", distinguishing between the additional occasion on which the arbitrator had been chosen by the law firm on behalf of Kazakhstan, and the multiple times he had been chosen by the same law firm on behalf of other clients. Following Daele's approach, it would seem that the number of counsel appointments and the number of party appointments should indeed be taken into account together, as both stakeholders act together in the eyes of the non-appointing party. Daele (2012), p. 362.

[69]Caratube v. Kazakhstan (2014), pars 90 and 93.

[70]*Ibid,* par 75.

[71]*Ibid,* par 107.

[72]Daele (2012).

author considers that the on-going nature of arbitrators' duty to disclose[73] may serve to restore the balance, leading sometimes to arbitrator's resignations or challenges. Indeed, it seems more reasonable to stress the long-lasting nature of the duty of disclosure with the aim of combating the negative effects of multiple appointments than to impose an *ex ante* all-encompassing disclosure obligation that would be difficult to frame and comply with in the investment praxis.[74]

To switch to a different scenario for a moment, the problems attributed to repeat appointments are likely to fade away in future contexts such as the MIC. EU texts like CETA, TTIP, the EU-Vietnam FTA, and JEFTA have clearly opted for committee-appointed tribunal members sitting in randomly formed divisions whose make-up cannot be predicted, while equal opportunities to serve will be available to every member.[75] These are important structural changes that can also be expected to lead to a reduction in the volume of challenges arising in this context.[76]

3.4.2 Issue Conflict

Secondly, several decisions on arbitrator challenges have dealt with the topic of issue conflict. This is a highly complex notion to define. The explanation provided by the engaging 2016 Report of the ASIL-ICCA Joint Task Force on Issue Conflicts in Investor-State Arbitration offers however a suitable starting point. Issue conflict can be explained as "an allegation that an arbitrator is biased towards a particular view of certain issues or has already prejudged them. The alleged predisposition or prejudgment [vis-à-vis certain factual or legal issues in dispute between the parties] involves an arbitrator's purported adherence to his or her pre-existing views on legal and factual questions, developed through experience as an arbitrator, as counsel, writing scholarly articles, and giving interviews or other public expressions of views."[77]

The IBA Guidelines address the troublesome question of arbitrator bias from different perspectives. While Article 3.1.5 of the Orange List refers to the convergence of issue-based conflicts and repeat appointments thus: "the arbitrator currently

[73] *Supra*, Sect. 2.4.

[74] In EnCana v. Ecuador—an arbitration pursuant to the UNCITRAL Rules with the London Court of International Arbitration acting as Secretariat- the partial award on jurisdiction states: "[the arbitrator] cannot reasonably be asked to maintain a "Chinese wall" in his own mind: his understanding of the situation may well be affected by information acquired in the other arbitration. The most he can be asked to do is to disclose facts so derived whenever they appear to be relevant to any issue before this Tribunal. The Tribunal does not propose to deal with this question in a categorical way by ordering full advance disclosure to the Claimant of the pleadings in the other arbitration." EnCana v. Ecuador, pars 45–46.

[75] Article 8.27.10 CETA, Article 9.7 TTIP, Article 12.7 EU-Vietnam FTA and Article 8.7 JEFTA.

[76] Schacherer (2016).

[77] International Council for Commercial Arbitration (2016).

serves, or has served within the past three years, as arbitrator in another case dealing with a related issue involving one of the parties, or an affiliate of one of the parties"; the IBA Guidelines examine the question of expressing legal views and draw the following distinction: while Article 4.1.1 of the Green List—no duty to disclose—refers to situations in which "the arbitrator has previously expressed a legal opinion (such as in a law review article or public lecture) concerning an issue that also arises in the arbitration (but this opinion is not focused on the case)",[78] Article 3.5.2 of the Orange List—duty to disclose—addresses the fact that "the arbitrator has publicly advocated a position on the case, whether in a published paper, or speech, or otherwise". The latter circumstance is restricted to the pending case and is also included in the ICC Note to Parties and Arbitral Tribunals as one of the circumstances that the arbitrator should take into account.[79]

Focusing on arbitrators' academic and professional writings and public statements, ICSID practice has addressed some cases involving this type of potential issue conflict.[80] The initial position was favourable towards arbitrators, a prime example being the dismissal of the alleged ground of issue conflict in the *Urbaser v. Argentina* case. The challenged arbitrator had fervently expressed his legal opinion on two key legal issues—the Most Favoured Nation clause and the defence of state of necessity—in a leading casebook and an academic paper. The claimants considered that the arbitrator lacked impartiality as he had prejudged the issues at stake in the case. Nevertheless, the other two tribunal members felt that: "the mere showing of an opinion, even if relevant in a particular arbitration, is not sufficient to sustain a challenge for lack of independence or impartiality of an arbitrator. For such a challenge to succeed there must be a showing that such opinion or position is supported by factors related to and supporting a party to the arbitration (or a party closely related to such party), by a direct or indirect interest of the arbitrator in the

---

[78]This text was worded slightly differently in the 2004 version of the IBA Guidelines: "the arbitrator has previously published a general opinion (such as in a law review article or public lecture concerning an issue which also arises in the arbitration (but this opinion is not focused on the case that is being arbitrated)". IBA (2004).

[79]The ICC Note states: "Each arbitrator or prospective arbitrator must assess what circumstances, if any, are such as to call into question his or her independence in the eyes of the parties or give rise to reasonable doubts as to his or her impartiality. In making such assessment, an arbitrator or prospective arbitrator should consider all potentially relevant circumstances, including but not limited to the following: (..) The arbitrator or prospective arbitrator or his or her law firm is or has been involved in the dispute, or has expressed a view on the dispute in a manner that might affect his or her impartiality. ICC (2017), p. 20.

[80]All the cases addressed in the main text refer to professional writing, but references have been found to an unpublished case on professional speech. In Canfor Corporation v. United States of America; Terminal Forest Products Ltd. v. United States of America, UNCITRAL, the NAFTA arbitrator was challenged as a result of a speech he had previously given to the Canadian government council, in which he commented from the legal perspective various aspects of the US softwood lumber industry. Daele (2012), pp. 404–405. Concretely, the challenged arbitrator stated: "This will be the fourth time we have been challenged. We have won every single challenge on softwood lumber, and yet they continue to challenge us with respect to these issues. Because they know the harassment is just as bad as the process". Legum (2005), p. 243.

outcome of the dispute, or by a relationship with any other individual involved, such as a witness or fellow arbitrator."[81]

This decision also addresses more general issues such as the arbitral system's proper functioning under the ICSID Convention,[82] the benefits of academic debate on investment arbitration, and the dangers—e.g., chilling effect—of recognizing that the issue conflicts in these contexts amount to a valid reason to disqualify an arbitrator.[83] It is not possible to be absolutely certain if, from an academic point of view, the statement made in this case that: "one of the main qualities of an academic is the ability to change his/her opinion as required in light of the current state of academic knowledge" pours oil on troubled waters, or does just the opposite when viewed from the perspective of consistency and the proper administration of justice.

After Urbaser v. Argentina, other ICSID cases have dealt to a greater or lesser extent with the topic of issue conflict in the context of arbitrators' general and abstract written opinions. While there is general agreement that this circumstance is not *per se* a cause for removal,[84] the CC/Devas v. India arbitration, substantiated

[81]Urbaser v. Argentina, par 46.

[82]The Decision states: "if Claimant's view were to prevail and any opinion previously expressed on certain aspects of the ICSID Convention be considered as elements of prejudgment in a particular case because they might become relevant or are merely argued by one party, the consequence would be that no potential arbitrator of an ICSID Tribunal would ever express views on any such matter, whether it may be procedural, jurisdictional, or touching upon the substantive rights deriving from BITs." Urbaser v. Argentina, par 48.

[83]The decision continues: "The wide spreading of ICSID awards has greatly contributed to dense exchanges of views throughout the world on matters of international investment law. This is very largely considered as a positive contribution to the development of the law and policies in this segment of the world's economy. It goes without saying that such a debate would be fruitless if it did not include an exchange of opinions given by those who are actually involved in the ICSID arbitration process, whether they are writing and speaking as scholars, arbitrators, or counsel. Such activity is part of the "system" as well known to all concerned. Therefore, it seems extremely strange that to the Two Members to accept the Claimants' position that a view previously expressed on an item relevant in an arbitral proceeding should be qualified as a prejudgment that demonstrates a lack of independence or impartiality". *Ibid*, par 48.

[84]In Repsol v. Argentina, the State considers that "el artículo del [árbitro] "hace suyo" el punto de vista del economista Sebastián Edwards en una publicación del 2008. Argentina sostiene que Edwards mantiene una visión despectiva de Argentina y que por lo tanto el [árbitro] tiene una visión "prejuiciosa y despreciativa de la República Argentina". (. . .) Este tipo de visiones, además de ser discriminatorias y haber dado lugar a la recusación de otros árbitros, constituye la negación misma de la imparcialidad y, en definitiva, de la justicia" ("the arbitrator's article "endorses" the point of view of the economist Sebastián Edwards in a publication of 2008. Argentina considers that Edwards maintains a derogatory view of Argentina and that therefore the arbitrator has a "prejudiced and contemptuous view of the Argentinian Republic". (...) This type of visions, in addition to being discriminatory and having led to the disqualification of other arbitrators, constitutes the very negation of impartiality and, ultimately, of justice") (author's translation). Nevertheless, the President of the ICSID Administrative Council considered in this case that: "esta publicación refleja una opinión sobre una disposición legal que no se encuentra presente en el instrumento jurídico invocado en este caso. Asimismo, las referencias del [árbitro] a una publicación de un tercero no constituyen evidencia de la carencia manifiesta de imparcialidad contra Argentina, tal y como requiere el Artículo 57 del Convenio" ("this publication reflects an opinion on a legal provision that is not present in the legal instrument invoked in this case.

by the PCA under UNCITRAL Arbitration Rules, sent shock waves through the scenario outlined so far. Although the challenge brought against the presiding arbitrator was denied, the ICJ President did uphold a challenge against a co-arbitrator with an academic background. The defendant state considered that the latter had already adopted a strong position on a legal issue—the "essential security interests" clause—in three previous arbitrations that were later partially or totally annulled, as well as in an academic paper on the issue.[85] The adjudicator of the challenge decision began by specifying his task: "to sustain any challenge brought on such a basis requires more than simply having expressed a prior view; rather, I must find, on the basis of the prior view and any other relevant circumstances, that there is an appearance of pre-judgment of an issue likely to be relevant to the dispute on which the parties have a reasonable expectation of an open mind".[86] Consequently, he ICJ President decided that: "In my view, being confronted with the same legal concept in this case arising from the same language on which he has already pronounced on the four aforementioned occasions could raise doubts for an objective observer as to [the arbitrator's] ability to approach the question with an open mind. The later article in particular suggests that, despite having reviewed the analyses of three different annulment committees, his view remained unchanged. Would a reasonable observer believe that the Respondent has a chance to convince him to change his mind on the same legal concept? [the arbitrator] is certainly entitled to his views, including to his academic freedom. But equally the Respondent is entitled to have its arguments heard and ruled upon by arbitrators with an open mind. Here, the right of the latter has to prevail. For this reason, I agree with the Respondent that [the arbitrator] should withdraw from this arbitration."[87]

The new stricter approach to arbitrators in cases of issue conflict has produced both controversy and legal debate. It is perhaps symptomatic that the most critical interpretation of the decision comes from the academic field, while some practitioners have reacted less strongly. Although some academics view the CC/Devas v. India case as an alarming departure that may restrict the freedom of legal

Likewise, the arbitrator's references to a publication of a third party do not constitute evidence of the manifest lack of impartiality against Argentina, as required by Article 57 of the Convention") (author's translation). Repsol v. Argentina, pars 30 and 79. In Saipem v. Bangladesh (unpublished challenge), the unchallenged arbitrators claimed that: "it is well established by national case law on the removal of arbitrators as well as in the practice of arbitration institutions that an arbitrator's doctrinal opinions expressed in the abstract without reference to any particular case do not affect that arbitrator's impartiality and independence, even though the issue on which the opinion is expressed may arise in the arbitration. It is not because a scholar has expressed general and abstract opinion that he or she will not consider the specificities of a given case and may not on such basis, form an opinion different from the one previously expressed." International Council for Commercial Arbitration (2016).

[85]It has been pointed out that: "the main sin would appear to be that the arbitrator did not repent of his earlier views when given an opportunity to support the new orthodoxy". Griffith and Kalderimis (2016), p. 611.

[86]CC/Devas v. India, par 58.

[87]*Ibid*, par 64.

academia, others favour distinguishing between bias with regard to the facts on one hand and to the law on the other. Whereas challenges should succeed if an arbitrator "has expressed views in prior academic writing that are fact-specific to the case at hand", they should not be upheld if the arbitrator has expressed "abstract views (...) on questions of law, that are outside the disposition of the parties to the arbitration proceedings."[88] However, some members of the legal profession feel that a closed-mind scenario may also arise from general views on unsettled legal issues. In this situation, the arbitrator's duty of impartiality and independence should prevail over arbitrator rights such as academic freedom.[89]

Analysing these cases has inevitably led to some final observations. It is noteworthy, for example, that the controversial—and certainly not arbitrator-friendly—criterion used in CC/Devas v. India has not emerged within ICSID context. Moreover, it could also be asked whether some of these challenges could have been avoided if the arbitrators had shown greater transparency and proactivity by voluntarily disclosing previous academic and professional writings, lectures and speeches to the parties. In the SGS v. Pakistan case, for instance, the arbitrator informed the parties that he had published a paper on the claim for fair and equitable treatment submitted by the investor—copies of which were distributed by the ICSID Secretariat.[90] It would be interesting to be able to verify whether this action influenced the fact that the subsequent challenge to the arbitrator was not based on the disclosed paper. Finally, in a global context in which it is common for individuals acting as investor arbitrators to pursue careers as international legal practitioners and academics, the most logical approach[91] for these "multiple role arbitrators"[92] may be to accept that the accrual of diverse professional commitments increases the likelihood of challenge.[93]

However, this general observation does not seem to be widely reflected in current arbitration practice on the whole. Conversely, the fact that arbitrators in several recent cases had also worked non-concurrently as lawyers did not result in successful challenges. In Saint-Gobain v. Venezuela, the investor claimed that the arbitrator [had] "acted as a zealous advocate for the most recalcitrant State party in ICSID

---

[88]Schill (2014), p. 6.

[89]Zamour (2015), pp. 227–245.

[90]8 ICSID Rep. 398 (2005).

[91]However, some commentators have observed that this approach would penalise the most-experienced arbitrators. International Council for Commercial Arbitration (2016), p. 65.

[92]In some cases, they have "quadruple versatility", as they also may intervene in arbitrations as legal experts. *Infra*, Sect. 3.4.3.

[93]In this sense: "it is not much more convincing to draw a strict dividing line between opinions expressed as a scholar and those to change and is unrelated to the pattern of facts and arguments related to a particular case, Claimants are right to the extent that they argue that such opinion may nevertheless be a factor of influence when it comes to considering the same or similar issues in a particular dispute. In other words, a legal scholar who becomes an ICSID arbitrator does not lose his/her capacity of being a scholar that conveys academic opinions, which might become relevant to the legal analysis undertaken in the resolution of a particular dispute". Urbaser v. Argentina par 52.

history", which presumably created an impression of possible bias.[94] The unchallenged arbitrators nevertheless argued forcefully that legal professionals, including arbitrators who had worked or were still working as counsels, are assumed to be capable of keeping a professional distance: "It is at the core of the job description of legal counsel—whether acting in private practice, in-house for a company, or in government—that they present the views which are favourable to their instructor and highlight the advantageous facts of their instructor's case. The fact that a lawyer has taken a certain stance in the past does not necessarily mean that he will take the same stance in a future case".[95]

Nevertheless, this adjudicator-friendly approach to consecutive service has been nuanced in various cases in which individuals acted as both arbitrator and counsel simultaneously. In circumstances such as these, either the challenge has been upheld[96] or the arbitrators have been required to choose between their roles.[97] The latter has generated in most cases a *de facto* cessation from the non-arbitrator role[98]

---

[94]Saint-Gobain v. Venezuela par 23.

[95]Saint-Gobain v. Venezuela, par 80.

[96]In ICS v. Argentina, the deciding authority referred to the IBA Guidelines in his decision to uphold the challenge.

[97]Academics have questioned whether this option should be allowed, since it has reasonably been considered that: "from the challenging party's perspective, its view of the arbitrator in all likelihood has already been tainted by the issue conflict, and the arbitrator's resignation as counsel thus would be insufficient to cure its concern that the dispute will be decided fairly". Mouawad (2008), p. 12. An important question that is open to debate in this kind of case refers to the reasons why an arbitrator does not renounce his or her role as arbitrator but decides to sacrifice the other position instead. While little academic interest seems to have been paid to the issue, some authors have indeed manifested clear opinions on the matter, for instance: "Arbitrators have a human incentive to market their services, even if indirectly, by making themselves better known and developing certain reputations (...) This role reversal has a simple explanation: a legitimate desire to earn as much fess as circumstances permit and obtain professional or academic recognition. A desire to earn more money normally does not influence issue conflicts for judges, while that desire can exert psychological pressure and be an important factor for arbitrators". Diaz-Candia (2012), pp. 7–8.

[98]For instance, as a consequence of the decision taken by the court of first instance of the Hague in the Republic of Ghana v. Telekom Malaysia Berhad case, the arbitrator resigned as attorney. The court had stated: "legitimate doubt will exist concerning [the arbitrator's] impartiality if he does not cease his activities as an attorney in the annulment action of RFCC versus Morocco. The challenge would be upheld if [the arbitrators] should fail to declare expressly and unreservedly within 10 days from the date of the decision that he would resign as attorney in the RFCC versus Morocco case" (reference included in the Decision of the District Court of The Hague, civil law section, 5 November 2004). As a consequence of the challenge in the Grand River v. United States case, the arbitrator ceased to represent or advise parties in two human rights bodies. The ICSID Secretary-General stated: "we concluded that representing or assisting parties in the later set of procedures would be incompatible with simultaneous service as arbitrator in the NAFTA proceeding, and asked that you inform us whether you would continue to represent or assist parties in the non-NAFTA procedures during your service as arbitrator in the present NAFTA proceeding". Grand River v. United States, 1, par 3.

or, occasionally, the arbitrator's resignation.[99] These situations highlighted the risks linked to issue conflict with regard to the adjudicators' impartiality and independence. In *Vito v. Canada*, for instance, the Deputy Secretary-General stated that: "By serving on a tribunal in a NAFTA arbitration involving a NAFTA State Party, while simultaneously acting as an advisor to another NAFTA State Party which has a legal right to participate in the proceedings, an arbitrator inevitably risks creating justifiable doubts as to his impartiality and independence (...) [the arbitrator] must therefore now choose whether he will continue to advise Mexico, or continue to serve as an arbitrator in this case".[100] In Blue Bank v. Venezuela, the Chairman of the ICSID Administrative Council upheld the proposal to disqualify the investor-appointed arbitrator, concluding that "a third party would find an evident and obvious appearance of lack of impartiality. This decision is consequence of a series of grounds, including the overlapping roles of the challenged arbitrator as, respectively, arbitrator and indirectly-involved lawyer in two on-going cases where similar issues were likely to be discussed".[101] Consecutive or concurrent circumstances of this kind, approached from very different angles by the IBA Guidelines, will be addressed in more detail in the sub-section on multiple hatting.[102]

The notion of issue conflict also covers cases in which arbitrators' predisposition or prejudgment may arise from having participated in one or more cases involving similar facts. Although an arbitrator's appointments may have a common origin, as they did in the Caratube v. Kazakstan case, there may be situations that do not fit into the repeat appointments typology,[103] and ICSID decisions have consistently rejected challenges to arbitrators in the latter situation. In some cases the rejection is based in the factual differences between the prior and present cases,[104] while in other the challenge fails because a distinction is established between the facts relevant to the

[99]In Glamis v. USA, the defendant state challenged the arbitrator appointed by the investor, as he was concurrently acting as a lawyer in a litigation case against the same state. The arbitrator resigned before a decision on the challenge was made, par 188. In Salini v. Jordan, the decision on jurisdiction does not specify whether the arbitrator resigned due to a concurrent or non-concurrent role as counsel, par. 9.

[100]Vito v. Canada (2009), pars 31 y 36.

[101]Blue Bank v. Venezuela, pars 67–69. Viewing this decision positively, Daele (2014), Horn (2014), p. 394.

[102]*Infra,* Sect. 3.4.3.

[103]*Supra,* Sect. 3.4.1.

[104]It is stated that: "In any event, it does not appear to be clear from the documents in the file that the two cases contain common factual evidence apart from the same context of privatization at the end of the 1990s". (author's translation) "En tout état de cause, il n'apparaît pas avéré au vu des pièces versées au dossier que les deux affaires présentent des éléments factuels communs en dehors d'un même contexte de privatisation à la fin des années 1990. Participaciones v. Gabon, par 32.

merits and the facts relevant to the interpretation of key legal provisions.[105] In this context, a petition for a reinforced duty of disclosure as a mechanism to overcome the problems posed by such cases may face practical difficulties: the adjudicator may lack sufficient information about the emerging case during the appointment process[106] or in the initial phases of the arbitration. This circumstance would prevent the arbitrator from detecting and consequently disclosing issue conflicts referring to past arbitrations.

Prior exposure to the same legal issues has been also subsumed under the notion of issue conflict. As indicated in the CC/Devas v. India case, it creates a fear that "an arbitrator will not approach an issue impartially, but rather with a desire to conform to his or her own previously expressed [legal] view".[107] Apart from this case, which addresses the strong position adopted by the arbitrator in various arbitrations and in an academic paper,[108] there are no further references to successful challenges focused solely on this category of issue conflict. The standard pro-arbitrator decision—which usually combine references to both factual and legal issues—stress that "the fact that an arbitrator made a finding of fact or a legal determination in one case does not preclude that arbitrator from deciding the law and the facts impartially in another case".

To conclude this subsection, it is worth observing that the great complexity and multiple nuances that issue conflict currently presents has led the ASIL-ICCA Joint Task Force to oppose the creation of formal "bright line" rules regulating inadequate prejudgment.[109] On the contrary, the task force decided—as commentators had also suggested[110]—to identify a series of factors to be taken into account when evaluating the arbitrator's relationship with the subject matter of the dispute, including the degree of commitment, concurrency, propinquity, specificity or proximity to the current case.[111]

The author would like to add that a strengthened duty of disclosure may play a constructive role when issue conflicts are tackled. The fact that there may be not enough information about the case during the opening stages of the arbitration, meaning that arbitrators would lack the requisite of certainty to disclose information, is not an insurmountable difficulty. Firstly, as already observed above, issue conflict addresses highly different cases, and a *sua sponte* disclosure of an arbitrator's

---

[105] It is affirmed that: "in the present case there is no overlap of facts relevant to the merits of the earlier arbitration and those relevant to the merits of the present case: the overlap merely concerns facts relevant to the interpretation of ArticleVII(2) of the BIT and related legal issues such as the scope of application of the MFN clause". İçkale v. Turkmenistan, par 119.

[106] Warning about the dangers of issue-based interviewing of arbitrators, International Council for Commercial Arbitration (2016), p. 19 (par 55).

[107] CC/Devas v. India, par 58.

[108] It cannot be ignored that this very same decision rejected the challenge to other co-arbitrator, who had also acted as adjudicator with the challenged arbitrator in two cases.

[109] International Council for Commercial Arbitration (2016), p. 64 (par 183).

[110] Brubaker (2008), pp. 111–152.

[111] International Council for Commercial Arbitration (2016), pp. 58–60.

academic publications seems a simpler task than anticipating the degree of similarity between factual or legal issues in two arbitration cases, for instance. Secondly, it should not be forgotten that arbitrators have an on-going duty of disclosure, which they must comply with. This may undoubtedly produce what are referred to as "late-in-the-day" arbitrator challenges, with all their consequences in terms of delays and increased costs.[112] However, the right to a neutral adjudicatory body is one of the pillars on which present and future of investment-related dispute resolution rests.

Looking ahead, the question arises as to whether there will be changes in the way this issue is dealt with in the future. The Codes of conduct incorporated in EU texts such as EU- Singapore IPA, TTIP, the EU-Vietnam FTA and JEFTA do no refer to issue conflict as such, but include a number of references that might be viewed as being connected with it; indicating, for instance, that: "members shall avoid direct and indirect conflicts of interest", "a member shall not be influenced by self-interest (...)", and "A member may not use his or her position as a member to advance any personal or private interests".[113] As has been pointed out in the context of the amendments to the ICSID Rules and Regulations,[114] it would be worthwhile devoting specific attention to issue conflict in any future code of conduct for investment adjudicators. Although eliminating party-appointed arbitrators in contexts such as the MIC may have consequences in terms of issue conflicts, controversial cases are still to be expected, since randomly appointed adjudicators are not completely exempt from the threat of prejudgment. Likewise, the possibility that new problems will arise at institutional level cannot be ruled out: for example, if there is scope for political parameters in the electing of MIC judges and tribunal members, controversial situations may arise similar to those recently experienced over re-appointment to the WTO Appellate Body.[115] To sum up, issue conflict is plainly a living concept, which will evolve side by side with the existing mechanisms of investment dispute resolution.

3.4.3 Multiple Hatting

Thirdly and lastly, one of the most common criticisms of the current ISDS system addresses the professional rotation effected by many jurists who fulfil more than one legal role in the system.[116] As outlined above, attention has mainly been focussed on situations in which the same individual consecutively or simultaneously serves as

[112]Levine (2015).

[113]Respectively, Articles 2, 5.1 and 5.3 of the Code of Conduct contained in the referred texts.

[114]Baker McKenzie (2017), p. 8.

[115]Claussen (2018).

[116]There is a clear example of this criticism in the document presented by more than 100 legal scholars, who called on Congress and the administration to protect democracy and sovereignty in U.S. trade deals. Alliance for Justice (2015).

both arbitrator and lawyer in several investment arbitration cases. This type of situation has given rise to the term "double hatting" commonly used by the academic community. The broader term "multiple hatting" is preferred here, however, since it enables other circumstances to be included in addition to the classic arbitrator-lawyer duality. Current practice shows that it is possible for a legal expert working in investment arbitration to act not only as legal counsel and arbitrator but also to serve as an expert witness, court secretary,[117] adviser to third-party funder,[118] government official,[119] corporation board member,[120] or lobbyist.[121] Besides that, this professional activity is sometimes combined with permanent or temporary academic work.[122]

This "multiple hat" scenario (mainly exemplified by arbitrator-lawyer double-hat scenario) has been condemned by many critics,[123] including the 2015 UNCTAD World Investment Report.[124] The reasons against this practice are well known: there is a risk of issue conflict, with the corresponding increase in the number of arbitrator challenges, which in turn leads many stakeholders to question the integrity of the whole ISDS. There is also a natural fear that this multiple role may jeopardize the independence and impartiality of these jurists, and that the arbitration parties may feel that their most basic procedural rights have been affected.[125] For this reason, voices have also been raised against these multiple roles and revolving doors during the current process of reforming the ICSID rules.[126]

Although some senior arbitrators have also severely criticized this revolving doors' approach, or have even voluntarily chosen to apply a restrictive strategy to

---

[117]Although it may be thought that the role of court secretary is secondary in principle and only occurs at a very early stage of an individual's professional career, a recent study ranking the "power brokers" of investment arbitration places an individual who has been court secretary in 38 cases but has never acted as either an arbitrator, legal counsel or expert witness in 20th position. Langford et al. (2017).

[118]UNCITRAL (2018), par 79.

[119]In Victor Pey Casado v. Chile (2008), a challenge against one of the arbitrators who was also Minister of Foreign Affairs of the Algerian Republic was upheld. Victor Pey Casado v. Chile, par 39.

[120]Compañía v. Argentina, pars 217–218.

[121]Myers v. Canada, par 28.

[122]Reflecting on the multiple hat phenomenon, Ziadé (2009).

[123]A devastating report in this sense is: Eberhardt and Olivet (2012).

[124]When focusing on the reforming of ISDS by replacing the existing system with other dispute resolution mechanisms the report suggests: "judges, unlike arbitrators in the present regime, would not be permitted to continue serving as counsel or expert witnesses". UNCTAD (2015), p. 152.

[125]Situations such as cross-appointments are also called into question by the same token. Cross-appointments have been defined thus: "Mr. X, as counsel in one case, agrees to appoint Ms. Y as arbitrator, and in return Ms. Y, when acting as counsel, will appoint Mr. X as arbitrator". Bernasconi-Osterwalder et al. (2010), p. 4.

[126]Claiming that this practice should be banned (Columbia Center on Sustainable Investment) or at least reduced to a minimum, Law Council of Australia (2017), p. 6.

their own professional careers,[127] the majority of the arbitral collective has in fact defended the current status quo, pointing out for instance that practical experience as counsel brings added value to the role of arbitrator and makes "double hatters" less dependent—e.g., financially—on appointments as arbitrators. Moreover, banning this practice would remove highly valued and experienced jurists from the arbitration market,[128] and it has been categorically stated that: "if arbitrators must be completely sanitized from all possible external influences on their decisions, only the most naïve or incompetent would be available".[129]

This subsection considers multiple hatting's present and future profile using a three-way internal distinction: the external activities carried out by adjudicators during their mandate; the *ex ante* quarantine period, and the *ex post* quarantine period. Separate observations are also made based on the various types of role reversibility that may occur, and the analysis also reflects on how reforming the much-criticized multiple hat scenario could influence adjudicators' duty of disclosure.

3.4.3.1 External Activities While Serving as Adjudicators

Various legal contexts have addressed some time ago the issue of international adjudicators and their external activities while serving on international tribunals.[130] In these cases, restrictive regulation was justified at theoretical level with the aim of ensuring these individuals' availability while also guaranteeing their independence and impartiality. However, in some milieus the practical application of these formal parameters has turned out to be laxer than originally expected.

The clearest example is undoubtedly the situation currently prevailing in the ICJ. The 1946 Statute embodied what academics have referred to as "relative incompatibility" and "absolute (functional) incompatibility".[131] Relative incompatibility is described as follows: "No member of the Court may act as agent, counsel, or

[127]US arbitrator Thomas Buergenthal, a former ICJ judge, stated that "arbitrators and counsel should be required to be one or the other", in order to "ensure that an arbitrator will not be tempted, consciously or unconsciously, to seek to obtain a result in an arbitral decision that might advance the interest of a client in a case he or she is handling as counsel". Perry (2012), p. 43. Sands has said: "it is possible to recognize the difficulty that may arise if a lawyer spends a morning drafting an arbitral award that addresses a contentious legal issue, and then in the afternoon as counsel in a different case drafts a pleading making arguments on the same legal issue". Sands (2012), pp. 31–32. Fernández-Armesto stated: "if self-policing does not work, in my opinion eventually there will be recommendations and eventually even outright prohibitions, following the precedent of CAS". Fernández-Armesto (2012). Another trend in the arbitral world is for senior "multiple hatters" to leave their big law firms and work solely as independent arbitrators, with the aim of minimising conflicts of interest.

[128]Derains and Gharavi (2017), pp. 5–6.

[129]Park (2009), p. 635.

[130]Shetreet (2003), pp. 127–161.

[131]Giorgetti (2015), pp. 7–13.

advocate in any case. No member may participate in the decision of any case in which he has previously taken part as agent, counsel, or advocate for one of the parties, or as a member of a national or international court, or of a commission of enquiry, or in any other capacity").[132] As a result of some controversial cases, this type of incompatibility is now interpreted more strictly, creating a significant number of self-recusals among ICJ judges.[133]

Absolute incompatibility is defined thus: "No member of the Court may exercise any political or administrative function, or engage in any other occupation of a professional nature".[134] This—in theory—categorical wording has prompted various judges to renounce civil service or academic positions when joining the ICJ. Nevertheless, later Court documents show that in practice some of its judges have in fact taken on various remunerated activities with the ICJ's approval. On the basis of the argument that these were exceptional situations, these judges have been allowed to act "as arbitrators in inter-state and private international arbitrations, serving in administrative tribunals or quasi-judicial organs of specialized agencies, lecturing, writing", among other positions.[135]

Recent statistics show that ICJ judges' participation in these permissible external activities is no longer simply anecdotal: "Yet at least 7 current ICJ judges and 13 former ICJ judges have worked—or are currently working—as arbitrators (or annulment committee members at ICSID) in investor–state dispute settlement (ISDS) cases during their ICJ terms. Those 20 individuals were appointed at least 92 times, either during or before the start of their ICJ terms, and served as arbitrators in at least 90 cases while sitting as ICJ judges (In two cases, two sitting ICJ judges served concomitantly as arbitrators in the same tribunal.) (...) This means that ICJ judges have sat as arbitrators in roughly 10% of all known investment treaty cases during their tenure".[136]

The data regarding ICJ judges' "moonlighting", to use its rather negative label, have rekindled the general debate on adjudicators' external activities. Opinions on the issue are highly polarized, and while some feel that such studies border on defamation, others value the fact that the studies dare to describe the following reality in writing: high financial incentives mean that some ICJ judges participate in arbitrations that appear incompatible with full-time ICJ positions.[137]

As indicated, the issue of external activities undertaken by international adjudicators during their term of service has been regulated to some extent in other legal

---

[132] Article 17. ICJ (1946).

[133] Giorgetti (2015), pp. 7–9.

[134] Article16. ICJ (1946).

[135] Giorgetti (2015), p. 11.

[136] Bernasconi-Osterwalder and Brauch (2017).

[137] A lively debate was generated on this matter in the OGEMID framework on 28 and 29 of November 2017.

contexts. If attention is focused on the issue's development in the 2007[138] and 2016 versions of the Code of Conduct for Members and Former Members of the CJEU,[139] it becomes clear from the Code's current wording that this issue is not only attracting ever-greater interest from international legislators, but that its regulation is also becoming increasingly detailed. Likewise, in the context of the ECHR, the 2008 Resolution on Judicial Ethics also addressed the issue of extra activities undertaken by judges. Although more concisely worded, it also requires that judicial duties take precedence over extrajudicial activities and that judges remain independent and impartial in spite of undertaking such activities.[140]

---

[138]Article 5 of the Code of Conduct proclaims: "Other activities: 1. Members who wish to take part in an external activity shall request prior authorisation from the Court or Tribunal of which they are a Member. They shall undertake, however, to comply with their obligation to be available so as to devote themselves fully to the performance of their duties. 2. Members may be authorised to participate in teaching activities, conferences, seminars or symposia, but may not receive any uncustomary financial remuneration for doing so. 3. Members may also be authorised to engage in activities of an academic nature and to assume unremunerated honorary duties in foundations or similar bodies in the cultural, artistic, social, sporting or charitable fields and in teaching or research establishments. In that connection, they shall undertake not to engage in any managerial or administrative activities which might compromise their independence or their availability or which might give rise to a conflict of interest. The expression 'foundations or similar bodies' means non-profit-making establishments or associations which carry out activities in the general interest in the fields referred to". CJEU (2007).

[139]Current Article 8 of the 2016 Code states: "External activities: 1. Members shall undertake to comply in all circumstances with their obligation to be available so as to devote themselves fully to the performance of their duties. 2. Members may engage in external activities only if they are compatible with their duties arising under Articles 2 to 4, 6 and 7 of this Code of Conduct. Without prejudice to the derogation provided for in the second paragraph of Article 4 of the Statute of the Court of Justice of the European Union, engaging in any professional activity other than that resulting from the performance of their duties shall be incompatible with the duties set out in this Code of Conduct. 3. Members may be authorised to engage in external activities that are closely related to the performance of their duties. In that context: — they may be authorised to represent the Institution or the Court or Tribunal of which they are a Member at ceremonies and official events, — they may be authorised to participate in activities of European interest that relate, inter alia, to the dissemination of EU law and to dialogue with national and international courts or tribunals. In this respect, Members may be authorised to participate in teaching activities, conferences, seminars or symposia. Only participation in teaching activities may give rise to remuneration in accordance with the rules of the teaching establishment concerned. The Members' activities authorised by the Court or Tribunal of which they are a Member shall be published on the Institution's website after the activity has taken place. 4. In addition, Members may be authorised to assume unremunerated duties in foundations or similar bodies in the legal, cultural, artistic, social, sporting or charitable fields and in teaching or research establishments. In that connection, they shall undertake not to engage in any managerial or administrative activities which might compromise their independence or their availability or which might give rise to a conflict of interest. The expression 'foundations or similar bodies' means not-for-profit establishments or associations which carry out activities in the general interest in the fields referred to. 5. Members who wish to take part in an activity covered by paragraphs 3 and 4 shall request prior authorisation from the Court or Tribunal of which they are a Member, by using a specific form. 6. Publications and the resulting copyright royalties shall be allowed without prior authorization". CJEU (2016)

[140]VII: "Additional activity. Judges may not engage in any additional activity except insofar as this is compatible with independence, impartiality and the demands of their full-time office. They shall

The same fundamental ideas appear in important soft law documents such as the 2002 Bangalore Principles of Judicial Conduct,[141] the 2005 Burgh House Principles on the Independence of the International Judiciary[142] and the 2011 Rhodes Resolution of the Institute of International Law on the Position of the International Judge.[143]

In the international arbitration context, since 2010, Section 18.3 of the Code of Sports-Related Arbitration applied by the Court of Arbitration for Sports has stated that: "CAS arbitrators and mediators may not act as counsel for a party before the CAS".[144]

There is no evidence, meanwhile, that the generous practical interpretation of these provisions in these frameworks has led to a generalized debate on the appropriateness of authorizing adjudicators to undertake external activities.

---

declare any additional activity to the President of the Court, as provided for in Rule 4 of the Rules of Court". ECHR (2008).

[141] Articles 4.11 and 4.12 of the Bangalore Principles: "Subject to the proper performance of judicial duties, a judge may: 4.11.1 write, lecture, teach and participate in activities concerning the law, the legal system, the administration of justice or related matters; 4.11.2 appear at a public hearing before an official body concerned with matters relating to the law, the legal system, the administration of justice or related matters; 4.11.3 serve as a member of an official body, or other government commission, committee or advisory body, if such membership is not inconsistent with the perceived impartiality and political neutrality of a judge; or 4.11.4 engage in other activities if such activities do not detract from the dignity of the judicial office or otherwise interfere with the performance of judicial duties. 4.12. A judge shall not practise law whilst the holder of judicial office". Judicial Group on Strengthening Judicial Integrity (2002).

[142] Article 8 of the Burgh House Principles: "Extra-judicial activity. 8.1. Judges shall not engage in any extra-judicial activity that is incompatible with their judicial function or the efficient and timely functioning of the court of which they are members, or that may affect or may reasonably appear to affect their independence or impartiality. 8.2. Judges shall not exercise any political function. 8.3. Each court should establish an appropriate mechanism to give guidance to judges in relation to extra-judicial activities, and to ensure that appropriate means exist for parties to proceedings to raise any concerns". International Courts and Tribunals, in association with the Project on International Courts and Tribunals (2004).

[143] Article 3 of the Rhodes Resolution: "2. They may not exercise political or administrative functions, or act as agents, counsel or advocates before any courts and tribunals. 3. Should judges engage in any other external activity, such as teaching or arbitration, if not prohibited by their statute, they shall afford absolute priority to the work of the international court or tribunal to which they belong. Moreover, they may not engage in any activity capable of impinging on their independence or susceptible of raising doubts on their impartiality in a given case. 4. It is undesirable for judges serving in courts and tribunals with a heavy workload to engage in arbitrations or in substantial teaching activities. 5. Special procedures should be set up within every international court or tribunal in order to regulate such matters. In any case, judges shall first request the authorization of the president of the court of which they are members. The president will decide, first and foremost, according to the interests and the needs of the international court or tribunal. Similar procedures are required when it appears that there is a risk of incompatibility in a particular case. 6. A former judge should not act as agent, counsel or advocate before the court or tribunal of which that judge has been a member during at least three years following the end of his/her term". Institute of International Law (2011).

[144] CAS (2010).

Having examined the way(s) in which the multiple hatting phenomenon—in the aspect of external activities undertaken while serving as an international adjudicator—has been tackled in different supranational contexts, attention now needs to turn to the future of this issue in the investment field. The inescapable starting point in this matter is highlighted in the introduction to the book: it cannot be denied that the EU's incursion into the ISDS scenario has awakened stakeholders' consciences. One example could be the fact that Paulsson's postulates have clearly resonated with the EU, which has chosen to abandon the practice of unilateral appointments in a way that can only be described as radical.[145]

The latest EU texts on ISDS all deal with multiple hatting to some extent, which is undoubtedly a positive development with respect to thousands of BITs, which do not expressly address the issue of role reversibility.[146] However, the EU texts fail to address all the potentially problematic facets of multiple hatting, and it is therefore necessary to consider their shortcomings and suggest mechanisms by which they could be improved.

As will be outlined in a subsequent chapter,[147] the EU texts state that adjudicators have a duty to be available, although using different wording: "The Judges/Members shall be available at all times and on short notice, and shall stay abreast of dispute settlement activities under this Agreement",[148] and "The Members of the Tribunal shall ensure that they are available and able to perform the functions set out under this Section".[149]

Furthermore, various points in these texts outline a type of multiple hatting ban:

Firstly, the EU-Singapore IPA,[150] EU-Vietnam FTA,[151] TTIP,[152] and the latest available version of JEFTA[153] use the same wording to define the characteristics of the tribunal of first instance and the appeal tribunal, and stress that members of the tribunal/judges that receive a regular salary, "shall not be permitted to engage in any

[145] Paulsson (2010), p. 344.

[146] The 2018 Netherlands draft model BIT addresses this issue, by stating in its Article 20.5 that: "Members of the Tribunal shall not act as legal counsel or shall not have acted as legal counsel for the last five years in investment disputes under this or any other international agreement". Netherlands (2018). The 2012 Southern African Development Community (SADC) Model Bilateral Investment Treaty also address this topic, stating that: "for greater certainty, the above requirements include the requirement not to act concurrently as counsel in another actual or potential treaty-based arbitration involving a foreign investor and a State". SADC (2012).

[147] *Infra*, Chap. 4.

[148] EU-Vietnam FTA 12.13 and 13.13; 9.11 and 10.11 TTIP; and JEFTA- 8.11. This text was inspired by Article 17 of the WTO DSU—Appellate Review-Standing Appellate Body: "All persons serving on the Appellate Body shall be available at all times and on short notice, and shall stay abreast of dispute settlement activities and other relevant activities of the WTO. They shall not participate in the consideration of any disputes that would create a direct or indirect conflict of interest." WTO (1994).

[149] Articles 8.27.11. CETA (2016).

[150] Article 3.9.15 and 3.10.13 EU-Singapore IPA (2018).

[151] Articles 12.17 and 13.17. EU-Vietnam FTA (2016).

[152] Articles 9.15 and 10.14. TTIP (2016).

[153] Articles 8.15 (tribunal of first instance and appeal tribunal). EU proposal, 14th round. JEFTA (2016).

occupation, whether gainful or not, unless exemption is exceptionally granted by the President of the Tribunal/of the Appeal Tribunal".

Secondly, when dealing with ethics, the 2016 CETA,[154] the EU-Vietnam FTA,[155] TTIP[156] and JEFTA[157] all state that: "upon appointment, they shall refrain from acting as counsel or as party-appointed expert or witness in any pending or new investment dispute under this or any other international agreement or domestic law."

At institutional level the EU has stated that, under this new regulation, "like in domestic and international courts, the judges won't be able to continue any activities which might interfere with their judicial functions".[158] This assessment has the support of eloquent authors such as Howse, who considers that: "it is much cleaner to have adjudicators who neither have a strong interest in being reappointed by parties in future cases as well as in cultivating a clientele for their services as counsel among the same universe of actors, more or less. The EU proposal does exactly this, by appointing judges to a standing tribunal (who are not therefore always out seeking further ad hoc appointments) and who are prohibited from further counsel work once appointed."[159]

Other stakeholders, however, have been far less enthusiastic in their assessments of the EU proposal, raising various criticisms. It has for instance been pointed out that texts such as CETA incomprehensibly omit the word "arbitrator" from the list of side roles that are prohibited for investment tribunal judges,[160] with all the serious consequences that this may entail.[161]

---

[154] Article 8.30 Ethics. CETA (2016).

[155] Article 14.1. EU-Vietnam FTA (2016).

[156] Article 11 of the Investment Chapter. TTIP (2016).

[157] EU proposal, 14th round. Article 8.1 (Ethics). JEFTA (2016).

[158] Malmström (2015).

[159] Howse (2015). The same author affirms: "Perhaps one of the most egregious ethical lapses in the existing system of investor-state arbitration is the tolerance of arbitrators who at the same time act as counsel in investor-state disputes. Many ISDS insiders see this as entirely normal and appropriate. I find it shocking. It is true that there is no *stare decisis* as a formal matter in ISDS and this is a problem (...) But how is it that an arbitrator who is in active practice can avoid being perceived, in the legal interpretation made as an arbitrator, as swayed either consciously or a subconsciously, by a wanting to create a jurisprudential universe on balance more rather than less favourable to the clients they continue to represent as counsel in other disputes? The perception of non-impartiality would have to be especially acute where an arbitrator is deciding a specific legal issue in one case have another case as counsel where how the very same legal issue is decided has high stakes for their client." Howse (last accessed in June 2018), pp. 10–11.

[160] Van Harten (2016). Footnote 6 to Article 11 of the TTIP has also been controversial ("*For greater certainty, this does not imply that persons who are government officials or receive an income from the government, but who are otherwise independent of the government, are ineligible*"). Dealing with this question, the Investment Treaty Working Group: "This provision raises questions about independence and the objective perception of bias, it must be read with the TTIP Code of Conduct which contains a specific provision on independence including "relationships" and financial interest". Investment Treaty Working Group: Task force report on the Investment Court System Proposal, Pag. 24. http://apps.americanbar.org/dch/thedl.cfm?filename=/IC730000/newsletterpubs/DiscussionPaper101416.pdf.

[161] That is, the current text would in principle allow judges to remain as arbitrators both in investment and commercial cases. Dias Simoes (2018). It has been stated by the Investment Treaty

There is also concern about the details of the incompatibilities regime applicable to these individuals when they are not serving on a full-time basis.[162] This leads to wider doubts about the relationship between the texts' provisions on ethics and the ban on engaging in additional occupations—unless exception is granted—established when the characteristics of these tribunals of first instance and appeal tribunals are being shaped.[163]

Questions could also be raised over the practical functioning of the exemptions regime, the application of which is in the hands of the president of the tribunal of first instance and appeal. The post of president is new, with all the uncertainty that this creates. Moreover, so far there are no further regulations or practical references to how the exceptional granting of exemptions could be handled (which is no trivial matter in the light of ICJ experience in practice).[164] Another major question that will need to be answered is whether it would be possible, or even necessary, to request an exemption during an *ex post* quarantine period as referred to below.[165]

Furthermore, it is believed that the modest monthly retainer fee that members of the tribunal of first instance are supposed to receive during the part-time-activity phase[166] may actually act as a deterrent for the most outstanding

---

Working Group that: "Investment Court members may also engage in potentially troubling conduct if they sit as arbitrators. In such a circumstance, the member may still have an interest in "siding" with one party for additional appointments to tribunals or advisory work taking place outside of the investment court. The context for the consideration of bias regarding members of the Investment Court must be considered in its entirety and not solely regarding the Investment Court". Investment Treaty Working Group (2016), p. 47.

[162]Ridderhof (2016).

[163]Focusing on the 2014 version of TTIP, some academics have interpreted that the ethics provision prohibits some of the multiple scenarios in which the judge/member of the court is acting on a part-time basis (as opposed to a situation in which he/she receives a regular salary because of working full-time). This approach has led to the following statement: "While the general, default rule (judges appointed on a part-time regime, prohibited from acting as counsel in other investment arbitrations [or, in other texts, prohibited also from acting as]) can limit the number of professionals interested in joining the investment court, the full-time option requires that they make an ever harder choice – judge at the investment court or nothing". Dias Simoes (2018). Although this interpretation is plausible, the aforementioned ICJ practice in this area raises the question of whether the EU legislator would in fact be willing to make the "default rule" also applicable to full-time judges.

[164]In this sense, a series of precautions taken into account in the international judicial context may be taken into account in the context of international investments. For example, point 17.3 of the Mont Scopus International Standards states that: "each court should establish an appropriate mechanism to give guidance to judges in relation to extra-judicial activities, and to ensure that appropriate means exist for parties to proceedings to raise any concerns". International Association of Judicial Independence and World Peace (2008).

[165]Article 9 of the 2016 states: "If in doubt as to the application of this article, a former Member may contact the President of the Court of Justice, who shall take a decision after obtaining the opinion of the Committee provided for in Article 10". CJEU (2016).

[166]Following the TTIP proposal, this monthly retainer fee will be around 2,000 euros per month (one third of the retainer fee for WTO Appellate Body Members). Titi (2017). Criticising the relatively low amount proposed for professional retainers and the severe system of incompatibility. EFILA (2016), pp. 55–56.

jurists,[167] as well as encouraging more middle-tier adjudicators to push back the boundaries and continue to undertake other types of professional activity. According to some authors, imposing a complete ban on the exercise of additional activities would mean having to choose investment dispute adjudicators who lacked the most suitable professional profiles,[168] creating circumstances that might impact negatively on key features of the new system, such as the adjudicators' expertise, the speed at which courts functioned, and the legal quality of their decisions.

To sum up, these EU texts currently fail to face a number of important aspects of the external activities undertaken by international adjudicators while serving on international tribunals such as those created by the ICS. In spite of this, the texts still represent a courageous step forward in the IISD context and should serve as a starting point for other contexts such as ICSID reform.

3.4.3.2 Ex-Ante and Ex-Post Quarantine Periods

As mentioned previously, another important question merits individual analysis: the cooling off periods that may be imposed on adjudicators. There are extremely varied and relevant interests at stake when the need to set quarantine periods is decided on, amongst which are confidentiality; adjudicator independence and impartiality; the adjudicators' reputations and that of the institution itself; the parties' right to be judged by highly qualified adjudicators; the adjudicators' right to advance their careers, and the avoiding of excessive restrictions that may affect the adjudicators' financial situation or their pensions.

---

[167] According to recent studies the individual fee per investment arbitrator amounts to USD 426,000 per case on average. Bernasconi-Osterwalder and Brauch (2017), p. 3. With this figures in mind, EFILA has declared that: "the opportunity of sitting on an investment appellate system with few cases to hear, comes at a high cost of being required at the same time to forfeit other professional opportunities. It is not unreasonable to suppose that the brightest and most experienced lawyers, who currently serve as counsel and arbitrators in investment disputes, could turn down an appointment to a less-than-busy appellate body, which would force them to abandon their profitable practice altogether. It is useful to recall that the retainer fee for WTO Appellate Body members amounts approximately to 7,000 Euros per month, a much lower sum than the average monthly income of top lawyers." EFILA (2016), pp. 55–56.

[168] It has been argued that: "Even if such arbitrators [who meet the stringent qualifications for members] could be persuaded, they almost all have full schedules for the next 3–5 years already set out, so would be hard pressed to assume the obligation to reserve time to hear CETA cases on an on-call basis. Academics can, and probably happily would, take on this role. However, it is problematic to only want, or cultivate conditions amenable, to academics serving as arbitrators? International investment law is a complex field, and practical experience arguing and arbitrating such cases is key, in additional to a dual scholar-practitioner or solely academic experience." Sardinha (2018). The author might also contemplate the possibility that, apart from arbitrators, other recognized professionals also have full schedules for the next 3–5 years. In any case, the crucial issue is whether these individuals are willing to forgo such commitments in order to provide an adequate service in courts like the MIC.

From a comparative perspective, pre-service limitations have been for example addressed by the ICJ Practice Direction VII, which refers solely to *ad hoc* judges.[169] Post-service limitations have also been tackled in various documents referring to international adjudicators,[170] such as the ICJ Practice Direction VIII,[171] Article 9 of the Code of Conduct for Members and Former Members of the CJEU,[172] and the Burgh House Principles on the Independence of the International Judiciary.[173]

From a *lege ferenda* perspective, support for a strict and detailed proposal to deal with pre- and post-service limitations in the investment dispute area is to be found in a French document entitled "Towards a new way to settle disputes between states and investors". The text makes a case for drawing up a compulsory code of conduct for arbitrators, which should include 5-year *ex ante* and *ex post* quarantine periods, during which arbitrators shall, respectively "not have acted as legal counsel either for one of the disputing parties or for any third party involved in a previous dispute related to similar facts as those considered in the dispute submitted to the Tribunal" and "act neither as legal counsel of one of the disputing parties, nor as legal counsel of any disputing party involved into another litigation lawsuit related to similar facts that were considered in the dispute on which the tribunal has ruled, unless a time period of 5 years has elapsed between the final award has been issued and the appointment of that former arbitrator as legal counsel".[174]

Article 6 of the Codes of conduct contained in the EU-Singapore IPA, the former EUSFTA, JEFTA, and TTIP offers only very general references that could be interpreted as imposing post-employment restrictions on investment court members: "All former members must avoid actions that may create the appearance that they were biased in carrying out their duties or derived advantage from the decision or

---

[169]Practice Direction VII: "The Court considers that it is not in the interest of the sound administration of justice that a person sit [sic] as judge *ad hoc* in one case who is also acting or has recently acted as agent, counsel or advocate in another case before the Court. Accordingly, parties, when choosing a judge *ad hoc* pursuant to Article 31 of the Statute and Article 35 of the Rules of Court, should refrain from nominating persons who are acting as agent, counsel or advocate in another case before the Court or have acted in that capacity in the three years preceding the date of the nomination. Furthermore, parties should likewise refrain from designating as agent, counsel or advocate in a case before the Court a person who sits as judge *ad hoc* in another case before the Court." ICJ (2013).

[170]This question has also been approached from the legal counsel's perspective in documents such as the Hague Principles on Ethical Standardsfor Counsel Appearing before International Courts and Tribunals, which states that: "The personal interests of counsel create an impermissible conflict where he or she: 4.3.4 has served as a judge or other officer of the international court or tribunal within the previous 3 years or such other period as the court or tribunal may establish by its rules; or 4.3.5 has previously dealt with the case in a judicial capacity". ILA Study Group on the Practice and Procedure of International Tribunals (2010).

[171]Practice Direction VIII. ICJ (2013).

[172]Article 9 CJEU (2016).

[173]Study Group (2004).

[174]French Government (2015).

award of the tribunal or Appeal Tribunal".[175] Although it is indeed a starting point, this type of provision does not fully cover the very broad issue of quarantine periods in contexts such as a prospective MIC.

Some critics consider that the future environment advocated by the EU—without full regulation of stand down periods—will be just as reprehensible as the situation in the past. They envisage "for-profit arbitrators"[176] who go straight "from lawyer to judge, and back again. In other words, the very same private lawyers who have until now driven the boom in investment arbitration and grown their own business—by encouraging investors to sue and by interpreting investment law expansively to encourage more claims—could simply walk through the revolving door and become the EU's new 'super-arbitrators', potentially deciding cases with the interests of previous clients and the arbitration industry in mind. After their term as super-arbitrators, they could directly go back into private practice, and use their past legal interpretations for private gain, including for the benefit of future employers. Also, during their time on the EU's pre-selected list, these super-arbitrators could still earn handsome fees as arbitrators in other cases and work for private law firms (even though they are banned from acting as counsel in other investment protection disputes)".[177]

If this imaginary scenario is not to become fact, future initiatives like the MIC will need to face a number of pre- and post- employment restriction issues head-on.[178] One such issue on which a decision has to be made revolves around whether it is more appropriate to refrain from all mention of specific banned activities by using generic wording such as "avoid actions", or whether it is preferable to take the opposite approach and actually list what will not be tolerated. While the French proposal referred to above solely alludes to various situations in which future or former arbitrators cannot "act as a legal counsel of...", ICJ Practice Direction VIII refers to "appear[ing] as an agent, counsel or advocate in a case before the Court". Another text that originated outside the investment arbitration milieu might also prove a useful reference if there were to be a requirement to list the professional activities that should be temporarily vetoed for future or former MIC judges/

[175]EU-Singapore IPA (2018), the former EUSFTA (2015), JEFTA (2016), and TTIP (2016).

[176]Corporate Europe Observatory (2016), p. 7.

[177]*Ibid*, 26.

[178]Connected with this issue to some extent, the question of renewable or non-renewable appointments is also currently being debated. The majority of the prefers the second option, in the sense that: "the non-renewable factor will maintain the independence of the judges, as there is little incentive to be partial to either side when there is no way to extend a judge's tenure and no way to remove a judge in retaliation". Howard (2018), p. 46. In this sense, this approach coincides with the following scholarly conclusion, which warns of the need for making trade-offs among the following three values: "it is not possible, either in principle or in practice, to maximize simultaneously the three fundamental values of judicial accountability, judicial transparency, and judicial independence (...) For these reasons, we endorse the approach taken by the ECtHR and the ICC, which combines the high transparency of open dissent and the high independence of secure judges with the acceptable decrease in judicial accountability associated with non-renewable terms". Dunoff and Pollack (2017), pp. 268 and 275.

members of the court: the 2014 WTO Post-Employment Guidelines in respect of former Appellate Body Members and former Appellate Body Secretariat staff. They specify the WTO policy regarding a series of legal roles: adviser, panellist, arbitrator, member of a delegation of a participant or third participant.[179]

Another clearly controversial issue with respect to pre- and post-employment restrictions is the time frame during which these measures should be applied.[180] While some proposals use non-specific references such as "during a reasonable time"[181] or "a certain period of grace",[182] the WTO Guidelines provide more precise information, as do documents such as the ICJ Practice Directions VII and VIII,[183] Article 9 of the Code of Conduct for Members and Former Members of the CJEU,[184] and the Burgh House Principles on the Independence of the International Judiciary.[185] These texts all agree that there should be a three year period during which former adjudicators should not participate in any new legal proceedings before the supranational institution on which they have previously served.[186] Likewise, a permanent quarantine period is imposed if the adjudicator actually participated in the legal proceedings or the case was simply raised during the period in which the adjudicator was serving in the court. There also seems to be agreement over not establishing *ex post* cooling off periods in respect of various types of legal work that former adjudicators may wish to carry out in legal contexts outside the body in which they previously held office.

---

[179]The Guidelines state: "A former Appellate Body Member shall not: a) be involved as an adviser or panelist in any dispute or matter the same as one that was before the Appellate Body during his or her term of office as an Appellate Body Member. A former Appellate Body Member may, however, accept appointment as an arbitrator in an arbitration under Article 21.3(c) of the DSU in respect of any dispute; b) for a period of three years following the end of his or her term of office, attend the oral hearing in any appeal before the Appellate Body as a member of a delegation of a participant or third participant; c) for a period of two years following the end of his or her term of office, accept appointment as a panelist in any WTO dispute." WTO (2014). This text also offers guidelines regarding former intern and former member of staff of the Appellate Body Secretariat.

[180]Against temporary prohibitions and vesting periods in investment arbitration, Cleis (2017), p. 204.

[181]Recommendations of the Spanish Arbitration Club (CEA) regarding the Independence and Impartiality of the Arbitrators: "Obligation to maintain independence and impartiality. Arbitrators shall maintain their independence and impartiality and neither they nor their offices shall accept professional assignments from the parties, while they are fulfilling their s functions and for a reasonable time after the termination."(author's translation). "Obligación de mantener la independencia e imparcialidad. Todo árbitro mantendrá su independencia e imparcialidad y ni él ni su despacho aceptarán encargos profesionales de las partes, en tanto no haya cesado en sus funciones y durante un tiempo razonable tras el cese". CEA (last accessed in June 2018).

[182]Baker McKenzie (2017), p. 8.

[183]ICJ (2013).

[184]CJEU (2016)

[185]Study Group (2004).

[186]The referred French proposal extends this period to 5 years but limits it to "dispute/litigation/lawsuit related to similar facts" French Government (2015).

In short, restrictive regulation of the legal activities open to adjudicators during both the *ex ante* and *ex post* quarantine periods and also during their mandate would lead to the gradual introduction of single-hat adjudicators. This would imply a rapprochement with the EU perspective, in which the ICS-MIC is perceived as a public service that is not entirely removed from national judicial contexts where judges cannot simultaneously be lawyers and vice versa. This separation of professional paths would impact on the profile of the duty of disclosure, which would become less onerous; that is, the more professional incompatibilities the fact of being a MIC member created, the fewer circumstances would need to be disclosed by anyone opting solely for this professional path. This correlation will become more evident when inadmissible professional activities are established in greater detail, together with the cooling-off periods.

As already noted, the imposition of single-task adjudicators is nevertheless a very controversial issue. There is clear opposition from powerful stakeholders to the "separate bar" rules, as well as practical doubts as to whether the prohibition will be enforced in the investment context. Under such circumstances, several authors have proposed retaining the double hat system and opting for a less radical and more feasible solution at the level of practice: strengthening current adjudicator disclosure requirements,[187] presently defined by some as merely "minimalistic".[188] The latter reflection is directly linked with adjudicators' duty of disclosure, a topic that is addressed in some depth in these pages.

References

Alliance for Justice (2015) More than 100 legal scholars call on Congress, administration to protect democracy and sovereignty in U.S. trade deals. http://economyincrisis.org/content/more-than-100-legal-scholars-call-on-congress-administration-to-protect-democracy-and-sovereignty-in-u-s-trade-deals

Arias D (2018) Soft law rules in international arbitration: positive effects and legitimation of the IBA as a rule-maker. Indian J Arbitr Law 6(2):29–42

Baker McKenzie (2017) Submissions to the ICSID Secretariat on amendments to the ICSID rules and regulations. https://icsid.worldbank.org/en/Documents/about/Public%20Comments%20to%20Amendment%20to%20ICSID%20Rules%20and%20Regulations.pdf

Ball M (2005) Probity deconstructed: how helpful, really, are the new international bar association guidelines on conflicts of interest in international arbitration? Arbitr Int 21(3):323–341

Bernasconi-Osterwalder N, Brauch MD (2017) Is "Moonlighting" a problem? The role of ICJ judges in ISDS. International Institute for Sustainable Development, Winnipeg. https://www.iisd.org/sites/default/files/publications/icj-judges-isds-commentary.pdf

Bernasconi-Osterwalder N, Johnson L, Marshall F (2010) Arbitrator independence and impartiality: examining the dual role of arbitrator and counsel. International Institute for Sustainable Development, Winnipeg. http://www.iisd.org/pdf/2011/dci_2010_arbitrator_independence.pdf

[187] Ziadé (2009), p. 64; Hwang and Lim (2011), p. 32.

[188] Mann (2005), p. 6.

Brubaker JR (2008) The judge who knew too much: issue conflicts in international adjudication. Berkeley J Int Law 26(1):111–152

Cinelli Moreira NF (2014) The arbitrator's duty of disclosure analyzed through case-law: are the IBA guidelines on conflict of interest in international arbitration enough to create consistency? Revista de Arbitragem e Mediaçao 40:115–150

Claussen K (2018) Tipping point challenges in international economic disputes. Law Pract Int Courts Tribunals 17(1):61–77

Cleis MN (2017) The Independence and impartiality of ICSID arbitrators. Brill Nijhoff, Leiden

Corporate Europe Observatory (2016) The zombie ISDS - rebranded as ICS, rights for corporations to sue states refuse to die. https://corporateeurope.org/sites/default/files/attachments/the_zombie_isds_0.pdf

Cristani F (2014) Challenge and disqualification of arbitrators in international investment arbitration: an overview. Law Pract Int Courts Tribunals 13:153–177

Daele K (2012) Challenge and disqualification of arbitrators in international arbitration. Kluwer, Alphen aan den Rijn

Daele K (2014) Saint Gobain v. Venezuela and Blue Bank v. Venezuela. The standard for disqualifying arbitrators finally settled and lowered. ICSID Rev 29(2):296–305

De Witt Wijnen OLO, Voser N, Rao N (2004) Background information on the IBA guidelines on conflicts of interest in international arbitration. Bus Law Int 5:433–458

Derains & Gharavi (2017) ICSID rules amendment project. https://icsid.worldbank.org/en/Documents/about/Public%20Comments%20to%20Amendment%20to%20ICSID%20Rules%20and%20Regulations.pdf

Dias Simoes F (2018) Hold on to your hat! Issue conflicts in the TTIP proposal for an investment court. Law Pract Int Courts Tribunals 17(1):98–116

Diaz-Candia H (2012) "Issue Conflict" in arbitration as apparently (un)seen in 2011 by a U.S. Court in STMicroelectronics vs. Credite Suisse Securities. Transnational Dispute Manag 9(3):1–10

Dunoff JL, Pollack MA (2017) The Judicial Trilemma. Am J Int Law 111(2):225–276

Eberhardt P, Olivet C (2012) Corporate Europe observatory and the Transnational Institute, profiting from injustice. How law firms, arbitrators and financiers are fuelling an investment arbitration boom. The Transnational Institute, Amsterdam. https://www.tni.org/en/briefing/profiting-injustice

EFILA (2016) Task force paper regarding the proposed International Court System. http://efila.org/wp-content/uploads/2016/02/EFILA_TASK_FORCE_on_ICS_proposal_1-2-2016.pdf

Feerick JD (2002) 1977 Code of Ethics for arbitrators: an outside perspective, the symposium: ethics in a world of mandatory arbitration. Ga State Univ Law Rev 18:907–925

Fernández-Armesto J (2012) Counsel and arbitrator in investment arbitration: does the mixing of the roles nix neutrality? In: IBA Arbitration Day 2012. http://jfarmesto.com/wp-content/uploads/2016/01/Counsel-and-Arbitrator-in-Investment-Arbitration-Does-the-mixing-of-the-roles-nix-neutrality.pdf

Fernández Pérez A (2018) Conflicts of interests of arbitrators in international law firms. Arbitr Int 34(1):1–24

French Government (2015) Towards a new way to settle disputes between states and investors. http://www.diplomatie.gouv.fr/fr/IMG/pdf/20150530_isds_papier_eng_vf_cle09912d.pdf

Freyer DA, Bédard J (2004) The concept of ethical rules or the new IBA guidelines on conflicts of interest in international arbitration. In: ADR & the Law, 21st. edn. Juris Publishing, Huntington, pp 225–244

Fry JD, Stampalija JA (2014) Forged independence and impartiality: conflicts of interest of international arbitrators in investment disputes. Arbitr Int 30(2):189–263

Giorgetti C (2015) The challenge and recusal of judges at the International Court of Justice. In: Giorgetti C (ed) Challenges and recusals of judges and arbitrators in international courts and tribunals. Brill, Leiden, pp 3–33

Giraldo-Carrillo N (2011) The repeat arbitrators' issue: a subjective concept. Int Law Revista Colombiana de Derecho Internacional 19:75–106

Griffith G, Kalderimis D (2016) "Pure" issue conflicts in Investment Treaty Arbitration. In: Caron DD et al (eds) Practising virtue, inside international arbitration. Oxford University Press, Oxford, pp 607–625

Hollander P (2008) Arbitrators' bias because of previous appointments. A civil law perspective. Transnational Dispute Manag 5(4):1–6

Horn P (2014) A matter of appearances: arbitrator independence and impartiality in ICSID arbitration. J Law Bus 11(2):349–395

Howard DM (2018) Creating consistency through a World Investment court. Fordham Int Law J 41 (1):46

Howse R (2015) "Courting the critics of investor-state dispute settlement: the EU proposal for a judicial system for investment disputes". https://cdn-media.web-view.net/i/fjj3t288ah/Courting_the_Criticsdraft1.pdf

Howse R (last accessed in June 2018) Courting the critics of investor-state dispute settlement: the EU proposal for a judicial system for investment disputes. https://cdn-media.web-view.net/i/fjj3t288ah/Courting_the_Criticsdraft1.pdf

Hwang M, Lim K (2011) Issue conflict in ICSID arbitrations. Transnational Dispute Manag 8 (5):1–33

IBA Subcommittee on Investment Treaty Arbitration (2016) Report on the subcommittee on Investment Treaty Arbitration's survey. http://www.ibanet.org/Document/Default.aspx?DocumentUid=65C2AE58-752F-4E8C-900C-1A1FC0C2FD8B

IBA Arbitration Guidelines and Rules Subcommittee (2016) Report on the reception of the IBA arbitration soft law products. https://www.ibanet.org/Document/Default.aspx?DocumentUid=105d29a3-6261-4437-84e2-1c8637844beb

International Council for Commercial Arbitration (2016) Report of the ASIL-ICCA joint task force on issue conflicts in Investor-State Arbitration, The ICCA Reports No. 3. https://www.asil.org/sites/default/files/ASIL_ICCA.pdf

Investment Treaty Working Group (2016) Task force report on the investment court system proposal. http://apps.americanbar.org/dch/thedl.cfm?filename=/IC730000/newsletterpubs/DiscussionPaper101416.pdf

Joelson MR (2015) A critique of the 2014 international bar association guidelines of conflicts of interest in international arbitration. Am Rev Int Arbitr 26(3):483–492

Krajewski M (2014) Modalities for investment protection and ISDS in TTIP from a trade union perspective. Friedrich Ebert Stiftung, Bonn. http://library.fes.de/pdf-files/bueros/bruessel/11044.pdf

Kuo H (2011) The issue of repeat arbitrators: is it a problem and how should the arbitration institutions respond? Contemp Asia Arbitr J 4(2):247–271

Langford M, Behn D, Lie RH (2017) The revolving door in international investment arbitration. J Int Econ Law 20(2):301–332

Law Council of Australia (2017) Potential rule amendments or improvements to the arbitration and conciliation procedures of ICSID, 6. https://icsid.worldbank.org/en/Documents/about/Public%20Comments%20to%20Amendment%20to%20ICSID%20Rules%20and%20Regulations.pdf

Lawson DA (2005) Impartiality and independence of international arbitrators. ASA Bull 1:22–44

Legum B (2005) Investor-State Arbitrator disqualified for pre-appointment statement on challenged measures. Arbitr Int 21(2):241–245. esp. p. 243

Levine J (2015) Late-in the-day arbitrator challenges and resignations. In: Giorgetti C (ed) Challenges and recusals of judges and arbitrators in international courts and tribunals. Brill, Leiden, pp 247–292

Longley N, Ngai J (2016) IBA guidelines on conflict of interest: the traffic lights flash amber. Mealey's Int Arbitr Report 31(4):1–5

Malmström C (2015) Blog Post, "Proposing an Investment Court System". https://ec.europa.eu/commission/2014-2019/malmstrom/blog/proposing-investment-court-system_en

Mann H (2005) The Emperor's clothes come off: a comment on Republic of Ghana v. Telekom Malasya Berhard, and the problem of arbitrator conflict of interest. Transnational Dispute Manag 2(1):1–7
Mouawad C (2008) Issue conflicts in Investment Treaty Arbitration. Transnational Dispute Manag 5(4):1–14
Mourre A, Fouret J (2015) Le chapitre X de l'accord économique et commercial global Canada-Union Européenne: une solution équilibrée au débat sur le recours à l'arbitrage dans le règlement des différends entre investisseurs et États? In: Heuzé V et al (eds) Mélanges en l'honneur du Professeur Pierre Mayer. LGDJ, Paris, pp 571–590
Mullerat Obe R (2012) The IBA guidelines on conflicts of interest revisited. Another contribution to the revision of an excellent instrument, which needs a slight daltonism treatment. Spain Arbitr Rev 14:61–99
Park W (2009) Arbitrator integrity: the transient and the permanent. San Diego Law Rev 46:629–647
Paulsson J (2010) Moral hazard in international dispute resolution. ICSID Rev- Foreign Invest Law J 25(2):339–355
Perry S (2012) Stockholm: the double-hat syndrome. Glob Arbitr Rev 7(2):43
Ridderhof R (2016) Investment protection: ISDS or ICS. Peace Palace Library, The Hague. https://www.peacepalacelibrary.nl/2016/05/investment-protection-isds-or-ics/
Rubins N, Lauterburg B (2010) Independence, impartiality and duty of disclosure in investment arbitration. In: Knahr C, Koller C, Rechberger W, Reinisch A (eds) Investment and commercial arbitration. Similarities and divergences. Eleven International Publishing, The Hague, pp 153–180
Sands P (2012) Conflict and conflicts in Investment Treaty Arbitration: ethical standards for counsel. In: Rovine A (ed) Contemporary issues in international arbitration and mediation: the Fordham papers. Brill, New York, pp 28–49
Sardinha E (2018) Party-appointed arbitrators no more: the EU-led investment tribunal system as an (Imperfect?) response to certain legitimacy concerns in Investor-State Arbitration. Law Pract Int Courts Tribunals 17(1):117–1332
Schacherer S (2016) TPP, CETA and TTIP between innovation and consolidation-resolving investor-state disputes under Mega-regionals. J Int Dispute Settlement 7(3):628–653
Schill S (2014) The new journal of World Investment and Trade: arbitrator independence and academic freedom. J World Invest Trade 15:1–11
Shetreet S (2003) Standards of conduct of international judges: outside activities. Law Pract Int Courts Tribunals 2:127–161
Sobota LA (2015) Repeat arbitrator appointments in international investment disputes. In: Giorgetti C (ed) Challenges and recusals of judges and arbitrators in international courts and tribunals. Brill, Leiden, pp 293–319
The IBA Conflicts of Interest Subcommittee (2010) The IBA guidelines on conflicts of interest in international arbitration: the first five years 2004–2009. Disput Resolut Int 4(1):1–52
Titi C (2017) The European Union's proposal for an international investment court: significance, innovations and challenges ahead. Transnational Dispute Manag 1:1–35
UNCITRAL (2018) Report of the Working Group III (Investor-State Dispute settlement reform) on the work of its thirty-fifth session. http://www.uncitral.org/uncitral/en/commission/working_groups/3Investor_State.html
UNCTAD (2015) World Investment Report 2015. http://unctad.org/en/PublicationsLibrary/wir2015_en.pdf, p 152
Van Harten G (2016) "Key flaws in the EC's proposals for foreign investor in TTIP". In: Osgoode legal studies research paper. https://papers.ssrn.com/sol3/papers.cfm?abstract_id=2692122
Zamour R (2015) Issue conflicts and the reasonable expectation of an open mind: the challenge decision in Devas v. India and its impact. In: Giorgetti C (ed) Challenges and recusals of judges and arbitrators in international courts and tribunals. Brill, Leiden, pp 227–245

Ziadé NG (2009) How many hats can a player wear: arbitrator, counsel and expert? ICSID Rev 24 (1):49–64

Legal and Arbitration References

IIAs

CETA (2014) http://trade.ec.europa.eu/doclib/docs/2014/september/tradoc_152806.pdf
CETA (2016) http://ec.europa.eu/trade/policy/in-focus/ceta/ceta-chapter-by-chapter/
EUSFTA (2015) http://investmentpolicyhub.unctad.org/Download/TreatyFile/3247
EU-Singapore IPA (2018) http://trade.ec.europa.eu/doclib/press/index.cfm?id=961
EU-Vietnam FTA (2016) http://trade.ec.europa.eu/doclib/docs/2016/february/tradoc_154226.pdf
Federal Ministry for Economic Affairs and Energy (2015) Project No. 83/15. Model Bilateral Investment Treaty with investor-state dispute settlement for industrial countries, giving consideration to the U.S. https://www.rph1.rw.fau.de/files/2016/02/150429-muster-bit-fr-industriestaaten-krajewski-englische-bersetzung.pdf
JEFTA (2016) https://trade-leaks.org/jefta-leaks/investment-dispute-resolution/
Kingdom of the Netherlands (2018) Netherlands draft model BIT. https://www.internetconsultatie.nl/investeringsakkoorden/document/3586
Kingdom of Norway (2015) Agreement between the Kingdom of Norway and for the promotion and protection of investments. https://www.regjeringen.no/contentassets/e47326b61f424d4c9c3d470896492623/draft-model-agreement-english.pdf
NAFTA (1994) Code of conduct. https://www.nafta-sec-alena.org/Home/Legal-Texts/Code-of-Conduct?mvid=1&secid=03428812-a551-4839-ab16-669c9d2a82e1
TTIP (2016) http://trade.ec.europa.eu/doclib/press/index.cfm?id=1230
Southern African Development Community (2012) Model Bilateral Investment Treaty. http://www.iisd.org/itn/wp-content/uploads/2012/10/sadc-model-bit-template-final.pdf

Arbitration Acts, Institutional Arbitration Rules, and Codes of Conduct

ABA, AAA, CPR Institute (2004) Code of ethics for arbitrators in commercial disputes. https://www.americanbar.org/content/dam/aba/migrated/dispute/commercial_disputes.authcheckdam.pdf
CAM (2010a) Arbitration rules. http://www.camera-arbitrale.it/Documenti/cam_arbitration-rules_2010.pdf
CAM (2010b) Code of ethics. https://www.camera-arbitrale.it/en/arbitration/arbitration-rules/code-of-ethics.php?id=104
CAM (2010c) Statement of independence of the arbitrator. Filling in notes. http://www.camera-arbitrale.it/Documenti/disclosure_en.pdf
CAS (2010) Code of sports-related arbitration. http://www.tas-cas.org/fileadmin/user_upload/Code_2017_FINAL__en_.pdf
CEA (last accessed in June 2018) Recommendations of the Spanish Arbitration Club regarding the independence and impartiality of the arbitrators. https://www.clubarbitraje.com/sites/default/files/recomendaciones_0.pdf

IBA (2004) Guidelines on conflicts of interest in international arbitration. http://www.ibanet.org/Document/Default.aspx?DocumentUid=21D27F55-134B-4791-A01C-F8B6658BAB24

IBA (2014) Guidelines on conflicts of interest in international arbitration. https://www.ibanet.org/Publications/publications_IBA_guides_and_free_materials.aspx#Practice%20Rules%20and%20Guidelines

ICC (2017) Note to parties and arbitral tribunals on the conduct of the arbitration under the ICC rules of arbitration. https://iccwbo.org/publication/note-parties-arbitral-tribunals-conduct-arbitration/

KLRCA (2013) Revised code of conduct for arbitrator. https://klrca.org/uploads/imguploadckc691e4fcd34a3f05e49b8eb477d2ec21.PDF

SIAC (2015) Code of ethics for an arbitrator. http://www.siac.org.sg/our-rules/code-of-ethics-for-an-arbitrator

TAB/BAC (2009) Code of ethics. http://www.tab.es/index.php?option=com_content&view=article&id=638:barcelona-arbitration-court-code-of-ethics&catid=29&lang=en&Itemid=426

Legal Documents

CJEU (2007) Code of conduct for members and former members of the court of justice of the European Union. http://eur-lex.europa.eu/LexUri-Serv/LexUriServ.do?uri=OJ:C:2007:223:0001:0002:EN:PDF

CJEU (2016) Code of conduct for members and former members of the court of justice of the European Union. http://eur-lex.europa.eu/legal-content/EN/TXT/PDF/?uri=OJ:C:2016:483:FULL&from=FR

ECHR (2008) Resolution on judicial ethics. http://www.echr.coe.int/Documents/Resolution_Judicial_Ethics_ENG.pdf

ICJ (1946) Statute of the ICJ. http://www.icj-cij.org/en/statute

ILA Study Group on the Practice and Procedure of International Tribunals (2010) Hague principles on ethical standards for counsel appearing before international courts and tribunals. http://www.ucl.ac.uk/laws/cict/docs/Hague_Sept2010.pdf

Institute of International Law (2011) Rhodes resolution of the institute of international law on the position of the international judge. http://www.idi-iil.org/app/uploads/2017/06/2011_rhodes_06_en.pdf

International Association of Judicial Independence and World Peace (2008) Mount Scopus approved revised international standards of judicial independence. http://www.cristidanilet.ro/docs/MtScopusInternationalStandrds.pdf

ICJ (2013) Practice directions. http://www.icj-cij.org/en/practice-directions

Judicial Group on Strengthening Judicial Integrity (2002) Bangalore principles of judicial conduct. https://www.unodc.org/pdf/crime/corruption/judicial_group/Bangalore_principles.pdf

Study Group of the International Law Association on the Practice and Procedure of International Courts and Tribunals, in association with the Project on International Courts and Tribunals (2004) Burgh House Principles on the Independence of the International Judiciary. https://www.ucl.ac.uk/international-courts/sites/international-courts/files/burgh_final_21204.pdf

WTO (1994) Understanding on rules and procedures governing the settlement of disputes. https://www.wto.org/english/tratop_e/dispu_e/dsu_e.htm

WTO (1996) Rules of conduct for the understanding on rules and procedures governing the settlement of disputes. WT/DSB/RC/1 (96-5267), https://www.wto.org/english/tratop_e/dispu_e/rc_e.htm

WTO (2014) Post-Employment Guidelines in respect of former Appellate Body Members and former Appellate Body Secretariat staff. https://www.wto.org/english/news_e/news14_e/ab_16apr14_e.htm

Chapter 4
The Duty of Personal Diligence and Integrity

This chapter aims to define the contours of the duty of personal diligence and integrity. This duty is highly complex, and this chapter deals with three different facets of this duty individually: non-delegation of responsibilities; time-related availability, and appropriate behaviour. Each section of this chapter examines the way in which these concepts have been shaped, in both commercial arbitration and in other contexts, such as the judicial, when necessary. The final aim is to put forward practical ideas on the specific content that should be attributed to these notions in the investment arbitration environment. It is also argued that these issues will need to be defined more clearly in the future, in contexts such as ICSID, the ICS, and a possible MIC.

Settling on the most appropriate wording for the title of this chapter ("The Duty of Personal Diligence and Integrity") was not easy, partly since the various texts analysed use different terms, and partly because the duties discussed here cannot be treated as watertight compartments. On the contrary, the vast majority of arbitrators' duties are interconnected to some extent. They can therefore be placed at different points within the general framework of arbitrator's duties contained for instance in Codes of conduct, without undermining the overall charter of duties.

4.1 Non-Delegation of Responsibilities

In a general sense, there is no debate as to whether arbitrators have a duty with regard to personal performance. An arbitrator's mandate arises from the disputing parties' exercise of their own autonomy, and is therefore viewed as an *intuitu personae* question.[1] However, the fact that international arbitrations are becoming

[1]According to academics, "It is axiomatic to say of an arbitrator's mission that it is *intuitu personae*. A party's choice of arbitrator is, of essence, personal, and so is the chosen arbitrator's mandate. In

K. Fach Gómez, *Key Duties of International Investment Arbitrators*,
https://doi.org/10.1007/978-3-319-98128-4_4

increasingly complex and lengthy and involving ever more actors and resources not only means that arbitrators need to possess highly specific personal characteristics and outstanding qualifications,[2] but also have to make themselves available for long periods of time.

For this reason, appointing an administrative secretary to save both time and money[3] is not unusual in international commercial and investment arbitration.[4] However, the practice also creates uncertainties and tensions, partly with regard to the individual arbitrators' duty to carry out their tasks in person, and partly when the array of different duties to be performed by either the arbitrator or the secretary have to be defined in detail.

Establishing which specific responsibilities can be delegated to third parties without breaching the duty referred to above is currently a highly controversial issue.[5] In addition, arbitration practice—mostly focused on commercial arbitration—has shown that inappropriate use of administrative secretaries on the part of arbitral tribunal members not only represents a betrayal of party expectations, but is also a harmful praxis that could lead to serious legal problems, such as the removal

---

accepting appointment, an arbitrator necessarily accepts a duty not to delegate that mandate". Partasides (2002), p. 147. This is also clearly stated, for example, in the FAI Note: "The mandate of an arbitrator is personal. By accepting appointment, an arbitrator undertakes not to delegate the mandate to any other person, including any tribunal-appointed secretary. An arbitrator may under no circumstances rely on a secretary to perform any essential duties of an arbitrator." Note FAI (2016).

[2]*Infra*, Sect. 6.2.

[3]An administrative secretary is paid less than an arbitrator, and the former's work allows the latter to concentrate on the essence of the case and issue the award more quickly.

[4]The 2012 International Arbitration Survey by White & Case and Queen Mary University indicates that tribunal secretaries are appointed in 35% of commercial cases (46% in civil law arbitrations and 24% in common law arbitrations). White & Case (2012), p. 44.

[5]What is unquestionable in all the texts consulted is that administrative secretaries are bound by the same duty of independence and impartiality as arbitrators. See, for instance: ICC Note: "Administrative Secretaries must satisfy the same independence and impartiality requirements as those which apply to arbitrators under the Rules" ICC (2017b), par 146; IBA Guidelines: "(5) Scope: (b) Arbitral or administrative secretaries and assistants, to an individual arbitrator or the Arbitral Tribunal, are bound by the same duty of independence and impartiality as arbitrators, and it is the responsibility of the Arbitral Tribunal to ensure that such duty is respected at all stages of the arbitration" IBA (2014); Research based report on the use of tribunal secretaries in international commercial arbitration: "5 b) Some arbitration institutions require arbitral or administrative secretaries and assistants to sign a declaration of independence and impartiality. Whether or not such a requirement exists, arbitral or administrative secretaries and assistants to the Arbitral Tribunal are bound by the same duty of independence and impartiality (including the duty of disclosure) as arbitrators, and it is the responsibility of the Arbitral Tribunal to ensure that such duty is respected at all stages of the arbitration. Furthermore, this duty applies to arbitral or administrative secretaries and assistants to either the Arbitral Tribunal or individual members of the Arbitral Tribunal", Berwin, Leighton, Paisner (2015); and Article 2.10 of the 2014 HKIAC Guidelines on the Use of a Secretary to the Arbitral Tribunal: "A tribunal secretary shall be subject to the same standards of impartiality and independence as the arbitral tribunal". HKIAC (2014). This idea is also conveniently reflected in the most recent EU texts on investment disputes.

of the arbitrator by a national court; the setting aside of the arbitral award; refusal to enforce the award, or—in specific contexts—a professional misconduct lawsuit being filed against the arbitrator(s).

4.1.1 International Commercial Arbitration

To take commercial arbitration as a starting point, an analysis of various texts addressing the issue of the administrative secretary's role shows that they contain dissimilarities at both terminological and drafting levels. Although these may appear trivial at first glance, in practice they may actually mark important differences. Accordingly:

The arbitrators' duty to perform their tasks personally is developed at some length in the ICC Note to parties and arbitral tribunals on the conduct of arbitration under the ICC rules of arbitration.[6] The text specifically states that, "Under no circumstances may the arbitral tribunal delegate decision-making functions to an Administrative Secretary. Nor should the arbitral tribunal rely on the Administrative Secretary to perform any essential duties of an arbitrator".[7] In the absence of any definition of the notions of arbitrators' "decision-making functions" or "essential duties", the examples provided by the Note of which are the "organizational and administrative tasks" that an administrative secretary could indeed perform show that the ICC does not intend this last notion to be interpreted expansively. For instance, the administrative secretary's functions with regard to procedural orders and awards are limited to "proof-reading and checking citations, dates and cross-references (. . .), as well as correcting typographical, grammatical or calculation errors".[8] This restrictive approach is also reflected in the Note when it specifically

---

[6]The essential ideas in this ICC Note (2017b) are reproduced by other arbitration institutions, such as Article 22 of the CIMA Arbitration Rules: "Administrative Secretary of the Arbitral Tribunal: "At any time during the arbitration proceedings and after seeking the express views of the parties, the Arbitral Tribunal may propose the appointment of an administrative Secretary. If any of the parties object to the proposal, the Arbitral Tribunal shall not proceed with the appointment. The administrative Secretary of the Arbitral Tribunal shall act, at all times, under the strict supervision of the Arbitral Tribunal and according to the directions and instructions given them. The Arbitral Tribunal shall, at all times, be responsible for the conduct of its administrative Secretary in relation with the arbitration. Under no circumstances shall the Arbitral Tribunal delegate its decision-making functions or the performance of any of its essential duties to its administrative Secretary, who will not participate in the deliberations of the Arbitral Tribunal. The appointment of an administrative Secretary of the Arbitral Tribunal shall not involve any additional cost to the parties. The Arbitral Tribunal shall not request of the Court any compensation for the activities of its administrative Secretary". CIMA (2015).

[7]ICC (2017a), par 151.

[8]*Ibid,* par 150. Very similar wording appears in the FAI Note on the Use of a Secretary: "In addition, a secretary may provide limited assistance to the arbitral tribunal in its decision-making process, as long as the arbitral tribunal ensures that the secretary does not assume any decision-making function of the tribunal, or otherwise influence the tribunal's decisions in any manner. Such

refers to the drafting of written notes or memoranda: "A request by an arbitral tribunal to an Administrative Secretary to prepare written notes or memoranda shall in no circumstances release the arbitral tribunal from its duty personally to review the file and/or to draft any decision of the arbitral tribunal".[9] This Note also reflects the arbitral tribunals' duty of supervision with respect to their administrative secretaries,[10] and also reinforces the ICC Secretariat's role should there be any doubts regarding the division of tasks.[11]

When dealing with this question, the LCIA makes an interesting clarification concerning the administrative secretary's somewhat limited range of functions. On the one hand, the LCIA Secretariat itself provides the tribunal and the parties with administrative support, such as to "finalise arrangements for hearing venues, transcripts and so on; provide any reminders that may be required on the procedural timetable; and deal with all matters required of it under the LCIA Rules". On the other hand, the administrative secretary's tasks should not constitute a delegation of the tribunal's authority. Therefore, if the court wishes to appoint an administrative secretary—provided that the parties agree, and subject to the usual conflict checks—the secretary's activities should be confined "to such matters as organising papers for the Tribunal, highlighting relevant legal authorities, maintaining factual chronologies, keeping the Tribunal's time sheets and so forth."[12]

Texts such as the HKIAC Guidelines on the Use of a Secretary to the Arbitral Tribunal contain an internal classification of possible tasks that can be assumed by the court secretary. This classification shows certain similarities to texts such as the 2014 IBA Guidelines on Conflict of Interest, which include green, orange and red lists. The HKIAC thus distinguishes between (a) the "organizational and administrative tasks", which are given the green light "unless the arbitral tribunal directs otherwise"; (b) more controversial tasks such as "preparing drafts of non-substantive letters for the arbitral tribunal and non-substantive parts of the tribunal's orders,

assistance may include, but is not limited to, the following tasks: (i) proofreading and checking the accuracy of cross-references, citations, dates and other figures in draft procedural orders and awards as well as correcting any clerical, typographical or computational errors found in the drafts". The FAI text continues specifying: "Such assistance may include, but is not limited to, the following tasks: "collecting case law or published commentaries on legal issues defined by the arbitral tribunal, preparing summaries from case law and publications as well as producing memoranda summarising the parties' respective submissions and the evidence supporting those submissions, provided that the arbitral tribunal refrains from relying solely on a secretary's work to the exclusion of its own review of the file and legal authorities". FAI (2016), point 3.4.

[9]ICC (2017b), par 153.

[10]*Ibid,* (2017), par 149: "Administrative Secretaries act upon the arbitral tribunal's instructions and under its strict supervision. The arbitral tribunal shall, at all times, be responsible for the Administrative Secretary's conduct in relation to the arbitration".

[11]*Ibid,* "When in doubt about which tasks may be performed by an Administrative Secretary, the arbitral tribunal or the Administrative Secretary should contact the Secretariat". ICC (2017b), par 154.

[12]LCIA (last accessed June 2018).

decisions and awards (such as procedural histories and chronologies of events)"[13] that can be undertaken by the secretary if the following circumstances co-exist: "Unless the parties agree or the arbitral tribunal directs otherwise (. . .) provided that the arbitral tribunal ensures that the secretary does not perform any decision-making function or otherwise influence the arbitral tribunal's decisions in any manner", and finally (c) the tasks that the secretary cannot assume, since they are the arbitral tribunal's personal duty, such as to "review the relevant files and materials, and to draft any substantive parts of its orders, decisions and awards".[14]

The 2014 Young International Council for Commercial Arbitration (ICCA) Guide on Arbitral Secretaries, drafted by the Young ICCA Task Force on the Appointment and Use of Arbitral Secretaries,[15] seems to advocate delegating a broader range of tasks to the arbitral secretary. The document begins by highlighting an arbitrator's duty: "It shall be the responsibility of each arbitrator not to delegate any part of his or her personal mandate to any other person, including an arbitral secretary".[16] Nevertheless, Article 3 contains a description of the specific tasks that may be delegated to an arbitral secretary, and in some points these go beyond purely administrative functions, for instance: "(h) Reviewing the parties' submissions and evidence, and drafting factual chronologies and memoranda summarizing the parties' submissions and evidence"; and "(j) Drafting appropriate parts of the award". The Commentary to this provision states: "The drafting of awards can be a time-consuming process for a sought-after arbitrator with a demanding schedule of commitments. To assist, an arbitral secretary may legitimately be used to prepare first drafts of certain sections of the award."[17] The Commentary to Article 3 goes into this question in more depth, recognizing that 67% of respondents in the 2013 Survey were opposed to tasking the arbitral secretary with drafting the whole award, and that only 31.9% felt comfortable about the arbitral secretary drafting the award's legal reasoning section. However, the Guide also emphasizes that the majority would allow the secretary to produce first drafts of other award sections, as follows: "Procedural Background" (84.9%); "Factual Background" (69.4%); and "Parties' Positions" (65.3%).[18]

---

[13]Likewise, Article 3.4.(c) of the HKIAC Guidelines also refer to "preparing summaries from case law and publications as well as producing memoranda summarising the parties' respective submissions and evidence". HKIAC (2014).

[14]Article 3. Duties. It is also relevant that the purely administrative tasks are an open list ("including, but not limited to, the following") while the more substantive functions are a closed list". HKIAC (2014).

[15]Young International Council for Commercial Arbitration (2014).

[16]*Idem,* Article 1(4), p. 5.

[17]*Idem,* Article 3, p. 11.

[18]*Ibid,* Article 3, p. 15. More recent studies indicate and reinforce this resistance to delegating certain non-administrative tasks to the administrative secretary: "Only a minority thought that it would be appropriate for the secretary to carry out functions that involved an assessment or analysis of evidence (14% in the case of a written legal analysis of the parties' arguments, 24% in relation to a review of evidence and 33% in connection with preparation of a summary of fact or expert

The broad approach advocated by the Young ICCA's Guide is perfectly understandable considering the document's authorship[19]: a stakeholder that would certainly be in favour of reducing the difficulties in accessing the closed world of international arbitration, and for whom the opportunity to act as administrative secretary may be excellent training for future arbitral appointments. Since it can be supposed that one priority for senior arbitrators is being appointed to a high number of disputes and having the support of efficient assistants so that the cases can be completed quickly and they can then be reappointed to new controversies, these powerful interests all converge in support of consolidating the role of administrative secretaries. Their functions in international commercial arbitration are therefore likely to be reinforced in the future, expanding into grey areas such as drafting the section of awards referring to the parties' positions. It consequently seems unrealistic to claim that arbitrators should decline appointment in cases in which they would require assistance from an administrative secretary. Although this would undoubtedly have the desired effect of opening up the arbitral market and increasing diversity, arbitrators are unlikely to withdraw just because they are politely reminded that they are free to do so whenever they are approached to resolve a case.[20]

All the above leads to the conclusion that it might be misleading to categorically state that arbitrators in the international commercial arbitration context have an unshakable duty to perform all their functions in person.[21] Reality in both this sector and the texts on which it is based shows that administrative secretaries currently play

evidence for inclusion in the award). Writing substantive parts of the award relating to the merits or a determination on the issues was a definite no-go area with only 10% of those responding expressing the view that this was an appropriate task for the tribunal secretary." Berwin, Leighton Paisner (2015), p. 11.

[19]The Young ICCA was established in 2010 and is a world-wide arbitration knowledge and skills network for young practitioners. Participation is open to law students, faculty members and young practitioners under the age of 40. Young ICCA (last accessed June 2018).

[20]Offering an interesting reflection on this issue: "often arbitrator candidates get too easily tempted by a seemingly interesting and lucrative arbitrator mandate without fully inquiring about the magnitude of the function (...) it would be wise (...) to remind [arbitrators] of Karl-Heinz Böckstiegel's admonishment that there is always the choice to "just say no" to another demanding engagement that might risk one's well-deserved reputation". Wilske (2014), p. 301.

[21]In addition to what has been discussed so far, this duty may be opposed by various exceptions. It is thus plausible that the delegation of the arbitrator's duty to personally perform decision-making functions may be imposed by the applicable law. For instance, Rule 7 of the CIArb Code states: "Conduct of the Process. A member shall not delegate any duty to decide to any other person unless permitted to do so by the parties or applicable law." CIArb (2009). It is also possible that, as the UNCITRAL Notes indicate, the delegation is a logical consequence of the very nature of a certain type of arbitration, in which non-legal adjudicators need legal advice from the legally trained administrative secretary. Point 36: "it is recognized that secretaries are not involved and do not participate in the decision-making of the arbitral tribunal, except in certain rare, specialized types of arbitration (for example, where the specific arbitration rules provide that secretaries are expected to provide legal advice in relation to the decision of the arbitral tribunal if and when the arbitral tribunal is composed only of non-lawyer, subject matter specialists)". UNCITRAL (2016). This admissible typology has to be clearly differentiated from other inadmissible cases. For example, the Italian Supreme Court clearly criticized the employment, without the parties' consent, of a lawyer

an active and relevant role in commercial arbitration. They are unquestionably in charge of multiple organizational and administrative tasks, and, while as a rule their tasks do not involve decision-making, they do sometimes exceed administrative tasks. Drawing a firm line between the two types of tasks is extremely complex, as shown by the current lack of unanimity among both institutional rules and scholars.

If administrative secretaries in commercial arbitration are here to stay, as they would seem to be, it appears that changes are needed to reduce the uncertainties arising from their participation as far as possible. Any such adjustments must be driven by two factors: party autonomy and the shockwave of new provisions and/or institutional rules and guidelines on the issue.

Party autonomy is a governing principle of arbitration, and its intervention in the question of arbitral secretaries may be reflected either via an ex ante party agreement accepting an administrative secretary and according her/him a specific level of involvement in the arbitration,[22] or via a detailed agreement on the issue within the framework of express consent when the arbitral tribunal has already informed the parties of its intention to appoint a secretary. However, if this type of precaution is to become more widespread in the future, arbitral institutions need to develop a stronger role. Supplying the parties with a detailed form covering issues such as those set out below, to ensure that all relevant points were dealt with, could be an effective means of enabling the parties to assign secretarial power on a case by case basis.

In addition, if provisions for arbitral secretaries were included within the procedural law applicable in the arbitration case, uncertainty in this matter would also be reduced.[23] In the same vein, the proliferation of well-grounded proposals in institutional arbitration may also encourage regulatory interest in national and supranational legislators.[24] Some points to consider in these texts may be the following: firstly, the issue of how the arbitrators' duty of transparency can be reinforced with

---

who was tasked with drafting the final award, which the non-legal arbitrators were not able to either draw up or critically examine. Galagan and Živković (2015).

[22]The standard arbitration agreement does not usually deal with the issue of the arbitral secretary. Altenkirch and Schmeil (2015) (referring to investment arbitration).

[23]Referring to an example of investment arbitration, this issue is not always developed in hard law: "In order to establish the job description of the arbitral secretary, one should consult the applicable procedural rules, which may differ from case to case. As set out above, the applicable procedural rules in this case are the Dutch Code of Civil Procedure and the UNCITRAL Rules. Because it concerns regulations that are applied in an international case, an interpretation must also take international practice into account (...) the Tribunal was appointed according to the UNCITRAL Rules. Like the Dutch Code of Civil Procedure, these arbitration rules do not contain any explicit provisions regarding the role of the arbitral secretary that are relevant here. This means that the job description of the arbitral secretary is mostly to be found in international practice". Writ of summons, par 485–486.

[24]Addressing the crucial issue of the hierarchy between these types of sources, see for example point 1.5 of the HKIAC Guidelines: "In the event of any discrepancy or inconsistency between these Guidelines and any contrary provisions of the parties' arbitration agreement or mandatory provisions of the applicable law, those provisions shall prevail." HKIAC (2014).

regard to the secretary's involvement in the arbitral proceedings needs to be addressed.[25] The fact that the transparency aim has not always been evident in recent arbitration practice will be discussed later.[26] Along these lines, the 2016 UNCITRAL Notes on Organizing Arbitral Proceedings offer the following suggestions regarding information to be shared with the parties: "If the arbitral tribunal wishes to appoint a secretary, it would normally disclose this fact to the parties, along with the identity of the proposed secretary, the nature of the tasks to be performed by the secretary, and the amount and source of any proposed remuneration. The parties may wish to agree on the role and practices to be adopted in respect of the secretaries, as well as on the financial conditions applicable to their services;"[27] A second relevant issue to be dealt with in this future regulation of arbitral secretary involves the fact that, regardless of the point at which party autonomy comes into play, the parties in the arbitration not only would have to consent to the appointment of a secretary to the court in a general sense, but would they also have to authorize the appointing of a specific individual.[28] Thirdly, it also has to be stressed that the secretary must comply with high levels of disclosure and other duties that are consistent with his/her relevant tasks. Fourthly, the individual's professional profile and the possible need for specific training should also be considered.[29] A decision should also be made on how to value the participation of an extremely well- or overqualified secretary, in terms of possible influence on the arbitrators' decision, for

[25]The contrary could lead to the argument that if the secretary's tasks go beyond what the parties have consented to, the arbitrators would be breaking their confidentiality obligation regarding the parties. This idea has been pointed out, for example, in the case Fábrica v. Venezuela: "these evidence (sic) would also demonstrate that [the arbitrator] "breached the confidentiality of this arbitration by granting unauthorized and undisclosed access to the record of the case to [the assistant] an employee of a law firm that is counsel of record to neither party in this arbitrator"". Fábrica v. Venezuela (2017), par 48.

[26]*Infra,* Chap. 5.

[27]UNCITRAL Notes (2016), point 38.

[28]Andersson (2015), p. 42.

[29]One recent initiative is the implementation of accreditation programmes for court secretaries. In 2015 the HKIAC launched an initiative of this type allowing participants that passed the exams to be eligible for appointment for any ad hoc or institutional arbitration. The programme involves a series of lectures, group discussions on case studies, and debates to educate the participants in all the skills required from competent court secretaries. The training also deals in detail with the harmful effects of a court's improper delegation of duties to court secretaries and prepares them to deal with this type of situation. Benson (2016). This initiative seems to become widespread, and the ICC Institute of World Business Law is offering a Training for Court Secretaries, which covers the following topics: What is expected from a tribunal secretary?, the appointment of tribunal secretaries, overview of the tribunal secretary's tasks and role in the organization of the proceedings, the support provided by tribunal secretaries from receipt of the case file until the signature of the terms of reference, the support provided by tribunal secretaries from the signature of the terms of reference until the evidentiary hearing, procedural aspects, technological aspects, and the award. ICC Institute of World Business Law (2018).

instance.[30] Fifthly, in connection with this, any supervisory measures to be undertaken by the arbitrators vis-à-vis the secretary should be specified,[31] and finally, the secretary's profile must be clearly drawn with respect to other actors that may concur in the arbitration, such as the person appointed by the arbitral institution to provide support during the proceedings.

4.1.2 International Investment Arbitration

Focusing attention in the context of international investment arbitration, Regulation 25 of the ICSID Administrative and Financial Regulations states that: "the Secretary-General shall appoint a Secretary for each Commission, Tribunal and Committee. The Secretary may be drawn from among the Secretariat of the Centre, and shall in any case, while serving in that capacity, be considered as a member of its staff".[32] All ICSID arbitrations therefore have an ICSID secretary,[33] whose non-decision-making tasks are specified in the Regulation.[34]

It is also clear from ICSID practice that the arbitrators making up the arbitral court may have an assistant during the arbitration in addition to the official ICSID secretary. This post is referred to as "(legal) assistant to the court" and while this

[30]Schwartz reports that: "in at least one case, the [ICC] Court required a tribunal to replace a secretary when the person originally appointed was a well-known arbitrator and arbitration authority in his own right." Schwartz (1995), p. 86.

[31]Some authors have proposed that a secretary should only be allowed to prepare draft procedural orders and non-substantive portions of awards if the tribunal gives the secretary detailed guidance before drafting, and the draft is scrutinized by the entire tribunal before it is finalised; thus, the responsibility for the contents remains with the members of the tribunal. With regard to the first requisite, Polkinghorne and Rosenberg state that it "ordinarily can be accomplished by having the secretary attend deliberations and be privy to the views of the tribunal". Polkinghorne and Rosenberg (2014).

[32]ICSID (2006).

[33]Unlike in ICSID, ICC staff members are not permitted to serve as Administrative Secretaries. ICC (2017b), point 146. On the other hand, other commercial arbitration institutions, such as HKIAC, do allow it: "A member of the HKIAC Secretariat may be appointed as a tribunal secretary subject to confirmation regarding his or her availability, impartiality and independence in accordance with paragraph 2.2. Such Secretariat member shall not act as a case manager in the same arbitration (...). The appointment of a tribunal secretary from the HKIAC Secretariat requires confirmation by HKIAC". HKIAC (2014).

[34]The secretary's tasks are specified in ICSID Regulation 25: "He shall (a) represent the Secretary-General and may perform all functions assigned to the latter by these Regulations or the Rules with regard to individual proceedings or assigned to the latter by the Convention, and delegated by him to the Secretary; (b) be the channel through which the parties may request particular services from the Centre; (c) keep summary minutes of hearings, unless the parties agree with the Commission, Tribunal or Committee on another manner of keeping the record of the hearings; and (d) perform other functions with respect to the proceeding at the request of the President of the Commission, Tribunal or Committee, or at the direction of the Secretary-General." ICSID (2006).

is not the norm in ICSID arbitrations, an analysis of ICSID awards and decisions issues over recent years shows that it is on the increase. When ICSID cases have employed an assistant, the initiative has usually come from the president of the court, who has sometimes expressly indicated that the assistant's role is to help him or her,[35] while at other times the assistant's remit has been to help the court as a whole. ICSID casuistry also permits an assistant to be appointed to provide support to a specific arbitrator—who is not the president—for example, when an arbitrator is disqualified and the replacement is forced to join a case that is already underway.[36]

ICSID arbitration assistants usually have a previous professional relationship with the chairman, and this is expressly stated in some awards.[37] Trust and a high degree of professional esteem between nominator and nominee are therefore essential elements of the relationship,[38] although naturally this does not prevent the assistant from being replaced in the course of the arbitration on a number of

[35]It is stated that: "The Parties signified their agreement (subject to final confirmation by the Respondent, later received) to the President's proposal to appoint a Legal Assistant from his Chambers to assist him in the proceedings", Rompetrol v. Romania, par 21.

[36]It is indicated that: "On 23 December 2013, the Tribunal informed the Parties that, given the short time between the appointment of [the arbitrator] and the date for the envisaged continuation of the hearing, [the arbitrator] envisaged the possibility to retain an assistant for the purpose of the preparation of the hearing. The Claimant and the Respondent consented to the appointment of such assistant on 24 December and 27 December 2013 respectively. It subsequently turned out that such support was eventually not needed", Crystallex v. Venezuela, par 118.

[37]It is stated that: "In particular, the Parties agreed on the application of the Rules of Arbitration in force since April 10, 2006 and on the appointment as assistant of the Arbitral Tribunal of (. . .), a lawyer in the firm H & VDB [being VDB the Tribunal President]" (English translation by the author) ("Les Parties se sont notamment accordées sur l'application du Règlement d'arbitrage en vigueur depuis le 10 avril 2006 et sur la nomination comme assistante du Tribunal arbitral de (. . .), avocate au sein du cabinet H&VDB [being VDB the Tribunal President])." Menzies v. Senegal, par 22. In Tenaris v. Venezuela, it is indicated that: "On November 5, 2014 the President proposed to the Parties the appointment of (. . .), associate of A & A, as Assistant to the Court, and requested their approval" (English translation by the author) ("El 5 de noviembre de 2014 el Presidente propuso a las Partes el nombramiento de (. . .) asociada de A&A, como Asistente del Tribunal, y solicitó su aprobación"), par 22. In Rompetrol v. Romania: "(. . .) to the President's proposal to appoint a Legal Assistant from his Chambers to assist him in the proceedings (. . .), a barrister, was subsequently duly appointed legal assistant to the Tribunal, and this was confirmed by ICSID by letter dated 21 September 2007", Tenaris v. Venezuela, par 21.

[38]Apart from the trust between arbitrator and secretary, they often have close relationship based on their previous professional relationship. This might explain the following British judge's decision: in P v. Q [2017] EWHC 194, an English High Court judge denied an application to remove two co-arbitrators from their positions in an on-going LCIA arbitration. The application was founded on the content of an email from the chairman to the tribunal secretary which was mistakenly sent to a paralegal working for one party's solicitors. The email contained a letter from the party to the tribunal and asked for 'Your [the secretary] reaction to the latest from [P]?', leading the party to question whether the arbitrator's duty not to delegate was being met and tasks carried out by the tribunal secretary. The High Court judge considered that "soliciting or receiving views from a tribunal secretary would not of itself demonstrate a failure to discharge the arbitrator's personal duty to perform the decision-making function and responsibility themselves".

grounds.[39] Another issue to consider, connected with this previous relationship between arbitrator and assistant, is that the connections and CV of the latter might end up producing serious legal effects in the position of the arbitrator, this being for example being challenged.[40] This is a question that could become increasingly important in the future, if the figure of the assistant is settling in the ICSID arbitrations.[41]

Most ICSID cases contain no reference to the specific tasks assigned to the assistant, but brief references have been found specifying that he or she has been employed “for logistical assistance on the file in this case”, for instance.[42] On other occasions, the tasks carried out de facto by the assistant can be deduced from the content of the award or decision.[43] These texts also reflect the procedural guarantees available to the arbitration parties with respect to employing the assistant: the parties are informed of the costs and invited to submit any comments they might have.[44] At the proposal of the arbitral tribunal, the appointment is made if the parties are in agreement[45] and if it is confirmed by ICSID, and finally the assistant’s signed statement is circulated to the parties.[46]

---

[39]Although no reason for the change is specified, see Vladislav. Kim v. Uzbekistan: “On 13 April 2015, the Parties agreed to the appointment of Ms. NM as the Assistant to the Tribunal. On 8 July 2016, the Parties agreed to the appointment of Dr. CCM to replace Ms. NM as the Assistant to the Tribunal” Vladislav. Kim v. Uzbekistan, par 31.

[40]This was alleged by Venezuela in ConocoPhillips v. Venezuela. The fact that the arbitral tribunal allegedly had a professional connection with a certain law firm encouraged Venezuela to file a fifth challenge against the arbitrator. In this case, their co-arbitrators considered that: “the Two Members cannot see that the facts relating to that appointment provide any support at all for the proposition that a limited tie with [the law firm] would lead a reasonable third person with knowledge of those facts to the conclusion that [the arbitrator] is manifestly lacking in the ability to act impartially between the parties in the present arbitration”. ConocoPhillips v. Venezuela (2016), par 35.

[41]In spite of the fact that the case refers to a law clerk who is not officially collaborating with the arbitral panel as an assistant, the case Tanesco v. Tanzania (unpublished) has generated an interesting situation: the investor challenged its own party appointed arbitrator because he had authorized that his law clerk published two articles in a Kluwer arbitration blog. Although the referred articles were supposed to be hypothetical, they described a case very similar to Tanesco, calling the defendant state “Nopayland”. The challenged arbitrator resigned. Daele (2012), pp. 399–400.

[42]Caratube v. Kazakhstan, par 14. A NAFTA-UNCITRAL arbitration included a more general reference (“to aid the Tribunal in its work”) which could cover many types of tasks. Glamis v. USA, par 189.

[43]In the non-ICSID case, Glamis v. USA referred to above, it was stated: “Procedural Order No. 9 postponed the deadlines for the submission of Claimant’s Reply until December 15, 2006, and Respondent’s Rejoinder until February 27, 2007. In addition, the final arbitral hearing was moved to May 2007, with the understanding that the Assistant to the Tribunal would work with the Parties to ascertain an exact date for the hearing” Glamis v. USA, par 262.

[44]Caratube v. Kazakhstan, par 14.

[45]Orascom v. Algeria, par 24; CEAC v. Montenegro, par 9.

[46]Crystallex v. Venezuela, par 97.

Lastly, a question of terminology needs to be taken into account: a clear distinction must be made between the ICSID notion of "assistant of the court" and the following ICSID terms: the secretary of each tribunal (Regulation 25), and the ICSID Secretariat, made up of the Secretary-General, one or more Deputy Secretaries-General and staff (Article 9 Convention and Chapter 2 of the Regulation). In spite of the way it has been interpreted by some authors,[47] the Additional Opinion put forward by a member of the ad hoc Committee in the Water Company v. Argentine case was not really expressing disagreement over a hypothetical assistant of the court, but with the expansive role that he felt the ICSID Secretariat had intended to play in this particular case. This ad hoc Committee member considered that the Secretariat was prepared to draft the recitals, for example, and in his opinion this was not suitable, since "choices need to be made and it is hardly the task of the Secretariat to make them. What are the key facts and relevant arguments and how they should be presented in the final decision or award is for Arbitrators or ad hoc Committee Members to select and decide".[48] The member stressed the importance of not letting control of the case slip out of the arbitrators' hands, pointing out that "if preparatory help of this nature is needed, Arbitral Tribunals or ad hoc Committees may be wiser to appoint their own assistant subject to their full control and direction. Any text tested in this manner might in appropriate cases then serve as part of the final award or decision".[49] In his Additional Opinion, the member emphasized the arbitral tribunal or Ad hoc Committee's independence and authority vis-à-vis the ICSID Secretariat, contrasting it with the hierarchical relationship between an arbitral tribunal and a legal assistant: "In sum, the Secretariat is not the fourth member of ICSID Tribunals or ad hoc Committees and is not an interested party in any other way. It also does not have powers of scrutiny in the manner of the ICC Court. Although in practice it acts as appointing authority - in the case of ad hoc Committees of all Members – these Committees do not thereby become the extension of the Secretariat".[50]

With regard to ICSID's future, the Public Comments to the Amendment of the ICSID Rules and Regulations (2016–2018) include some suggestions regarding the secretaries' role there. Clearly inspired by some of the reflections pointed out in the commercial arbitration context is a proposal for ICSID Rules to incorporate a list of legal assistants' tasks, which explicitly distinguishes between organizational or administrative issues and decision-making functions. An alternative proposal is for

[47] Polkinghorne and Rosenberg (2014), p. 114.

[48] Compañía de Aguas v. Argentina, par 4. Along the same lines: "For the Secretariat also to draft part or all of the decisions and reasoning would appear wholly inappropriate, even if following basic instructions of Arbitrators or *ad hoc* Committee Members whilst the final version would naturally still be left to them for approval. This would not appear to be sufficient to legitimize the text." Compañía de Aguas v. Argentina, par 7.

[49] *Ibid,* par 6.

[50] *Ibid,* par 21.

the Rules to incorporate a reference stating that a specific administrative secretary's tasks should be set out in consultation with the parties.[51]

ICSID's hegemony in investment arbitration dispute resolution has already been mentioned on various occasions. However, the most paradigmatic case in terms of the "arbitrator's personal performance of duties versus tasks carried out by the administrative secretary" binomial is actually outside ICSID's sphere. This case merits detailed analysis.

On 18 July 2014, the PCA issued three parallel final awards in favour of the former shareholders of OAO Yukos Oil Company (Yukos).[52] The arbitral tribunal felt that the Russian Federation had deliberately expropriated Yukos and therefore awarded the claimants astronomical damages of around US$ 50 billion.[53] A few months later, the Russian Federation asked the District Court of the Hague to reverse the awards pursuant to Article 1065(1)(c) of the Code of Civil Procedure of the Netherlands (DCCP) ("the arbitral tribunal has not complied with its mandate"), among other grounds.[54]

Concentrating on this specific ground for the reversal, the Russian Federation alleged that "the arbitrators did not personally fulfill their mandate, based on information recently provided to the parties showing that an assistant to the Tribunal, previously represented by the Tribunal to be responsible only for administrative tasks, instead devoted substantially more time to the Arbitrations than did any of the Tribunal members, and thus almost certainly performed a substantive role in analysing the evidence, in the Tribunal's deliberations, and in preparing the Final Awards, in breach of the Tribunal's mandate to personally perform these tasks."[55]

In these three awards, two members of PCA staff acted as Secretary to the Tribunal and as Assistant Secretary to the Tribunal, carrying out administrative tasks,[56] and the awards additionally refer to a lawyer acting as assistant to the Tribunal. According to the writ of summons presented by the Russian Federation

[51]Baker McKenzie (2017) and EFILA (2017).

[52]Yukos v. Russia, Hulley v. Russia and Veteran v. Russia.

[53]Analysing the main legal issues addressed by these awards, Brauch (2014).

[54]The content of Article 1065(4) DCCP might have been relevant in the resolution of the Dutch claim, as Russia might have needed to establish that it had not knowingly accepted the role actually played by the secretary: "The ground mentioned in paragraph (1)(c) above shall not constitute a ground for reversal if the party who invokes this ground has participated in the arbitral proceedings without invoking such ground, although it was known to him that the tribunal did not comply with its mandate". DCCP (1986).

[55]Writ of Summons, par 102.

[56]Terms of Appointment agreed by the parties, dated October 31, 2005, Article 7(c): "The Tribunal may appoint a member of the Registry [the PCA] to act as Administrative Secretary. The Administrative Secretary and other members of the International Bureau [of the PCA] shall carry out administrative tasks on behalf of the Tribunal".

in 2015, at the time of his appointment the assistant to the Tribunal was an associate at the chairman's law firm.[57]

To delve a little deeper into the referred Russian writ, it states that the assistant's appointment was in fact a *fait accompli*,[58] communicated to the parties by the Chairman of the Tribunal at the first organizational hearing and justified thus: "I would like to bring to the attention of the parties that I have asked one of my colleagues in my office in Montreal to assist me in the conduct of this case. Because, like all of us, I travel a lot, if at any time I am unreachable, you could always contact him. . .It may come to pass that you wish to find out something with respect to the tribunal that the [tribunal secretary, of the PCA] might not be aware of [the assistant] at my office in Montreal could be reached and hopefully will have the answer for you".[59] Russia also pointed out that the assistant concerned did not make a personal statement regarding his impartiality and independence from the parties, but that this was merely stated by the Chairman in an e-mail to the parties.[60]

Due to the fact that the assistant's fee amounted to €970,562.50,[61] and taking into account that his hourly rates were much lower than the arbitrators', the Russian Federation requested from the PCA Secretariat further details of the Tribunal and the assistant's time, expenses and activities. The parties received a Statement of Account, on the basis of which the claimant concluded that the assistant had only invoiced for 381 hours' work from the opening of the arbitrations to the jurisdiction and admissibility hearings, but had charged for 2625 hours during the period covering the merits hearing and the drafting of the Yukos Awards.[62] From his perspective: "This means that the "assistant's" hours were about 65% greater than the number of hours spent by the chairman, and more than 70% and 40% greater than the hours spent by co-arbitrators on the substantive hearing of the disputes and drawing up the Yukos awards".[63] The additional fact that the PCA Secretariat had already charged for a total of 5232.1 hours for performing administrative duties, together with the PCA statement that "the attached Statement of Account provides the Parties with the appropriate level of detail [on the assistant's tasks] while assuring the confidentiality of the Tribunal's deliberations", led the Russian

---

[57]The same assistant had been selected by the same chairman in a previous arbitration (Duke v. Peru).

[58]As has humorously been pointed out: "Husband's Hiring Secretaries without Wives' Input: Arbitrators Preempting Party Autonomy". Restemayer (2012), p. 337.

[59]Writ of Summons, par 488.

[60]*Ibid*, par 487.

[61]Naturally, the amount gave rise to some surprised comments: "But hey let's get real: the million-dollar bill plus for Valasek cannot but raise serious questions. *Yukos* is only *one* case (admittedly a complex one) and Valesek's invoice is about 10 times the *annual* salary of a judicial clerk for a US Supreme Court Justice. Those of us in the US law school world appreciate just what kind of top legal talent the clerks represent." Howse (2017).

[62]Writ of Summons, pars 494–496.

[63]*Ibid*, par 497.

Federation to conclude that the assistant had in fact participated not only in the Arbitral Tribunal's deliberations but also in drafting parts of the awards in question.

In 2016 the District Court of Hague set aside the three referred PCA awards on the grounds that it lacked jurisdiction over the investor's claims, as the Russian Federation had never ratified the *Energy Charter Treaty*. The decision did not cover Russia's other claims, including the contention that the chairman's assistant had acted as a fourth arbitrator. Nevertheless, since the Yukos saga had triggered numerous judicial proceedings, this argument had been repeatedly raised. For instance, in the course of a Petition to Confirm Award filed with U.S. District Court for the District of Columbia in 2015, the counsel for the Russian Federation presented an extensive legal expert opinion addressing the following question: "Whether the Tribunal's appointment and, more important, its use of what it called an" assistant "to the Tribunal so disappointed the parties' entitlement to have their dispute decided in all relevant respects entirely by the arbitrators whom they had chosen that the resulting Awards should be denied enforcement under Article V(l) (d) of the New York Convention as a violation of the arbitral mandate".[64]

The legal expert offered detailed explanations on the current use of arbitral secretaries and assistants,[65] outlining a strict approach that he also defended in his own arbitration activities[66]: "the prevailing international practice dictates that secretaries should neither participate in nor influence the arbitral tribunal's core functions, and thus not participate at all in evaluating the parties' submissions and evidence or deciding the legal and factual issues in the case (. . .) It is generally viewed as impermissible for arbitral secretaries to produce even a preliminary draft of substantive portions of an award."[67] The application of these parameters in the

[64]Expert Opinion of Professor GAB, par 9 D.

[65]The legal expert made an interesting observation regarding terminology "As the term "secretary" suggests, such an individual is meant to perform tasks of an essentially administrative character, and it is so understood. By contrast, the term "assistant," which has surfaced in this case is of no certain meaning. It is difficult to tell precisely from this term alone which functions that person can be expected to perform". *Ibid*, par 83. As the Yukos cases have indicated, arbitral secretaries—but not assistants—are mentioned in the DCCP.

[66]The legal expert stated: "Other tribunals, however, task secretaries with producing first drafts of certain portions of awards, but only those typically early portions of an award that identify, among other things the parties and counsel (and other factual items such as applicable law or language of the arbitration), or recite the basic procedural history of the case, or even possibly (though even this is controversial) a summary of the parties' positions. The reason why secretarial drafting of these portions is commonly allowed is that it is viewed as a largely ministerial task. As chair, I myself studiously avoid assigning arbitral secretaries any greater drafting role than that (and I do not in fact allow them to summarize, even in draft form, the positions of the parties)." *Ibid*, par 91.

[67]*Ibid*, pars 86, 94. The expert also provides important doctrinal references arguing that certain lines cannot be crossed: "Even a careful review by an arbitrator of a secretary's first draft does not entirely remove the scope given to the secretary to make judgements as to what to emphasize and what to omit, judgements that the arbitrator reviewing the draft may not even be able to identify never mind control. The act of writing is the ultimate safeguard of intellectual control. An arbitrator should be reluctant to relinquish it. Partasides (2002), p. 163. Likewise: "As a general rule, the drafting of the substantive parts of the final award, which include its operative part, must be reserved

Yukos case led the legal expert to consider that the assistant had "overstepped the above referred accepted role in international arbitral practice of an arbitral assistant".[68] At this point, the legal expert also brought up an expert linguist's report submitted to the District Court of The Hague, which stated: "it is" extremely likely "that [the assistant] wrote the majority of at least three substantive - and unquestionably vital - sections of the Final Awards, namely, 78.57% of the Preliminary Objections section, 65.38% of the Liability section and 71.43% of the Quantification of Claimant's Damages".[69]

Meanwhile, ripples from the Yukos case spread to other arbitrations such as ConocoPhillips. On November 2015, for the fourth time in the case, Venezuela proposed the disqualification of the former Yukos chairman, who was acting as a claimant-appointed arbitrator, stressing that the arbitrator had refused to give an explicit answer to the question as to: "whether as a matter of fact [the assistant's] activity in the Yukos cases did indeed include writing the reasoning and conclusions of the Yukos awards".[70] The arbitrator denied that he had failed to answer the question regarding the authorship of the Yukos awards and referred to a previous letter in which he had stated: "[the assistant] undertook numerous tasks assigned to him by the Tribunals, including summarizing evidence, researching specific issues of law and organizing the massive case file. Notwithstanding any press reports to the contrary and the speculation of the Respondent, [the assistant] was not involved and did not play any role in the Tribunal's decision-making process This is a true and correct description of [the assistant's] role in the Yukos cases".[71] The co-arbitrators dismissed Venezuela's proposal to disqualify the arbitrator, affirming that: "[they] understand that, in this statement, [the arbitrator] fully answers the Respondent's question to him about the authorship of the Yukos tribunal's reasoning and conclusions of the awards (. . .) The Respondent has not established that [the arbitrator] manifestly lacks the ability to act independently and impartially in the current arbitration".[72]

The possibility that similar cases may arise in the future, together with the likelihood of new controversial issues along the same lines emerging, justifies introducing more detailed specifications and changes such as those proposed

---

for the arbitral tribunal. It is particularly in this substantive section where writing one's own text instead of reading the text prepared by someone else remains the ultimate means of intellectual control of the tribunal's decision of the dispute as the essential tool for safeguarding the proper performance of the arbitrators' personal decision-making duty owed to the parties that have appointed them, thereby preserving the integrity of the arbitral process as such". Berger (2015). In favour of a (restrictive) "non-adjudicative delegation", see also Hong-Lin and Masood (2016).

[68] Expert Opinion of Professor GAB, par 96.

[69] *Ibid,* par 118. Reflecting on linguistic issues in international arbitration, Wilske (2016).

[70] ConocoPhillips v. Venezuela, par 27.

[71] *Ibid,* par 17.

[72] *Ibid,* pars 39 and 40.

throughout this section, which are also generally valid in the investment arbitration framework (ICSID and non-ICSID cases).[73]

The same can be said of future scenarios such as the MIC, in which party-appointed arbitrators would no longer exist. The most recent EU texts on the matter (the EU-Singapore IPA,[74] the former EUSFTA,[75] the Vietnam FTA,[76] TTIP,[77] and the latest available version of JEFTA[78]) deal in their Codes of conduct with the question of the arbitrator's personal performance of duties using almost clone-like drafting: the judges/members of the tribunal shall consider only those issues raised in the proceeding and which are necessary for a decision or award/ruling and shall not delegate this duty to any other person. This text in turn bears many similarities to the NAFTA Code of Conduct,[79] which states: "A member shall consider only those issues raised in the proceeding and necessary to a decision and shall not delegate the duty to decide to any other person, except as provided in the applicable rules". Having pointed out all the problems and queries that more detailed rules than that indicated above have already caused in practice, it seems clear that a prospective MIC should not be content with solely stating that the judge/member "shall not delegate the duty to decide to any other person".[80] Further development on this issue is therefore required.

An interesting final question to examine more closely in the future is whether the EU's encouragement of initiatives such as the MIC might lead to the imposition of some approaches and structures that may seem to exist in the EU context. It is no secret that the judges and advocates generals' chambers in the European Court of Justice (ECJ) includes a number of legal assistants (*référendaires*).[81] Exporting such concept to the world of the investment dispute resolution might open Pandora's Box, since, in the words of a jurist that is an unquestionable expert on the matter: "somewhat hidden in the shadows of the collegiate bench or the individual

[73]This issue has also been addressed in other legal contexts such as the WTO. Its Rules of Conduct state that: "III. Observance of the Governing Principle: "Pursuant to the Governing Principle, each covered person, shall be independent and impartial, and shall maintain confidentiality. Moreover, such persons shall consider only issues raised in, and necessary to fulfil their responsibilities within, the dispute settlement proceeding and shall not delegate this responsibility to any other person. Such person shall not incur any obligation or accept any benefit that would in any way interfere with, or which could give rise to, justifiable doubts as to the proper performance of that person's dispute settlement duties." WTO (1996).

[74]Article 4. Code of Conduct. EU-Singapore IPA (2018).

[75]Article 4. Code of Conduct. EUSFTA (2015).

[76]Article 4. Code of conduct. EU-Vietnam FTA (2016).

[77]Article 4. Code of Conduct. TTIP (2016).

[78]Article 4. Code of Conduct. JEFTA (2016).

[79]NAFTA (1994) Code of Conduct.

[80]The first question that arises is in how broad sense the duty to decide has to be understood.

[81]Adopting a series of good conduct rules for ECJ legal secretaries, which does not include details of their duties and / or the limits of these, see ECJ (2009). *Focusing on the référendaires' role: McAuliffe* (2012), pp. 203–209.

Advocates Generals are the legal secretaries or in French the *référendaires*. Not members of the ECJ or the GC, they are *just* assisting (…) 'assisting' may mean anything between researching the case law and writing memoranda down to the function of a ghost writer, drafting but never signing a judgment or opinion (…) [we have to take into account] the hardly deniable fact that legal secretaries do exercise intellectual influence over the judicial decision-making of the ECJ".[82] Comparisons that other authors have drawn between these ECJ *référendaires* and law clerks in the US also reveal the legal scope of the tasks entrusted to the former.[83]

In short, shaping a MIC will also require a clear outlining of the concept of legal assistants in the investment context. This implies that it will be necessary to specify all the aspects mentioned above, including the crucial question of whether this new institution will allow its assistants to carry out any kind of decision-making functions. So far, in the documents issued by the EU only the following quantitative information appears: each adjudicator will be assigned with three members of staff.[84]

4.2 Time-Related Availability

4.2.1 International Commercial Arbitration

In the commercial arbitration context, many arbitral institution rules and Codes of ethics deal with the question of arbitrators' availability time-wise one way or another, both when appointments are accepted and throughout the subsequent arbitration procedure. According to these texts, arbitrators have a duty to be available, which is sometimes subsumed within broader concepts such as the duties of diligence and efficiency.[85]

---

[82]The author was appointed Advocate General at the Court of Justice in October 2015. Bobek (2014), pp. 14–15.

[83]Richman (2008), p. 16; Kenney (2000).

[84]EC (2017), 303 final.

[85]For instance, the IBA Rules of Ethics for International Arbitrators 1987 refer to the duty of diligence thus: "All arbitrators should devote such time and attention as the parties may reasonably require having regard to all the circumstances of the case, and shall do their best to conduct the arbitration in such a manner that costs do not rise to an unreasonable proportion of the interests at stake" IBA (1987). The ICC Note declares: "Arbitrators have a duty to devote to the arbitration the time necessary to conduct the proceedings as diligently, efficiently and expeditiously as possible" Note (2017); the Standard 7 of the Barcelona Arbitration Court Code of Ethics states that: "Duty of diligence: All arbitrators must devote as much time and attention as the parties may reasonably require taking into account all of the circumstances of the case, and must do everything possible to conduct the arbitration in such a way that costs do not rise in a unreasonable proportion in relation to the interests at stake". (On 16th March 2009, this institution decided to adhere to the guidelines of the International Bar Association's Code of Ethics for International Arbitration, eliminating or reformulating parameters of TAB requirements to set possibly even higher setting standards). TAB (2009).

4.2.1.1 Appointment Stage

If the texts covering arbitrator availability at the appointment stage are systemised, it becomes clear that in some cases it is left to the arbitrators themselves to judge whether they are available—and for long enough- to be able to accept an appointment, and they are thus not required to provide any further guarantee of this when accepting the position. Partially inspired by the 1987 IBA Rules of Ethics for International Arbitrators,[86] the Code of Ethics of Arbitrators of the CAM for instance states: "When accepting his/her mandate, the arbitrator shall, to the best of his/her knowledge, be able to devote the necessary time and attention to the arbitration to perform and complete his/her task as expeditiously as possible".[87]

The arbitration rules themselves sometimes implement mechanisms to facilitate the arbitrators' task of making availability-related decisions. An example in point is the relaxing of the restrictions on *ex parte* communications[88] to allow arbitrators to enquire as to the anticipated time frame for the arbitration before accepting an appointment.[89] Some degree of freedom notwithstanding, texts such as the 2013 revised KLRCA Code of Conduct for Arbitrator reminds arbitrators that dedicating their time to the arbitration as required is, in short, a party right that has to be taken seriously ("An arbitrator shall only accept an appointment if he (...) is able to give to the proceedings the time and attention which parties are reasonably entitled to expect").[90]

In other cases, arbitral institutions do not leave the issue of availability entirely in the hands of the arbitrators, but impose certain explicit controls on them.[91] For instance, the 2015 Code of Ethics for arbitrators of the SIAC requires prospective

---

[86]Rule 2.3 of the IBA Rules states: "A prospective arbitrator should accept an appointment only if he is able to give to the arbitration the time and attention which the parties are reasonably entitled to expect". IBA (1987). In relation to the validity of this 1987 text, the 2014 IBA Guidelines state that: "In 1987, the IBA published Rules of Ethics for International Arbitrators. Those Rules cover more topics than these Guidelines, and they remain in effect as to subjects that are not discussed in the Guidelines. The Guidelines supersede the Rules of Ethics as to the matters treated here". IBA (2014).

[87]Article 4. CAM (2010).

[88]*Infra,* Chap. 5.

[89]Article 4.1. SIAC-Communications: "Before accepting an appointment, an arbitrator may only enquire as to the general nature of the dispute, the name of the parties and the expected time period required for the arbitration". SIAC (2015) Article 4 of the Code of Ethics for an Arbitrator of CIICA also indicates: "Before accepting an appointment, an arbitrator can only inquire about the general nature of the dispute, the names of the parties and the expected time period required for the arbitration". CIICA (2016). Article 4.2 of the KLRCA's revised Code of Conduct for Arbitrator: "Before accepting an appointment, an Arbitrator may only enquire as to the general nature of the dispute, the names of the parties, the amount in dispute and the expected time period required for the proceeding". KLRCA (2013).

[90]*Ibid,* Article 2.2.

[91]In other cases, the arbitration institution's control is affirmed but no further details are given. It is affirmed: "(5) The SCC takes into account the efficiency of the dispute and the issue of availability when selecting arbitrators." SCC (2017).

arbitrators to disclose any potential time constraints they may have over the next 12 months to the SIAC Registrar.[92] This time frame is duplicated in the ICC context, which also requires arbitrators to provide detailed information as to their availability ("Accordingly, prospective arbitrators must indicate in the Statement the number of arbitrations in which they are currently acting, specifying whether they are acting as president, sole arbitrator, co-arbitrator or counsel to a party, as well as their availability over the next 24 months").[93] Arbitration parties are also provided with safeguards in the PCA framework, as the institution allows following optional paragraph to be included in the Model statements of impartiality and independence pursuant to Article 11 of the Rules: "Note — Any party may consider requesting from the arbitrator the following addition to the statement of impartiality and independence: I confirm, on the basis of the information presently available to me, that I can devote the time necessary to conduct this arbitration diligently, efficiently and in accordance with the time limits in the Rules".[94]

If arbitration institutions do require arbitrators to disclose their availability, serious consequences may result. The SIAC, for example, "reserves the right to refuse to appoint the prospective arbitrator should it take the view that the prospective arbitrator will not be able to discharge his duties due to such potential time constraints."[95] Certain institutions may reject candidates that do not abide the rules on the duty of disclosure with regard to availability.[96] From the perspective of arbitration's protection, it seems reasonable that arbitration institutions may have the final say on arbitrators' appointment.[97]

---

[92]Article 1.2 SIAC: "Appointment: Should the prospective arbitrator be aware of any potential time constraints un the next 12 months in his ability to discharge his duties if he is appointed as an arbitrator, he shall, without breaching any existing confidentiality considerations and/or obligations, disclose details of such time constraints to the Registrar of SIAC in the attached Disclosure Sheet. SIAC reserves the right to refuse to appoint the prospective arbitrator should it take the view that the prospective arbitrator will not be able to discharge his duties to such potential time constraints." SIAC (2015).

[93]Note (2017), par.25.

[94]PCA (2012).

[95]Article 1.2. Appointment. SIAC (2015).

[96]The Arbitration Rules state: "The concealment of all or any objective circumstances affecting their availability, impartiality or independence by a candidate from the parties, the Court or the other Arbitrators shall entitle the Court to deny, where applicable, confirmation of the proposed candidate. Should the concealed circumstance giving rise to a conflict of interest come to be known to a party who challenges the Arbitrator concerned on this basis, the previous concealment will be an element to be weighed by the Court in its decision, depending on the circumstances of the case". CIMA (2015).

[97]The strict approach supported by Rivkin deserves detailed reading: "Most importantly, arbitrators have to commit that they have sufficient time in their schedule to conduct the case efficiently and – here is a key point – that they will not in the future schedule themselves so fully that they do not have time for the work to be done on the case. This does not just mean time having the time to slot in a week's hearing and perhaps a procedural conference some time soon after appointment. This means having enough time to read all submissions promptly when they are made, so that if procedural issues arise, they can be determined based on actual knowledge of the case at the

4.2.1.2 Arbitration Proceedings

In addition, the rules of arbitral institutions dealing with commercial disputes mainly reflect an interest in the entire proceedings being carried out without any unnecessary delays, which is also linked to arbitrator availability. Although minimizing delay is a more general aim, in which other stakeholders such as parties are equally involved, it seems clear that the arbitrator's availability is a crucial factor in preventing unnecessary hold-ups in the proceedings.[98] Some rules also emphasize the importance of avoiding unwarranted delays at specific key moments in the arbitration. The Code of Ethics of Arbitrators of the CAM, for instance, states that "the arbitrator shall refrain from any obstructive or non-cooperative behaviour and promptly participate in the deliberation."[99]

It is interesting to note here that other arbitration frameworks are rather more demanding, in the sense that avoiding unnecessary delays is no longer enough. CAS, for instance, requires arbitrators to "complete the arbitration expeditiously".[100] Ascertaining exactly what is meant by these general terms is not always a simple task.[101]

---

time. It means having sufficient time for some pre-hearing deliberations by the arbitrators, so that the hearing itself can be focused on the issues that are truly relevant to their decision. It means having and scheduling enough time after the hearing to deliberate and to write the award. Frankly, too many arbitrators schedule themselves so fully that they move from hearing to hearing, week to week, and never leave themselves time to undertake their other responsibilities (reading the papers and particularly deliberating and writing the award). Arbitrators now commit to sit in their chair through a hearing, but they also must commit to sit in their chair in their office, or wherever they want to work, to write the award afterwards. Deliberations and award drafting cannot simply be fit into the free days and weekends that happen to occur between hearings in other matters (. . .) I must add that arbitrators who have dozens of cases simply cannot reasonably commit that they have time to devote sufficient attention to each matter, and they should turn down new appointments when that is the case. Arbitrators often justify taking on new matters even when they are too busy by saying that rejecting the appointment would deprive a party – or an institution – of its choice of arbitrators. I strongly disagree with such an assertion. Once appointed, each arbitrator owes a duty to both parties, and to any institution administering the case, and if he or she cannot fulfill that duty, he or she must politely decline the appointment. I have done so on more than a few occasions. Excessively busy arbitrators also justify nevertheless taking on new cases because some cases settle. That is of course true, but the possibility of settlement can be dealt with by applying appropriate cancellation fees; it should not justify taking on a new matter that will impact the arbitrator's ability to fulfill his or her obligations to an already existing matter." Rivkin (2015), pp. 5–6.

[98]Rule 7 of the CIArb Code of Professional and Ethical Conduct for Members states that: "A member shall not unduly delay the completion of the dispute resolution process". CIArb (2009).

[99]Article 11. CAM (2010).

[100]R33- Independence and Qualifications of Arbitrators. CAS (2013).

[101]The comment on rule 2.5 of the ABA Model Code of Judicial Conduct is useful here, as it specifies that: "A judge should seek the necessary docket time, court staff, expertise, and resources to discharge all adjudicative and administrative responsibilities. Prompt disposition of the court's business requires a judge to devote adequate time to judicial duties, to be punctual in attending court and expeditious in determining matters under submission, and to take reasonable measures to ensure

Avoiding unnecessary hold-ups during the entire arbitral proceedings is associated with a further highly desirable objective from the arbitration institution's perspective: avoiding unnecessary expense.[102] These aims,[103] which arbitration regulations usually group together,[104] are also linked with the even more general goal of efficiency.[105]

In commercial arbitration, important legal effects may ensue should arbitrators fail to act without undue delay during the arbitration proceedings. Article 14 of the UNCITRAL Model Law on International Commercial Arbitration,[106] which has inspired many national legislations and regulations of arbitral institutions, is paradigmatic here, establishing a hierarchy of consequences: "his mandate terminates if he withdraws from his office or if the parties agree on the termination. Otherwise, if a controversy remains concerning any of these grounds, any party may request the court or other authority specified in Article 6 to decide on the termination of the mandate, which decision shall be subject to no appeal".[107] The *travaux préparatoires* for Article 14, adopted in 1985, refer to a series of factors that determine whether or not arbitrators have met their obligation to act without undue

---

that court officials, litigants, and their lawyers cooperate with the judge to that end. In disposing of matters promptly and efficiently, a judge must demonstrate due regard for the rights of parties to be heard and to have issues resolved without unnecessary cost or delay. A judge should monitor and supervise cases in ways that reduce or eliminate dilatory practices, avoidable delays, and unnecessary costs". ABA (2011).

102 *Infra,* Sect. 6.1.

103 However, avoiding unnecessary delay and expense are not absolute objectives. There are a series of crucial procedural precautions, that cannot be ignored, such as assuring equality of treatment and safeguarding the parties' rights to present claims and defences fairly. Article 21.2 of the International Dispute Resolution Procedures of the ICDR states: "Exchange of Information - The arbitral tribunal shall manage the exchange of information between the parties with a view to maintaining efficiency and economy. The tribunal and the parties should endeavour to avoid unnecessary delay and expense while at the same time avoiding surprise, assuring equality of treatment, and safeguarding each party's opportunity to present its claims and defenses fairly". ICDR (2014). See also Canon IV of the Code of Ethics for Arbitrators in Commercial Disputes: "An arbitrator should conduct the proceedings fairly and diligently (...)." ABA (2004).

104 For example, Article 4.4 of the LCIA Arbitration Rules: "Under the Arbitration Agreement, the Arbitral Tribunal's general duties at all times during the arbitration shall include: (...) (ii) a duty to adopt procedures suitable to the circumstances of the arbitration, avoiding unnecessary delay and expense, so as to provide a fair, efficient and expeditious means for the final resolution of the parties' dispute". LCIA (2014).

105 For instance, Article 14. 2 of the DIA Rules: "If an arbitrator does not act timely and efficiently, or if the arbitrator's other duties according to the Rules are not fulfilled, a party may request the Chairman's Committee to decide whether the arbitrator shall be replaced. Even in the absence of such a request, the Chairman's Committee may replace an arbitrator on the grounds mentioned in the 1st sentence of this paragraph". DIA (2013).

106 UNCITRAL (1985a).

107 Article 14 does not cover situations in which an arbitrator's appointment is questioned on the basis of doubts as to impartiality or independence as this issue is dealt with in Article 12 of the UNCITRAL Model Law on International Commercial Arbitration. UNCITRAL (1985a).

delay,[108] and the UNCITRAL Digest of Case Law on the Model Law on International Commercial Arbitration—a compilation of national case law—considers that arbitrator failure to render an award within the time limit agreed on by the parties constitutes a failure to act without undue delay.[109]

In the same sense, the excessive delays of the arbitrator at key moments such as the delivery the final award have generated drastic consequences in the praxis of international commercial arbitration. For example, the CIArb Disciplinary Tribunal has come to expel a member from the Institute and ordered him to pay a fine due to a significant delay -4 years- in rendering the award.[110]

4.2.2 International Investment Arbitration

Where arbitrator time-related availability in investment arbitration is concerned, it is worth maintaining the distinction between availability when accepting an appointment and then later throughout the arbitration procedure.

4.2.2.1 Appointment Stage

In relation to the first issue, investment arbitration cases are currently resolved by party-appointed arbitrators selected for each specific dispute. It is worth pointing out here that ICSID arbitration rules have not yet devoted specific attention to arbitrator availability at the appointment stage, an issue that will be discussed in more detail in the final pages of this sub-section. Nevertheless, it should also be emphasised that both the latest EU texts and the MIC project would introduce substantial changes to the selection procedure, which would also affect arbitrator availability at the time of appointment. The EU-Singapore IPA, Vietnam FTA, TTIP, 2016 CETA and the last available version of JEFTA clearly refer to a tribunal of members/judges (6, 9, 15, 15 and 15 persons respectively) appointed by the corresponding committee for a specific term (8, 4, 6, 5 and 6 years respectively) and renewable once. These

[108] The *travaux préparatoires* state that: "courts should take into consideration the following factors: what action was expected or required of the arbitrator in light of the arbitration agreement and the specific procedural situation; if the arbitrator has not done anything in this regard, whether the delay has been so inordinate as to be unacceptable in light of the circumstances, including technical difficulties and the complexity of the case; if the arbitrator has done something and acted in a certain way, whether his conduct clearly falls below the standard of what could reasonably be expected. The *travaux préparatoires* also mentioned that "[a]mongst the factors influencing the level of expectations are the ability to function efficiently and expeditiously and any special competence or other qualifications required of the arbitrator by agreement of the parties." UNCITRAL (1985b).

[109] *Ibid.*

[110] Hutcheon (2012).

tribunals will hear each case in a division made up of three persons, appointed by the president of the tribunal on a rotation basis. All these texts note that every tribunal division should be made up in such a way as to ensure that their composition is both random and unforeseeable, while also giving all the judges an equal opportunity to serve. The texts analysed state that "the Members/judges shall be available at all times and on short notice",[111] thus reproducing the wording of the Article 17 of the WTO Dispute Settlement Understanding.[112] They also agree on the payment of a (low) monthly retainer "in order to ensure their availability", and there is provision for the committee to convert the retainer and other fees into a regular salary as and when appropriate.

The disappearance of party-appointed arbitrators (or, following the EU's terminology, "detaching adjudicators from the disputing parties")[113] is therefore a novel shift in circumstances in these contexts.[114] As the power to appoint the group of experts making up a tribunal is transferred to the committees, whose mechanisms remain unregulated, the question in the ICS arises as to whether these committees will establish sufficiently detailed guidelines capable of addressing the issue of their appointees' availability.

4.2.2.2 Arbitration Proceedings

In the world of investment arbitration, ICSID has not yet devoted specific attention to the availability of arbitrators throughout the proceedings. An essential text on this issue is the 1994 NAFTA Code of Conduct, Part III of which (The Performance of Duties by Candidates and Members) states: "A candidate who accepts an appointment as a member shall be available to perform, and shall perform, a member's duties thoroughly and expeditiously throughout the course of the proceeding. A member shall ensure that the Secretariat can, at all reasonable times, contact the member in order to conduct panel or committee business. A member shall carry out all duties fairly and diligently".[115]

As has already been pointed out with respect to other arbitrator duties, the NAFTA Code of Conduct is also a pioneer text in this specific context. More than 20 years later, the EU expressly reproduced the three-faceted wording in NAFTA (be available to perform; perform the duties thoroughly and expeditiously throughout the course of the proceeding, and carry out all duties fairly and diligently) in the

[111] CETA introduces a variation into the wording in its Article 8.11, stating that: "The Members of the Tribunal shall ensure that they are available". CETA (2016).

[112] Article 17. WTO (1994).

[113] EC (2017).

[114] In favour of this radical change, Howse (2015), pp. 6–7; Titi (2017). Reflecting on this issue, *supra*, Chap. 1.

[115] NAFTA (1994).

Codes of conduct contained in the recent EU-Singapore IPA,[116] the former EUSFTA,[117] the EU-Vietnam FTA,[118] TTIP,[119] and the latest available version of the leaked EU-Japan Trade Agreement (JEFTA).[120] Other texts drafted specifically for investment arbitration context were however inspired by the tone of the documents previously discussed with reference to commercial arbitration, (e.g., "determine the case in a prompt and efficient manner").[121] Implementing texts such as those reproduced in the EU context would undoubtedly entail the consolidating in writing of the arbitrators' duty to be available throughout the entire proceedings.

With a view to the future, it is important to note that the Public Comments to the Amendment of ICSID's Rules and Regulations (2016–2018) include various proposals linked with the issue of arbitrator availability. It is generally suggested that ICSID could show greater interest in the question, both at the stage at which the arbitration tribunal is constituted and at then all times during the subsequent arbitration. There are also intimations that the content of the declaration referred to in Rule 6.2 may also be expanded to stipulate that a confirmation of a prospective arbitrator must also be incorporated with respect to "(i) his/her commitment to conduct the proceedings fairly and efficiently, by adopting procedures suitable to the circumstances of the arbitration, (ii) the days or weeks in the next two years that he/she has already committed to other cases or other obligations that make him/her unavailable and (iii) his/her commitment that he/she will not take on now appointments that will conflict with his/her responsibilities to the case subject to the appointment". There is also a proposal to incorporate a new rule detailing tribunal duties such as "(ii) a duty to adopt procedures suitable to the circumstances of the arbitration, avoiding unnecessary delay and expense, so as to provide a fair, efficient and expeditious means for the final resolution of the parties' dispute".[122]

In addition, various recommendations linked one way or another with arbitrator availability at certain crucial points during the ICSID arbitration have also been

[116]Article 4. Code of conduct: "a member shall perform his or her duties throughout the course of the proceeding and with fairness and diligence." EU-Singapore IPA (2018).

[117]Article 4. Code of conduct: "Upon selection, an arbitrator shall perform his or her duties thoroughly and expeditiously throughout the course of the proceeding and with fairness and diligence." EU-Singapore FTA (2015).

[118]Article 4. Code of conduct: "Upon confirmation of her or his selection, an arbitrator shall be available to perform and shall perform her of his duties thoroughly and expeditiously throughout the course of the proceeding, and with fairness and diligence.". EU-Vietnam FTA (2016).

[119]Article 4. Code of Conduct: "Duties of members- Members shall perform their duties thoroughly and expeditiously throughout the course of the proceeding and shall do so with fairness and diligence". http://trade.ec.europa.eu/doclib/docs/2015/november/tradoc_153955.pdf. TTIP (2016).

[120]Article 4. Code of conduct: "Duties of members- A member shall perform his or her duties thoroughly and expeditiously throughout the course of the proceeding and shall do so with fairness and diligence". JEFTA (2016).

[121]Rule 10.3: "The Court (appointing authority) shall also consider whether the arbitrator has sufficient availability to determine the case in a prompt and efficient manner that is appropriate given the nature of the arbitration". SIAC (2017).

[122]Debevoise & Plimpton (2017).

issued. For instance, with regard to the key stage at which arbitration awards are drafted and issued, it has been proposed that a code of conduct for arbitrators should set out estimated deadlines within which arbitrators have to undertake to issue awards (e.g., "arbitrators undertake to take all reasonable measure to issue an award within 120 days at the minimum and 180 days in exceptional circumstances").[123] A further suggestion favours setting a time limit for the rendering of awards, after which any delay would result in the withholding of a percentage of the arbitrator's fee.[124] However, this proposal, a legal transplant that would come from the ICC context[125] and that also exists in some national spheres,[126] does not have unanimous support, and has been criticised on the basis that the ICC policy gives rise to unnecessary post-hearing briefs as a mechanism used by the arbitral tribunal when there are delays in finalising the award with the aim of avoiding financial penalties, among other issues. One possible solution could be the ICSID Secretariat's taking responsibility for a series of measures, such as issuing regular reminders to arbitration tribunal presidents on the importance of respecting timeframes and award deadlines, requesting regular progress reports from tribunals at the award drafting stage when the hearing is concluded, etc.[127] It has also been pointed out that the parties feel powerless if arbitrators postpone, reduce or cancel scheduled hearings as a result of obligations deriving from a later arbitration to which they have committed themselves—a situation known as "double booking". A possible solution would be ensuring that any changes could only be made with the ICSID Secretary General's express authorisation.[128] In short, stakeholders feel that ICSID must firmly address

[123]Baker McKenzie (2017).

[124]Freshfields, Bruckhaus, Deringer (2017) and Law Council of Australia (2017).

[125]Egger (2010), p. 112.

[126]For instance, the 2015 version of the Indian Arbitration and Conciliation (Amendment) Ordinance stated: "29A. (4) If the award is not made within the period specified in sub-section (1) or the extended period specified under sub-section (3), the mandate of the arbitrator(s) shall terminate unless the Court has, either prior to or after the expiry of the period so specified, extended the period: Provided that while extending the period under this sub-section, if the Court finds that the proceedings have been delayed for the reasons attributable to the arbitral tribunal, then, it may order reduction of fees of arbitrator(s) by not exceeding five per cent. for each month of such delay. (5) The extension of period referred to in sub-section (4) may be on the application of any of the parties and may be granted only for sufficient cause and on such terms and conditions as may be imposed by the Court". India (2015). A new version of this text has added some nuances to this issue: "In section 29A of the principal Act, (a) for sub-section (1), the following sub-section shall be substituted, namely: "(1) The award in matters other than international commercial arbitration shall be made within a period of twelve months from the date of completion of pleadings under sub-section (4) of section 23."; (b) in sub-section (4), after the proviso, the following provisos shall be inserted, namely: "Provided further that where an application under sub-section (5) is pending, the mandate of the arbitrator shall continue till the disposal of the said application: Provided also that the arbitrator shall be given an opportunity of being heard before the fees is reduced." India (2018).

[127]Derains & Gharavi (2017), p. 8.

[128]*Ibid,* p. 10.

the issue of arbitrator availability, both when they accept an appointment and throughout the subsequent proceedings.

This is a logical consequence of the clear demand posed by stakeholders regarding the availability of the adjudicator in the international arbitration milieu: more information on the matter is required. The 2018 White & Case International Arbitration Survey firmly states that: "respondents are concerned with all relevant data that would indicate the degree of arbitrators' availability. Specifically, users would appreciate knowing the number of, and more information on, their ongoing cases, including how many proceedings they are presiding over. Respondents also showed interest in data regarding the overall efficiency of arbitrators. Mentions of the time spent on each previous arbitration (or the average duration thereof) and of the amounts of time elapsed between the closing of the proceedings and the rendering of the awards (or the average duration thereof) were particularly recurrent in the responses. Once again, arbitral institutions would appear to be the key sources for much of this data."[129]

4.3 Appropriate Behaviour

Adjudicator behaviour has been the object of reflection in the national and international judicial context for some time.[130] The ABA Model Code of Judicial Conduct, for instance, is a well-grounded and extremely detailed soft law text on this subject. Rule 2.3 focuses on bias, prejudice and harassment of the judge and proclaims that: "A judge shall not, in the performance of judicial duties, by words or conduct, manifest bias or prejudice, or engage in harassment, including but not limited to bias, prejudice or harassment based upon race, sex, gender, religion, national origin, ethnicity, disability, age, sexual orientation, marital status, socioeconomic status, or political affiliation, and shall not permit court staff, court officials or others subject to the judge's direction and control to do so". In addition, Rule 2.8 affirms that "a Judge shall be patient, dignified, and courteous to litigants, jurors, witnesses, lawyers, court staff, court officials and others with whom the judge deals in an official capacity, and shall require similar conduct of lawyers, court staff, court officials, and others subject to the judge's direction and control".[131]

In the field of commercial arbitration, the arbitrators' duty to behave appropriately has been expressed in writing in very different ways, using a range of qualifying adjectives that *strictu sensu* are not completely synonymous but share a common

[129] White & Case (2018), p. 22.

[130] For instance, values 3 and 4 of the 2002 Bangalore Principles of Judicial Independence refer to integrity and propriety. Judicial Group on Strengthening Judicial Integrity (2002). More international texts dealing with these issues are to be found in and Shetreet and Forsyth (2011).

[131] ABA (2011).

concern for arbitrators' personal dignity.[132] Some texts connect this duty with the procedural guarantees that must be extended to participants in arbitration proceedings ("An arbitrator should conduct the proceedings in an even-handed manner. The arbitrator should be patient and courteous to the parties, their representatives, and the witnesses and should encourage similar conduct by all participants.").[133] Other texts also stress that the duty to behave appropriately also extends to arbitrators' relationships with their peers ("The arbitrator shall refrain from any obstructive or non-cooperative behaviour (...) in the deliberation").[134] Scholars have also highlighted the importance of an arbitrator's appropriate behaviour, by stating for instance that: "integrity is to arbitration what location is to the price of the real state: Without it, other things do not matter all that much".[135]

In the investment arbitration field, the NAFTA Code of Conduct is once again a pioneer text, stating on this issue that: "Every candidate, member and former member shall avoid impropriety and the appearance of impropriety and shall observe high standards of conduct so that the integrity and impartiality of the dispute settlement process is preserved".[136] The EU nowadays concurs with the importance of both avoiding impropriety and the appearance of impropriety and its connection with arbitrator independence and impartiality. In recent Codes of conduct such as the ones contained in the EU-Singapore IPA,[137] the former EUSFTA,[138] the EU-Vietnam FTA,[139] TTIP,[140] and the leaked EU-Japan Trade Agreement (JEFTA)[141] this appears as one of the arbitrators' responsibilities to the proceedings.

On a practical level,[142] it is probably true that "the truly harmful cases remain unknown, because improper behaviour is shrouded in urbane subterfuge and hypocrisy. It is extraordinarily difficult to police this type of behaviour".[143] Nevertheless, some interesting references in the fields of international commercial and investment arbitration have been found, and they show that instances of improper behaviour on

[132]The present analysis does not cover the kind of situation analyzed in the commercial context by the following piece: Hanotiau (2003), pp. 261–287.

[133]Canon IV of the Code of Ethics for Arbitrators in Commercial Disputes: "An arbitrator should conduct the proceedings fairly and diligently". ABA (2004).

[134]Art. 11 Code of ethics of arbitrators of the CAM- Deliberation of the award. CAM (2010).

[135]Park (2012) In the same sense, Park (2009), p. 100.

[136]Part I: Responsibilities to the Process. NAFTA (1994).

[137]Article 2. Code of Conduct. EU-Singapore IPA (2018).

[138]Article 2. Code of Conduct. EUSFTA (2015).

[139]Article 2, Code of Conduct. EU-Vietnam FTA (2016).

[140]Article 2. Code of Conduct. TTIP (2016).

[141]Article 2. Code of Conduct. JEFTA (2016).

[142]An example of this issue in the commercial field is the following: "whilst the co-arbitrator expressed views on certain issues and sometimes adopted an attitude which could be perceived as rude, 'preliminary views' and 'strong terms' on the arbitrator's side, albeit 'it would have been wiser to keep his thoughts for himself', do not qualify as a basis for a challenge". LCIA Reference N° 81224, Decision Rendered 15 March 2010. Challenge Digests.

[143]Paulsson (2010), p. 344.

the part of arbitrators have been indeed considered by parties in some challenges. Such behaviour is usually associated with the issue of a challenged arbitrator's perceived lack of independence and impartiality, and also sometimes with the issue of confidentiality.

An analysis of these cases reveals that unsuitable behaviour has neither proved to be a major motive for challenging individual arbitrators, nor has it been felt to be a sufficiently weighty matter to be alleged as a sole reason in challenge procedures. This reality is thrown into relief in the ICSID environment for instance by the investment case of RSM v. Saint Lucia.[144] The claimants considered that: "the description [given by the challenged arbitrator] of third-party funders as "mercantile adventurers" and the association with "gambling" and the "gambler's Nirvana: Heads I win and Tails I do not lose" are radical in tone and negative and prejudge the question whether a funded claimant will comply with a costs award".[145] Nevertheless, the co-arbitrators stated: "we regard the language in the Assenting Reasons as radical and perhaps extreme in tone, but not to a degree as to justify a disqualification. [The arbitrator] may well, with the expressions used, have stepped close to the edge of what can be considered as an objective reasoning. However, we believe that he has not actually stepped over the demarcation line between radical and extreme language on the one hand and clearly inappropriate and hence inacceptable expressions in the context of an arbitration on the other hand".[146]

In this context, the doctrine also refers to a case decided by the PCA under UNCITRAL rules in which one party unsuccessfully accused the challenged arbitrator of having "made sarcastic comments to ridicule counsel for respondent, conducted himself intemperately and insensitively" among other transgressions.[147]

---

[144]In another case, allegations that "the arbitrator was discourteous and showed animosity and contempt", were radically ruled out by the co-arbitrators: "Regarding the first ground for recusal, the Tribunal does not share the Claimants' position. In her First Clarification the arbitrator limited herself to answering the Claimants' questions in one of ICSID's official languages, in on-going proceedings in which the first session between the Parties and the Tribunal members to agree on the language of the proceeding, among other issues, had not yet been held. Neither does the Court find, as the Claimants assert, that the Arbitrator's First Clarification contains discourteous language or expressions that lead one to believe the arbitrator under recusal feels animosity towards the Claimants. The arbitrator answered the questions amiably, and also always showed herself willing to clarify any other questions that the Claimants may have" (English translation by the author) ("En cuanto al primer motivo de recusación el Tribunal no comparte la postura de las Demandantes. La [árbitro] se limitó en su Primera Aclaración a contestar a las preguntas de las Demandantes en uno de los idiomas oficiales del CIADI, en un procedimiento incipiente, en el que no se había celebrado la primera sesión entre las Partes y los miembros del Tribunal para fijar, entre otras cuestiones, el idioma del procedimiento. Tampoco encuentra el Tribunal en la Primera Aclaración de la [árbitro], tal como afirman las Demandantes, un lenguaje descortés, o expresiones que lleven a pensar que exista animadversión de la árbitro bajo recusación contra las Demandantes. La [árbitro], respondió a las preguntas de forma afable, y además mostró siempre su disposición para aclarar cualesquiera otras dudas que les surgieran a las Demandantes"). Highbury v. Venezuela (2015b) pars 101–102.

[145]RSM v. Saint Lucia, par 42.

[146]*Ibid* par 86.

[147]Without identifying the case referred to, see Levine (2015), p. 269.

However, there is one example of successful challenge in the sphere of arbitrator's behaviour. In the Burlington v. Ecuador case, a proposal to disqualify the arbitrator was indeed upheld by the Chairman of the Administrative Council on the basis of the written explanation provided by the challenged arbitrator. The problem raised by the explanation was not the arbitrator's language or tone, but the allegations he made about the ethics of the counsel for the defendant state.[148] In the chairman's view: "a third party undertaking a reasonable evaluation of the July 31, 2013 explanations would conclude that the paragraph quoted above manifestly evidences an appearance of lack of impartiality with respect to the Republic of Ecuador and its counsel".[149] In this case, therefore, it seems that the arbitrator's inability to avoid unsuitable behaviour in his explanations concerning the challenge brought with it an apparent lack of impartiality that in turn justified the challenge.

There is also another case—Perenco v. Ecuador—of successful challenge deriving from the arbitrator's remarks, which connects with the notions of issue conflict and prejudgment.[150] In this case the controversy did not arise from comments in a document produced within the arbitration procedure framework, but from the arbitrator's remarks in an external media interview. The arbitrator in fact stated the following to the legal magazine The Metropolitan Corporate Counsel: "There is an issue of acceptance and the willingness to continue participating in it, as exemplified by what Bolivia has done and what Ecuador is doing. Ecuador currently is expressly declining to comply with the orders of two ICSID tribunals with very stiff interim provisional measures, but they just say they have to enforce their national law and the orders don't make any difference. But when recalcitrant host countries find out that claimants are going to act like those who were expropriated in Libya, start bringing hot oil litigation and chasing cargos, doing detective work looking for people who will invoke cross-default clauses in loan agreements, etc., the politics may change. After a certain point, no one will invest without having something to rely on."[151] In this case, the PCA Secretary General decided that "from the point of view of a reasonable third person having knowledge of the relevant facts, the

[148]The challenged arbitrator stated: "[l]astly there are some ethical assertions that cannot be left unanswered. [The law firm] admonishes this arbitrator to resign on ethical grounds as if [the law firm]'s views were proven correct. This is certainly not the case. Moreover, the real ethical question seems to lie with [the law firm]'s submissions and the handling of confidential information. To the best of this arbitrator's knowledge the correspondence concerning disclosure and other matters in Pan American v. Bolivia is part of the confidential record of that case. [The law firm] is in the knowledge of such correspondence as counsel for Bolivia, but it does not seem appropriate or ethically justified that this information be now used to the advantage of a different client of [the law firm], a use that in any event should be consented to by the other party to that case." Burlington v. Ecuador, par 79.

[149]*Ibid*, par 80.

[150]*Supra*, Sects. 2.1 and 3.2.

[151]Perenco v. Ecuador, par 27.

comments (. . .) constitute circumstances that give rise to justifiable doubts as to [the arbitrator's] impartiality or independence."[152]

Although it falls outside this chapter's scope, it is important to point out here that there are also examples of requests for investment awards to be annulled on the basis of inappropriate behaviour on the part of the arbitrators.[153] Thus, in Klöckner v. Cameroon the investor unsuccessfully argued before the *ad hoc* committee that the hostility towards the claimant reflected in the award involved a lack of tribunal impartiality that was subsumable under Article 52(1)(d) of the ICSID Convention; that is, serious departure from a fundamental rule of procedure.[154]

Cases such as these underline the usefulness of maintaining the reference to dignified behaviour of the investment adjudicator in future Codes of conduct or other soft or hard law instrument dealing with investment adjudicator's duties. As already noted, despite the inherent difficulties, it would also be useful if the notion were defined or at least outlined by means of examples, along the lines of for instance the ABA Model Code of Judicial Conduct's comments to the rules.[155]

Finally, it is worth making a brief comment on a topic that is related to some extent with arbitrators' duty of personal diligence and integrity: their duty of loyalty towards the arbitral institution. This issue has already been addressed in the context of supranational courts: for instance, Article 6 of the current Code of Conduct for Members and former Members of the CJEU[156] states: "Members shall comply with their duty of loyalty towards the Institution. Members shall make use of the services of officials and other servants of the Institution, in particular those allocated to their

---

[152]*Ibid,* par 70. The assessment of the challenged arbitrator himself on this case can be read in: Brower, Melikian and Daly (2015), pp. 320–335.

[153]For instance, due to an obstructive arbitrator. Schneider (2011), p. 275.

[154]Klöckner v. Cameroon, pars 82 bis-113.

[155]Rule 2.3 of the ABA Model Code of Judicial Conduct: "[1] A judge who manifests bias or prejudice in a proceeding impairs the fairness of the proceeding and brings the judiciary into disrepute. [2] Examples of manifestations of bias or prejudice include but are not limited to epithets; slurs; demeaning nicknames; negative stereotyping; attempted humor based upon stereotypes; threatening, intimidating, or hostile acts; suggestions of connections between race, ethnicity, or nationality and crime; and irrelevant references to personal characteristics. Even facial expressions and body language can convey to parties and lawyers in the proceeding, jurors, the media, and others an appearance of bias or prejudice. A judge must avoid conduct that may reasonably be perceived as prejudiced or biased. [3] Harassment, as referred to in paragraphs (B) and (C), is verbal or physical conduct that denigrates or shows hostility or aversion toward a person on bases such as race, sex, gender, religion, national origin, ethnicity, disability, age, sexual orientation, marital status, socioeconomic status, or political affiliation. [4] Sexual harassment includes but is not limited to sexual advances, requests for sexual favors, and other verbal or physical conduct of a sexual nature that is unwelcome." Rule 2.8: "the duty to hear all proceedings with patience and courtesy is not inconsistent with the duty imposed in Rule 2.5 to dispose promptly of the business of the court. Judges can be efficient and businesslike while being patient and deliberate". ABA (2011).

[156]The 2007 version of the Code of Conduct of the CJEU affirmed in its Article 1.3: "General principles- "Members shall refrain from making any statement outside the Court which may harm the reputation of the Court or which may be interpreted as the adoption of a position by the Court on Issues falling outside its institutional role". CJEU (2007).

Chambers, in a respectful manner. Members shall manage the material resources of the Institution in a responsible manner. Members shall refrain from making any statement outside the Institution which may harm its reputation".[157] This idea also underlies the provisions on integrity and freedom of expression in the 2008 ECHR Resolution on Judicial Ethics.[158] Similar references can be found in the commercial arbitration context, such as Rule 1 of the Code of Professional and Ethical Conduct for Members of the CIArb: "A member shall not behave in a manner which might reasonably be perceived as conduct unbecoming a member of the Institute."[159] In the investment arbitration framework, it is also relevant to reflect on the need for making explicit statements of this kind.

References

Altenkirch M, Schmeil B (2015) The Substantial involvement of arbitral secretaries. Global Arbitration News. https://globalarbitrationnews.com/the-substantial-involvement-of-arbitral-secretaries-20150917/

Andersson S (2015) A Fourth Arbitrator or an Administrative Secretary? A Study on the Appointment and Authority of Arbitral Secretaries in Swedish Arbitral Proceedings. http://uu.diva-portal.org/smash/get/diva2:817193/FULLTEXT01.pdf

Baker McKenzie (2017) Submissions to the ICSID Secretariat on amendments to the ICSID Rules and Regulations. https://icsid.worldbank.org/en/Documents/about/Public%20Comments%20to%20Amendment%20to%20ICSID%20Rules%20and%20Regulations.pdf

Benson L (2016) HKIAC pioneers accreditation of tribunal secretaries. https://afiaasiablog.wordpress.com/2016/04/19/hkiac-pioneers-accreditation-of-tribunal-secretaries/

Berger KP (2015) 27 Scenario: deliberation of the tribunal and rendering of the award. In: Berger KP (ed) Private dispute resolution in international business. Negotiation, mediation and arbitration, 3rd rev edn. Wolter Kluwers, Alphen ann den Rijn, pp 1–38

Berwin, Leighton, Paisner (2015) Research based report on the use of tribunal secretaries in international commercial arbitration. http://www.blplaw.com/media/International_Arbitration/BLP_International_Arbitration_Survey_2015.pdf

Bobek M (2014) The Court of Justice of the European Union, Research Papers in Law. College of Europe. https://www.coleurope.eu/sites/default/files/.../researchpaper_2_2014_bobek.pdf

Brauch MB (2014) Yukos v. Russia: The issues and legal reasoning behind US$50 billion awards. Investment Treaty News. https://www.iisd.org/itn/2014/09/04/yukos-v-russia-issues-and-legal-reasoning-behind-us50-billion-awards/

Brower CN, Melikian S, Daly MP (2015) Tall and small tales of a challenged arbitrator. In: Giorgetti C (ed) Challenges and Recusals of Judges and arbitrators in international courts and tribunals. Brill, Leiden Boston, pp 320–335

[157] CJEU (2016).

[158] III. Integrity: "Judges' conduct must be consistent with the high moral character that is a criterion for judicial office. They should be mindful at all times of their duty to uphold the standing and reputation of the Court". VI. Freedom of expression: "Judges shall exercise their freedom of expression in a manner compatible with the dignity of their office. They shall refrain from public statements or remarks that may undermine the authority of the Court or give rise to reasonable doubt as to their impartiality". ECHR (2008).

[159] CIArb (2009).

Daele K (2012) Challenge and disqualification of arbitrators in international arbitration. Kluwer, Netherlands

Debevoise & Plimpton, Proposed Amendments to 2006 ICSID rules, 31 March 2017. https://icsid.worldbank.org/en/Documents/about/Public%20Comments%20to%20Amendment%20to%20ICSID%20Rules%20and%20Regulations.pdf

Derains & Gharavi (2017) ICSID Rules Amendment Project. https://icsid.worldbank.org/en/Documents/about/Public%20Comments%20to%20Amendment%20to%20ICSID%20Rules%20and%20Regulations.pdf

EFILA (2017) Response of the European Federation for Investment Law and Arbitration to the Invitation to File Suggestions for ICSID Rules Amendments. https://icsid.worldbank.org/en/Documents/about/Public%20Comments%20to%20Amendment%20to%20ICSID%20Rules%20and%20Regulations.pdf

Egger PW (2010) Independence, impartiality and disclosure in international arbitration: recent developments. Yearb Int Arbitr 1:103–113

Freshfields, Bruckhaus, Deringer LLP (2017) Proposals from the International Arbitration Group. https://icsid.worldbank.org/en/Documents/about/Public%20Comments%20to%20Amendment%20to%20ICSID%20Rules%20and%20Regulations.pdf

Galagan D, Živković P (2015) The Challenge of the Yukos Award: an Award Written by Someone Else – a Violation of the Tribunal's Mandate? Kluwer Arbitration Blog. http://arbitrationblog.kluwerarbitration.com/2015/02/27/the-challenge-of-the-yukos-award-an-award-written-by-someone-else-a-violation-of-the-tribunals-mandate/

Hanotiau B (2003) Misdeeds, wrongful conduct and illegality in arbitral proceedings. In: Van den Berg AJ (ed) International commercial arbitration: important contemporary questions. Kluwer Law International, The Hague/London/New York, pp 261–287

Hong-Lin Y, Masood A (2016) Keeping the invisible hand under control? Arbitrator's mandate and assisting third parties. Vindobona J Int Commer Law Arbitr 19(2):1–38

Howse R (2015) Courting the Critics of Investor-State Dispute Settlement: the EU proposal for a judicial system for investment disputes. https://cdn-media.web-view.net/i/fjj3t288ah/Courting_the_Criticsdraft1.pdf

Howse R (2017) The Fourth Man: an intriguing sub-plot in the Yukos arbitration. ISDS Platform. http://isds.bilaterals.org/?the-fourth-man-an-intriguing-sub

Hutcheon P (2012) High-profile QC kicked out of disputes body. The Herald. http://www.heraldscotland.com/news/13046496.High-profile_QC_kicked_out_of_disputes_body/

ICC Institute of World Business Law (2018) Training for Court Secretaries. https://iccwbo.org/event/icc-institute-training-tribunal-secretaries-miami/#1489599116575-1e41f4d5-9907

Kenney S (2000) Beyond principals and agents-seeing courts as organizations by comparing Référendaires at the European Court of Justice and Law Clerks at the U.S. Supreme Court. Comp Polit Stud 33(5):593–625

Law Council of Australia (2017) Potential rule amendments or improvements to the arbitration and conciliation procedures of the ICSID. https://icsid.worldbank.org/en/Documents/about/Public%20Comments%20to%20Amendment%20to%20ICSID%20Rules%20and%20Regulations.pdf

LCIA (last accessed June 2018) Frequently Asked Questions. http://www.lcia.org/frequently_asked_questions.aspx#Secretaries.

Levine J (2015) Late-in the-day arbitrator challenges and resignations. In: Giorgetti C (ed) Challenges and Recusals of Judges and arbitrators in international courts and tribunals. Brill, Leiden Boston, pp 247–292

McAuliffe K (2012) Language and law in the European Union. In: Tiersma PM, Solan L (eds) The Oxford handbook of language and law. OUP, Oxford, pp 203–209

Park WW (2009) Arbitrator integrity and investor-state disputes. Contemp Issues Int Arbitr Mediation 3:100–129

Park WW (2012) Investment claims and arbitrator comportment. Transnl Dispute Manage 9(1)

Partasides C (2002) The Fourth Arbitrator? The role of secretaries to tribunals in international arbitration. Arbitr Int 18(2):147–163

Paulsson J (2010) Moral Hazard in international dispute resolution. ICSID Rev - Foreign Invest Law J 25(2):339–355

Polkinghorne M, Rosenberg CB (2014) The role of the tribunal secretary in international arbitration: a call for a uniform standard. Dispute Resol Int 8(2):107–128

Restemayer CJ (2012) Secretaries always get a bad rep: identifying the controversy surrounding administrative secretaries, current guidelines, and recommendations. Yearb Arbitr Mediation 4:328–342

Richman DJ (2008) How to be a great law clerk. Litigation 35(4):16

Rivkin DW (2015) HKIAC Arbitration Week Keynote Address. A new Contract Between Arbitrators and Parties. http://www.sccinstitute.com/media/93206/1000973790v2-hkiac-keynote-address.pdf

Schneider ME (2011) Forbidding unilateral appointments of arbitrators- a case of vicarious hypochondria? ASA Bull 29(2):275

Schwartz E (1995) The Rights and Duties of ICC Arbitrators. ICC International Court of Arbitration Bulletin. Special Supplement. The Status of the Arbitrator

Shetreet S, Forsyth C (2011) The culture of judicial independence: conceptual foundations and practical challenges. Brill Nijhoff, Leiden

Titi C (2017) The European Unión's proposal for an international investment court: significance, innovations and challenges ahead. Transnl Dispute Manage, 1

White & Case and Queen Mary University (2012) International Arbitration Survey: Current and Preferred Practices in the Arbitral Process. www.whitecase.com/files/Uploads/Documents/Arbitration/Queen-Mary-University-London-International-Arbitration-Survey-2012.pdf

White & Case (2018) International Arbitration Survey: The Evolution of International Arbitration. https://www.whitecase.com/sites/whitecase/files/files/download/publications/2018-international-arbitration-survey-the-evolution-of-ia.pdf.

Wilske S (2014) The ailing arbitrator-identification, abuse and prevention of a potentially dangerous delaying and obstruction tool. Contemp Asia Arbitr J 7(2):279–308, 301

Wilske S (2016) Linguistic and language issues in international arbitration-problems, pitfalls and Paranoia. Contemp Asia Arbitr J 9(2):159–196

Young International Council for Commercial Arbitration (2014) (ICCA)'s Guide on Arbitral Secretaries. https://pca-cpa.org/wp-content/uploads/sites/175/2016/01/ICCA-Reports-No.-1_Young-ICCA-Guide-on-Arbitral-Secretaries.pdf

Young ICCA (last accessed June 2018) About Young ICCA. http://www.arbitration-icca.org/YoungICCA/AboutYoungICCA.html

Legal and Arbitration References

International Conventions

UNCITRAL (1985a) Model Law on International Commercial Arbitration. http://www.uncitral.org/uncitral/en/uncitral_texts/arbitration/1985Model_arbitration.html

UNCITRAL (1985b) Travaux Préparatoires. http://www.uncitral.org/uncitral/en/case_law/digests.html

IIAs

CETA (2016) http://ec.europa.eu/trade/policy/in-focus/ceta/ceta-chapter-by-chapter/
EU-Singapore IPA (2018) http://trade.ec.europa.eu/doclib/press/index.cfm?id=961
EU-Vietnam FTA (2016) http://trade.ec.europa.eu/doclib/docs/2016/february/tradoc_154226.pdf
EUSFTA (2015) http://investmentpolicyhub.unctad.org/Download/TreatyFile/3247
JEFTA (2016) https://trade-leaks.org/jefta-leaks/investment-dispute-resolution/
NAFTA (1994) Code of Conduct. https://www.nafta-sec-alena.org/Home/Legal-Texts/Code-of-Conduct?mvid=1&secid=03428812-a551-4839-ab16-669c9d2a82e1
TTIP (2016) http://trade.ec.europa.eu/doclib/press/index.cfm?id=1230

Arbitration Acts, Institutional Arbitration Rules, and Codes of Conduct

ABA, AAA, CPR Institute (2004) Code of Ethics for Arbitrators in Commercial Disputes. https://www.americanbar.org/content/dam/aba/migrated/dispute/commercial_disputes.authcheckdam.pdf
ABA (2011) Model Code of Judicial Conduct. https://www.americanbar.org/groups/professional_responsibility/publications/model_code_of_judicial_conduct.html
CAM (2010) Code of Ethics. https://www.camera-arbitrale.it/en/arbitration/arbitration-rules/code-of-ethics.php?id=104
CAS (2013) Statutes of the bodies working for the settlement of sports-related disputes. http://www.tas-cas.org/fileadmin/user_upload/Code20201320corrections20finales20_en_.pdf
CIArb (2009) Code of Professional and Ethical Conduct for Members. http://www.ciarb.org/docs/default-source/ciarbdocuments/guidance-and-ethics/practice-guidelines-protocols-and-rules/code-of-professional-and-ethical-conduct-october-2009.pdf?sfvrsn=6
CIICA (2016) Code of Ethics for an Arbitrator. http://ciica.org/arbitration/code-of-ethics-for-an-arbitrator/
CIMA (2015) Arbitration Rules. http://arbitrajecima.com/wp-content/uploads/2015/12/Reglamento-CIMA-2015-ingles.pdf
DCCP (1986) Code of Civil Procedure of the Netherlands. http://www.dutchcivillaw.com/legislation/civilprocedure044.htm
DIA (2013) Rules of Arbitration Procedure. https://voldgiftsinstituttet.dk/wp-content/uploads/2015/01/rules_1_may_2013_-_pdf-uden-logo.pdf
FAI (2016) Note on the Use of a Secretary. Proceedings conducted under the Finland Arbitration Institute (FAI) Arbitration Rules and FAI Expedited Arbitration Rules effective as of 1 June 2013. https://arbitration.fi/wp-content/uploads/sites/22/2016/07/note-on-the-use-of-a-secretary.pdf
HKIAC (2014) Guidelines on the Use of a Secretary to the Arbitral Tribunal. http://www.hkiac.org/images/stories/arbitration/HKIAC%20Guidelines%20on%20Use%20of%20Secretary%20to%20Arbitral%20Tribunal%20-%20Final.pdf
IBA (1987) Rules of Ethics for International Arbitrators. https://www.trans-lex.org/701100/_/iba-rules-of-ethics-for-international-arbitrators-1987/
IBA (2014) Guidelines on Conflicts of Interest in International Arbitration. https://www.ibanet.org/Publications/publications_IBA_guides_and_free_materials.aspx#Practice%20Rules%20and%20Guidelines

ICC (2017a) Arbitration Rules. https://iccwbo.org/dispute-resolution-services/arbitration/rules-of-arbitration/

ICC (2017b) Note to Parties and Arbitral Tribunals on the conduct of the arbitration under the ICC rules of arbitration. https://iccwbo.org/publication/note-parties-arbitral-tribunals-conduct-arbitration/

ICDR (2014) International Dispute Resolution Procedures. https://www.adr.org/sites/default/files/ICDR%20Rules_0.pdf

India (2015) The Arbitration and Conciliation (Amendment) Ordinance. http://www.adrassociation.org/pdf/acact2015.pdf

India (2018) The Arbitration and Conciliation (Amendment) Bill. http://www.arbitrationindia.org/pdf/acbill2018.pdf

KLRCA (2013) Revised Code of Conduct for Arbitrator. https://klrca.org/uploads/imguploadckc691e4fcd34a3f05e49b8eb477d2ec21.PDF

LCIA (2014) Arbitration Rules. http://www.lcia.org/Dispute_Resolution_Services/lcia-arbitration-rules-2014.aspx

PCA (2012) Arbitration Rules. https://pca-cpa.org/en/services/arbitration-services/pca-arbitration-rules-2012/

SIAC (2015) Code of Ethics for an Arbitrator. http://www.siac.org.sg/our-rules/code-of-ethics-for-an-arbitrator

SIAC (2017) Investment Arbitration Rules. http://www.siac.org.sg/our-rules/rules/siac-ia-rules-2017

SCC (2017) Stockholm Chamber of Commerce Policy on Appointment of Arbitrators, amended by the SCC board on 8 September 2017. http://www.sccinstitute.com/media/220131/scc-policy-appointment-of-arbitrators-2017.pdf

TAB/BAC (2009) Code of Ethics. http://www.tab.es/index.php?option=com_content&view=article&id=638:barcelona-arbitration-court-code-of-ethics&catid=29&lang=en&Itemid=426

Legal Documents

CJEU (2007) Code of Conduct for Members and former Members of the Court of Justice of the European Union. http://eur-lex.europa.eu/LexUri-Serv/LexUriServ.do?uri=OJ:C:2007:223:0001:0002:EN:PDF

CJEU (2016) Code of Conduct for Members and former Members of the Court of Justice of the European Union. http://eur-lex.europa.eu/legal-content/EN/TXT/PDF/?uri=OJ:C:2016:483:FULL&from=FR

EC (2017) Commission Staff Working Document. Executive summary of the impact assessment. Accompanying the document. Recommendation for a Council Decision authorizing the opening of negotiations for a Convention establishing a multilateral court for the settlement of investment disputes. SWD (2017) 303 final. https://ec.europa.eu/transparency/regdoc/rep/10102/2017/EN/SWD-2017-303-F1-EN-MAIN-PART-1.PDF

ECJ (2009) Décision *de la Cour du* 17 février 2009 portant adoption des règles de bonne conduite des Référendaires. https://www.amicuria.com/presentation

ECHR (2008) Resolution on Judicial Ethics. http://www.echr.coe.int/Documents/Resolution_Judicial_Ethics_ENG.pdf

ICSID (2006) ICSID Administrative and Financial Regulations https://icsid.worldbank.org/en/Pages/icsiddocs/Administrative-and-Financial-Regulations.aspx

Judicial Group on Strengthening Judicial Integrity (2002) Bangalore Principles of Judicial Conduct. https://www.unodc.org/pdf/crime/corruption/judicial_group/Bangalore_principles.pdf

UNCITRAL (2016) Notes on organizing arbitral proceedings. http://www.uncitral.org/pdf/english/texts/arbitration/arb-notes/arb-notes-2016-e.pdf

WTO (1994) Understanding on Rules and Procedures Governing the Settlement of Disputes. DSU. https://www.wto.org/english/docs_e/legal_e/28-dsu_e.htm#17

WTO (1996) Rules of Conduct for the Understanding on Rules and Procedures Governing the Settlement of Disputes. WT/DSB/RC/1 (96-5267), https://www.wto.org/english/tratop_e/dispu_e/rc_e.htm

Chapter 5
The Duty of Confidentiality

5.1 The Duty of Confidentiality

It is useful to provide a broader conceptual framework within which the duty of confidentiality of investment arbitrators can be understood. This Chapter therefore begins with the premise that confidentiality is an extremely broad and polysemic term in the international arbitration context, and even when it has been demarcated from other terms such as privacy[1] or *ex parte* communications,[2] additional distinctions still need to be made. Firstly, there are notable differences between the regulation and practice of confidentiality in the commercial and investment arbitration spheres, and one consequence of this is that notions such as transparency are interpreted, structured and valued differently in the two arbitration areas. Secondly, there are usually dissimilarities in these two spheres between the profile of the duty of confidentiality that is attributed to the arbitrator and to other arbitration participants, such as the parties.

5.1.1 International Commercial Arbitration

Although they are not intended to be exhaustive, some important transversal ideas in the commercial arbitration sphere are outlined below: while the mantra that

[1]Academics draw the following distinction: privacy in arbitration refers to the inability of unauthorised third parties to attend arbitral hearings or participate in the arbitral proceedings. On the other hand, confidentiality refers to the obligation not to disclose to third parties any information or documents concerning the arbitration. Born (2012), p. 196.

[2]The avoidance of specific ex parte communications is another arbitrator's duty. This book does not contain a chapter dealing with this topic, as the author is preparing an article on this issue. Fach Gómez (2019).

K. Fach Gómez, *Key Duties of International Investment Arbitrators*,
https://doi.org/10.1007/978-3-319-98128-4_5

confidentiality is one of modern commercial arbitration's great virtues lives on,[3] several comparative law studies in the commercial arbitration context have shown that the perimeters of confidentiality applicable to the different actors in arbitral proceedings are far from homogeneous.[4]

Firstly, dealing with the arbitration's parties, the fact that most national commercial arbitration legislation does not expressly address the confidentiality issue, coupled with the fact that the parties sometimes fail to reach explicit confidentiality agreements, has led many national courts to reflect on the issue. In general terms, this has created a division between countries whose courts consider that an agreement to arbitrate generates a "confidentiality by default" rule, and those that not recognize that an implicit duty of confidentiality derives from the mere existence of an arbitration agreement between the parties.[5] This lack of unanimity on confidentiality in judicial practice has in turn prompted various national legislators and arbitration institutions to draw up new provisions in this broad area, either defending confidentiality[6] or promoting greater transparency.[7] Moreover, it has not contributed to repairing the fragmented nature of the current system dealing with confidentiality and parties.[8] In short, the parties' positioning on confidentiality is an open-ended topic in many ways, which will undoubtedly continue to give rise to much debate in the international commercial arbitration context.

Conversely, the situation regarding commercial arbitrators' duty of confidentiality seems to be rather more consolidated, possibly in part because of the of the traditional judicial sphere's influence in this non-judicial context.

That is, the duty of confidentiality is widely considered to be inherently linked to the figure of the adjudicator. In the judicial context, in which accessibility, transparency and publicity are key guarantees,[9] judges are clearly still bound by a duty of

[3]The 2018 White & Case survey states that: "87% of respondents believe that confidentiality in international commercial arbitration is of importance. Most respondents think that confidentiality should be an opt-out, rather than an opt-in, feature". White & Case (2018), p. 3. Nevertheless, it has recently been contended that commercial arbitration would benefit from shifting towards transparency. Carmody (2016).

[4]Fortier (1999), pp. 131–139; Noussia (2010) and UNCITRAL (2016), pars 31–32.

[5]Poorooye and Feehili (2017).

[6]For instance, Article 30.1 LCIA Arbitration Rules: "The parties undertake as a general principle to keep confidential all awards in the arbitration, together with all materials in the arbitration created for the purpose of the arbitration and all other documents produced by another party in the proceedings not otherwise in the public domain, save and to the extent that disclosure may be required of a party by legal duty, to protect or pursue a legal right, or to enforce or challenge an award in legal proceedings before a state court or other legal authority." LCIA (2014).

[7]Malatesta and Sali (2013) and Buys (2003).

[8]Some academics have supported the creation of a model confidentiality clause, as a means to achieve harmonization. Sarles (2002).

[9]The Magna Carta of Judges states the following in points 14–16: "Access to justice and transparency. Justice shall be transparent and information shall be published on the operation of the judicial system. Judges shall take steps to ensure access to swift, efficient and affordable dispute resolution; they shall contribute to the promotion of alternative dispute resolution methods. Court documents

confidentiality. In the international sphere, texts like the 2016 Code of Conduct for Members and former Members of the CJEU[10] and the 2008 Resolution on Judicial Ethics of the ECHR[11] both express the judges' duty of discretion with regard to proceedings in general terms. The adjudicators' duty to respect the secrecy of deliberations, a key stage in the proceedings, is also sometimes explicitly emphasized. The Burgh House Principles on the Independence of The International Judiciary, for instance, state that "deliberations of the court shall remain confidential".[12] On the basis of such postulations, international texts such as the UN Basic Principles on the Independence of the Judiciary affirm the professional secrecy of the judiciary, who "shall be bound by professional secrecy with regard to their deliberations and to confidential information acquired in the course of their duties other than in public proceedings, and shall not be compelled to testify on such matters".[13]

Where commercial arbitration is concerned, multiple institutional arbitration rules and arbitrator codes of conduct contain provisions that specifically address the scope of arbitrators' duty of confidentiality.[14] The starting point of these texts, which will be discussed in more detail later, is that arbitration proceedings must be confidential where arbitrators are concerned, a duty that is felt to be justified by an adjudicator's

and judicial decisions shall be drafted in an accessible, simple and clear language. Judges shall issue reasoned decisions, pronounced in public within a reasonable time, based on fair and public hearing. Judges shall use appropriate case management methods." Consultative Council of European Judges (2010). Mahoney (2008).

[10]Article 7 of the Code of Conduct: "Discretion. 1. Members shall preserve the secrecy of the deliberations. 2. Members shall comply with their duty to exercise discretion in dealing with judicial and administrative matters. 3. Members shall act and express themselves with the restraint that their office requires". CJEU (2016).

[11]Article V of the Resolution: "Discretion. Judges shall exercise the utmost discretion in relation to secret or confidential information relating to proceedings before the Court. They shall respect the secrecy of deliberations". ECHR (2008).

[12]Article 1.4. Study Group (2004).

[13]Point 15. UN (1985).

[14]Some other arbitration acts and institutional rules contain a reference on confidentiality, common to various arbitration actors. For instance, Article 24.2 of the Spanish Arbitration Act states that: "the arbitrators, the parties and the arbitral institutions, if applicable, are obliged to maintain the confidentiality of information coming to their knowledge in the course of the arbitral proceedings". Kingdom of Spain (2013). Article 34 of the Danish Institute Arbitration Rules lists the different persons composing the DIA who are obliged by the referred confidentiality duty: "the members of the Arbitral Tribunal, the members of the Board or the Board of Representatives, the Chairman's Committee, the Secretariat and the Secretary General of DIA shall treat all matters relating to the arbitration as confidential." DIA (2013); and Article 3 of the Arbitration Rules of the Stockholm Chamber of Commerce: "Unless otherwise agreed by the parties, the SCC, the Arbitral Tribunal and any administrative secretary of the Arbitral Tribunal shall maintain the confidentiality of the arbitration and the award." SCC (2017) Outside of the commercial arbitration's framework: R43 of the Procedural Rules of the Court of Arbitration for Sport indicates: "Confidentiality. Proceedings under these Procedural Rules are confidential. The parties, the arbitrators and CAS undertake not to disclose to any third party any facts or other information relating to the dispute or the proceedings without the permission of CAS. Awards shall not be made public unless all parties agree or the Division President so decides". CAS (2017).

relationship of trust with the parties in an arbitration.[15] Moreover, it is generally held that confidentiality—including arbitrator confidentiality—protects the parties' business relationship and shelters them from the excessive curiosity of, for example, competitors and social media.[16] This facet of the duty of confidentiality means that commercial arbitrators should not use "confidential information acquired during the course of proceedings to gain personal advantage for others, or to affect adversely the interest of another."[17] The duty is also long-lasting, in the sense that an arbitrator's duty "not [to] disclose or use any confidential information acquired in the course of or for the purposes of the process"[18] does not only exist during the arbitration proceedings, but also "after completion of the dispute arbitration process"[19] or "at any time".[20] Certain ex post considerations have also sometimes been connected with the duty of confidentiality, such as: "after an arbitration award has been made, it is not proper for an arbitrator to assist in proceedings to enforce or challenge the award".[21] In addition, there are commercial arbitration texts that refer to the measures that arbitral tribunals can take to ensure confidentiality,[22] and provisions on arbitrators' duty of confidentiality also appear in other kinds of texts, such as the IBA Rules on the Taking of Evidence in International Arbitration.[23] However, many texts stress that confidentiality should not be interpreted as an

---

[15]Canon VI of the Code of Ethics for Arbitrators in Commercial Disputes states that: "An arbitrator should be faithful to the relationship of trust and confidentiality inherent in that office". ABA (2004).

[16]Gu (2005).

[17]Article 8 of the KLRCA's revised Code of Conduct for Arbitrator: "Confidentiality. The proceedings shall remain confidential. An Arbitrator is in a relationship of trust to the parties and should not, at any time, use confidential information acquired during the course of proceedings to gain personal advantage for others, or to affect adversely the interest of another". KLRCA (2013).

[18]Rule 8 of the CIArb Code: "Trust and Confidence. A member shall abide by the relationship of trust which exists between those involved in the dispute and (unless otherwise agreed by all the parties, or permitted or required by applicable law), both during and after completion of the dispute resolution process, shall not disclose or use any confidential information acquired in the course of or for the purposes of the process". CIArb (2009).

[19]*Ibid.*

[20]Article 7.1. SIAC (2015).

[21]Canon VI. C of the Code of Ethics. ABA (2004).

[22]For instance, Article 37.2 of the Arbitration Rules of ICDR: "Unless the parties agree otherwise, the tribunal may make orders concerning the confidentiality of the arbitration or any matters in connection with the arbitration and may take measures for protecting trade secrets and confidential information". ICDR (2014). With a very similar drafting, Article 22.3 of the ICC Arbitration Rules. ICC (2017).

[23]Article 3.13 of the IBA Rules on the Taking of Evidence in International Arbitration: "Any Document submitted or produced by a Party or non-Party in the arbitration and not otherwise in the public domain shall be kept confidential by the Arbitral Tribunal and the other Parties, and shall be used only in connection with the arbitration. This requirement shall apply except and to the extent that disclosure may be required of a Party to fulfil a legal duty, protect or pursue a legal right, or enforce or challenge an award in bona fide legal proceedings before a state court or other judicial authority. The Arbitral Tribunal may issue orders to set forth the terms of this confidentiality. This

absolute duty for commercial arbitrators, and some provisions even expressly envisage circumstances in which the duty of confidentiality would lapse; for instance, if agreed on by the parties or required by the applicable law.[24]

As mentioned above with reference to the international judicial context, several texts in the commercial arbitration field pay specific attention to the duty of confidentiality during the arbitral tribunal's deliberations, underlining the seminal importance of complying with this duty.[25] An example in the national legislation sphere is provided by the French Code of Civil Procedure, which states that "arbitrators' deliberations are secret".[26] Article 9 of the 1987 IBA Rules of Ethics for International Arbitrators is a pioneering text on this matter in the sphere of institutional arbitration rules. The provision, which has also inspired later institutional rules,[27] states that: "The deliberations of the arbitral tribunal, and the contents of the award itself, remain confidential in perpetuity unless the parties release the arbitrators from this obligation. An arbitrator should not participate in, or give any information for the purpose of assistance in any proceedings to consider the award unless, exceptionally, he considers it his duty to disclose any material misconduct or fraud on the part of his fellow arbitrators".[28] The article opens with a statement concerning the permanent nature of the duty of confidentiality with respect to arbitrators' deliberations. However, the provision also foresees that certain circumstances may override the duty (party waivers, co-arbitrator material misconduct and fraud). Further provisions on arbitral tribunal deliberations contribute new circumstances that would also justify a decline in the duty of confidentiality; for example, if required by the applicable law, or if co-arbitrators have to reveal that an arbitrator has refused to participate in an arbitration.[29]

---

requirement shall be without prejudice to all other obligations of confidentiality in the arbitration." IBA (2010).

[24]Article 37.1 of the Arbitration Rules of ICDR: "Confidential information disclosed during the arbitration by the parties or by witnesses shall not be divulged by an arbitrator or by the Administrator. Except as provided in Article 30, unless otherwise agreed by the parties or required by applicable law, the members of the arbitral tribunal and the Administrator shall keep confidential all matters relating to the arbitration or the award". ICDR (2014).

[25]For instance, Article 5 of the Code of Ethics of the Court of Arbitration at the Polish Chamber of Commerce of Warsaw, when dealing with confidentiality, states that: "It is particularly inadmissible to disclose the content of the award before it is served upon the parties". Polish Chamber (n.a.).

[26]Article 1469. French Code of Civil Procedure (2011).

[27]For instance, article 44.2 of the Swiss Rules of International Arbitration affirms that: "the deliberations of the arbitral tribunal are confidential". Swiss Chamber's Arbitration Institution (2012). Likewise, Article 9 of the Barcelona Arbitration Court Code of Ethics states that: "Confidentiality of deliberations. The deliberations of the arbitration tribunal, and the content of the award, shall remain confidential in perpetuity unless the parties release the arbitrators from this obligation. An arbitration may not take part in or provide any information in order to assist in any proceeding designed to analyse the award unless, exceptionally, the said arbitrator considers it is his duty to reveal any reprehensible or fraudulent conduct on the part of his co-arbitrators." TAB (2009).

[28]Article 9 IBA Rules. IBA (1987).

[29]Article 30.2. LCIA Arbitration Rules (2014).

5.1.2 International Investment Arbitration

An essential idea in the current context of the duty of confidentiality in the investment arbitration framework is that the study of the notion of confidentiality must go hand in hand with the notion of transparency. While the profiles of this confidentiality/transparency duality seem to remain blurred in the commercial context, in investment arbitration they are more clearly defined.

Confidentiality's multiple facets and its relationship with transparency are reflected in current ICSID provisions and practices. In simple terms,[30] the degree of confidentiality and transparency of ICSID cases depend on the parties' agreements and the applicable provisions, a broad concept that encompasses both investment treaties[31] and other legal texts. In the absence of party agreements and applicable legal sources, confidentiality and transparency levels are set by the ICSID arbitral tribunal.[32]

When addressing transparency, an extremely important international text should be referred to: the 2014 UNCITRAL Rules on Transparency in Treaty-based Investor-State Arbitration,[33] which aims to establish what has been referred to as an information-centric notion of transparency.[34] This set of procedural rules aims to ensure that relevant information, documents and hearings are accessible to the public. The Rules also allow submissions from both third parties and non-disputing treaty parties and create a repository of published information.[35] Naturally, the transparency objective is not absolute, and the Rules include a list of exceptions.[36]

Article 1.1 of the referred Rules states that they are applicable to investor-state arbitration initiated under the UNCITRAL Arbitration Rules if they have been included in investment treaties concluded on or after 1 April 2014, and also in UNCITRAL arbitrations regarding investment treaties concluded before that date, provided that the treaty parties or the parties to the dispute agree. It is important to stress that the UNCITRAL Rules are also relevant in the ICSID context, as the door

[30]A more detailed information is provided by ICSID (last accessed in June 2018).

[31]A number of recent IIAs address the issue of transparency of arbitral proceedings in a very detailed way. For example, Article 11.21 of the Australia-Korea FTA requires hearings to be open to the public and demands key documents to be made publicly available—with the exceptions to disclosure listed in the referred provision. This is complemented by the regulation of amicus curiae submissions performed by third (non-disputing) parties contained in Article 11.20. Australia-Korea FTA (2014).

[32]This kind of decision of the arbitration panel finds its legal support in articles 44 and 47 of the ICSID Convention (Articles 44-inherent powers of the tribunal and 47-provisional measures) and in the corresponding Arbitration Rules (Articles 19 and 39). ICSID (1966).

[33]UNCITRAL Rules (2014).

[34]Maupin (2013), p. 7.

[35]Euler et al. (2015), Malintoppi and Limbasan (2015), pp. 31–57; Shirlow (2016) and Yu and Olmos Giupponi (2016).

[36]Article 7. UNCITRAL Rules (2014).

opened by Article 1.9[37] has enabled these rules to be applied in ICSID arbitrations. In BSG v. Guinea, for instance, the parties agreed on a tailor-made transparency regime for the arbitration, based primarily on the UNCITRAL Rules on Transparency amended according to the parties' will, as reflected in Procedural Order No. 2 issued by the arbitral tribunal.[38] Furthermore, according to the 2014 United Nations Convention on Transparency in Treaty-based Investor-State Arbitration,[39] the UNCITRAL Rules on Transparency also apply to ICSID arbitrations in certain circumstances.[40] It has also been predicted that even in ICSID cases where the Rules are not formally applied, this new legal environment will lead to increased pressure for transparency in investment arbitration.[41]

If secrecy is indeed a habit and not a need, as has been stated,[42] the UNCITRAL initiative constitutes a decisive and transparency-fostering step forward in the Treaty-based Investor-State arbitration sphere. The existence of the two international texts mentioned above would seem to suggest that the recent era, during which the rule of confidentiality was in practice gradually eroded through leading cases in which transparency increased,[43] has been consigned to the past. In short, where the public's relationship with investment arbitration is concerned, the UNCITRAL initiative can be expected to bring about the gradual establishment of transparency as the default rule,[44] and in this specific context arbitrators emerge as significant guarantors of the transparency objective. Articles 1.4, 1.5 and 1.6 of the referred text, for instance, recognize both arbitral tribunals' discretion and authority, and Article 1.3.b affirms their power to adapt the Rules' requirements to the particular circumstances of given cases.

However, it must be borne in mind that while the UNCITRAL Rules focus on the transparency level applicable to investment arbitration's relationship with the public, they do not address the issue of investment arbitrators' duty of confidentiality, not even from the perspective of the exceptions to transparency. The degree of transparency of an investor-State arbitration and the degree of confidentiality applicable

[37] Article 1.9: "These Rules are available for use in investor-State arbitrations initiated under rules other than the UNCITRAL Arbitration Rules or in ad hoc proceedings". UNCITRAL Rules (2014).

[38] BSG v. Guinea, pars 1–18.

[39] The Convention entered into force on October 18, 2017. Canada, Mauritius and Switzerland are so far the three parties to the Convention.

[40] Agreement of the State parties based on investment treaties concluded before April 1, 2014; subject to any reservation allowed under the so-called Mauritius Convention; and in regard to cases commenced after the Convention enters into force. ICSID (last accessed in June 2018).

[41] Buntenbroich (2014).

[42] Juratowitch (2017).

[43] For instance: Knahr and Reinisch (2007), pp. 97–118; Kawharu (2007), pp. 159–172; Newcombe (2010). The arbitration praxis regarding transparency has also generated in the past legislative reforms, such as the amendment of the ICSID Arbitration Rules in 2006.

[44] Some authors refer to this as "court-like" transparency. Puig (2015). Moreover, the ICSID system contains a set of pro-transparency provisions on the publication of arbitration requests, awards and other arbitration documents to be applied by the Secretariat.

to the arbitrators resolving the arbitration are therefore two separate issues, which have diverse legal justifications. On the one hand, to use UNCITRAL terminology, it is recognized that the public has the right to access a certain amount of information about the investment arbitration, and it requires the active cooperation of key figures such as investment arbitrators to achieve this objective. On the other hand, on the basis of the underlying arguments already analysed in the judicial and international arbitration context, investment arbitrators are still required to comply with a certain level of confidentiality. Although it may sound paradoxical, what transparency in investor-state arbitration and confidentiality of investment arbitrators have in common, within their respective field of action, is their positive impact on the legitimacy of the investment arbitration system.

The duty of confidentiality attributable to investment arbitrators has been addressed by other pre-existing legal frameworks such as ICSID. Rule 6 (2) of the Arbitration Rules is expressed in these broad terms: "Before or at the first session of the Tribunal, each arbitrator shall sign a declaration in the following form: (. . .) I shall keep confidential all information coming to my knowledge as a result of my participation in this proceeding, as well as the contents of any award made by the Tribunal", and Rule 15 states that: "the deliberations of the Tribunal shall take place in private and remain secret".[45]

ICSID thus clearly imposes a duty of confidentiality on investment arbitrators and the breaching of some facets of this duty has consequently been alleged in a few ICSID cases.[46] The duty is sometimes linked to the notion of prohibited ex parte communications.[47] A clear example of this was provided by Victor Pey Casado v. Chile, in which one of the party-appointed arbitrators was proved to have advised his appointing party of the partial award project's content proposed by the president of the ICSID arbitral tribunal.[48] The arbitrator duly resigned from the case. Another aspect of the duty of confidentiality to have been addressed in the ICSID context is its application vis-à-vis the arbitral institution. In Compañía v. Argentina, one of the members of the second ad hoc committee issued an additional opinion making a clear argument in favour of the privacy and secrecy of the arbitration tribunal's deliberations and drafts, in keeping with Arbitration Rule 15. In this case, the committee member claimed that the Secretariat was de facto exceeding its original

---

[45]ICSID (2006).

[46]Outside the ICSID sphere, the arbitral tribunal of the Croatia v. Slovenia inter-state arbitration—constituted under the auspices of the *Permanent Court of Arbitration*—has also dealt with a case connected to the prohibition of *ex parte* communications. The arbitrator appointed by Slovenia reported details of the tribunal's deliberations in two telephone conversations held with one of its agents. The arbitrator later resigned. Croatia v. Slovenia, par 173.

[47]Fach Gómez (2019).

[48]Victor Pey Casado v. Chile (2008), pars 33–36.

powers, and questioned whether the ICSID Secretariat was also acting according to this duty or not.[49]

It is useful to go a step further at this point and reflect on the future of investment arbitrators' duty of confidentiality in the framework of the ICS system and a prospective MIC. It is well-known that Chapter 8 of the 2016 CETA,[50] which is devoted to investment, contains a provision dealing with ethical issues concerning the members of the tribunal, yet lacks a code of conduct. Article 8.44 entrusts the Committee on Services and Investment with obtaining parties' agreement as to the adoption of a "Code of Conduct for the Members of the Tribunal to be applied in disputes arising out of this Chapter, which may replace or supplement the rules in application". As confidentiality is one of the three topics expressly referred to in Article 8.44 CETA, it would seem to be a particularly relevant issue in this context.

The other texts that have been or are being negotiated by the EU within the ICS framework (EU-Singapore IPA,[51] former EUSFTA,[52] EU-Vietnam FTA,[53] JEFTA,[54] and TTIP[55]) do devote a provision in their codes of conduct -Article 7- to confidentiality. They all open with a general paragraph that was clearly inspired by the NAFTA Code of Conduct[56]: "No member or former member shall at any time disclose or use any non-public information concerning a proceeding or acquired during a proceeding, except for the purposes of the proceeding, and shall not, in any case, disclose or use any such information to gain personal advantage or advantage for others or to adversely affect the interest of others". It is clear from this that the duty of confidentiality also extends to former tribunal members. The text uses wording that is well-known in the commercial arbitrage context -gain advantage/ adversely affect-, and emphasizes the relationship of trust and loyalty that should prevail between present and past tribunal members and parties to investment cases.

The provision's next two paragraphs, which should perhaps appear in reverse order,[57] are devoted to two specific points during arbitral proceedings: the adjudicatory body deliberations -7.3- and the disclosure of a decision before its publication -7.2.

---

[49]The member states: "It should be noted in this regard that the Secretariat, whilst receiving any of this information, appears to be under no similar secrecy obligation." Compañía v. Argentina, Additional Opinion. par 14.

[50]CETA (2016).

[51]EU-Singapore IPA (2018).

[52]EUSFTA (2015).

[53]EU-Vietnam FTA (2016).

[54]JEFTA (2016).

[55]TTIP (2016).

[56]Part VI: Maintenance of Confidentiality. NAFTA (1994). Stressing the importance of NAFTA in matters of transparency: Bjorklund (2016), pp. 291–310.

[57]The order of these paragraphs may originate in the NAFTA Code of Conduct, whose clauses B, C, and D of Part VI refer to the non-disclosure of different opinions, reports and decisions, whereas E refers to the non-disclosure of panel deliberations. NAFTA (1994).

With regard to the deliberations, which are to be understood in a broad sense and not only as referring to the final discussion before an award is agreed on,[58] the texts state[59]: "No member or former member shall at any time disclose the deliberations of the Tribunal or Appeal Tribunal, or any member's views, whatever they may be".[60] This duty seems to be outlined entirely without any type of palliative, since there are no caveats along the lines of that appearing in the NAFTA Code of Conduct ("except as required by law.")[61]

All the texts analysed use very similar wording with respect to the premature full or partial disclosure of a decision or award: ("a member shall not disclose a decision or award or parts thereof prior to its publication in accordance with (. . .)"),[62] prohibiting present members from engaging in such conduct, as it constitutes a breach of the duty of confidentiality. Some of these texts (the EU-Singapore IPA,[63] and former EUSFTA[64]) refer explicitly to their own sets of transparency rules, which appear in annexes and are inspired by the UNCITRAL Rules on Transparency—rules on public access to documents, hearings and the possibility of third persons to make submissions-, while others (CETA,[65] EU-Vietnam FTA,[66] JEFTA,[67] TTIP[68]) have incorporated—with slight differences-[69] a provision referring to the UNCITRAL Rules in their investment chapters. Texts such as these show a convergence of two important areas, which come together in the figure of the

[58]Considering the deliberations ("a process which extends throughout the entire duration of the proceedings from their very beginning up to the delivery of the award") to be a tangible example of cooperation among international arbitrators, Draetta (2016), p. 144. Systematizing various categories of arbitrator deliberations, Derains (2012).

[59]The penultimate version of the TTIP includes a single paragraph, with no express reference to this issue or to the disclosure of a decision before its publication. European Commission (2015).

[60]A slightly different drafting appears in both texts referring to Singapore: "A Member or former Member shall not at any time disclose the deliberations of the Tribunal or Appeal Tribunal, or any Member's view regarding the deliberations". EU-Singapore IPA (2018) and former EUSFTA (2015).

[61]Article 37 of the 2017 SIAC Investment Arbitration Rules does contain a long list of grounds for disclosure. SIAC (2017).

[62]The text presents the following variants: "no member shall disclose a decision or award or parts thereof prior to its publication in accordance. . ." (TTIP, JEFTA, EU-FTA Vietnam); "an arbitrator shall not disclose an arbitration panel ruling or parts thereof prior to its publication in accordance with (...)" (EUSFTA).

[63]Annex 8. EU-Singapore IPA (2018).

[64]Annex 9-G. EUSFTA (2015).

[65]In this case, CETA still does not provide a Code of Conduct containing a provision on confidentiality. Article 8.36. CETA (2016).

[66]Article 20. EU-Vietnam FTA (2016).

[67]Article 11. JEFTA (2016).

[68]Article 18: "with the following additional obligations". TTIP (2016).

[69]These provisions recognize that the application of the UNCITRAL Rules presents the following nuances: "as modified by chapter 8, investment-" (CETA); "subject to the following rules" (EU-Vietnam FTA); "with the following additional obligations" (JEFTA and TTIP).

investment adjudicator: his/her duties as guarantor of transparency vis-à-vis the public, and his/her duty of confidentiality with respect to the participants in the proceedings.

The fact that individual provisions in the ICS sphere demonstrate the connection between the areas of transparency and confidentiality, which seemed to be in conflict in the past, is both positive and illuminating. However, in the face of future developments such as the MIC, it is necessary to reflect on whether the current regulations in the ICS scheme are wholly coherent.

At first glance, Article 7 of the Codes of conduct that make up part of the ICS may give the impression that the duty of confidentiality is outlined in very broad terms. This is in fact a consequence of the provision's wording, which has been extrapolated in part from other legal fields. That is, coming from contexts in which the notion of transparency may be less rooted.[70] However, a more thorough analysis of the article in its full ICS context reveals that the duty of confidentiality should be interpreted more narrowly than first appears. While the influence of increasingly pro-transparency regulation has already been analysed in this Chapter, it is also necessary to reflect on the way or ways in which transparency regulation affects the notion of "public information", which in turn has an impact on the real scope of the adjudicators' duty of confidentiality.

In this last sense, the truly key notion of the ICS is the concept of "non-public information"[71] that appears in the first paragraph of the referred Article 7.[72] Practical reflections on the content of this term were already being expressed in the ICSID framework around a decade ago. Thus, the decision on the arbitrator challenge in Perenco v. Ecuador—previously referred to from the perspectives of appropriate behaviour for arbitrators and issue conflict,[73] also addresses a possible breach of confidentiality by the challenged arbitrator. The defendant state considered that the fact that the arbitrator gave an interview to a legal magazine justified the arbitrator's disqualification. The Secretary General of the PCA upheld the challenge, but solely

[70] Also dealing with international investment and commercial arbitration, Brown and Winch (2019).

[71] Similar terms are used in the commercial context, such as "not publicly available". Article 44.1. DIS (2014).

[72] A reference to the "public domain" is also included in arbitration contexts outside the investment sphere. For instance, Article 78 of the WIPO Arbitration Rules state that: "Maintenance of Confidentiality by the Center and Arbitrator. (a) Unless the parties agree otherwise, the Center and the arbitrator shall maintain the confidentiality of the arbitration, the award and, to the extent that they describe information that is not in the public domain, any documentary or other evidence disclosed during the arbitration, except to the extent necessary in connection with a court action relating to the award, or as otherwise required by law. (b) Notwithstanding paragraph (a), the Center may include information concerning the arbitration in any aggregate statistical data that it publishes concerning its activities, provided that such information does not enable the parties or the particular circumstances of the dispute to be identified". WIPO (2014).

[73] *Supra*, Sect. 3.4.2.

on the basis of reasoning that focused on justifiable doubts as to the arbitrator's impartiality or independence.[74]

It is worth noting that this breach of confidentiality was not accepted as a valid ground per se for the arbitrator's disqualification from the Perenco case. The Secretary General's decision showed clearly that the scope of investment arbitrators' duty of confidentiality has been reduced in practice, as a result of both the transparency rights exercised by the parties and the amplifying effect of the mass media's information work. The ICSID decision in this case states: "The IBA Guidelines do not provide for breach of confidentiality as a ground for disqualification of an arbitrator. In any event, having reviewed the documents provided by both Parties and [the challenged arbitrator], it is clear that [the challenged arbitrator] did not say anything in the interview that revealed confidential information from the arbitration. Ecuador's withdrawal from the ICSID Convention is public knowledge. The fact of Perenco's dispute with Ecuador is public knowledge. The provisional measures decisions by the tribunals in the Perenco and Burlington ICSID arbitrations are publicly available on the ICSID website and have been the subject of media attention. The Parties' public statements and conduct in reaction to the decisions have also been widely covered by the international media and oil industry press."[75]

The scope of the notion of public information has increased further in the internet era. As outlined above, transparency regulations are being established in the investment arbitration sector, and this has made arbitration parties and their counsels fully aware that the development and implementation of a sophisticated strategy with regard to media coverage is one of the issues that must be addressed in any contemporary investment arbitration. In some cases, the parties are so proactive in developing their media strategy[76] that in practice an important part of the case content has to be labelled as public information. In these circumstances, there is little information that can still be classified as non-public—to use the terminology in Article 7.1 ICS of the ICS texts—and therefore little information whose disclosure

[74]Within the framework of these reflections on impartiality and independence, Ecuador argued that "the very fact that [the arbitrator] 'decided to go public' with his comments in a published interview, against the background of the escalating dispute between Perenco and Ecuador, demonstrates a lack of impartiality". Nevertheless, the Secretary General of the PCA affirmed that: "there is no general or absolute prohibition in the IBA Guidelines against international arbitrators speaking with the press or making public statements about pending cases. The IBA Guidelines instead focus on an inquiry into justifiable doubts brought about by *particular* "facts or circumstances" in any given challenge. Obviously, if arbitrators choose to discuss a pending case with the press, they risk opening up the possibility of making statements that could give rise to justifiable doubts as to their impartiality. However, there is no basis in the IBA Guidelines on which to accept the Respondent's argument that [the arbitrator's] decision to give the interview *in and of itself* should lead to his disqualification". Perenco v. Ecuador, par 59–61.

[75]*Ibid,* par 68. The non-existence of a presumption of confidentiality with respect to the parties to the arbitration had been affirmed in other ICSID arbitrations. Kinnear and Diop (2010), pp. 46–49.

[76]This strategy can be very controversial and requires the intervention of the arbitral tribunal. For instance, see United Utilities v. Estonia—a case in which the UNCITRAL Rules on Transparency do not apply.

by investment adjudicators could entail a breach of the duty of confidentiality. It would therefore make sense for the drafting of provisions such as Article 7.1 to be updated so as to include an express reference to the existing regulation on transparency, which progressively broadens the outline of the notion of "public information". The impact of new technology in the sector will undoubtedly continue to reinforce this trend.

However, the fact that breaches of the duty of confidentiality may continue to occur in the area of adjudicators' personal actions should not be ignored. As set out in situations referred to in paragraphs 2 and 3 of Article 7 of the ICS Codes of conduct, disclosure sometimes depends solely on the adjudicators themselves. As the parties are not present at tribunal deliberations or during the drafting of decisions or awards, transparency is not only not required but is also prohibited at these times. In this kind of context, then, it makes sense to continue to require confidentiality from the only individuals who can legitimately participate in them: ICS tribunal members/judges.

Ultimately, the duty of confidentiality that falls to these adjudicators will not disappear completely in the future, but the practical effects of transparency will be noticeable in the duty's breadth. The latter has to be taken into account in contexts such as the ICSID reform, the future MIC and/or the UNCITRAL initiative.

References

Bjorklund A (2016) NAFTA Chapter XI's contribution to transparency in investment arbitration. Austrian Yearb Int Arbitr 10:291–310

Born GB (2012) International arbitration: law and practice. Wolters Kluwer, The Netherlands, p 196

Brown C, Winch P (2019) The confidentiality and transparency debate in commercial and investment mediation. In: Titi C, Fach Gómez K (eds) International commercial and investment mediation. Oxford University Press, Oxford., in press

Buntenbroich D (2014) All parties in investment arbitration will need to adapt to new UNCITRAL rules on transparency. https://www.dlapiper.com/en/spain/insights/publications/2014/03/international-arbitration-newsletter-q1-2014/new-uncitral-rules-on-transparency-in-force-4-2014/

Buys CG (2003) The tensions between confidentiality and transparency in international arbitration. Am Rev Int Arbitr 14:121–138

Carmody M (2016) Overturning the presumption of confidentiality: should the UNCITRAL rules on transparency be applied to international commercial arbitration? Int Trade Bus Law Rev 16:96–179

Derains Y (2012) Fifth annual international commercial arbitration lecture. The arbitrator's deliberation. Am Univ Int Law Rev 27(4):911–923

Draetta U (2016) Cooperation among arbitrators in international arbitration. Indian J Arbitr Law 5 (1):107–146

Euler D, Gehring M, Scherer M (eds) (2015) Transparency in international investment arbitration: a guide to the UNCITRAL rules on treaty-based investor-state arbitration. Cambridge University Press, Cambridge

Fach Gómez K (2019) The avoidance of ex parte communications in international arbitration and its possible effects on the recognition and enforcement of foreign arbitral awards. In: Fach

Gómez K, López Rodríguez AM (eds) 60 Years of the New York Convention. Key Issues and Future Challenges, in press
Fortier U (1999) The occasionally unwarranted assumption of confidentiality. Arbitr Int 15 (2):131–139
Gu W (2005) Confidentiality revisited: blessing or curse in international commercial arbitration. Am Rev Int Arbitr 15:607–637
Juratowitch B (2017) Departing from confidentiality in international dispute resolution. Br Inst Int Comp Law. https://www.biicl.org/documents/1676_2017.pdf?showdocument=1
Kawharu A (2007) Public participation and transparency in international investment arbitration: Suez v. Argentina. N Z Yearb Int Law 4:159–172
Kinnear M, Diop A (2010) Use of the media by counsel in investor-state arbitration. In: ICCA Congress Series. Arbitration Advocacy in Changing Times 15. Wolters Kluwer, Netherlands, pp 40–51.
Knahr C, Reinisch A (2007) Transparency versus confidentiality in international investment arbitration- The Biwater Gauff Compromise. Law Pract Int Courts Tribunals 6:97–118
Mahoney P (2008) The international judiciary-independence and accountability. Law Pract Int Courts Tribunals 7(3):313–349
Malatesta A, Sali R (2013) The rise of transparency in international arbitration. Juris, Huntington, New York
Malintoppi L, Limbasan N (2015) Living in glass houses? The debate on transparency in international investment arbitration. BCDR Int Arbitr Rev 2(1):31–57
Maupin JA (2013) Transparency in international investment law: the good, the bad and the Murky. https://papers.ssrn.com/sol3/papers.cfm?abstract_id=2058195
Newcombe A (2010) Confidentiality in investment treaty arbitration (Giovanna A Beccara and others v. The Argentine Republic). Kluwer Arbitration Blog. http://arbitrationblog.kluwerarbitration.com/2010/03/03/confidentiality-in-investment-treaty-arbitration/
Noussia K (2010) Confidentiality in international commercial arbitration. Springer, Berlin
Poorooye A, Feehili R (2017) Confidentiality and transparency in international commercial arbitration: finding the right balance. Harv Negot Law Rev 22:275–323
Puig S (2015) The social cost of secrecy in international investment arbitration. Kluwer Arbitration Blog. http://arbitrationblog.kluwerarbitration.com/2015/11/18/the-social-cost-of-secrecy-in-international-investment-arbitration/
Sarles JW (2002) Solving the arbitral confidentiality conundrum in international arbitration. https://www.josemigueljudice-arbitration.com/xms/files/02_TEXTOS_ARBITRAGEM/01_Doutrina_ScolarsTexts/confidentiality/Confidentiality_in_International_Arbitrations_-_Sarles.pdf
Shirlow E (2016) Dawn of a new era? The UNCITRAL Rules and UN Convention on transparency in treaty-based investor-state arbitration. ICSID Rev 31(3):622–654
White & Case (2018) International arbitration survey: the evolution of international arbitration. https://www.whitecase.com/sites/whitecase/files/files/download/publications/2018-international-arbitration-survey-the-evolution-of-ia.pdf
Yu HL, Olmos Giupponi B (2016) The Pandora's Box effects under the UNCITRAL transparency rules. J Bus Law 5:347–369

Legal and Arbitration References

International Conventions

ICSID (1966) Convention on the Settlement of Investment Disputes between States and Nationals of Other States. https://icsid.worldbank.org/en/Documents/icsiddocs/ICSID%20Convention%20English.pdf
UN (2014) Convention on Transparency in Treaty-based Investor-State Arbitration. http://www.uncitral.org/uncitral/uncitral_texts/arbitration/2014Transparency_Convention.html
UNCITRAL (2014) UNCITRAL Rules on Transparency in Treaty-based Investor-State Arbitration. http://www.uncitral.org/uncitral/en/uncitral_texts/arbitration/2014Transparency.html

IIAs

Australia-Korea FTA (2014) http://investmentpolicyhub.unctad.org/Download/TreatyFile/2971.
EU-Singapur IPA (2018) http://trade.ec.europa.eu/doclib/press/index.cfm?id=961
EU-Vietnam FTA (2016) http://trade.ec.europa.eu/doclib/docs/2016/february/tradoc_154226.pdf
EUSFTA (2015) http://investmentpolicyhub.unctad.org/Download/TreatyFile/3247
JEFTA (2016) https://trade-leaks.org/jefta-leaks/investment-dispute-resolution/
CETA (2016) http://ec.europa.eu/trade/policy/in-focus/ceta/ceta-chapter-by-chapter/
NAFTA (1994) Code of Conduct. https://www.nafta-sec-alena.org/Home/Legal-Texts/Code-of-Conduct?mvid=1&secid=03428812-a551-4839-ab16-669c9d2a82e1
European Commission (2015) Draft Text on Investment Protection and Investment Court System in the TTIP. http://trade.ec.europa.eu/doclib/docs/2015/september/tradoc_153807.pdf
TTIP (2016) http://trade.ec.europa.eu/doclib/press/index.cfm?id=1230

Arbitration Acts, Institutional Arbitration Rules, and Codes of Conduct

ABA (2004) Code of Ethics for Arbitrators in Commercial Disputes. https://www.americanbar.org/content/dam/aba/events/dispute_resolution/committees/arbitration/Code_Annotated_Final_Jan_2014_update.authcheckdam.pdf
CAS (2017) Procedural Rules of the Court of Arbitration for Sport. http://www.tas-cas.org/en/arbitration/code-procedural-rules.html
CIArb (2009) Code of Professional and Ethical Conduct for Members. http://www.ciarb.org/docs/default-source/ciarbdocuments/guidance-and-ethics/practice-guidelines-protocols-and-rules/code-of-professional-and-ethical-conduct-october-2009.pdf?sfvrsn=6
DIA (2013) Rules of Arbitration Procedure. https://voldgiftsinstituttet.dk/wp-content/uploads/2015/01/rules_1_may_2013_-_pdf-uden-logo.pdf
DIS (2018) Arbitration Rules. http://www.disarb.org/upload/bgbl/2018-DIS-Arbitration-Rules.pdf
French Code of Civil Procedure (2011) http://www.jus.uio.no/lm/france.arbitration.code.of.civil.procedure.1981/doc.html#117
IBA (1987) Rules of Ethics for International Arbitrators. https://www.trans-lex.org/701100/_/iba-rules-of-ethics-for-international-arbitrators-1987/

IBA (2010) Rules on the Taking of Evidence in International Arbitration. https://www.ibanet.org/ENews_Archive/IBA_30June_2010_Enews_Taking_of_Evidence_new_rules.aspx
ICC (2017) Arbitration Rules. https://iccwbo.org/dispute-resolution-services/arbitration/rules-of-arbitration/
ICDR (2014) International Dispute Resolution Procedures. https://www.adr.org/sites/default/files/ICDR%20Rules_0.pdf
ICSID (2006) Arbitration rules. https://icsid.worldbank.org/en/Pages/icsiddocs/ICSID-Convention-Arbitration-Rules.aspx
KLRCA (2013) Revised Code of Conduct for Arbitrator. https://klrca.org/uploads/imguploadckc691e4fcd34a3f05e49b8eb477d2ec21.PDF
LCIA (2014) Arbitration Rules. http://www.lcia.org/Dispute_Resolution_Services/lcia-arbitration-rules-2014.aspx
Polish Chamber of Commerce of Warsaw (n.a.) Code of Ethics of the Court of Arbitration. https://www.sakig.pl/en/arbitration/arbitrators/code-of-ethics
SIAC (2015) Code of Ethics for an Arbitrator. http://www.siac.org.sg/our-rules/code-of-ethics-for-an-arbitrator
SIAC (2017) Investment Arbitration Rules. http://www.siac.org.sg/our-rules/rules/siac-ia-rules-2017
Kingdom of Spain (2013) Spanish Arbitration Act https://www.boe.es/buscar/act.php?id=BOE-A-2003-23646
SCC (2017) Arbitration Rules. http://www.sccinstitute.com/dispute-resolution/rules/
Swiss Chamber's Arbitration Institution (2012) Swiss Rules of International Arbitration. https://www.swissarbitration.org/
TAB/BAC (2009) Code of Ethics. http://www.tab.es/index.php?option=com_content&view=article&id=638:barcelona-arbitration-court-code-of-ethics&catid=29&lang=en&Itemid=426
WIPO (2014) Arbitration Rules. http://www.wipo.int/amc/en/arbitration/rules/#conf2

Legal Documents

Study Group of the International Law Association on the Practice and Procedure of International Courts and Tribunals, in association with the Project on International Courts and Tribunals (2004) Burgh House Principles on the Independence of The International Judiciary. https://www.ucl.ac.uk/international-courts/sites/international-courts/files/burgh_final_21204.pdf
Consultative Council of European Judges (2010) Magna Carta of Judges (Fundamental Principles) https://rm.coe.int/16807482c6
CJEU (2016) Code of Conduct for Members and former Members of the Court of Justice of the European Union. http://eur-lex.europa.eu/legal-content/EN/TXT/PDF/?uri=OJ:C:2016:483:FULL&from=FR
ECHR (2008) Resolution on Judicial Ethics. http://www.echr.coe.int/Documents/Resolution_Judicial_Ethics_ENG.pdf
ICSID (last accessed in June 2018) Confidentiality and Transparency. https://icsid.worldbank.org/en/Pages/process/Confidentiality-and-Transparency.aspx
UN. Human Rights Office of the High Commissioner (1985) Basic Principles on the Independence of the Judiciary. http://www.ohchr.org/EN/ProfessionalInterest/Pages/IndependenceJudiciary.aspx
UNCITRAL (2016) Notes on Organising Arbitral Proceedings. https://www.uncitral.org/pdf/english/texts/arbitration/arb-notes/arb-notes-e.pdf

Chapter 6
Other Duties. Control of Arbitration Costs and Continuous Training

This chapter briefly covers other duties that investment arbitrators—and in the future, judges and members of the court—may have to fulfil. The key aspects of two of these duties (the duty to control arbitration costs and the duty of continuous training) are outlined, and attention is paid to relevant issues that prospective initiatives would need to deal with. The present chapter does not include an exhaustive list of adjudicators' other duties. Certain further duties that have been recognized in the normative and academic contexts, such as the duty to decline or resign, the duty to grant equal treatment to the parties, the duty to render a decision that is enforceable, and post-award duties are also addressed,[1] although this does not mean that they are of little importance. Other obligations that UNCITRAL has recently indicated as "possibly relevant to ethics of arbitrators",[2] such as nationality and arbitrator involvement in settlement, equally merit studies that are beyond the scope of this book.[3]

6.1 The Duty to Control Arbitration Costs

6.1.1 International Commercial Arbitration

Costs are a highly controversial issue in the world of commercial arbitration. Their overriding tendency to increase has meant that the alleged advantages of arbitration over litigation have frequently been questioned, and some critics have also justified the rise of other ADR mechanisms. On the other hand, in their role of service

[1]Referring to these issues—in some cases from a commercial arbitration perspective: Wyss (2017), Karton (2018) and Hausmaninger (1995).

[2]UNCITRAL (2017b).

[3]Berger and Jensen (2017).

K. Fach Gómez, *Key Duties of International Investment Arbitrators*,
https://doi.org/10.1007/978-3-319-98128-4_6

providers, arbitral institutions have in fact implemented a variety of mechanisms to control costs (expedited procedures, online cost calculators, etc.) with the aim of maintaining arbitration's dominant position as a conflict resolution mechanism.

With respect to the arbitrators themselves and the nature of their relationship with arbitration costs, two types of reference are usually included in institutional arbitration rules or in the codes of conduct established for their commercial arbitrators. Some texts consider that, as part of their duty of diligence,[4] "the arbitrators shall do their best to conduct the arbitration in such a manner that costs do not rise to an unreasonable proportion of the interests at stake".[5] Other texts connect costs with effectiveness: "At all stages of the proceedings, the arbitral tribunal normally takes into consideration the need to control costs and preserve the cost-effectiveness of the overall process."[6] Arbitrators therefore have a duty to control all the costs of arbitration.

Moreover, many texts referring to commercial arbitration establish detailed rules on the cost of the arbitrators themselves. Simply put, the tasks of setting arbitrators' fees and reimbursing expenses are mainly left to arbitral institutions, which have drawn up a series of fee tables or schedules establishing *ex ante* information and thus enhancing transparency in this area. Adopting a different fee scale is admissible in some cases, provided that all the parties involved accept it.[7] Consequently, unilateral fee arrangements between an arbitrator and any of the parties or their counsels are usually prohibited, especially if the arbitral institution is not duly informed.[8]

---

[4]*Supra*, Chap. 4.

[5]Article 7 of the IBA Rules of Ethics for International Arbitrators. IBA (1987). Inspired by this provision, Standard 7 of the Barcelona Arbitration Court Code of Ethics states: "Duty of diligence: All arbitrators (. . .) must do everything possible to conduct the arbitration in such a way that costs do not rise in an unreasonable proportion in relation to the interests at stake". TAB (2009). Reflecting this idea, Article 12.3 of the Code of Ethics of the CAM proclaims: "The arbitrator shall avoid superfluous expenses that can increase the costs of the proceedings in an unjustified manner". CAM (2010).

[6]UNCITRAL (2016), par 47.

[7]For example, Article 7 of the KLRCA's revised Code of Conduct for Arbitrator: "For matters conducted under KLRCA Rules, an Arbitrator must adopt the KLRCA Schedule of Fees and adhere to the KLRCA Notes on Schedule of Fees. However, an Arbitrator may adopt a different scale of fees subject to the agreement of parties as provided for in KLRCA Rules. In the event parties agree to adopt a different scale of fees, an Arbitrator must disclose and explain the basis of his fees and expenses to the parties on or before the first preliminary meeting. Immediately after the first preliminary meeting, the Arbitrator shall notify KLRCA, in writing, of the agreed fees and expenses. The Arbitral Tribunal shall keep KLRCA informed, in writing, of any changes in the amount of dispute during the proceeding as it affects the scale of fees applicable". KLRCA (2013).

[8]For instance, Article 5.1 of the Code of Ethics for an arbitrator of the SIAC states: "In accepting an appointment, an arbitrator agrees to the remuneration as settled by the SIAC, and he shall make no unilateral arrangements with any of the parties or their counsel for any additional fees or expenses, except with the express agreement of the Registrar". Article 3.5 of Appendix 1—Administrative Charge and Arbitrators' Fees—of the DIA 2013 Rules of Arbitration Procedure states that: "Separate fee arrangements between the parties and the arbitrators shall be considered contrary to the Rules". SIAC (2015).

The quantifying of arbitrators' fees and expenses has also been approached from an ethical perspective, and some arbitral institutions have chosen to set down in writing an arbitrator's duty to adhere to standards of integrity and fairness when arranging remuneration and reimbursement of expenses.[9] Arbitrators have for instance been required to ensure that: "only reasonable fees and expenses having regard to all the circumstances" are charged.[10] In practice, this is linked with an increasing number of administrative and accounting requirements that arbitrators have to fulfil: some arbitral instances require all payments claimed to be justified; expense reimbursement claims must be supported by receipts or evidence, requests for payment must be submitted within a specific time framework, etc.[11] Likewise, an ethical approach justifies statements such as the following: "the arbitrator shall also not accept directly or indirectly gifts or privileges from any of the parties to the arbitration or their representatives, whether before the commencement of the arbitral proceedings, during or after it."[12] The firm resolve in Article 45.10 of the Arbitration Rules of the Cairo Regional Center for International Commercial Arbitration (CRCICA) may also be seen from an ethical approach of the cost perspective: "the arbitrator who is removed according to Article 12 [de jure or de facto impossibility of performing his or her functions or in the event that he or she deliberately delays the commencement or the continuation of the arbitral proceedings] or successfully challenged according to Article 13 [challenge if circumstances exist that give rise to justifiable doubts as to the arbitrator's impartiality or independence] shall not be entitled to any fees."[13]

6.1.2 International Investment Arbitration

In the investment arbitration context, ICSID specifies that the cost of proceedings governed by their rules include three main items: parties' legal fees and expenses, advance payments to ICSID, and lodging fees.[14] The broad notion of advance payments includes fees and expenses of Tribunal, Commission and *ad hoc* Committee members. The arbitrator's fee entitlement appears in the ICSID Schedule of Fees,[15] and expense entitlements are detailed in the Memorandum on the Fees and Expenses of ICSID Arbitrators.[16] Other investment rules such as the 2017

[9] Canon VII. ABA (2004).

[10] Rule 9 of the CIArb Code. CIArb (2009).

[11] Note to Parties. ICC (2017).

[12] Article 11. CRCICA Arbitration Rules (2011).

[13] *Ibid,* Article 45.10.

[14] ICSID (last accessed in June 2018a).

[15] ICSID (last accessed in June 2018b).

[16] ICSID (2005).

Investment Arbitration Rules of the SIAC also have a written arbitrator fee schedule.[17] From an ethical approach, the ICSID Declaration proclaims: "I shall not accept any instruction or compensation with regard to the proceeding from any source except as provided in the Convention on the Settlement of Investment Disputes between States and Nationals of Other States and in the Regulations and Rules made pursuant thereto".[18]

At the practical level of investment arbitration, both the cost of arbitration itself and the cost of arbitrators remain a highly controversial issue.[19] In the recent case Getma v. Guinea, the increased fees unilaterally imposed by the arbitrators is the core argument of both the annulment decision and the US rejection of enforcement.[20] Besides this specific case, information such as the fact that "the presiding arbitrator in the case between Chevron and Texaco v. Ecuador, received US $ 939,000"[21] gave rise to a generalized heated debate in the investment arbitration sector, and also created a demand for rationalizing costs in investment treaty arbitration.[22] Various proposals for improving the current situation are brought together in the Public Comments to Amendment of ICSID's Rules and Regulations (2016–2018). With regard to the costs of the arbitral proceedings themselves, it has for instance been suggested that time limits for rendering awards should be included.[23] Where payments to arbitrators are concerned, it has been suggested that arbitrations could be more efficiently administered if arbitrators were paid after specific milestones were reached, instead of on an on-going basis with the money advanced by the parties.[24] As mentioned above,[25] it is also proposed that undue delays may be sanctioned by a reduction in the arbitrator's fees.[26]

The EU has recently taken the helm on both these cost issues (cost of the arbitration and cost of the arbitrator) and has so far devoted more attention to it than ICSID. Within the ICS framework, recent EU texts contain a series of novel proposals that seek to modify the current investment arbitration status quo in terms of costs. With respect to the two-instance proceedings sketched in the ICS, these include: prevention of parallel or multiple claims; a simplified objection procedure for claims manifestly without legal merit or unfounded as a matter of law; specific support measures for small and medium-sized investors; provisions dealing with security for costs, arbitration costs and third-party funding; incorporation of the loser

[17]SIAC Investment Arbitration Rules. SIAC (2017).

[18]*Supra*, Sect. 2.2.

[19]Apart from the compensation that may be granted to an investor in the award, the legal costs of investment arbitration are gigantic. Gaukrodger and Gordon (2012).

[20]Rogers (2016).

[21]Eberhardt and Olivet (2012), p. 35.

[22]Franck (2011).

[23]Baker McKenzie (2017).

[24]Freshfields Bruckhaus Deringer LLP (2017).

[25]*Supra*, Sect. 4.2.

[26]Law Council of Australia (2017).

pays principle regarding apportionment of legal costs; specific deadlines for issuing awards in both first instance and appeals, etc.[27] Where members of the tribunal/judges are concerned, the EU supports a system that combines a retainer fee with other fees and expenses (quantified in the first instance à la ICSID—unless there is a Committee ruling on the issue-, or directly by the Committee in the appeal tribunal), and which can be transformed into a regular salary set by the Committee should adjudicators serve on a full-time basis. This is undoubtedly a major change for the better, if attention is paid to the many criticisms raised by the ICSID system in terms of costs.

The Codes of conduct for members of the Court, Appeal Tribunal and Mediators in the EU-Singapore IPA,[28] former EUSFTA,[29] EU-Vietnam FTA,[30] JEFTA[31] and TTIP[32] all include an Article 8—Expenses—worded as follows: "Each member shall keep a record and render a final account of the time devoted to the procedure and of the expenses incurred". The EU-Vietnam FTA, JEFTA, and TTIP also add: "as well as the time and expenses of their assistant and staff". This last sentence is certainly positive in terms of the adjudicators' commitments with respect to these individuals and is linked to the proposals put forward throughout in this book.[33]

Apart from this explicit reference to adjudicators' duty to control their own costs and sometimes those of their subordinates, it is necessary to read both the EU Codes of conduct and other EU texts in some detail to obtain a clear outline of the scope of the adjudicators' duty regarding cost control. Generic references in the Codes of conduct to duties such as performing "his or her duties thoroughly and expeditiously" and "with fairness and diligence", for instance, can be interpreted from the perspective of the adjudicators' duty to control costs. Academics have pointed out that arbitration costs are an ethical issue, and thus "arbitrators have an obligation, at the very least, to be sensitive to cost issues and to keep costs down as far as possible (...) as a matter of fairness to the parties, fairness being an overarching ethical responsibility that includes many facets in the arbitral process".[34] Likewise, various ICS provisions may also be understood as rendering adjudicators accountable not only for delays but also for costs. Some of the EU texts referred to above, for example, set a fixed deadline for issuing provisional awards and require justification for delays.[35]

---

[27]Titi (2017).

[28]EU-Singapore IPA (2018).

[29]EUSFTA (2015).

[30]EU-Vietnam FTA (2016).

[31]JEFTA (2016).

[32]TTIP (2016).

[33]*Supra,* Sect. 4.2.

[34]Referring to commercial arbitration: Rovine (2009), at 133.

[35]Article 27.6 Vietnam-FTA, Article 12.6 JEFTA, Article 3.18.4 EU-Singapore IPA (2018), and Article 28.6 TTIP.

In short, outlining the duty to control arbitration costs in greater detail, including those generated by arbitrators themselves, would be a positive development. For instance, a MIC should be capable of adopting a more systematic and detailed approach than the one outlined in the ICS context,[36] one that explicitly reflects the multiple aspects encompassed by this duty. Finally, it has to be borne in mind that transitioning from the ICS system to the MIC mechanism[37] would bring with it the need for new decisions regarding costs, such as cost allocation in a multilateral system, a topic of crucial importance which lies outside the scope of this book.[38]

6.2 The Duty of Continuous Training

Competence is a necessary capacity for arbitrators in the commercial and investment arbitration context, and is usually expressly required in various legal texts. Although different wording is used in each case, this requisite is reflected in the investment milieu in the texts of international conventions,[39] arbitration institution regulations,

[36]For instance, an express reference to the fact that the adjudicator's expenses have to be reasonable would do no harm. This is explicitly stated in Appendix I. III. 2 of the China International Economic and Trade Arbitration Commission International Investment Arbitration Rules: "The arbitrator's expenses shall include all reasonable expenses actually incurred during the arbitrator's arbitration activities". Likewise: "The Convention should include appropriate provisions aimed at ensuring the access of small and medium-sized enterprises and natural persons to the multilateral court by seeking, inter alia, to reduce costs". European Union (2018a).

[37]This transition is explained by the EU as follows: "the EU approach since 2015 has been to institutionalise the system for the resolution of investment disputes in EU trade and investment agreements through the inclusion of the ICS. However, due to its bilateral nature, the ICS cannot fully address all the aforementioned problems (. . .)". EC (2017).

[38]The EU has already raised the issue of cost allocation in a multilateral system. EC (2016). The importance of this issue is also underlined by UNCITRAL (2017a), p. 6.

[39]Article 14 of the ICSID Convention: "(1) Persons designated to serve on the Panels shall be persons of high moral character and recognized competence in the fields of law, commerce, industry or finance, who may be relied upon to exercise independent judgment. Competence in the field of law shall be of particular importance in the case of persons on the Panel of Arbitrators". ICSID (1966).

Codes of ethics,[40] and recent IIAs,[41] among others. The concept's specific definition and its practical expression raise many burning questions, some of which the author has addressed by in a recent work.[42]

When dealing with the notion of continuous training, it has been stated in the international judicial sphere that training is both a duty and a right for judges, first when they take up their positions, and then throughout their professional careers. Institutions such as the Council of Europe have committed themselves to playing an active role in this training, since it is believed to lead to benefits in terms of enhanced adjudicator competence and independence, and increased quality and efficiency in the adjudicatory system.[43] It is therefore considered that the training has to meet a series of quality markers; that is, it must be detailed; in depth; diversified; open; impartial; assessable, and have an adequate budget.[44]

---

[40]Article 3 of the CAM Code of Ethics states: "When accepting his/her mandate, the arbitrator shall, to the best of his/her knowledge, be able to perform his task with the necessary competence with respect to his/her adjudicating function and the subject matter of the dispute". CAM (2010). Documents such as the ABA Code of Ethics for Arbitrators in Commercial Disputes, the 1987 IBA Rules of Ethics for International Arbitrators and the Code of Professional and Ethical Conduct for Members of the CIArb have addressed this issue from the perspective of the arbitrator's own responsibility. Canon I.3 of the ABA Code states that: "One should accept appointment as an arbitrator only if fully satisfied that he or she is competent to serve", ABA (2004); Article 2.2 of the Rules, when dealing with the accepting of appointments affirms that: "A prospective arbitrator shall accept an appointment only if he is fully satisfied that he is competent to determine the issues in dispute, and has an adequate knowledge of the language of the arbitration", IBA (1987); and Rule 4.1 of the CIArb Code proclaims: "a member shall accept an appointment or act only if appropriately qualified or experienced", CIArb (2009).

[41]Article 8.27.4 CETA: "The Members of the Tribunal shall possess the qualifications required in their respective countries for appointment to judicial office, or be jurists of recognised competence. They shall have demonstrated expertise in public international law. It is desirable that they have expertise in particular, in international investment law, international trade law and the resolution of disputes arising under international investment or international trade agreements". CETA (2016). The same wording appears in Article 12.4 of the EU-Vietnam FTA, in Article 9.4 of TTIP, and in Article 8.6 of JEFTA.

[42]Fach Gómez (2016). A recent OECD consultation paper summarizes the status quo on this issue: Gaukrodger (2018), pp. 68–71.

[43]Point 8 of the Magna Carta of Judges defines training as a guarantee of independence, as follows: "initial and in-service training is a right and a duty for judges. It shall be organized under the supervision of the judiciary. Training is an important element to safeguard the independence of judges as well as the quality and efficiency of the judicial system". Consultative Council of European Judges (2010).

[44]For instance, Action 2.5 of the Plan of Action on Strengthening Judicial Independence and Impartiality launched by the Council of Europe is entitled "Ensure comprehensive and effective training of the judiciary in effective judicial competences and ethics", and the remedial action by member States says that: "Judges should receive detailed, in-depth and diversified training to enable them to perform their duties satisfactorily. The quality of initial and in-service training for judges should be reinforced by allocating sufficient resources to guarantee that training programmes meet the requirements of competence, openness and impartiality inherent in judicial office. Training programmes should be subject to frequent assessments by the organs responsible for judicial

A supranational judicial institution like the ECHR also treats the issue of the continuous development of professional skills as one of a judge's duties, approaching the issue from the perspective of judicial ethics.[45] In the EU framework, multiple regional and national initiatives have also been implemented in recent years, with the aim of improving European judicial training and ensuring the full application of EU law.[46] This question has been approached from different angles at academic level as well.[47]

However, there appear to be no generalized references to the need for international arbitrators to participate in continuous training programmes throughout their professional lives. In some commercial arbitration contexts, jurists may be required to complete a series of courses provided by the arbitration institution in the form of continuing training requirements to keep their names on the potential arbitrators list.[48] This does not mean, however, that the current international arbitration framework imposes generalized compulsory training on commercial or investment arbitrators. On the contrary, the system basically relies on self-regulation, in the hope that arbitrators who accept appointments do so because they possess the necessary suitable and up-to-date skills. The following mentions—outside the investment context-, which point in the direction of fostering adjudicators' continuous training, are remarkable: for instance, from the perspective of the duties of arbitral institutions, it has been stated that: "the arbitral institutions, by themselves or in collaboration with other institutions, will try to offer permanent training programmes that promote the professionalization of arbitration practice."[49] The reference in the WTO DSU, which has been reproduced in recent EU texts,[50] might also be interpreted—albeit indirectly—in this sense: "All persons serving on the Appellate Body (. . .) shall stay abreast of dispute settlement activities and other relevant activities of the WTO".[51]

In practice, professionals who act as arbitrators within the framework of an arbitration institution are assumed to have access to a relevant range of training resources. While they may be able to use multiple legal resources paid for by the institution—online databases, law libraries, etc., it is also well known that all

---

training. Candidates for judicial office should receive proper training, including practical training by assisting sitting judges". Council of Europe (2016).

[45]The ECHR 2008 Resolution on Judicial Ethics states: "IV. Diligence and competence. Judges shall perform the duties of their office diligently. In order to maintain a high level of competence, they shall continue to develop their professional skills". ECHR (2008).

[46]EU (2018b).

[47]Some pieces have been written from a comparative perspective: Neil (2014), pp. 893–950; and other papers are dealing with a specific subject matter: Weiner (2015).

[48]The author raised this issue in OGEMID on April 18, 2018 and wishes to thank all participants who offered their opinions on the subject.

[49]Duty 27 of the CEA Code of Good Arbitration Practices. (Author's translation). CEA (2005).

[50]Articles 9.11 and 10.11 TTIP (2016); Articles 12.13 and 13.13 EU-Vietnam FTA (2016); Article 8 JEFTA (2016).

[51]Article 17 DSU. WTO (1994).

arbitration institutions are very active in the training field.[52] Providing a variety of arbitration courses is a way of publicizing the organization itself, and in some cases, of obtaining important financial resources. Individuals who appear on arbitration lists or/and who have already acted as arbitrators are likely to receive detailed information about these activities and may even benefit from preferential fees when registering.

While key stakeholders seem to accept this state of affairs, it has emerged from informal conversations with representatives of civil society who are actively involved in investment arbitration that they take a very dim view of the situation. In short, they pointed out that due to the investment arbitrators' daunting profiles and their weight as a lobby, nobody dares to stick their neck out,[53] and it is suggested that they might benefit from further training. They do feel that investment arbitrators' participation in compulsory training programmes is essential both for the sake of the quality of arbitral decisions and the legitimacy of the whole system, and that this should therefore somehow be formalised.

If changes are to be implemented in the investment context, as would be desirable, we need to look once again to arbitral institutions and new players such as the EU or UNCITRAL. The issue of continuous training for adjudicators should be examined and discussed in depth in the course of projects such as the reform of the ICSID rules or the creation of a MIC.

Previous lifelong learning programmes implemented by other institutions could be used as models in these investment frameworks; face-to-face courses could be combined with a sound e-learning platform, for example. Likewise, training could be an ideal response to a classic complaint in the investment arbitration context: adjudicators' lack of sensitivity with respect to issues such as human rights.[54] The training could also cover issues of the type addressed in these pages, included within the generic concept of "ethics for investment adjudicators".[55] It may even deal with

[52]For instance, ICSID has a section in its website entitled "Events and Training", but the activities are not expressly offered to its arbitrators and mediators. ICSID (last accessed in June 2018c).

[53]The issue of the arbitrators' qualifications is rarely raised in the context of investment challenges, and even less the issue of a potential duty regarding continuous training. Exceptionally, in Alpha v. Ukraine the respondent dared to suggest that the arbitrator "lacked the kind of arbitration experience that would be exceptional of a person appointed to serve in such an obviously complicated investment arbitration case". However, the other members of the tribunal concluded that the arbitrator "possesses competence in the field of law as required by Article 14.1." Alpha v. Ukraine, pars 67 and 70.

[54]Termacic and Pastrana (2017) and Mahoney (2009).

[55]When describing the AAA training program, a reflection is made that can be extrapolated to the context of investment arbitration: "Each training program focuses heavily on issues of arbitrator ethics and disclosures. The rationale in parte here is that an ethical arbitrator in typically an efficient one". Slate (2004), p. 86.

linguistic[56] or cybernetic[57] issues, which may become increasingly relevant in the future. Introducing a duty to acquire continuous training delineated through a transparent system would also have positive repercussions on the adjudicators' CVs, an issue that has also been addressed in these pages.[58] Finally, the *ex novo* creation of an institution like a prospective MIC would also enable its regulations to address the question of adjudicators' continuous training from the very beginning.[59]

References

Baker McKenzie (2017) ICSID rules and regulations. submissions to the ICSID Secretariat on revisions to the ICSID rules and regulations. https://icsid.worldbank.org/en/Documents/about/Public%20Comments%20to%20Amendment%20to%20ICSID%20Rules%20and%20Regulations.pdf

Berger KP, Jensen JO (2017) The arbitrator's mandate to facilitate settlement. Fordham Int Law J 40(3):887–918

Cohen S, Morril M (2017) A call to Cyberarms: the international arbitrator's duty to avoid digital intrusion. Fordham Int Law J 40(3):981–1021

Eberhardt P, Olivet C (2012) Profiting from injustice. https://www.tni.org/files/download/profitingfrominjustice.pdf

Fach Gómez K (2016) The US-EU transatlantic trade and investment partnership: should it leave a door open for non-legal arbitrators? Confl Resol Q 34(2):189–224

Franck SD (2011) Rationalizing costs in investment treaty arbitration. Wash Univ Law Rev 88:769–852

Freshfields Bruckhaus Deringer LLP (2017) Proposals from Freshfields Bruckhaus Deringer LLP (International Arbitration Group). https://icsid.worldbank.org/en/Documents/about/Public%20Comments%20to%20Amendment%20to%20ICSID%20Rules%20and%20Regulations.pdf

Gaukrodger D (2018) Appointing authorities and the selection of arbitrators in investor-state dispute settlement: an overview. http://www.oecd.org/investment/investment-policy/ISDS-Appointing-Authorities-Arbitration-March-2018.pdf

Gaukrodger D, Gordon K (2012) Investor-state dispute settlement: a scoping paper for the investment policy community. In: OECD Working Papers on International Investment. http://www.oecd.org/investment/investment-policy/WP-2012_3.pdf

Hausmaninger C (1995) Rights and obligations of the arbitrator with regard to the parties and the arbitral institution – a civil law viewpoint. In: ICC (ed) The status of the arbitrator. ICC Publishing Corporation, New York, pp 36–44

[56]In National Grid v Argentina, it seems that the language was a key issue in the challenge decision: "the Division wishes to state that [the arbitrator's] challenged statement may have been unfortunate and could have been the result of linguistic infelicity because Spanish is not Mr Kessler's native language." National Grid v Argentina, par 102.

[57]The future of investment arbitration will have to face multiple cyber challenges, such as: security and confidentiality threats connected to the use of shared platforms for data storage and transmission; cybersecurity training and education programs for the arbitration's participants, etc. Cohen and Morril (2017).

[58]*Supra,* Sect. 2.6.

[59]Offering an ex ante trainings to potential adjudicators may also generate positive effects in terms of increased adjudicator's diversity. In the UNCITRAL setting has been stated that: "training should be provided to expand the pool of potential international arbitrators". UNCITRAL (2018), par 74.

Karton J (2018) The international investment arbitrator's duty to apply the law. Law Pract Int Courts Tribunals 17(1):159–176
Law Council of Australia (2017) Potential rule amendments or improvements to the arbitration and conciliation procedures of the ICSID. https://icsid.worldbank.org/en/Documents/about/Public%20Comments%20to%20Amendment%20to%20ICSID%20Rules%20and%20Regulations.pdf
Mahoney P (2009) A European judicial training institute on human rights. Eur Human Rights Law Rev 2:123–134
Neil C (2014) The faces of judicial independence: democratic versus bureaucratic accountability in judicial selection, training, and promotion in South Korea and Taiwan. Am J Comp Law 62 (4):893–950
Rogers C (2016) When arbitrators and institutions clash, or the strange case of Getma v. Guinea. Kluwer Arbitration Blog. http://arbitrationblog.kluwerarbitration.com/2016/05/12/when-arbitrators-and-institutions-clash-or-the-strange-case-of-getma-v-guinea/
Rovine AW (2009) Cost concerns in the drafting of arbitral awards-an issue of ethics. Contemp Issues Int Arbitr Mediation, 133–145
Slate WK (2004) Fostering and rating arbitrators' efficiency. The view of the appointing authorities. J World Invest Trade 5(1):85–88
Termacic T, Pastrana E (2017) Human Rights Education for Legal Professionals (HELP): Council of Europe programme. http://help.elearning.ext.coe.int
Titi C (2017) The European Union's proposal for an international investment court: significance, innovations and challenges ahead. Transnl Dispute Manage, 1
Weiner P (2015) The right to a competent judge: selecting, training and assigning international criminal judges. In: Sarvarian A, Baker R, Fontanelli F, Tsevelekos V (eds) Procedural fairness in international courts and tribunals. British Institute of International and Comparative Law, London
Wyss L (2017) Expedient and efficient arbitrations need strong arbitrators- but how "strong" should and may arbitrators get? Int Arbitr Law Rev 2 and 3:69–90

Legal and Arbitration References

International Conventions

ICSID (1966) Convention on the Settlement of Investment Disputes between States and Nationals of Other States. https://icsid.worldbank.org/en/Documents/icsiddocs/ICSID%20Convention%20English.pdf

IIAs

EU-Vietnam FTA (2016) http://trade.ec.europa.eu/doclib/docs/2016/february/tradoc_154226.pdf
EUSFTA (2015) http://investmentpolicyhub.unctad.org/Download/TreatyFile/3247
EU-Singapore IPA (2018) http://trade.ec.europa.eu/doclib/press/index.cfm?id=961
JEFTA (2016) https://trade-leaks.org/jefta-leaks/investment-dispute-resolution/
CETA (2016) http://ec.europa.eu/trade/policy/in-focus/ceta/ceta-chapter-by-chapter/
TTIP (2016) http://trade.ec.europa.eu/doclib/press/index.cfm?id=1230

Arbitration Acts, Institutional Arbitration Rules, and Codes of Conduct

ABA, AAA, CPR Institute (2004) Code of Ethics for Arbitrators in Commercial Disputes. https://www.americanbar.org/content/dam/aba/migrated/dispute/commercial_disputes.authcheckdam.pdf

CAM (2010) Code of Ethics. https://www.camera-arbitrale.it/en/arbitration/arbitration-rules/code-of-ethics.php?id=104

CEA (2005) Código de buenas prácticas arbitrales. Code of Good Arbitration Practices. (Author's translation). https://www.clubarbitraje.com/sites/default/files/090216_buenas_practicas_arbitrales_castellano_1.pdf

CIArb (2009) Code of Professional and Ethical Conduct for Members. http://www.ciarb.org/docs/default-source/ciarbdocuments/guidance-and-ethics/practice-guidelines-protocols-and-rules/code-of-professional-and-ethical-conduct-october-2009.pdf?sfvrsn=6

CIETAC (2017) International Investment Arbitration Rules. http://www.cietac.org/index.php?m=Page&a=index&id=390&l=en

CRCICA (2011) Arbitration Rules. http://crcica.org/Arbitration_rules.aspx#_idTOCAnchor-101

DIA (2013) Rules of Arbitration Procedure. https://voldgiftsinstituttet.dk/wp-content/uploads/2015/01/rules_1_may_2013_-_pdf-uden-logo.pdf

IBA (1987) Rules of Ethics for International Arbitrators. https://www.trans-lex.org/701100/_/iba-rules-of-ethics-for-international-arbitrators-1987/

ICC (2017) Note to Parties and Arbitral Tribunals on the conduct of the arbitration under the ICC rules of arbitration. https://iccwbo.org/publication/note-parties-arbitral-tribunals-conduct-arbitration/

KLRCA (2013) Revised Code of Conduct for Arbitrator. https://klrca.org/uploads/imguploadckc691e4fcd34a3f05e49b8eb477d2ec21.PDF

SIAC (2015) Code of Ethics for an Arbitrator. http://www.siac.org.sg/our-rules/code-of-ethics-for-an-arbitrator

SIAC (2017) Investment Arbitration Rules. http://www.siac.org.sg/our-rules/rules/siac-ia-rules-2017

TAB/BAC (2009) Code of Ethics. http://www.tab.es/index.php?option=com_content&view=article&id=638:barcelona-arbitration-court-code-of-ethics&catid=29&lang=en&Itemid=426

Legal Documents

Consultative Council of European Judges (2010) Magna Carta of Judges (Fundamental Principles) https://rm.coe.int/16807482c6

Council of Europe (2016) Plan of Action on Strengthening Judicial Independence and Impartiality. https://rm.coe.int/1680700285

EC (2016) Expert meeting. Establishment of a multilateral investment dispute settlement system. http://trade.ec.europa.eu/doclib/docs/2017/january/tradoc_155267.12.12%20With%20date_%20Discussion%20paper_Establishment%20of%20a%20multilateral%20investment%20Geneva.pdf

EC (2017) Recommendation for a Council Decision authorizing the opening of negotiations for a Convention establishing a multilateral court for the settlement of disputes. https://eur-lex.europa.eu/legal-content/EN/TXT/?uri=CELEX%3A52017SC0303

EU (2018a) Negotiating directives for a Convention establishing a multilateral court of the settlement of investment disputes". 12981/17 ADD 1 DCL 1. http://data.consilium.europa.eu/doc/document/ST-12981-2017-ADD-1-DCL-1/en/pdf
European Court of Human Rights (2008) Resolution on Judicial Ethics. http://www.echr.coe.int/Documents/Resolution_Judicial_Ethics_ENG.pdf
EU (2018b) Working together to improve European judicial training. https://e-justice.europa.eu/content_the_european_judicial_training_policy-121-en.do
ICSID (2005) Memorandum on the Fees and Expenses. https://icsid.worldbank.org/en/Pages/icsiddocs/Memorandum-on-the-Fees-and-Expenses-FullText1.aspx
ICSID (last accessed in June 2018a) Cost of Proceedings. https://icsid.worldbank.org/en/Pages/services/Cost-of-Proceedings.aspx.
ICSID (last accessed in June 2018b) Schedule of fees. https://icsid.worldbank.org/en/Pages/icsiddocs/Schedule-of-Fees.aspx
ICSID (last accessed in June 2018c) Events and Training. https://icsid.worldbank.org/en/Pages/about/Upcoming-Events-and-Training.aspx
UNCITRAL (2016) Notes on Organizing Arbitral Proceedings. http://www.uncitral.org/uncitral/en/uncitral_texts/arbitration/2016Notes_proceedings.html
UNCITRAL (2017a) Note by the Secretariat. Possible reform of investor-State dispute settlement, A/CN.9/WG.III/WP.142, https://documents-dds-ny.un.org/doc/UNDOC/LTD/V17/067/48/PDF/V1706748.pdf?OpenElement
UNCITRAL (2017b) Possible future work in the field of dispute settlement: Ethics in international arbitration. United Nations Working Group III. http://www.uncitral.org/uncitral/en/commission/working_groups/3Investor_State.html
UNCITRAL (2018) Report of the Working Group III (Investor-State Dispute Settlement Reform) on the work of its thirty-fifth session. http://www.uncitral.org/uncitral/en/commission/working_groups/3Investor_State.html
WTO (1994) DSU. https://www.wto.org/english/docs_e/legal_e/28-dsu_e.htm#17

Chapter 7
Conclusion. A New Code of Conduct for Present and Future Investment Adjudicators

The practice of investment arbitration shows that dilemmas closely related to the figure of the investment arbitrator frequently arise in the course of arbitral proceedings. This book analyses and systematizes such situations, which are highly controversial at both legal and ethical level, and links them with some of the duties that are usually attributed to investment arbitrators. There is a strong transnational element in this study, since the origins of the institution of international investment arbitration itself and many of the texts dealing with investment arbitrators' duties are transnational in nature.

This book undertakes a detailed analysis of a range of investment arbitrator duties selected by the author. These duties not only have outstanding practical importance, but also merit individual study, with the aim of creating a debate that may give rise to *lege ferenda* proposals. However, other significant duties do not receive individual attention here, partly because of the limited word length, and partly because they have already been dealt with in previous works by the author.

Chapter 1 presents an overview of the transformational period that the ISDS regime is currently undergoing. Various policy papers published by the EU in recent years, together with the fact that these papers' key points have materialised in the latest EU FTAs, have caused the winds of change to blow through the investment discipline, including crucial modifications to the figure of the investment adjudicator.

The EU's specific concern over their investment adjudicators' ethics is reflected in a provision entitled "Ethics" contained in the referred EU FTAs. This provision continues to accommodate traditional figures such as adjudicator challenge and potential disqualification, and also regulates the removal of adjudicators. As a noteworthy novelty, the EU texts also include a Code of Conduct for Members of the Court and the Appeal Tribunal. Texts such as this, which public opinion views in a positive light, constitute an advance in terms of systematization, visibility, transparency and accountability. They may also be a weapon for combatting systemic adulterations, such as the well-known guerrilla tactics sometimes employed in the course of arbitration proceedings. EU-driven codes of conduct may also spark a race

K. Fach Gómez, *Key Duties of International Investment Arbitrators*,
https://doi.org/10.1007/978-3-319-98128-4_7

to the top among stakeholders, contributing to a situation in which arbitrators' duties are also addressed in a more orderly way in other forums such as ICSID. It is important to be aware, however, of the fact that codes of conduct for investment adjudicators are still embryonic mechanisms which are criticised for their ambiguity and lack of completeness. In other words, whether we like it or not, we are currently faced with a work in progress. The same can be said with regard to the content of the specific investment arbitrators' duties that would give shape to the code of conduct.

There is an unquestionable reality with respect to many crucial issues pertaining to the investment arbitration milieu, which also comprises investment arbitrators' ethics: the great interest shown by a range of stakeholders, who are willing to encourage public debate and see their opinions reflected in a regulatory metamorphosis. It would not be overstating the case to say that there has recently been a clear rise in expectations with respect to investment arbitrators' conduct. However, the regulatory framework of investment arbitration has reflected this increasingly significant reality only in a partial and piecemeal fashion. As detailed in Chap. 1, the current system presents certain transversal uncertainties and challenges, such as the following: in spite of the fact that investment arbitrators' duties are currently mentioned in a plurality of sources that have varying origins and binding effects, there are no clear uniform guidelines on how to deal with possible contradictions arising from the diverse content of these potentially applicable sources. Other troublesome facts are the non-existence of a finely-tuned system to determine the consequences that may derive from a breach of investment arbitrators' duties, and the absence of any general clarification regarding the entities in charge of exercising disciplinary power in the investment adjudicator context.

It is not possible to be certain about the reason(s) slowing down changes in the issue of investment arbitrators' ethics, but it is possible to pinpoint a few contributory factors: firm resistance on the part of the arbitral collective itself, who mainly agree with the current status quo; stagnation and a kind of fear of facing crucial changes on the part of service providers, and the fact that some of the stakeholders who favour introducing changes might suffer from a lack of unity. In any case, this asymmetry between a collective will on the rise and the present regulatory framework is unlikely to be able to sustain itself in the future. That is why, faced with this current scenario, the Codes of conduct for Investment Adjudicators could be an optimal tool to encourage and facilitate a transition that would overcome the phase of the classic ISDS system.

The interest recently expressed by UNCITRAL Working Group III in an ISDS reform suggests that there may be new developments on a truly global level in the area of investment adjudicators' duties in the future. So far, the desire of relevant stakeholders such as the EU to create a MIC, and all that this entails for investment adjudicators, has remained unwavering. This fact also reinforces the likelihood of future changes.

It is impossible to ignore that fact that the issue here is about making a large-scale transition from ad hoc arbitral panels to a permanent global court, and from party-appointed arbitrators to court members with quasi-civil servant status, etc. If this transformation does come about, it will certainly not be a trouble-free. It is therefore to be expected that the path taken by the reform of the current ISDS system will be long and complicated, and a similar fate probably awaits investment adjudicators' duties. However, and since a number of key principles in the ISDS system (legitimacy, transparency, accountability, etc.) cannot be waived, it is no longer possible to continue to sidestep the question of arbitrators' ethical duties. This book therefore wishes to encourage debate among international scholars and practitioners on the fascinating issue of investment adjudicators' dilemmas and duties.

The duty of disclosure that falls to investment arbitrators is linked with their duty of independence and impartiality. *A priori*, it seems reasonable for arbitrators to be obliged to disclose circumstances that may connect them with the case or its participants, all the more so since party-appointed arbitrators are crucial figures in the investment arbitration setting. Nevertheless, in contemporary ISDS, the exact profile and extent of the duty to disclose is a highly controversial issue, which usually arises in the framework of a challenge brought by one of the parties against one or more investment arbitrators.

The marked increase of challenges in the course of ICSID arbitrations has set alarm bells ringing among practitioners and scholars, in the sense that unnecessary challenges aimed at stalling proceedings—one of the most noteworthy manifestations of so-called "guerrilla tactics"—are subjecting the undoubtedly trustworthy collective of arbitrators to excessive scrutiny and stress. However, from another perspective it is argued that the existence and use of the challenge mechanism is a fair price that must be paid, as one of ISDS's ultimate aims is to protect arbitration parties' most fundamental rights—which include the right to fair proceedings.

These divergent opinions about the benefits or evils of investment arbitrator challenges come hand in hand with a fundamental controversy over the contours of the duty of disclosure. While some authors consider that a strong *ex ante* policy on the matter of disclosure gives the whole ISDS system legitimacy, others consider that an overblown duty of disclosure would be counterproductive.

It is therefore clear that the duty of disclosure attributable to investment arbitrators currently presents a significant number of contentious features. Many ICSID challenges have addressed issues such as the formal features and content of the statement of impartiality and independence, as well as the scope of the duty of disclosure and the applicable disclosure standards. The detailed analysis of the decisions resulting from these challenges in Chap. 2 leads to the conclusion that unchallenged co-arbitrators, who are in most cases responsible for settling challenges brought by parties, may sometimes have erred on the side of leniency when judging their colleagues' actions or omissions in connection with the duty of disclosure. The author believes that the very wording of ICSID provisions and a sense of endogamy among the somewhat limited group of arbitrators are two factors that may have prevented breaches of this duty from being sanctioned with disqualification.

Chapter 2 sets out and argues for a series of regulatory reforms that seek a firmer reshaping of the profile of the duty of disclosure while avoiding any over-exploitation of the referred duty that would damage ISDS praxis. To this end, the chapter offers some specific suggestions that may be incorporated into the work initiated by ICSID on November 2016 to update and modernise current Rules and Regulations. The EU ICS scheme, the EU proposal for a MIC and the recent UNCITRAL initiative on ISDS may equally benefit from a new approach to the duty of disclosure, giving the prospective system greater legitimacy. In summary, the main proposals developed in Chap. 2 are the following:

Where the wording of the ICSID Arbitration Rule 6 (2), the ICSID Declaration and the ICSID statement of impartiality and independence are concerned, both a brief analysis of the documents drafted by other institutions and the practical doubts raised by these documents in various arbitration proceedings suggest that there is room for improvement in this area. Chapter 2 therefore suggests various formal amendments with regard to the current ICSID Declaration and its statement of impartiality and independence. More specifically, it would be appropriate to add a standard text to the Declaration, clearly stating the independence and impartiality of all arbitrators—even for those who consider that there is no basis for attaching the statement in their case. In addition, the content of the ICSID Declaration itself should be broadened, for instance, by including a reference to further issues, such as the crucial topic of arbitrator availability, which is dealt with in Chap. 4. Likewise, ICSID should draft an "attached statement" for arbitrators that is technically advanced. Reflecting current practice in many other arbitration institutions, this statement should equally contain clear guidelines that are capable of ring-fencing the ICSID investment arbitrators' current flexibility of disclosure, thus helping to establish the content of this duty. These suggestions also apply to other future non-ICSID settings in which the duty of disclosure of investment adjudicators will have to be addressed.

The practical implementation of the disclosure standard included in clause (b) of ICSID Rule 6(2) ("any other circumstance that might cause his/her reliability for independent judgment to be questioned by a party") is another highly controversial issue. Chapter 2 shows that the parties' subjective standard in Rule 6(2)—which it is not the majority standard in the international arbitration context—has been ousted by a subjective standard referring to the arbitrator in various ICSID cases. The author considers that this trend is to be avoided, as the duty of disclosure is weakened by reliance on arbitrator subjectivism. On the other hand, other ICSID decisions have shifted towards objectivism when the "any other circumstance" clause has been applied. Faced with a current scenario in which there is a clear disconnection between the original drafting of Rule 6 (2) and its implementation, Chap. 2 argues for either redrafting the contentious ICSID Rule or using procedural means to promote a genuine return to party-centred standards.

In addition, Chap. 2 offers various suggestions on the timing, celerity and addressees of the duty of disclosure; proposals which may be taken into account both in the course of the ICSID reform and also when other rules dealing with the duty of disclosure in the international investment context are drafted. By way of an example, the regime needs to be shaped in such a way as to expressly recognize the existence of both pre- and post-appointment adjudicator duties and the duty's continuing nature. The current ICSID regime gives the arbitrators considerable scope time-wise with regard to their duty of disclosure, and is an exception that should be overridden. It is also important to address other relevant aspects of the duty of disclosure in practice, such as the persons to whom the adjudicator must disclose information.

Chapter 2 further argues that the specific content of the duty of disclosure still needs to be properly outlined because ICSID "case law" has so far failed to produce fully harmonized results. The high degree of transparency implemented by ICSID has led to the understanding in various challenge proceedings that a range of data—such as previous appointments—belongs in the public domain. In practical terms this has meant that disclosure was therefore not essential, but may be merely undertaken "out of an abundance of caution". This book makes a case for drafting a definition of the notion of the public domain that does not impose an excessive information-gathering burden onto the parties to the dispute. In keeping with this, Chap. 2 advocates de-dramatizing the duty of disclosure; in the framework of a new system that provides adjudicators with a series of clear guidelines to assist them in performing this significant duty of disclosure, it is preferable for the adjudicators to disclose too much information than too little. However, the arbitral collective feels strongly that an over-fed duty of disclosure could begin to prey on the current system. These divergent positions are reflected in a range of different issues, such as the lack of consensus as to the degree of relevance of the facts that investment arbitrators should disclose.

Chapter 2 also contains detailed reflections on two issues that are closely connected to the duty of disclosure: the importance of having access to a reliable CV for every investment adjudicator, and the adjudicators' duty to investigate. Where the former question is concerned, it is clear from a good number of arbitration institutions' written rules and practices that there is a general tendency not to put much pressure on arbitrators to make their full up-to-date CVs available, despite noteworthy efforts of transparency such as those made by ICSID. Although *a priori* CVs might be considered key documents in the context of the duty to disclose, contemporary praxis in the sector reveals that, in the absence of major institutional demands, parties and other participants in investment arbitrations often need to resort to alternative sources (informal chats with colleagues; information that is publicly available on internet; specialist companies, novel online initiatives, etc.) to obtain this much-needed information. This is consistent with some stakeholders' view of the arbitration milieu as a small, mysterious and powerful group of high-profile professionals with a tendency to exclude new blood. The current situation regarding investment arbitrators' CVs seems to lack efficiency, and a system in which the arbitrators themselves are held responsible for providing their own full CVs is encouraged in this chapter. In this scenario, more active participation on the part of arbitration institutions would of course be welcomed.

Chapter 2 also argues that investment arbitrators' duty to investigate should be specified in more detail. For instance, the sector's key rules need to make it clear that arbitrators have a non-delegable, personal obligation to investigate. Some investment disputes have demonstrated the importance of clarifying this issue in the ICSID setting. With respect to the adjudicator duty to investigate, this chapter argues that instead of being governed by a standard based on what is reasonable for a person, adjudicators should have to meet an appropriate standard of enquiry for well-organized professionals, a more demanding parameter that may lead to a rise in the currently small number of successful challenges to arbitrators. On this basis, the scope of the duty to investigate should cover personal records and additional sources of information, which could be specified in contexts such as ICSID or a prospective MIC. It seems reasonable not to impose any specific investigation methods on adjudicators while this on-going duty is being fulfilled, but to accept any that enable them to comply with the reinforced duty of disclosure supported here.

A recurrent underlying theme in Chap. 2 is the role that traditional arbitral institutions and new stakeholders such as the MIC should adopt vis-à-vis the adjudicators' duty of disclosure in the investment milieu. The arguments put forward here lead to the contention that arbitration institutions should both be more involved in various issues connected with the duty of disclosure and should also establish a more demanding framework for investment arbitrators. The chapter identifies a series of issues such as institutional training tailored to adjudicators or the use of sanctions as a consequence of non-compliance with duties; these are discussed in greater detail in Chaps. 1 and 6.

Chapter 3 reflects on the impact that the regulation on conflicts of interest may have on the investment arbitrators' duty of disclosure. The first part of the chapter focuses on the IBA Guidelines on Conflicts of Interest in International Arbitration, presenting the key aspects and pondering the Guidelines' present and future role in the international investment arbitration context. The analysis of ICSID cases shows that although the IBA Guidelines have frequently been cited as a benchmark and also praised in multiple investment arbitrator challenges, the ICSID adjudicators do not consider them to be binding in the vast majority of cases. The study also assesses the approach to the Guidelines taken by investment arbitration tribunals outside the ICSID context, and indicates that these tribunals have generally been more inclined to take into account and apply the Guidelines.

Chapter 3 also explores the role granted to the IBA Guidelines by diverse IIAs, which is of little quantitative significance so far. Although CETA and two recent national model Agreements state that adjudicators must indeed comply with the IBA Guidelines, these texts also envisage that the Guidelines will eventually be supplemented or even replaced by other existing or future texts. In addition, most IIAs contain no reference to the Guidelines whatsoever. This may be linked with the lack of unanimity among academics regarding the suitability of applying the IBA Guidelines in contexts outside commercial arbitration.

The IBA Guidelines' future in the investment milieu is therefore not guaranteed. However, Chap. 3 foresees various prospective scenarios in which they may play a prominent role: if the EU imposes compliance with the Guidelines in its entire ICS framework; if the Guidelines are incorporated as ICSID policy in the course of the institution's current reform, or if the IBA itself reforms the Guidelines with the aim of incorporating specific references to the investment milieu. Furthermore, were codes of conduct or similar texts to be developed for instance in the prospective MIC context, these would also undoubtedly borrow from the IBA Guidelines.

Taking all these circumstances into account, key institutions such as ICSID, the EU-via the ICS-, UNCITRAL, ICSID or the IBA may soon decide to address the important question of investment adjudicators' conflicts of interest. This is a fundamental issue in investment praxis and there is believed to be sufficient scope for this type of intervention. Accordingly, the second part of the chapter tackles three highly controversial topics pertaining to the conflicts of interest sphere: repeat appointment, issue conflict and multiple hatting. The objective of this analysis is to outline the status quo with respect to these three issues and develop a series of feasible proposals on the matter.

Chapter 3 accepts in a general sense that the duty of disclosure is not *per se* the universal remedy for the somewhat disparaged ISDS system as it currently exists. Nevertheless, the author feels that emphasising the duty of disclosure's continuous nature, for instance, may be a useful tool in the struggle against the procedural inequality between parties that is created with the collapsing of the "Chinese wall" in an arbitrator's mind. Despite the lukewarm nature of some ICSID decisions regarding the institution of multiple arbitral appointments, international praxis has managed to show that repeat appointments may give rise to a range of negative consequences that revolve around arbitrators' loss of independence and impartiality. Chapter 3 argues that the on-going nature of arbitrators' duty to disclose may serve to restore the balance, in some cases leading to resignations or challenges. Looking to the future, the chapter also takes into account the fact that the characteristics of the ICS as well as future initiatives such as the MIC will probably reduce the problems deriving from repeat appointments.

Likewise, the arbitrators' duty to avoid issue conflicts and keep an open mind may be facilitated by a strengthened and continuous duty of disclosure. Some possibly adverse effects of this duty—such as the generating of late-in-the-day arbitrator challenges—will have to be accepted, as the right to a neutral adjudicatory body should be one of the pillars of the present and future investment system. To reach this conclusion, Chap. 3 first reflects on the definition and practical relevance of the notion of issue conflict in investment arbitration context. There have been various cases both in and outside the ICSID context in which issue conflict was suspected as a consequence of the arbitrators' academic and professional writings and public statements. As detailed in the book, arbitrator challenges have not been upheld in such circumstances in most of the cases studied. However, neither the deep debate arising from the stricter decision in CC/Devas v. India, nor the legal consequences deriving from some challenges on the basis of concurrent service (arbitrator resignation or cessation from the non-arbitrator role) can be ignored.

A reinforced duty of disclosure may also prove to be a useful tool for fighting against the harmful effects that may derive from the current multiple hat scenario. The fact that legal experts working in the investment arbitration setting usually play different roles (arbitrator, counsel, expert witness and many others) throughout their professional careers is extreme controversial. Despite the risks that this practice may entail in terms of the system's integrity and legitimacy, the arbitrator collective mainly defends a revolving door system that enables it to benefit from experienced jurists and enables arbitrators to be less financially dependent.

The question of the external activities undertaken by international adjudicators during their terms of service has been regulated in contexts such as the ICJ, and has been highly polemical on a practical level. The latest EU FTAs do refer to the phenomenon of multiple hatting, which is a step forward with respect to the pre-ICS phase. Nevertheless, Chap. 3 details a plurality of questions deriving from these EU-negotiated texts that raise interpretative doubts or require more detailed development. The question of possibly imposing cooling off periods on adjudicators has been addressed only tangentially in some specific legal contexts, and the recent ICS does not devote detailed attention to it either. Chapter 3 offers a series of proposals on specific issues of pre- and post-employment restrictions that should be addressed in future regulations. Finally, it must be borne in mind that the implementation of the proposed measures would lead to a primary role being allotted to single-hat adjudicators, which would in turn have the effect of progressively reducing the weight of adjudicators' duty of disclosure in this new scenario.

Chapter 4 focuses on defining the contours of the highly complex duty of personal diligence and integrity. Three different but sometimes interconnected facets of the duty are studied individually: non-delegation of responsibilities; time-related availability, and appropriate behaviour. Each section examines the way in which these concepts have been shaped, and at times a comparative analysis of other legal sectors such as commercial arbitration and the justice system is employed. The chapter's ultimate aim is to put forward practical ideas on the specific content that should be attributed to these notions in the investment arbitration environment. It is also argued that these issues will need to be more clearly defined in the future in contexts such as ICSID, the ICS, and a possible MIC.

Where the issue of non-delegation of responsibilities is concerned, it is a proven fact that administrative secretaries (also referred to as arbitrator secretaries, legal assistants and assistants to the court) intervene in international arbitrations with some frequency. In spite of the fact that the arbitrators' mandate is classified in law as *intuitu personae,* practice shows that they do actually delegate a range of tasks to these secretaries. Legal assistants usually have well-established relationships of trust and professional esteem with arbitrators, and one of the reasons for their participation in arbitration proceedings is to speed up the process and reduce costs. Despite these potential benefits, their profiles have long been highly controversial in the international arbitration setting.

The analysis of various institutional rules operating in the commercial arbitration context undertaken in Chap. 4 reveals that the specific responsibilities that can be delegated to the secretaries are not always foreseen *ex ante*, and although arbitration institutions and stakeholders have made attempts in this direction, the results have not been entirely convergent. The debate surrounding arbitral secretaries has so far focused mainly on the importance of distinguishing between decision-making functions (non-delegable) and those that are merely organizational or administrative (and therefore delegable). Undoubtedly, the uncertainties deriving from the lack of definition in this respect must be avoided, but many other questions related to the future of assistants of this sort also need to be dealt with. These include further clarification of the secretaries' profile, training, duties and levels of disclosure, as well as the degree of control that arbitrators have over them, and the formers' duty of transparency vis-à-vis this issue with respect to arbitration parties. If these points are to be clarified, various non-exclusive actions such as those detailed in Chap. 4 are possible: new provisions focusing on arbitral secretaries could be drafted; or key actors such as arbitral institutions could give their active support for a new culture in which, as a general rule, details of the arbitral secretary's profile were agreed on by the arbitration parties with the support of the service provider.

Similar issues also clearly need to be addressed in the investment arbitration field. ICSID praxis has already tackled various cases in which controversial issues have been raised with respect to the figure of the assistant to the court; issues which could be adequately addressed in the sense suggested in this chapter by the reform currently promoted by ICSID. In addition, this chapter presents a detailed analysis of the doubts about non-delegation of responsibilities posed by the Yukos case, pointing out that not all professional arbitrator-secretary relationships seem to be appropriate. The possible creation of a MIC also reinforces the need to address the institution of the assistant to the court in further detail, as the brief reference contained in the Codes of Conduct of the latest generation of EU FTAs is clearly insufficient.

With respect to investment arbitration's future and the role that should be allotted to arbitrator availability when accepting appointments, it would seem reasonable for ICSID and other investment arbitration management institutions to echo not only some of the safeguards already applied in the commercial arbitration context, but also the concerns about this precise issue recently voiced by various stakeholders.

To these ends, Chap. 4 puts forward a series of proposals that revolve around adjudicator availability. They originally arose in the commercial arbitration context but can be extrapolated to the current ICSID-led investment arbitration scenario. First and foremost, arbitrators should provide accurate details of their availability time-wise from the outset. This would be more feasible if they were given access to information about the calls on their time entailed by accepting the appointment to the new case, without this causing problems in the context of restrictions on *ex parte* communications. Nevertheless, the principle of trusting arbitrators' judgement regarding their availability should not be absolute, and arbitration institutions must have the final say on appointments, which in turn means that these institutions need access to information about arbitrators' short and medium-term commitments. It would therefore be helpful if ICSID, for example, were to extend the content of the Declaration referred to in Rule 6.2 asking would-be-arbitrators to specify all their arbitration commitments within a reasonable timeframe. Once the full picture has emerged, it might turn out that an arbitrator's assessment of his or her own availability did not match that of the arbitration institution. For instance, an arbitrator may have given an affirmative response with regard to availability, but failed to take sufficiently into account other essential values supported by the arbitral institution itself (promptness, efficiency, process and award quality, etc.). Chapter 4 also suggests that in these cases arbitration institutions need to be able to refuse to appoint such arbitrators, just as inadequate or incomplete disclosures of arbitrators' workloads may lead to negative institutional decisions regarding their appointment.

Possessing detailed information about an arbitrator's availability at the appointment stage is thus certainly very useful, but it is not always enough. To prevent subsequent appointments from producing "double bookings" and the corresponding delays and inconvenience, it would make sense if arbitrators had to commit themselves at the appointment stage not to take up subsequent appointments that clashed with their responsibilities in the original case. Any failure to fulfil this commitment that subsequently caused unjustified delays in the original arbitration could be a useful argument in favour of arbitration institutions using some of the measures addressed in this book against such arbitrators, such as rejecting their appointment.

The scenario outlined above will no longer apply in the frameworks of the latest generation of EU FTAs and the prospective MIC, in which the figure of the party appointed arbitrator disappears. Nevertheless, this does not mean that the availability of members of tribunals/judges will *ipso facto* cease to be a problem. It is true that the matter's relative importance will be associated with the new professional incompatibilities regime imposed on court members, as detailed in Chap. 3. However, it is also felt that safeguards such as those previously indicated should be available to whichever institution—committee or similar—supervises the appointment of tribunal members/judges in each case.

With respect to arbitrator availability time-wise throughout the entire arbitral proceedings, eliminating unnecessary delays is indisputably an essential aim in the settling of investment-related conflicts, regardless of whether they are resolved by an ad hoc triumvirate of arbitrators that includes party-appointed arbitrators, or by a randomly created permanent tribunal division. For these reasons, a duty capable of guaranteeing the various aspects of the availability of adjudicators involved in international investment disputes must be committed to paper, irrespective of whatever specific terminology is used. Other major issues that also need to be pinned down are the specific degree of engagement required from an adjudicator in terms of compliance with time frames; the detail in which the duty should be defined in writing, and the consequences that may derive from any breach of this duty on the part of an adjudicator. Implementing some of the consequences suggested in Chap. 4, such as fee reduction as a result of delays in issuing awards, or non-appointment in future cases on the basis of double bookings, would undoubtedly mean that this aspect of the duty of diligence and integrity would acquire greater importance in the future practice of the resolution of conflicts arising from international investments.

Focusing on the arbitrator's behaviour throughout the arbitration proceedings, the contemporary arbitral practice analysed by Chap. 4 reveals a range of examples of arbitrator's attitudes and actions that arbitration parties may consider unsuitable. Texts in the commercial and investment arbitration sphere use a range of terminology to refer to circumstances of this type, requesting appropriate behaviour from arbitrators in a fairly general sense.

So far, few successful arbitration challenges have been justified by the investment arbitrator's unsuitable behaviour alone although in some cases challenges on the basis of lack of impartiality have their origin in remarks made by arbitrators that have been negatively assessed by the challenging party. Looking ahead, it would be advisable for future Codes of Conduct or other texts applicable in the investment milieu to keep an express reference to dignified arbitrator behaviour. The current standard drafting contained in the ICS is a suitable starting point ("avoid impropriety and the appearance of impropriety (. . .) observe high standards of conduct so that the integrity and impartiality of the dispute settlement mechanism is preserved") that, if possible, should strive to provide as much detail as possible on the issue of adjudicator's appropriate behaviour. Likewise, the incorporation of written recognition of the adjudicator's loyalty towards the arbitration institution would be welcome.

The content of Chap. 5 revolves around the notion of confidentiality in international arbitration, a very complex term whose exact content varies according to time, legal sector (commercial/investment) and the subject under analysis (party/arbitrator/etc.). The chapter firstly explores the controversial profile of the duty of confidentiality applicable to the parties in the commercial arbitration milieu. It also studies how this duty affects international commercial arbitrators. This initial comparative analysis leads into a discussion of the question at the heart of the chapter: the meaning, content and current relevance of the duty of confidentiality that falls to investment arbitrators.

To reach a proper understanding of the contemporary facets of this duty, appropriate consideration needs to be given to existing provisions on transparency with respect to the public. In the past, the opacity traditionally imputed to investment arbitration was mitigated via specific ad hoc arbitral tribunal decisions and normative amendments such as that endorsed by ICSID in 2006 regarding open hearings, the publication of awards and amicus curiae briefs. The UNCITRAL Rules on Transparency and the entry into force of the UN Convention on Transparency in Treaty-based Investor-State Arbitration represent a step forward in this matter, consolidating as they do a series of pro-transparency practices and thus responding to a long-standing demand from civil society. In this context, the investment adjudicator is a key subject, committed to protecting what has been referred to as an information-centric notion of transparency.

Along with this obligation to guarantee the objective of transparency vis-à-vis the public, investment adjudicators are also subject to a duty of confidentiality which is currently affirmed in frameworks such as ICSID and ICS. Various provisions, often inspired by texts from other areas such as commercial arbitration or the national judicial system, not only express the adjudicators' duty of confidentiality in very general wording, but also emphasize the duty's importance at certain key moments during arbitration proceedings (the deliberations of the arbitral tribunal or any of its members, and the final drafting of a decision or award before its publication).

In the ISDS setting the duty of confidentiality falling to investment adjudicators, which various ICSID decisions have also addressed, nowadays coexists with the key notion of transparency. Chapter 5 explains that investment provisions reflecting the adjudicators' duty of confidentiality have to be understood in accordance with the ascertainment that when transparency and confidentiality converge in the figure of the investment adjudicator, they may in fact act like two communicating vessels.

In this dual context, it is therefore important to stress the practical importance acquired by notions such as "non-public information" referred to in Article 7.1 of the codes of conduct in various EU-pushed FTAs. At first glance, such provisions may appear to establish a broad duty of confidentiality. However, the reality is that a great deal of the information connected to investment disputes may become public, given the potential scope of the legal transparency regime and its practical implementation by arbitration parties and their counsels.

Taking into account the fact that the generic duty of confidentiality attributable to investment adjudicators is *de facto* reduced if the sphere of transparency vis-à-vis the public is increased, the confidentiality duty nevertheless retains its scope with respect to specific documents or situations that are under investment adjudicators' control; the disclosure of a decision or award or parts thereof prior to its publication, and the disclosure of the tribunal's deliberations or members' views, for instance. The basic characteristics of such circumstances seem unlikely to be altered by future changes in the investment dispute resolution system. In the latter context, it is both predictable and natural for confidentiality to continue to be required from investment adjudicators.

Chapter 6 brings the book to a close by briefly analysing two more increasingly relevant issues in the practice of investment dispute resolution. Where arbitration costs are concerned, the issue is currently covered from a formal point of view in a series of ICSID tables and quantitative scales, although their practical application has created a great deal of controversy. In this investment arbitration context, some stakeholders seem genuinely interested in addressing the issue of arbitrators' duty to control arbitration costs and the costs created by the arbitrators themselves, but this has not so far been reflected in any far-reaching changes in the system. Commercial arbitration seems to be more advanced in this issue, as shown by the examples connecting the control of various aspects of expenditure with adjudicators' ethical duties. In the ICS framework, a brief reference to court members' expenses has been incorporated into their Code of Conduct and there are also various scattered references to the costs of proceedings. Although this is clearly a step forward, the author considers that the adjudicators' duty to control costs should receive more systematic and detailed attention where the shaping of initiatives such as a future MIC is concerned.

The second duty analysed concerns investment adjudicators' continuous training. While the international judicial context contains examples of institutions that are actively involved in systematically providing continuous training for their judges, some stakeholders consider that initiatives of this type are still insufficiently consolidated in the international arbitration world, especially in investment. Confidence in adjudicator competence is the starting point in the investment context, which is why imposing a learning programme on professionals who are already considered to be highly qualified is viewed as unnecessary. Nevertheless, some interested parties do advocate implementing a range of measures in this area, arguing that an all-encompassing, up-to-the-minute and transparent training programme may enhance key values among investment adjudicators—e.g., competence, independence and impartiality—as well as improving the quality and efficiency of the adjudicatory system. A continuous training programme in the investment milieu might also increase adjudicators' knowledge and sensitivity with respect to issues such as human rights or their own ethical duties when acting as investment adjudicators. A comprehensive multidisciplinary training system is even more justified given the intention to create an international institution as crucial as the MIC from scratch.

Other adjudicator duties—such the duty to decline or resign, the duty to grant equal treatment to the parties, the duty to render enforceable decisions, post-award duties, duties regarding settlement, etc.—have not been expressly addressed in this section, but this does not diminish their interest as objects of future analysis. It is highly advisable for initiatives such as the ICSID reform or the future MIC to help investment adjudicators to envisage this wide range of "other duties".

In short, this book makes a case throughout its pages for the elaboration of a new code of conduct for present and future investment adjudicators, considering that this initiative is necessary and would be beneficial in the international investment setting.

List of ICSID Investment Cases

Unless stated otherwise all these decisions and awards are available free of charge on the ITALAW website and/or the ICSID website.

Abaclat v. Argentina	Abaclat and Others v. Argentine Republic, (formerly Giovanna a Beccara and Others v. The Argentine Republic), ICSID Case No. ARB/07/5, Decision on the Proposal to Disqualify a Majority of the Tribunal, 21 December 2011.
Alpha v. Ukraine	Alpha Projektholding GmbH v. Ukraine, ICSID Case No. ARB/07/16, Decision on Proposal for Disqualification of an Arbitrator, 19 March 2010.
Blue Bank v. Venezuela	Blue Bank International & Trust (Barbados) Ltd. v. Bolivarian Republic of Venezuela, ICSID Case No. ARB 12/20, Decision on the Parties' Proposals to Disqualify a Majority of the Tribunal, 12 November 2013.
BSG v. Guinea	BSG Resources Limited, BSG Resources (Guinea) Limited and BSG Resources (Guinea) SÀRL v. Republic of Guinea. ICSID Case No. ARB/14/22, Procedural Order No. 2 on Transparency, 17 September 2015.
Burlington v. Ecuador	Burlington Resources INC v. Republic of Ecuador, ICSID Case N° ARB/08/5, ICSID Case N° ARB/08/5, Decision on the Proposal for Disqualification of Professor Francisco Orrego Vicuña, 13 December 2013.

K. Fach Gómez, *Key Duties of International Investment Arbitrators*,
https://doi.org/10.1007/978-3-319-98128-4

Caratube v. Kazakhstan	Caratube International Oil Company LLP v. The Republic of Kazakhstan, ICSID Case No. ARB/08/12, Award, 5 June 2012.
Caratube v. Kazakhstan (2014)	Caratube International Oil Company LLP & Mr. Devincci Salah v. The Republic of Kazakhstan, ICSID Case No. ARB/13/13, Decision on the proposal for disqualification of Mr. Bruno Boesch, 20 March 2014.
CEAC v. Montenegro	Central European Aluminium Company (CEAC) v. Montenegro, ICSID Case No. ARB/14/8, Award, 26 July 2016.
Compañía v. Argentina	Compañía de Aguas del Aconquija S.A. and Vivendi Universal S.A. v. Argentine Republic, ICSID Case No. ARB/97/3, Decision on Argentina's Request for Annulment of the Award, 10 August 2010.
ConocoPhillips v. Venezuela	ConocoPhillips Petrozuata B.V., ConocoPhillips Hamaca B.V. and ConocoPhillips Gulf of Paria B.V. v. Bolivarian Republic of Venezuela, ICSID Case No. ARB/07/30, Decision on the Proposal to Disqualify L. Yves Fortier, Q.C., Arbitrator, 27 February 2012.
ConocoPhillips v. Venezuela (2016)	Conoco Phillips Petrozuata B.V., ConocoPhillips Hamaca B.V. and ConocoPhillips Gulf of Paria B.V. v. Bolivarian Republic of Venezuela, ICSID Case No. ARB/07/30, Decision on the Proposal to Disqualify L. Yves Fortier, Q.C., Arbitrator, 15 March 2016.
Crystallex v. Venezuela	Crystallex International Corporation v. Bolivarian Republic of Venezuela, ICSID Case No. ARB(AF)/11/2, Award, 4 April 2016.
Duke v. Peru	Duke Energy International Peru Investments No. 1 Ltd. v. Republic of Peru, ICSID Case No. ARB/03/28, Award, 18 August 2008.
EDF v. Argentina	EDF International S.A., SAUR International S.A. and León Participaciones Argentinas S.A. v. Argentine Republic, ICSID Case No. ARB/03/23, Challenge Decision Regarding Professor Gabrielle Kaufmann-Kohler, 25 June 2008.

Electrabel v. Hungary	Electrabel S.A. v. Republic of Hungary, ICSID Case No. ARB/07/19, Decision on the Claimant's Proposal to Disqualify a Member of the Tribunal, 25 February 2008.
Fábrica v. Venezuela (2015)	Fábrica de Vidrios Los Andes, C.A. and Owens-Illinois de Venezuela, C.A. v. Bolivarian Republic of Venezuela, ICSID Case No. ARB/12/21, Decision on the Proposal to Disqualify a Majority of the Tribunal, 16 June 2015.
Fábrica v. Venezuela (2016a)	Fábrica de Vidrios Los Andes, C.A. and Owens-Illinois de Venezuela, C.A. v. Bolivarian Republic of Venezuela, ICSID Case No. ARB/12/21, Reasoned Decision on the Proposal for Disqualification of Arbitrator L. Yves Fortier, Q.C., 28 March 2016.
Fábrica v. Venezuela (2016b)	Fábrica de Vidrios Los Andes, C.A. and Owens-Illinois de Venezuela, C.A. v. Bolivarian Republic of Venezuela, ICSID Case No. ARB/12/21, Decision on the Proposal to Disqualify L. Yves Fortier, Q.C., Arbitrator, 12 September 2016.
Fábrica v. Venezuela (2017)	Fábrica de Vidrios Los Andes, C.A. and Owens-Illinois de Venezuela, C.A. v. Bolivarian Republic of Venezuela, ICSID Case No. ARB/12/21, Decision on the Proposal to Disqualify L. Yves Fortier, Q.C., Arbitrator, 5 May 2017.
Highbury v. Venezuela (2015a)	Highbury International AVV, Compañía Minera de Bajo Caroní AVV, and Ramstein Trading Inc. v. Bolivarian Republic of Venezuela, ICSID Case No. ARB/14/10, Disqualification of Professor Brigitte Stern (Spanish), 9 January 9 2015.
Highbury v. Venezuela (2015b)	Highbury International AVV, Compañía Minera de Bajo Caroní AVV, and Ramstein Trading Inc. v. Bolivarian Republic of Venezuela, ICSID Case No. ARB/14/10, Decisión sobre la propuesta de recusación de la profesora Brigitte Stern (Spanish), 9 June 2015.

İçkale v. Turkmenistan	İçkale İnşaat Limited Şirketi v. Turkmenistan, ICSID Case No. ARB/10/24, Decision on Claimant's Proposal to Disqualify Professor Philippe Sands, 11 July 2014.
Klöckner v. Cameroon	Klöckner Industrie-Anlagen GmbH and others v. United Republic of Cameroon and Société Camerounaise des Engrais, ICSID Case No. ARB/81/2, Ad hoc Committee Decision on Annulment. 3 May 1985. https://academic.oup.com/icsidreview/article-pdf/1/1/89/2272172/1-1-89.pdf
Menzies v. Senegal	Menzies Middle East and Africa S.A. and Aviation Handling Services International Ltd. v. Republic of Senegal, ICSID Case No. ARB/15/21, Award, (French), 5 August 2016.
Nations Energy v. Panama	Nations Energy, Inc. and others v. Republic of Panama, ICSID Case No. ARB/6/19, Decision on the Proposal to Disqualify Dr. Stanimir Alexandrov, Arbitrator - Spanish (Original), 7 September 2011.
Opic v. Venezuela	OPIC Karimum Corporation v. The Bolivarian Republic of Venezuela, ICSID Case No. ARB/10/14, Decision on the Proposal to Disqualify Professor Philippe Sands, Arbitrator, 5 May 2011.
Orascom v. Algeria	Orascom TMT Investments S.à r.l. v. People's Democratic Republic of Algeria, ICSID Case No. ARB/12/35, Final Award, 31 May 2017.
Perenco v. Ecuador	Perenco Ecuador Limited v. Republic of Ecuador, ICSID Case No. ARB/08/6, Decision on Challenge to Arbitrator, 8 December 2009.
PIP v. Gabon	Participaciones Inversiones Portuarias SARL v. Gabonese Republic, ICSID Case No. ARB/08/17, Decision on the Proposal to Disqualify an Arbitrator, 12 November 2009.

Repsol v. Argentina	Repsol, S.A. and Repsol Butano, S.A. v. Argentine Republic, ICSID Case No. ARB/12/38, Decision on the Proposal for Disqualification of Francisco Orrego Vicuña and Claus von Wobeser (Spanish), 13 December 2013.
RSM v. Saint Lucia	RSM Production Corporation v. Saint Lucia, ICSID Case No. ARB/12/10, Decision on Claimant's Proposal for the Disqualification of Dr. Gavan Griffith QC (October 23, 2014), Award, 5 August 2016.
Saba v. Turkey	Saba Fakes v. Republic of Turkey, ICSID Case No. ARB/07/20, Decision on Disqualification of an Arbitrator (not public), 26 April 2008.
Saint-Gobain v. Venezuela	Saint-Gobain Performance Plastics Europe v. Bolivarian Republic of Venezuela, ICSID Case No. ARB/12/13, Decision on Claimant's Proposal to Disqualify Mr. Bottini from the Tribunal under Article 57 of the ICSID Convention, 27 February 2013.
Salini v. Jordan	Salini Costruttori S.p.A. and Italstrade S.p.A. v. The Hashemite Kingdom of Jordan, ICSID Case No. ARB/02/13, Decision on Jurisdiction, 9 November 2004.
SGS v. Pakistan	SGS Société Générale de Surveillance S.A. v. Islamic Republic of Pakistan, ICSID Case No. ARB/01/13, Decision on Claimant's Proposal to Disqualify Arbitrator, 19 December 2012, published at 8 ICSID Rep. 398 (2005).
Suez v. Argentina	Suez, Sociedad General de Aguas de Barcelona S.A. and Interagua Servicios Integrales de Agua S.A. v. Argentine Republic, ICSID Case No. ARB/03/17, Decision on a Second Proposal for the Disqualification of a Member of the Arbitral Tribunal, 12 May 2008.
TANESCO v. Tanzania	Tanzania Electric Supply Company Limited v. Independent Power Tanzania Limited, ICSID Case No. ARB/98/8, Challenge documents unpublished.

Tenaris v. Venezuela	Tenaris S.A. and Talta - Trading e Marketing Sociedade Unipessoal Lda. v. Bolivarian Republic of Venezuela, ICSID Case No. ARB/11/26, Award (Spanish), 29 January 2016.
Tidewater v. Venezuela	Tidewater Investment SRL and Tidewater Caribe, C.A. v. Bolivarian Republic of Venezuela, ICSID Case No. ARB/10/5, Decision on the Proposal for the Disqualification of a Member of the Arbitral Tribunal, 23 December 2010.
Total v. Argentina	Total S.A. v. Argentine Republic, ICSID Case No. ARB/04/1, Decision on the Proposal to Disqualify Teresa Cheng, 26 August 2015.
United v. Estonia	United Utilities (Tallinn) B.V. and Aktsiaselts Tallinna Vesi v. Republic of Estonia, ICSID Case No. ARB/14/24, Decision on Respondent's Application for Provisional Measures, 12 May 2016.
Universal v. Venezuela	Universal Compression International Holdings, S.L.U. v. Bolivarian Republic of Venezuela, ICSID Case No. ARB/10/9, Decision on the Proposal for the Disqualification of two Members of the Arbitral Tribunal, 20 May 2011.
Urbaser v. Argentina	Urbaser S.A. and Consorcio de Aguas Bilbao Bizkaia, Bilbao Biskaia Ur Partzuergoa v. The Argentine Republic, ICSID Case No. ARB/07/26, Decision on Claimants' Proposal to Disqualify Professor Campbell McLachlan, Arbitrator, 12 August 2010.
Victor Pey Casado v. Chile (2008)	Victor Pey Casado and President Allende Foundation v. Republic of Chile, ICSID Case No. ARB/98/2, Award, 8 May 2008.
Victor Pey Casado v. Chile (2017a)	Victor Pey Casado and President Allende Foundation v. Republic of Chile, ICSID Case No. ARB/98/2, Decision on the Proposal to Disqualify Sir Franklin Berman QC and Mr V.V. Veeder QC (English), 21 February 2017.

Victor Pey Casado v. Chile (2017b)	Victor Pey Casado and President Allende Foundation v. Republic of Chile, ICSID Case No. ARB/98/2, Decision on the Proposal to Disqualify Mr V.V. Veeder and QC Sir Franklin Berman QC, 13 April 2017.
Vladislav. Kim v. Uzbekistan	Vladislav. Kim and others v. Republic of Uzbekistan, ICSID Case No. ARB/13/6, Decision on Jurisdiction, 8 March 2017.

List of Non-ICSID Investment Cases

CC/Devas v. India	CC/Devas (Mauritius) Ltd., Devas Employees Mauritius Private Limited and Telecom Devas Mauritius Limited v. India, UNCITRAL, PCA Case n° 2013-09, Decision on the Respondent's Challenge to the Hon. Marc Lalonde and Prof. Francisco Orrego Vicuña, 30 September 2013.
EnCana v. Ecuador	EnCana Corporation v. Republic of Ecuador, LCIA Case No. UN3481 UNCITRAL, Partial Award on Jurisdiction, 27 February 2004.
Glamis v. USA	Glamis Gold, Ltd. v. The United States of America, NAFTA/UNCITRAL, Award, 8 June 2009.
Grand River v. USA	Grand River Enterprises Six Nations, Ltd., et al. v. United States of America, UNCITRAL Decision on the Challenge to Arbitrator James Anaya, 28 November 2007.
Hulley v. Russia	Hulley Enterprises Limited (Cyprus) v. The Russian Federation, PCA Case No. AA 226, Award, 18 July 2014.
ICS v. Argentina	ICS Inspection and Control Services Limited (United Kingdom) v. The Republic of Argentina, UNCITRAL PCA Case No. 2010-9, Decision on Challenge to Arbitrator, 17 December 2009.
LCIA Reference N° 81224	Decision Rendered 15 March 2010. Challenge Digests.
Myers v. Canada S.D.	Myers, Inc. v. Government of Canada, UNCITRAL, Partial Award, 13 November 2000.

K. Fach Gómez, *Key Duties of International Investment Arbitrators*,
https://doi.org/10.1007/978-3-319-98128-4

National Grid plc v. Argentina	National Grid plc v. The Argentine Republic, UNCITRAL, Decision on the Challenge to Mr Judd L. Kessler, 3 December 2007.
Pope v. Canada	Pope & Talbot Inc. v. The Government of Canada, UNCITRAL, Decision by Tribunal (II), 27 September 2000.
Veteran v. Russia	Veteran Petroleum Limited (Cyprus) v. The Russian Federation, PCA Case No. AA 228, Award, 18 July 2014.
Vito v. Canada (2009)	Vito G. Gallo v. The Government of Canada, UNCITRAL, PCA Case No. 55798, Decision on the Challenge to Mr. J. Christopher Thomas, QC in the Arbitration, 14 October 2009.
Vito v. Canada	Vito G. Gallo v. The Government of Canada, UNCITRAL, PCA Case No. 55798, Award, 15 September 2011.
Yukos v. Russia	Yukos Universal Limited (Isle of Man) v. The Russian Federation, PCA Case No. AA 227, Award, 18 July 2014.

Court Judgments and Related Documents

- [2016] EWHC 422 (Comm). Case No: CL-2015-000344, http://www.bailii.org/ew/cases/EWHC/Comm/2016/422.html.
- Case C-284/16, Judgment of the Court (Grand Chamber) of 6 March 2018. Slowakische Republik v. Achmea BV. http://curia.europa.eu/juris/document/document.jsf?text=&docid=199968&pageIndex=0&doclang=EN&mode=lst&dir=&occ=first&part=1&cid=554136.
- Expert Opinion of Professor George A. Berman regarding the Yukos awards in Respondent Motion to Dismiss Petition to Confirm Award filed with U.S. District Court of District of Columbia, 20 October 2015.
- Judgment of the US Court of Appeals Upholding the Decision to Refuse the Enforcement of Award (July 7, 2017), referring to the case Getma International and others v. Republic of Guinea, ICSID Case No. ARB/11/29.
- P v. Q [2017] EWHC 194. https://www.judiciary.gov.uk/wp-content/uploads/2017/03/p-v-q-and-ors-2017-ewhc-194-comm-20170209.pdf.
- Raoul Duval v. V., Cour de cassation, chambre civile 1, du 16 décembre 1997, 95-15.921. https://www.legifrance.gouv.fr/affichJuriJudi.do?idTexte=JURITEXT000007367685.
- Republic of Ghana v. Telekom Malaysia Berhad, Decision of the District Court of The Hague, Civil Law section, 5 November 2004, Case No. HA/RK 2004, 788, https://www.italaw.com/cases/documents/1201.
- Writ of Summons regarding the Yukos awards, District Court in The Hague, 28 January 2015.

K. Fach Gómez, *Key Duties of International Investment Arbitrators*,
https://doi.org/10.1007/978-3-319-98128-4

Index

K. Fach Gómez, *Key Duties of International Investment Arbitrators*,
https://doi.org/10.1007/978-3-319-98128-4

D

MIX
Papier aus verantwortungsvollen Quellen
Paper from responsible sources
FSC® C105338
FSC
www.fsc.org

If you have any concerns about our products,
you can contact us on
ProductSafety@springernature.com

In case Publisher is established outside the EU,
the EU authorized representative is:
Springer Nature Customer Service Center GmbH
Europaplatz 3, 69115 Heidelberg, Germany

Printed by Libri Plureos GmbH
in Hamburg, Germany